ACTION and CONDUCT

ACTION and CONDUCT

Thomas Aquinas and the Theory of Action

Paperback Edition
with New Appendix,
"The Specification of Action in St. Thomas"

STEPHEN L. BROCK

Foreword by
RALPH MCINERNY

The Catholic University of America Press
Washington, DC

Previously published by T&T Clark, 1998.
Paperback edition copyright © 2021
The Catholic University of America Press
All rights reserved

ISBN: 978-0-8132-3425-0

To my parents, in memoriam

Contents

Foreword by Ralph McInerny — ix

Acknowledgments — xi

Abbreviations — xii

Introduction — 1

Chapter 1 The Analogy of Action — 5
  A. The Equivocity of 'Action' and Analogical Equivocation — 5
  B. The Order of Agents: Actions and Their Subjects — 14
  C. The Analogy of 'Action' — 27
  D. Common Features of Action — 39

Chapter 2 Agency as Efficacy — 47
  Introduction: Action at Its Lowest Level — 47
  A. The Act of the Agent is in the Patient — 51
  B. What Do Actions Consist In? — 59
  C. Motion as an Irreducible Event — 65
  D. Actions as Events that Consist in Causations — 74
  E. Agent and Patient in the Specification of Action — 81

Chapter 3 Agent-Causality and Finality — 91
  A. Finality as a Common Feature of Action — 91
  B. The Origin of the Notion of a Cause — 98
  C. Active Power — 104
  D. Action, Inclination and Causality — 110
  E. Direct and Indirect Agency — 122

Chapter 4 The Agency of the Will — 133
  A. Autonomy or Agency? — 135
  B. Wanting as a Causal Disposition — 145
  C. The Distinction of Understanding and Willing — 156
  D. The Twofold Relation of the Will to Its Object — 167
  E. The Will and Conduct — 181

Chapter 5 *Praeter Intentionem* ... 193
Introduction: Some Terminology ... 193
A. Indirect Objects of Intention and Act-specification ... 196
B. The Diffusiveness and Non-divisiveness of Intention ... 204
C. Evil as Praeter Intentionem ... 212
D. Praeter Intentionem, *the Involuntary through Ignorance, and the Specifiability of Action* ... 221

Appendix *The Specification of Action in St. Thomas: Nonmotivating Conditions in the Object of Intention* ... 239

Bibliography ... 265

Index of References to the Works of St Thomas Aquinas ... 271

Index of Names ... 277

Index of Subjects ... 279

Foreword

There are three reasons why this book is important.

First, it represents a sustained effort to grasp the basic points of Thomas Aquinas's account of human action. It will of course be appreciated that it is no easy matter to pluck from the vast ocean of Thomas's writings a single concept and deal with it as if it were a land animal. Stephen Brock could have presupposed that his readers already are certified oceanographers, but then why would they want this book? What he does do is illustrate, as he develops his analysis of human action, how, as a type of action, it arises out of simpler and more widespread instances of action. This admirably conveys the basic pedagogy of Thomas. Our minds bear naturally on the nature of physical things and it is only by careful extrapolation and analogy that we can extend the vocabulary developed in talking about physical change to the change brought about by an agent endowed with reason and will. The account accordingly is at once assimilative and narrative. The reader is given not only an historically accurate picture of Thomistic theory of action; he participates in the reenactment of the thinking that led to it.

Second, Brock's book will be welcomed by contemporary philosophers who, while schooled in other and latter day traditions, come to see that earlier discussions of human action are philosophically interesting. We have witnessed another one of those resurgences of interest in Aristotle which stud the history of the philosophical community, this time rescuing the Stagyrite from the pale cast of merely philological thought. This in turn has led to an interest in medieval commentaries on Aristotle. It has not been sufficiently stressed that Thomas Aquinas would command our attention if he had done nothing other than the twelve commentaries—not all completed—on Aristotelian works. Those on the *Nicomachean Ethics* and *De anima* are particularly relevant to the topic of this book. Brock's discussion of Chisholm's views makes clear that he intends to stress this relevance.

Third, our author has given us a discussion, in context, of matters of great moment for recent disputes in moral theology. Much dissent from traditional moral doctrine is based on understandings of such conceptions as *praeter intentionem*, or perhaps one should say based on misunderstandings of it. Brock's book is anything but polemic, but he could not possibly have been unaware of the indirect contribution his analysis will make to moral theology.

Chiefly for these reasons, but for others as well, I welcome this book. Stephen Brock has been a participant in the *soi disant* Thomistic Seminars held annually in July at the University of Notre Dame. The aim of those seminars is to bring together scholars whose work is influenced by their faith and who, accordingly, take seriously the reiterated recommendation by the Magisterium that we take Thomas for our mentor in philosophy as well as theology. By bringing together senior thinkers, whose work, while exhibiting family resemblances, is scarcely redundant, as well as scholars just coming on the scene, junior scholars and graduate students are provided with living models of great variety. There are many ways in which one can respond to the invitation of John of St. Thomas: *philosophandum in fide*. Stephen Brock has found his distinctive way and, with this book, he consolidates his claim to be numbered among the best and the brightest of the new generation of Catholic philosophers.

RALPH MCINERNY
University of Notre Dame

Note to the Paperback Edition

My sincere thanks to the Catholic University of America Press for hereby making the book more widely available. Readers should note that the original pagination has not been preserved. The major change is the addition, as an appendix, of my article, 'The Specification of Action in St. Thomas: Nonmotivating Conditions in the Object of Intention,' *The Thomist* 83 (2019), pp. 321–55. I am grateful to the editors of *The Thomist* for their permission to include it here. (The style of the citations has been modified so as to conform with the rest of the book, but the content is the same.) On the reason for adding it, see the note inserted at the beginning of Chapter 5, Section A.

Otherwise, I have made some very small corrections and alterations here and there.

Stephen L. Brock
Chicago, Illinois
March 19, 2021

Abbreviations

Except for *Quaestiones disputatae de potentia*, the *Scriptum* on the *Sentences*, and *In libros Metaphysicorum expositio*, references to the works of St Thomas may be found in the Leonine edition. For convenience, the Marietti subdivisions of the chapters of the *Summa contra gentiles*, and of the *lectiones* of the commentaries on Aristotle, are also given. The *Summa theologiae* is usually cited without title, beginning with the *pars* (e.g. I–II). Other works of Aquinas are cited by the following abbreviations:

De malo	*Quaestiones disputatae de malo*
De pot.	*Quaestiones disputatae de potentia*
De ver.	*Quaestiones disputatae de veritate*
In De an.	*Sententia libri De anima*
In Eth.	*Sententia libri Ethicorum*
In Meta.	*In libros Metaphysicorum expositio*
In Peri herm.	*In libros Peri hermeneias expositio*
In Phys.	*Commentaria in libros Physicorum*
In Post an.	*Expositio libri Posteriorum analyticorum*
In Sent.	*Scriptum super libros Sententiarum*
SCG	*Summa contra gentiles*

Unless otherwise indicated, translations are mine. See the Bibliography for the full references to works of contemporary authors cited. Wherever applicable, page references to articles by G. E. M. Anscombe are taken from the *Collected Papers*.

Introduction

Part of the usual task of the introduction to a philosophical study is to locate it in the scheme of the philosophical sciences. In the present case this task is well-nigh hopeless. In its intention, what follows must be said to pertain to ethics. Its aim is to shed some light on the nature of human action, and the science of human action *is* ethics. A large portion of it, however, concerns non-human action, what we may call merely physical action, and so belongs to natural philosophy. Yet again, the point of the voyage into the domain of physical action is to establish certain general principles also governing human action, and to show that both the distinction and the connection between physical and human action are essential elements in the understanding of human action itself; and since the establishment of general principles, and the distinction and co-ordination of the subjects of the particular sciences, are works normally assigned to metaphysics, the present investigation may also be said to be metaphysical in its scope. But it is certainly not a study in the 'metaphysics of morals' or 'meta-ethics', as these are normally understood.

Whether or not all this scientific promiscuity is justified will be left to the reader to judge. Something in its favor, though, is indicated by the (somewhat) traditional name for this branch of inquiry: the 'psychology of human action.' This means the account of human action in relation to its principles in the human soul. For the human soul is, as they say, 'in a way' all things.

The study draws heavily on the thought of Thomas Aquinas. Its overall aim is not that of a systematic exegesis of his writings on human action. For that reason, I have for the most part not entered into questions of the evolution of his doctrine, and I have concentrated primarily on his more mature writings, especially the *Summa theologiae*. Still, it does involve a good deal of exegesis. Overall, it is an investigation of certain problems in the theory of action, carried out mainly under the direction and inspiration of Thomas's writings. It will not be possible to give exhaustive textual support for every one of the positions attributed to him, but some defense will be adduced in the case of the more controversial interpretations. There will also be some effort to clear up possible misunderstandings of his doctrine, to draw out certain points that he leaves implicit, and above all to present his thought in a manner suitable for participation in current debates. So, if the interpretation of Aquinas offered in the following pages should prove to be substantially mistaken, then the study can hardly but have failed philosophically as well; but, as goes without saying, the correctness of its interpretation is not the same as its philosophical success. Nor, I might add, does its philosophical success depend upon its persuading anyone to go so far as to take to himself the epithet 'Thomist.'

The larger portion of the specific problems addressed are issues current in contemporary work on action among Anglo-Saxon, 'analytical' philosophers. The choice of these problems has several motives, not the least of which is simply that they are, in my estimation, serious problems. Nor are they foreign to the sorts of questions that a treatment of human action from a Thomistic viewpoint needs to take up. On the contrary, studying them can enhance one's grasp of Aquinas's own doctrine significantly. At least, such has been my experience. This is not, after all, very surprising; it is enough to consider the serious attention paid to Aristotle in analytical thought. (I have no intention of entering here into the question whether it is proper to call Thomas, who after all was a theologian by profession, an 'Aristotelian.' But no apology is needed for regarding him as at least a powerful interpreter of Aristotle, and as having *some* dependence upon 'the Philosopher.')

Thomas, too, is by no means a stranger in Anglo-Saxon philosophy. More and more is being published on him in English. Anthony Kenny, for example, has shown the great relevance of Thomas's thought in a number of areas, including or perhaps even especially in the theory of action. Many other prominent authors have also clearly been influenced by Aquinas. In fact, among contemporary authors, those to whom I shall be giving the larger share of attention expound theories of action which have very much in common with that of Aquinas, and evidently not by chance. These include G. E. M. Anscombe, Joseph Boyle, Roderick Chisholm, the late Alan Donagan, and Peter Geach.

My giving more attention to these authors may seem to be begging some questions. However, this study in no way pretends to be a 'dialogue' between Thomism and analytical philosophy, whatever such a thing would or ought to be, and however it might be possible for *one* writer to carry it out. Besides, analytical philosophy hardly constitutes more of a 'school' than does 'scholasticism.' The aim is neither to reach some sort of compromise nor to draw up battle-lines, but simply to try to gain a better understanding of human action, in a Thomistic vein and in a contemporary setting. My consideration of analytical writers will be frankly rather piecemeal (if not pedestrian). I do not think this is a vice, or need make for bad philosophy. The parts are only fully understood in light of the whole, but we often get at the whole by way of the parts.

The choice of problems has been determined, above all, by their bearing on the main theme: the relation between physical and voluntary action. This too arises, in part, from my reading (again, not exhaustive) of the analytical work on action. Time and again I have been left with the impression of a need for clarifying that relation. This is not meant as a criticism. It has also cost me a good deal of work to unravel the lines of Aquinas's thought on the matter, if indeed I have unraveled them. It may be, though, that studying Aquinas does help to instill a certain sensitivity to the question; my reasons for saying this should come out as the work unfolds. It will be the thesis of this book that understanding the relation between physical and voluntary action is crucial for understanding voluntary action itself, and that Thomas can help a great deal toward furthering such understanding. Although many things have been written on one aspect or another of this topic, in Aquinas and in analytical thought, I know of no general presentation of it such as the one I have proposed to undertake.

The question hinges mainly on the way in which a few key notions ought to be understood, distinguished, and co-ordinated. These are the notions of causality, intention, action, and 'acts of will.' Very generally speaking, and aside from the occasional attribution of something like intention to some of the higher brute animals, the analytical philosophy of action shows a tendency to confine the applicability of the last three notions to the human domain. It also shows a tendency to present the first notion, causality, in such a way as to deprive it of any generally definable connection with the other three. For Aquinas, by contrast, it is only the last notion, 'acts of will,' that expresses something exclusively human; at the same time, it expresses something decidedly causal. Any one of these notions could, of course, serve as the subject of an investigation even longer than the present one. Here, though, the treatment of them is subordinated to the goal of giving general delineation to a notion that (it is claimed) embraces them all, the notion of human action, or what the title of the present work calls 'conduct.'

The absence or near-absence of certain topics which are unquestionably essential to a complete account of human action will be immediately and glaringly apparent. For instance, I have deliberately shied away from a thematic discussion of practical reasoning, or of things like habits and passions. All of these pertain to what one might call the inner workings of human action, the particular elements or principles which enter into its genesis or formation, and its full explanation. The present work stays more on the 'surface' of human action, to mark off its shape, seen both in distinction from and in connection with physical action.

This is not to say that there will be no lengthy discussion of things *proper* to human action. The notions of freedom, the voluntary, and acts of will shall figure heavily. But again, the aim will not be to give a full explanation for these things, by getting at their root principles in the human soul or by considering how reality must be in order to make them possible. Thus, I do not enter at all into the question of freedom and determinism, or into the equally vexed question of the structure of the interdependence between intellect and will. These would call for another book. I do take up the question of how intellect and will are *distinguished*, in Thomas, simply in order to get *at* what he means by 'will' and 'act of will.' I also enter into Thomas's differentiation of kinds of acts of will, or of what I would call formal principles of volitional relation, but with unequal attention to the various kinds. My aim there is to isolate the properly causal moment, or form, of the will's operation. This, I believe, turns out to be one of the Thomistic acts of will which has received very little attention, even from Thomists: the act called *usus*, use.

I said there was no aim to draw up battle-lines. In relation to the notion of causality, this needs some qualification. I shall be at some pains to bring out

Thomas's understanding of causality in opposition to that of Hume—whose influence in Anglo-Saxon thought goes without saying. Also, although in no way part of the original point of this inquiry, one of its chief results has turned out to be to underscore the disparity between Aquinas and Kant, or at any rate a standard reading of Kant, on the subject of human action. This disparity is hardly a new discovery, particularly as concerns the theme of the relation between physical and moral action. It is discussed here only by way of setting the Thomistic position in sharper relief. A systematic analysis and evaluation of Kant's theory of action would go far beyond both the limits of the present study and the competence of the author. But the comparison with Kant will help to bring out the fact that the questions of the relation between physical and human action, and of the causality of the will, are not only illuminating as regards the conceptualization of human action, but also decisive for the way in which the *morality* of human action is understood. And Kant's presence in contemporary Anglo-Saxon moral thought is at least comparable to Hume's. Indeed, one author, Henry Veatch, calls Kant its 'grey eminence.'

(I would also like to say something about the fact that part of my treatment of questions connected with Kant, and of other questions related to these, leads me to take issue with certain positions held by the late Alan Donagan. What I wish to say is simply that my debt to his work is of far greater magnitude than my criticisms, despite what the space devoted to the latter might make it seem; and that I am much more sure of the things in which I agree with him than of those in which I do not.)

The rationale of the book's structure derives from the thesis laid out in Chapter 1, that 'action' is an analogical term. Its primary referent is human or personal action—the action of an agent who is 'master of his acts.' By analogical extension it is also attributed to non-personal subjects. The analogy is such as to permit us to isolate certain features of action common to personal and non-personal actions. The feature which I propose to investigate, again for reasons laid out in Chapter 1, are those of efficacy (agent-causality), finality, and the agent-patient relation. These are the concern of Chapters 2 and 3. The fourth chapter may be regarded as the principal one, bringing the analysis of the common features of action to bear on the understanding of properly human, voluntary action. The final chapter gives consideration to a topic which is almost unavoidable, that of indirect human agency, or actions which somehow fall 'outside' the voluntary agent's will or intention, *praeter intentionem*. I do not pretend to give anything like a full treatment of this topic. My main concern is to bring out two points. One is what seems to me to be a very useful distinction, in Thomas, between two very different senses of *praeter intentionem*; this distinction will be explained with the help of preparation provided at the end of Chapter 3, where I attempt to expound an important and not very well known text from Thomas on indirect causality. The other point, which rests on the connection between intention and specification, is the futility of trying to specify things done out of ignorance.

Chapter 1
The Analogy of Action

A. THE EQUIVOCITY OF 'ACTION' AND ANALOGICAL EQUIVOCATION

1. The Apparent Equivocity of 'Action'

Generally speaking, when contemporary philosophers refer to the theory of action, what they mean by 'an action' is fairly specific. It is not nearly as broad as 'an activity' or 'a doing.' For one thing, it is taken to signify only doings engaged in by human beings. Nor does it cover everything that men do or every activity whose subject may be a man. Rather, the problems addressed by the theory of action are, at least for the most part, problems concerning what Aquinas calls *actus humani*, human acts.[1] Not everything a man does is a human act. A human act is a deliberate or voluntary doing.[2]

This usage of the term 'action,' however, is not wholly exceptionless, even among philosophers. Anthony Kenny, for instance, maintains that non-rational and even non-living subjects engage in action.[3] Similarly, Eric D'Arcy insists that the English term 'action' is applicable to the doings of many things besides man. He can offer no single term that properly designates voluntary actions, although in his judgment there is one that always signifies *actus hominis*, i.e. doings with a personal subject but not necessarily voluntary: the term 'act.'[4]

Non-philosophical speech seems to display a similar uncertainty as to the proper domain of the term 'action.' Surely Kenny and D'Arcy are right that English-speakers do not always restrict the term to the doings of men. For example, falling is said to result from the action of gravity; rust is the effect of the action of oxygen upon iron; for every action there is an equal and opposite reaction; etc. Nor does there seem to be any special reason to ascribe such usage to the anthropomorphism of ruder ancestors. On the other hand, within the domain of the doings of human beings, non-philosophical English does seem inclined to reserve the term 'action' for those that are voluntary or human. At least it seems somewhat odd to speak of a sudden sneeze or an idle stroking of the beard as an action. It is

---

1. See Anscombe, 'Action, Intention and "Double Effect," ' pp. 12f.
2. *Summa theologiae* I–II, q. 1, a. 1.
3. *The Metaphysics of Mind*, pp. 33–34.
4. D'Arcy, *Human Acts*, pp. 6–8, 132–33.

not entirely clear, however, that this is on account of the intrinsic sense of 'action,' as one might argue that it is in the case of the Anglo-Saxon term 'deed.' It may be merely that when speaking of the action that a human being *as a whole* is engaged in, one naturally tends to have in mind deliberate or voluntary action, as in some way the kind of action proper to a person as a whole and as such.[5] As Anscombe notes, when one simply looks at a man and reports what he is doing, what activity he is engaged in, in most cases (of course not all) the report will be of something that he is doing intentionally.[6]

Thomas Aquinas himself employs the term 'action' somewhat equivocally. 'Action' corresponds to the Latin *actio* and, in Aquinas's usage, to the infinitive *agere*, taken as a substantive.[7] Often he applies these terms, and the finite forms of *agere*, quite straightforwardly to the doings of non-human and non-personal subjects. One of his favorite examples of an action is that of fire heating something.[8] On other occasions, however, he makes an explicit call for restricting the term to human or voluntary doings. Commenting on Book II of Aristotle's *Physics*, for instance, he remarks that action belongs properly to that which is master of its act: *eius autem proprie est agere, quod habet dominium sui actus*.[9] The expression 'master of one's act' is one of his ways of describing agents that have free choice, i.e. agents capable of voluntary or human acts. This same doctrine is repeated in several places in the *Summa theologiae*.[10] Yet, strikingly, both the *Physics* commentary and the *Summa theologiae* also contain lengthy treatments of the 'action' of physical, non-voluntary subjects. Some of these are located very near the passages in which he appropriates the term to human acts.[11]

2. Analogical Equivocation; the Example of Actus

Equivocation is not always a sign, or a source, of confusion. There is no reason why the same word should not bear several senses, even in scientific discourse. What matters is that the sense intended in any given use of it remain clear. The peril of confusion is least, perhaps, when the senses are unrelated. This is what Aristotle calls equivocation by chance.[12] In this case, the mere context usually suffices to show which sense was meant. But sometimes a word's various senses overlap, or bear a certain intrinsic connection to each other. When they do, the mind risks slipping from one to another. Yet even in this case, the term's

---

5. See III, q. 19, a. 2: an act not arising from reason and will *non est simpliciter operatio humana, sed convenit homini secundum aliquam partem humanae naturae*. Cf. Eudemian Ethics II, ch. 8, 1224b8–37.
6. *Intention*, pp. 8–9.
7. See Ramírez, *De hominis beatitudine*, p. 234: *agere humanum et actio humana idem sonant*.
8. See e.g. I, q. 1, a. 3; II–II, q. 58, a. 2.
9. *In II Phys.* lect. x, § 229.
10. I, q. 29, a. 1; q. 22, a. 2 ad 4; q. 103, a. 5 ad 2; I–II, q. 1, a. 2; q. 93, a. 5.
11. E.g. *In III Phys.* lects. iv, v; I–II, q. 1, a. 2; I, q. 105, a. 5.
12. *Nicomachean Ethics* I, ch. 4, 1096b27.

equivocity may not be something to be deplored. There may well be compensations for the risk of misunderstanding. Artificially restricting the term's meaning for the sake of precision might entail a certain reduction, not only of sense, but also of doctrinal richness. This point bears developing, by way of an example.

Picking up Aristotle's distinction between chance equivocation and equivocation by design, Aquinas calls this second sort, in which the several senses of a term retain a certain unity or order among themselves, equivocation by analogy. A good example of a term he holds to be equivocal in an analogical way is 'act,' *actus*. The usage he ascribes to this term could hardly be further removed from the narrow acceptation urged by D'Arcy for 'act.' As Aquinas uses it, *actus* by no means signifies only acts of personal subjects. It is not even restricted to doing or activity in general. Not only activity but also form, existence, and in general any sort of positive characteristic, any perfection or fullness, can be designated by *actus*.

What is noteworthy is that in ascribing so broad a range of reference to the term *actus*, Aquinas is not merely adopting common usage. On the contrary, he explicitly maintains that such a broad application departs from the common usage. It is precisely for scientific purposes that the term's significance has been extended.

> As it seems from the common understanding of men, the name *actus* was first attributed to operation; for almost everyone understands *actus* in this way. Subsequently however it was thence transferred to form, insofar as form is a principle and end of operation.[13]

Clearly, the broad meaning of *actus* is an analogical extension from *actus* in the narrow sense of operation. As the text just quoted indicates, the term *actus*, as a term of art, is not merely a synonym for (say) 'perfection' or 'fullness,' even if it is convertible with them. Terms are convertible when each of them can be truly predicated of whatever the other can. This does not entail identical meanings. In comparison with *actus*, 'perfection' furnishes a rather more formal vision of what it is predicated of. That is, the point of reference is not activity or operation as such, but rather some sort of model or rule against which a thing is judged. The 'perfect' is that which is lacking in nothing, that which fills up its measure. This is so even though, in Aquinas's view, what is primarily *judged* perfect, namely a perfect substance, is precisely that which has reached its proper capacity to operate; for it is then that a substance is fully developed or mature.[14] But in the case of *actus*, the *meaning* is either operation itself, or something having some sort of relation to operation. Even when it refers to mere form, *actus* retains a certain connotation of operation. It is operation that is *actus* in the primary, unqualified sense.

---

13. *Sicut videtur ex communi hominum intellectu, nomen actus primo fuit attributum operationi; sic enim quasi omnes intelligunt actum; secundo autem exinde fuit translatum ad formam, inquantum forma est principium operationis et finis* (*De pot.* q. 1, a. 1).

14. See I, q. 5, a. 4. Cf. Aristotle, *Metaphysics* IX, ch. 8, 1050a15–23.

This account of the analogy of *actus* fits Aquinas's notion of analogical equivocation in general. The unity of the several definitions or senses of an analogically equivocal term consists in the fact that all derive from or center upon one primary sense. Some reference to this primary sense must be included in the account of the other senses. There is no single, completely definite common meaning or notion that can be abstracted from these several meanings. If one wishes to assign a common meaning to the term, it will be necessary to allow for a certain indefiniteness in the meaning itself, if such a thing is possible. By 'indefiniteness in the meaning,' I do not mean merely that the things of which the term is predicable are indefinitely many; this is true of any common term, even if it is univocal. Rather, I mean that the very account of the term's meaning, its definition, must itself remain indefinite or incomplete; it must, so to speak, have a blank waiting to be filled in. Thus, the 'common notion' of *actus* would be '_____ operation.' Remove the blank, and you have the primary sense, *actus simpliciter*. Each secondary sense will call for filling in the blank, and doing so in such a way as to qualify the term's reference to operation.

One might say that with analogical terms such as *actus*, whose multiple meanings all point to a single primary one, there are good reasons *both* for restricting the term's application to the things covered by its primary sense *and* for extending it to what falls under the other sense or senses. Because the primary (and, for Aquinas, primitive) sense of *actus* is operation, it is this sense that can be taken as the standard one, the one intended when no qualification or special context dictates otherwise. Thus, in his actual use of the term, St Thomas often simply goes along with 'what almost everyone understands' by it. Seldom, if ever, in his various treatments of human 'acts,' voluntary 'acts,' and so forth, does he see any need to caution the reader that he is speaking of act precisely in the sense of operation. On the other hand, he is highly aware that not everything pertaining to the notion of operation is altogether proper to it. The domain of influence of operation extends beyond operation itself; and the extension of the term *actus* beyond operation seems to have been a quite conscious effort to draw attention to the connection between operation and other entities. If a multiplicity of terms is useful for making precise distinctions between different things, the grouping of several senses under one term is also useful for expressing the unity still remaining among the things distinguished (precisely *as* distinguished).

Not to notice such unity can have serious consequences. Neglect of the point about form as act, for instance, seems to play a part in the rather sophomoric criticism sometimes directed against 'classical' metaphysics for being 'substance-based' and, therefore, for promoting a view of reality as fundamentally 'static,' which is to say, lifeless, inert, merely 'given.'

Moreover, Aquinas's treatment of form as sharing in the nature of act, 'insofar as it is a principle and end of operation,' reflects important elements in his analysis of operation itself. One need only consider the role played in his doctrine by the principle that 'operation follows upon being,' i.e. that the operation proper to each thing is a function of what it is. What a thing is, for Thomas, derives chiefly from its form. The denomination of form as act is a way of expressing this proportion between form and operation.

3. Names, Conceptions and Natures

As the reader will have surmised, I am dwelling at such length on the notion of analogical equivocation because it seems to me that this sort of equivocation is at work in Aquinas's uses of the term 'action.' Showing this, together with the grounds for it, as I intend to do in the rest of this chapter, should already shed some light on his understanding of its nature, and will also provide the rationale for the discussion in the chapters to follow. However, before entering into the Thomistic analogy of 'action' and the grounds for it, I will mention one other general distinction, which figures in one of St Thomas's discussions of analogy. This is the distinction between what later scholastics call nominal and real definitions.

This distinction, which I shall explain shortly, is pertinent on account of the fact that that analogy is a matter of meanings or definitions.[15] Definitions are expressions of knowledge. Now obviously, one and the same thing can fall under people's knowledge in various ways. As a result, a term's meaning, and hence its unity or multiplicity of meaning, can vary according to the cognitive context in which it is employed. This implies, for instance, that analogy has a place both outside and within scientific discourse, and that one and the same term may be analogical within one domain of discourse, and not so in another. Noting this will help us at least to be wary of confusing the domain of discourse in which St Thomas carries out his treatment of action with other possible domains.

This is not a merely imaginary danger, I believe. As we shall see in a moment, Thomas calls attention to a situation of this sort in the case of the term 'body.' I strongly suspect that 'action,' and also some other terms connected with it, may also be susceptible of such analysis. Even though I do not intend to follow up on it at length here, I wish at least to indicate this suspicion. Doing so will also provide a convenient opportunity to introduce those other terms into the discussion.

Now, as Thomas reads it, Aristotle's doctrine of the meaning of words rests on a distinction between the conception or *ratio* that a term immediately signifies, and the *res*—the nature—that it also signifies, though only mediately.[16] Also from Aristotle is the view that in many instances, we begin with a merely confused or superficial conception of a nature, and that we name the nature accord-

---

15. Of course, one might extend the meaning of 'analogical' itself in an analogical way; St Thomas seems to indicate that he is extending it in this way when he says in I, q. 13, a. 5 ad 1 that something 'might be called an analogical agent,' owing to a certain similarity with analogical predicates.

16. See Aristotle, *De interpretatione* ch. 1, 16a4–9; Aquinas, *In I Peri herm.* lect. ii, §§ 13, 15, 19. On the importance of this distinction in Aristotle, see Anscombe, 'Aristotle,' esp. pp. 41–46. The study of the immediate significations of names is a matter of 'dialectic' in a broad sense. See Aristotle, *De anima* I, ch. 1, 403a30–b17; Thomas, *In XI Meta.* lect. iii, § 2204 and *In VII Meta.* lect. xvii § 1658.

ingly, e.g. by reference to some merely extrinsic sign or accompaniment. Only later do we arrive at a clearer and more proper understanding of the nature, scientific knowledge of it. Such knowledge perfects the conception or definition that the name originally signifies.

Would the scientific definition be a mere secondary, qualified sense of the term, an analogical derivation from the definition originally signified? Surely not. It would be precisely a more perfect *primary* signification. It would be the definition of which the original one is but the germ or sketch.

On the other hand, the original, imperfect definition is the one that attaches most immediately and universally to the name. It would be the more suitable answer to the merely lexical question of what the name means. One can know what 'man' means and yet wonder what it is to be a man. This seems to be why later scholastics call the original, imperfect definition the 'nominal' definition of the *thing* named. The scientific definition, framed by a mind that has fully assimilated the thing, is called the thing's 'real' definition.

What has this to do with analogy? Sometimes a term is said equally of certain subjects according to the nominal definition, but only unequally—analogically—according to the real or scientific definition. Even though they share equally in the features by which a nature was originally designated, the subjects may turn out not to share equally in that nature. This does not mean merely that they differ in nature. Man and dog differ in specific nature, but they share equally in the generic nature of animal; man may be the more perfect animal, but he does not have animality more perfectly. 'Animal' is said of them univocally. Its definition applies equally to both. A name is analogous when the definition applies only with qualification in some cases.

According to Thomas, a name which *is* analogous in this way is 'body,' taken as signifying a genus of substance.[17] The original or nominal definition of bodily substance differentiates it only by way of a sign, namely three-dimensionality. (This is only a sign, since it is not itself a substantial feature; it belongs to the accidental genus of quantity.) Taken merely as signifying this conception, or from a merely 'dialectical' point of view, the name 'body' is said univocally of all three-dimensional substances. But in Aquinas's world, real corporeal nature is not the same in all three-dimensional substances. To be a body is not the same thing—cannot be defined in the same way—for a heavenly body and a terrestrial one. This is because what primarily distinguishes bodily substance from incorporeal substance is that bodies have matter. Aquinas believed that celestial matter is not the same thing as terrestrial matter. The matter of terrestrial bodies is a principle of corruption for them, a potentiality for diverse substantial forms. In heavenly bodies, which were thought to be incorruptible, the only potential diversity following upon their matter is diversity of place. The matter of heavenly

---

17. *In I Sent.* d. 19, q. 5, a. 2 ad 1; *ST* I, q. 66, a. 2; *In V Meta.* lect. xvii, § 1124–27.

bodies is matter in only a qualified sense; and so they are bodies in only a qualified or analogical sense.

The upshot of this would be that there is not one generic science of body for Aquinas. There would be a science of celestial body, and a science of earthly body. On this view, the original or 'nominal' conception of body would need to be rather sharply distinguished from the scientific one, since the scientific one is in fact not one but two. At the same time, the very fact that the two ways of being a body do have things in common (e.g. three-dimensionality) would seem at least to allow for a general study of the 'common features' of body. A good deal of the knowledge we have of terrestrial bodies (which are obviously the ones better known to us) could be applied to the science of heavenly ones—with care, of course, and only to the extent that the knowledge falls within the scope of some common feature.

Now, at least from an Aristotelian perspective, considerations similar to the ones just presented about (a medieval notion of) 'body' might well be applicable to a term which we have already discussed, the term 'operation.' That is, this term may, at least in certain settings, possess a merely nominal or dialectical univocity which conceals an equivocity belonging to it from the scientific standpoint. The basis for this discrepancy would be, as in the case of body, the use of a mere sign or accompaniment as the basis for the concept. For instance, in the setting of much contemporary philosophy, the initial concept of 'operation' might be found to be based on the fact that operations are expressed in speech by way of *verbs*. Being expressed in verbs would be a sign naturally accompanying operation. This is true, and certainly very important; at the same time, it is also obviously compatible with profound differences among operations, perhaps differences even with respect to what being an operation is for each of them. In this respect, the term 'operation' may be equivocal, and operations may not fall under it equally, even though they are all equally 'verbal.'

Aristotle suggests something like the equivocity of 'operation' in his discussion of *energeia*. *Energeia* is broader than 'operation,' since it also covers existence and form;[18] but he points out that (just like the Latin *operatio*) it derives from 'work' (*ergon/opus*), and one of the equivocities of *energeia* that he signals is precisely in the domain of operation. In general, for him, the gist of *energeia* is marked out by its opposition to potentiality. This is the basis for the connection between it and *entelecheia*; *energeia* is a kind of ultimate, a term to which something else, potentiality, is ordered. But as he notes, some things which are called *energeia* are such that part of their very nature is precisely to be in potency, to be ordered to something else. These are motions (*kineseis*). And therefore, he calls for withholding the term *energeia* from such 'operations,' and restricting it to 'perfect' operations.

---

18. See *Metaphysics* IX, ch. 6, 1048a32 and IX, ch. 8, 1050a15.

For every motion is incomplete, as in losing weight, learning, walking, and building. These, then, are motions, and they are incomplete; for one is not walking and at the same time has walked, nor is he building and has built, nor is a thing being generated and has been generated, nor is it being moved and has moved, but they are distinct; and moving another thing is distinct from having moved another thing. On the other hand, the same thing has seen and is seeing at the same time, and likewise it is thinking and has thought. I call each of the latter 'an *actuality*' [*energeia*], but each of the former 'a motion.'[19]

Motion is the 'act of what is in potency, as such,' and essentially imperfect or incomplete operation. So long as it exists, some part of it has yet to be exercised. Its full achievement, its reaching its term, is simultaneous with its cessation. But to say this is to qualify the very way in which 'operation' is said of it; for 'operation' *means* a certain term or perfection, precisely the opposite of being in potency.

This distinction comes out only by examining the natures of the things in question. It may or may not show up clearly in the signs, the *verbs* by which they are signified and which provide a first and, so to speak, merely 'dialectical' account of them. For instance, as seems to fit with Aristotle's thesis, the orchestra is playing a symphony but has not played it. Yet, in apparent contrast with his view of cognitive operations such as seeing or hearing, it would also seem to be the case that you are listening to the symphony but have not listened to it. The listening, it seems, cannot be complete until the playing is. But this is to miss Aristotle's point, which is that the listening does not *add* any process to the process which is the playing of the symphony. All the movement is in the playing, not the listening, and if the listening is incomplete, it is merely because only a part of the symphony has been played, not because there is any such thing as part of a listening. It is not the grammar of the verbs 'playing' and 'listening to' which is decisive.[20] This point is made very forcefully by Terry Penner in his article 'Verbs and the Identity of Actions.'[21]

---

19. *Metaphysics* IX, ch. 6, 1048b29–35 (Apostle translation). For the connection between *energeia* and *entelecheia*, see *Metaphysics* IX, ch. 8, 1050a23; cf. *Summa theologiae* I, q. 4, a. 1, together with q. 5, a. 1 ad 1 and q. 5, a. 4.

20. At the same time, as is often the case, the difference could also be brought back up to the level of linguistic expression. For instance, instead of saying that you are listening to the symphony, you can say that you are listening to *the orchestra playing* the symphony, and it is simultaneously the case that you have listened to the orchestra playing the symphony; but obviously you cannot say that the orchestra is playing *the orchestra playing* the symphony. The objects of 'listening' and 'playing' are not altogether identical.

21. The objection about the symphony was raised in J. L. Ackrill's paper, 'Aristotle's Distinction between *energeia* and *kinēsis*'; Penner's article is mostly a reply to this paper. Also very helpful for working out act-differences similar to the kinds signaled by Aristotle, in relation to their verbal expressions in English, is Kenny, *Action, Emotion and Will*, ch. 8 ('States, Performances and Activities'), pp. 171–86.

I suspect that a similar point may be made about 'action.' The verbal expression does not always answer directly to the nature of the thing expressed. For example, St Thomas makes much of the distinction between what he calls 'immanent' and 'transitive' action. The former is action which is seated or takes place in the very agent which performs it, and in virtue of the very power by which he performs it; the latter takes place in something distinct from the agent, or at least in virtue of a (passive) power distinct from the active power by which the agent performs it. Loosely, transitive action is doing something *to* something, while immanent action is simply doing something. But this is not always reflected in the verbal expression. That is, not all transitive verbs signify transitive actions, and not all intransitive verbs signify immanent ones. Transitive verbs can signify immanent actions, because even immanent actions can have 'objects'; not objects upon which they are performed, but objects with which they are concerned. Hitting Socrates' nose is doing something to his nose, whereas seeing Socrates' nose is merely an operation concerned with Socrates' nose, but not affecting the nose; and yet the form of expression is altogether identical. On the other hand, 'to grow' is an intransitive verb in many of its senses, and yet even in these senses, what it signifies, for Aquinas at least, is a transitive operation: an action which a living thing performs, in virtue of its vegetative powers and by means of food, upon itself. The living thing receives that action in virtue of the passivity of its body. The only truly immanent actions, he holds, are operations of cognition and appetite.[22]

One other point that was mentioned in connection with Aquinas's understanding of 'body' also seems to have a bearing on action. If 'action' does turn out to be an equivocal term, at least from the point of view of the real or scientific definition signified by it, then there may very well not be one generic science of it. As it happens, St Thomas investigates something called 'action' within both of what he regards as generically diverse sciences: physics and ethics. Physics, the science of natural things, is a speculative science, and it studies operations and actions whose principles are in the things themselves, not in the knower (*qua* knower). Ethics, the science of voluntary things, is a practical science, bearing upon actions whose principles are in the knower himself. This then is another sign that for Thomas, the term 'action' is scientifically equivocal. What I shall now try to show is that its equivocity is that of analogy. This will justify the more general project of this study, which is to contribute to the understanding of human action through consideration of features common to being a human action and being a physical action. The foregoing observations add a note of caution: such a project must be very careful not to blur the distinction between these fundamentally diverse ways of being actions.[23]

22. See *SCG* II, ch. 23, § 993: *Huiusmodi autem non sunt nisi actiones cognoscentis et appetentis.*

23. This concern is the theme of Eileen C. Sweeney's 'From Determined Motion to Undetermined Will.' She in fact claims that in Thomas, the analogies between natural agents and agents of a higher level—human, divine—take on more and more the character of *metaphors* as one goes up the

B. THE ORDER OF AGENTS: ACTIONS AND THEIR SUBJECTS

We may now begin to consider the analogical equivocity with which St Thomas uses the term 'action' and related terms such as 'agent.' There are several texts which indicate that he judges that voluntary and non-voluntary actions receive the name 'action' in an analogical way. As fits with the passages mentioned in Section A.1, the chief meaning of 'action' remains human, voluntary action.

Instead of presenting a string of texts from Aquinas which indicate the analogy of 'action,' I propose to concentrate on just one of them, an especially instructive one. This is question 29, article 1 of the *prima pars* of the *Summa theologiae*. This article is devoted to defending and interpreting Boethius's definition of the term 'person' as 'individual substance of a rational nature.'

Aquinas's primary aim in the corpus of the article is to explain why a special term has been adopted to signify those individual substances whose nature is rational. The reason, he argues, is that, in a certain way, rational individuals possess the character of individuals in a more special way than do the rest. What he adduces to show this is the special way in which rational individuals are subjects of action. The whole argument merits our attention. What follows is the entire corpus of the article. I shall be examining it, together with some of the article's objections, throughout this section.[24]

> Granted that the universal and the particular are found in all genera, nevertheless the individual is found in a certain special way in the genus of substance. For substance is individuated through itself, whereas accidents are individuated through their subject, which is substance. For a whiteness is called 'this' insofar as it is in this subject. Whence individuals of substance, in preference to the others, fittingly have some special name: for they are called hypostases, or first substances. But the particular and individual is found in a still more special and perfect way in rational substances, which have mastery of their act, and are not

---

scale. I suspect, although I cannot enter into the matter here, that this claim involves a conception of analogy and metaphor which is radically different from the one I am assuming. She holds that analogy *is* a kind of metaphor (p. 209, n. 6); compare McInerny, *The Logic of Analogy*, pp. 144–52.

24. *Licet universale et particulare inveniantur in omnibus generibus, tamen speciali quodam modo individuum invenitur in genere substantiae. Substantia enim individuatur per seipsam, sed accidentia individuantur per subiectum, quod est substantia. Dicitur enim haec albedo, inquantum est in hoc subiecto. Unde etiam convenienter individua substantiae habent aliquod speciale nomen prae aliis; dicuntur enim hypostases, vel primae substantiae. Sed adhuc quodam speciali et perfectiori modo invenitur particulare et individuum in substantiis rationalibus, quae habent dominium sui actus, et non solum aguntur, sicut alia, sed per se agunt. Actiones autem in singularibus sunt. Et ideo etiam inter ceteras substantias quoddam speciale nomen habent singularia rationalis naturae. Et hoc nomen est persona. Et ideo in praedicta definitione personae ponitur substantia individua, inquantum significat singulare in genere substantiae, additur autem rationalis naturae, inquantum significat singulare in rationalibus substantiis.* I have slightly altered the punctuation of the Leonine edition, making *actiones autem in singularibus sunt* a new sentence.

merely operated, as the others are, but operate on their own. Now actions are in singulars. And therefore, even among the other substances, singulars of a rational nature have a certain special name. And this name is 'person.' And therefore in the aforesaid definition of 'person' is placed 'individual substance,' insofar as it signifies a singular in the genus of substance; while 'of a rational nature' is added, insofar as it signifies a singular in rational substances.[25]

1. *Actiones in singularibus sunt*

The text begins with a consideration drawn from Aristotle's *Categories* (ch. 2). This is that the distinction between the general and the particular cuts across all the genera of beings, i.e. substance and the nine accidental genera. There is both man and this man, both blue and this (patch of) blue, both fatherhood and this man's fatherhood, etc.

That Aquinas begins his discussion of individuals and persons with a point taken from the *Categories* fits with the fact that for him, the term 'individual' is first of all a logical notion. It has to do with the way things are known and named by us. As he notes in the third objection of this same article, 'individual' refers to the object of a certain kind of name, or to a certain kind of meaning or *intentio: individuum . . . est nomen intentionis*. It is in this sense that individuals are properly opposed to universals.[26] When something is called an individual, in this sense, the focus is precisely on how its name functions; an individual is something which cannot be predicated of many subjects, something whose name cannot stand for many subjects except by equivocation. It is logically 'incommunicable,' fit to have what we would call a proper name, such as 'Socrates.' A universal is just the opposite: something which can be predicated of many subjects, or whose name can stand for many subjects without equivocation—something with a common name, such as 'horse.'

Individuals are thus opposed to the objects of common names and general expressions, things which are susceptible of being shared or 'divided up' and applied to many subjects. To the extent that the individual is opposed to the general, the chief distinguishing feature of the individual is clearly the exclusion of multiplicity. An individual is what there cannot be many of, but only one. There can be many men, but not many Aristotles (unless 'Aristotle' is used equivocally).

Thomas goes on to note that although particularity or individuality is found in all the categories, it is found in a special way in substances. Substances are

---

25. The terms 'operated' and 'operate' may be a bit jarring; I have chosen them, instead of expressions using the term 'act,' in order to keep a closer grammatical parallel with *non solum aguntur, . . . sed per se agunt*, and also for reasons which will be discussed below, pp. 29–39. But I will grant that *aguntur* might also be rendered 'are made to act'; or even better, in the final analysis, 'are led to act.'

26. See *In I Peri herm.* lect. x, § 121 (commenting on *De interpretatione* 7, 17a38–b2): if the distinction between individuals and universals is taken as a division of *things*, it can only be of things precisely insofar as they are signified by names, not of things taken absolutely.

'individuated through themselves,' whereas accidents are individuated through their subjects, which are substances. To distinguish one instance of an accidental kind, e.g. one patch of red, from another requires designating the subject in which it inheres, either directly or by way of some other accident inhering in the same subject; whereas distinguishing one substance from another of the same kind means finding another designation for the substance itself, not finding any other subject which it is 'of.' For this reason, there is a special name for individual substances: 'hypostases,' or the 'first substances' of the *Categories*.

We may note that the focus continues to be logical. That is, Thomas is continuing to speak of individuals in opposition to universals. What he is telling us is that there is both this white and this man, but the reason why this white is 'this,' i.e. is just this one and not common to many, is that it belongs to this man; whereas it is not by belonging to anything else that this man is just *this* man. A substance is something which does not 'exist in' a subject, as an accident does. Not being received in something else, an individual substance cannot be individuated through anything other than itself.

To be sure, Aquinas will insist in many other places that matter ('signate' matter, 'this stuff over here') is the 'principle of individuation' of corporeal substances. But this is not opposed to the thesis that individual substances are individuated *per se*. For the matter of a substance is a part or component of that substance, not a distinct subject in which the substance is received. What is received in matter is not the substance but only the substantial form, e.g. the soul of a living body. However, this does mean that not only accidents, but also substantial forms, are individuated by 'something else,' at least to the extent that individuation means exclusion of universality or community.

Having explained the grounds for giving a special name to individual substances, Aquinas now goes on to argue that among individual substances, rational ones have a further special individuality about them. He bases this judgment on the special way in which they act: *habent dominium sui actus, et non solum aguntur, sicut alia, sed per se agunt*. They have mastery of their act, and are not merely operated, as other things are, but operate on their own. As regards the question of the analogy of action, this is the key thesis in the article.

Before examining it, however, I would first like to give some consideration to the basis upon which Thomas judges that this thesis leads to the conclusion that rational individuals have a special mode of individuality. As he immediately indicates, that basis is the fact that the actions of things, as opposed to other possessions they may enjoy, bear a particularly close relationship to their individuality. *Actiones autem in singularibus sunt*. Actions are in singulars.

Now, it seems to me that in this phase of the argument, Thomas is in fact shifting from a 'logical' to a 'real' perspective, or from a consideration of things as they are known and named to a consideration of them as they are in themselves. I will explain this in a moment. But even from a logical perspective, i.e. the perspective of the comparison between particulars and universals, the thesis that actions are in singulars has its validity, and is worth developing, because it is also rather delicate. The validity of it is simply that universals or kinds are not proper subjects of action. As Aristotle says, it is not man that is generated, but this man.

But it is a delicate point, easily misunderstood; for there are many things which it may seem to mean but in fact does not. It certainly does not mean that there are no *kinds* of action, or that actions themselves cannot be considered in a general way. Action-theory would be in pretty serious trouble if they could not. Nor does it mean that actions *are* individuals. This is a thesis dear to many action-theorists;[27] and certainly for Aquinas there are individual actions.[28] But he already indicated this, at the beginning of the *respondeo*, when he said that there are particulars or individuals in *every* category. The special point that he is now making about actions is a different one.

Neither is it that nothing belonging to the sphere of action can be attributed to kinds or general subjects. For instance, we say that dogs bark, people talk, stars shine, and so forth. But what each of these statements attributes to the subject is only something *pertaining* to action, not action itself. That is, none of these statements implies that anything *is* barking, talking or shining, or that anything ever has done so or ever will do so. They only attribute some kind of potential for action; or, if you prefer, they only attribute action in the manner of something potential—which means precisely *not* in the manner of action.

To put the point in Thomistic language, part of the very *meaning* of action-terms, or at least the primary meaning, is 'being in act.' And being in act requires individuals. 'Man is mortal' does not imply that any man actually exists; and 'man talks' does not imply either that any man exists, or that any man is doing anything, even talking. Universals are 'always and everywhere,' which means they are indefinite as regards time and place;[29] but an action-predicate contracts the sense of the sentence to a definite time and place, that of the action itself (even if its definite time is 'forever' and its place 'everywhere').

What makes this point slippery is perhaps, in part, that for English-speakers it is almost too obvious. In Latin, *Homo currit* can stand for both 'Man runs' and 'A man is running.' Hence a philosopher writing in Latin might feel the need to call special attention to the distinction between the potential and actual senses of *currere*, and to the fact that the *actual* sense calls for an individual subject.

Of course, linguistic usage is not the final arbiter here; nothing prevents us from attributing genuine actions to general subjects or to kinds by synecdoche. Indirectly or *per accidens*, universals may be said to act. We might say that in

---

27. See Davidson, 'The Individuation of Events,' in *Essays*, pp. 163–80; Donagan, *Choice*, pp. 26ff.

28. This is what allows him to treat circumstances as 'accidents' of action (see I–II, q. 7, a. 1); for it is in individuals, not universals, that are found things that are one *per accidens* (see *In V Meta.* lect. xi, § 910).

29. See I, q. 16, a. 7 ad 2.

1969, man went to the moon. But the point remains that such a statement implies that there was *some* man who, in 1969, went to the moon; and it does not at all imply that whatever was a man in 1969 went to the moon. Whereas in statements like 'man is mortal,' there is no implication that 'there is some man who . . .'; and the sense of such statements is precisely to the effect that *whatever* is a man is mortal.

2. Actiones sunt suppositorum

As I said, however, it seems to me that the drift of the text on 'person' is better captured if, at this point, we take Aquinas to be shifting from a 'logical' to a 'real' perspective. Such a shift would certainly be appropriate, since, as he noted in that objection in which 'individual' was said to be the name of an *intentio*, 'person' is *not* the name of an *intentio* but the name of a *res*.[30] To call something a person is to consider it, not in relation to its name or concept, but in itself, in its own reality. Hence, he says in the reply to the objection, when it is used in the definition of person, 'individual' does not mean an *intentio*, but is taken in an extended sense according to which it applies to real things. In this sense, he says, it designates what he calls the 'mode of subsisting that belongs to particular substances.'

The shift is appropriate also because the statement 'actions are in singulars' is not altogether rigorous unless here 'singulars' has come to mean precisely individual *substances*—opposed, not to universals, but to accidents, forms, and other mere ingredients of substances. For in fact not all singulars, in the sense in which these are opposed to universals, are subjects of action. As with universals, some singulars can be said to act only indirectly or *per accidens*; e.g. an individual triangle. Only substantial singulars, *subsisting* things, can either act or be acted upon, properly speaking. Thus, later in the *Summa theologiae*, Aquinas says that 'actions are of *supposita* [hypostases] and wholes, but not, properly speaking, of parts and forms, or of powers; for it is not said properly that the hand strikes, but that the man strikes with his hand, nor is it said properly that heat heats, but that fire heats through its heat.'[31] Seen from this perspective, what 'actions are in singu-

---

30. I, q. 29, a. 1 obj. 3. See also I, q. 30, a. 4: *hoc nomen persona non est nomen negationis neque intentionis, sed est nomen rei*.

31. *Actiones autem sunt suppositorum et totorum, non autem, proprie loquendo, partium et formarum, seu potentiarum; non enim proprie dicitur quod manus percutiat, sed homo per manum, neque proprie dicitur quod calor calefaciat, sed ignis per calorem* (II–II, q. 58, a. 2). So of course, when I say that Thomas has now shifted from a logical to a real perspective, I do not mean to suggest that he thinks that only individual names, as opposed to universal names, signify anything real. I mean that he is no longer talking about a logical distinction, but about one of the terms of the real distinction which forms the basis of the logical one. The real distinction is between a whole, concrete subject and a form inhering in it. By 'abstracting' the form, the mind frames the notion of the universal, the species. And so although the species does not subsist *per se*, its definition is predicable not only of it but also of the individuals possessing the form which is its principle.

lars' means is precisely that actions belong to things having that 'mode of subsisting that belongs to particular substances.'

One might object to this account on the grounds that it seems to render 'substance' in the definition of 'person' superfluous. If 'individual' is taken precisely in the sense of 'proper subject of action,' then it includes substance in its very meaning, rather than functioning as a quasi-differentia of substance. However, the definition is not Aquinas's invention, but Boethius's; and in fact Boethius arrives at it by a purely logical method of division.[32] Such a method cannot suffice, by itself, to achieve Aquinas's aim in this article, which is not merely to identify the class of things called 'persons,' but to *explain* what it is about that class which merits it a special name.

Moreover, and more importantly for our purposes, even if 'individual' stands for 'subject of action,' a place could still be found for 'substance' in the definition of 'person.' It could stand generally for *subsisting* things, in such a way as to include both subsistent *wholes* and subsistent *parts* (e.g. a bone or a leg or a human soul). Then 'individual' would restrict the definition precisely to the *wholes*, the subsistent entities naturally apt to exist *separately*. There is nothing at all forced about such a distinction. Aristotle repeatedly calls the parts of animals 'substances.' And St Thomas himself, in his discussion of the subsistence of the human soul, goes into considerable detail in explaining the sense in which subsistence can be attributed not only to whole substances but also to their parts. Their 'being in the whole' is not at all the same as that of accidents or 'material forms.'[33] He even grants that it is not altogether improper to speak of the subsisting parts of substances as subjects of action.[34]

In any case, no matter how the objection is answered, it would seem to be precisely this, existing separately and not as an inherent form or as a part,

---

32. *Liber de persona et duabus naturis contra Eutychen et Nestorium*, 2–3, PL 64, 1342–43. Interestingly, looking at the definition from the 'logical' perspective, Thomas himself has to face a similar objection to the one mentioned here: the article's second objection is that 'individual' either yields a contradiction *in adiecto*, or else is superfluous, depending upon whether 'substance' stands for second substance or first substance. His preferred reply is simply that 'substance' stands commonly for both, and that 'individual' contracts it to first substance. The more general point to note is that the terms of the definition do not stand in strict logical subordination. There are individuals outside the class of substances, and substances outside the class of individuals. This is not an objection to the definition, since 'person' is not presumed to name a species of a genus. The definition does not state an essence. This allows Thomas to be rather free with his use of it in the treatise on the divine Persons. For instance, sometimes he uses 'individual' in the sense of 'distinct' or 'incommunicable'; on other occasions he uses it in the sense of 'subsistent.' This is why, although I certainly do not mean to insist that my present account of the definition is how Aquinas 'really' understands it, I also do not think it deviates significantly, if at all, from his doctrinal intentions.

33. I, q. 75, a. 2 ad 1 and 2. Cf. Aristotle's insistence that the sense in which accidents are 'present in' the substance is not that in which the substance's parts are, and that therefore we can still call the parts substances (*Categories*, 2, 1a25, 3a29–31).

34. I, q. 75, a. 2 ad 1 and 2; see below, pp. 24–25.

which Aquinas has in mind in speaking of the 'mode of subsisting belonging to *particular* substances.' Evidence for this is found in the reply to the fifth objection of the article on 'person.' There he denies that a human soul is an individual substance, even though it subsists, precisely because it lacks the nature of something *separate*. Even when it is *in fact* separate (after death), this is contrary to its nature, which is that of something meant to be united (*unibilis*).[35]

Generally speaking, to subsist is to be a subject of existence, to exist *per se* rather than *per accidens*. Accidents and 'material forms' are not subjects of existence, but exist only by belonging to or accompanying an existing subject. They are called 'beings' only in a secondary sense, that of things 'by which' a subject exists (either absolutely, as a substance, or in some qualified mode). By contrast, the parts of substances are subjects of existence, or subsistent; they exist *per se* rather than *per accidens*. But the existence of which they are subjects is not strictly their own, not belonging to them as to its *primary* subject. 'Something can sometimes be called a *per se* existent if it is not inherent as an accident or a material form, even if it is a part; but what is properly and *per se* called subsistent is what is neither inherent, in the aforesaid manner, nor a part.'[36] What subsists properly and *per se*, the most proper subject of existence, is the whole individual substance, the one which is not a part of something else, but rather whole and fully distinct from everything else, separate. The discussion thus continues to be quite Aristotelian; for separateness is one of the chief marks, in Aristotle, distinguishing whole individual substances in act—substances in the highest sense—not only from universals but also from individual accidents, forms, and even matter, parts, and any sort of substance existing merely in potency.

Further clarification of this point may be provided by reference to a formula for 'individual' which Aquinas gives a little later in question 29: an individual, he says, is what is 'indistinct in itself, and distinct from others' (I, q. 29, a. 4). 'Distinct from' means 'divided from.' What is 'indistinct in itself' is what is one and not many, what is not divided into separate parts, either in the fashion of a species or genus (divided into subjective parts) or in the fashion of a mere aggregate (divided into independently existing integral parts). In the highest sense, it is what holds together, not in just any fashion, but by nature.[37] What is 'distinct from others' is precisely what is separate, having its own existence. For 'distinct from others' does not mean merely 'distinct from the others of the same kind';

---

35. *Anima est pars humanae speciei, et ideo, licet sit separata, quia tamen retinet naturam unibilitatis, non potest dici substantia individua quae est hypostasis vel substantia prima; sicut nec manus, nec quaecumque alia partium hominis. Et sic non competit ei neque definitio personae, neque nomen.*

36. *Per se existens quandoque potest dici aliquid si non sit inhaerens ut accidens vel ut forma materialis, etiam si sit pars. Sed proprie et per se subsistens dicitur quod neque est praedicto modo inhaerens, neque est pars* (I, q. 75, a. 2 ad 2).

37. See *Metaphysics* V, ch. 6, 1015b35–1016a16; X, ch. 1, 1052a19–29.

individual accidents and forms are also 'distinct' in this way. Rather, it means distinct *simpliciter*, distinct from the other *beings*.

It may be noted that *this* sort of distinction, both for Aristotle and for Aquinas, is not merely through matter, but also and chiefly through substantial *form*, which is both the proper principle of subsistence[38] and the proper principle of the highest degree of undividedness or unity (the other aspect of 'individual'), namely unity by nature. Thus, in this same context (I, q. 29, a. 4), Thomas says that the 'principles individuating a man' are 'this flesh and these bones and *this soul*.' Here it is not a question of the principles distinguishing individuals within a species, 'logical' individuation; in that sense, even soul is individuated by something else, namely matter.[39] Instead, here the individuating principles are the very principles which constitute the subject of existence, as such. And it is through its form that a subject is perfected in its capacity to exist, and at the same time made whole and definite, set fully apart from its surroundings. 'Everything which is in act must be distinct from the rest; for one thing is divided from another through its act and through its form.'[40]

It is surely along these lines that we are to understand the general notion of one substance's having individuality in a 'more special and perfect way' than another. Mere logical particularity, within the genus of substance, does not seem to admit of grades. All individual substances are individual *per se*. As Aristotle says in the *Categories* (ch. 5, 2b26–28), an individual man is not 'more' a first or individual substance than is an individual ox.

But clearly some substances are more distinct beings, stand out more, than others. Again according to Aristotle, many of the things called 'substances' are mostly potentialities: not only the parts of animals, but also inanimate substances like earth, fire or air, which exist 'like a heap,' waiting to be formed and made into a unity.[41] There is no such thing as 'a water' or 'an air' or 'a gold'; there is only a body of water, a current or pocket of air, a lump of gold. In things like these, the particulars do not *per se* divide themselves up or hold themselves together in any special way. Their separateness is haphazard and unstable. The manner in which they stand out or are set apart is mostly a function of what surrounds them or what has happened to them. It is only once they are given a further form, beyond their own nature and to which they relate as matter, that it is possible to speak of intrinsically definite individuals: this lake (of water), that medal (of gold). And truly stable separateness, having an intrinsic principle in the

---

38. See I, q. 29, a. 2 ad 5: *quod [individuum compositum ex materia et forma] per se subsistat, habet ex proprietate suae formae, quae non advenit rei subsistenti, sed dat esse actuale materiae, ut sic individuum subsistere possit.*

39. See I, q. 76, a. 2 ad 1.

40. *Omne . . . quod est actu oportet esse ab aliis distinctum; quia res una dividitur ab alia per suum actum et per formam* (*In VII Meta.* lect. xvi, § 1633).

41. See *Metaphysics* VII, ch. 16, 1040b5–10.

thing, really only seems to appear definitively at the level of living things. These actively resist not only being divided up but also being blended with or assimilated by anything else.

Still, even inanimate substances, although their separateness is indefinite and unstable, *are* genuinely separable; and, to repeat, in this they already differ from mere accidents or forms. The difference between the individuality of accidents, and that of substances, is not *merely* a logical one, a matter of how they are distinguished from others in their species. It is not just that the red of the apple is distinguished by making some kind of reference to the apple, while the apple is distinguished by making a different reference to the apple itself; it is also that the red is *inseparable* from the apple, whereas the apple is not inseparable from the red. For while that red never has been and never will be the red of anything else, that very same apple was previously not red but green, and later it may be some other color. In fact, already in the *Categories* (ch. 2, 4a10–4b18), Aristotle makes the 'most distinctive' feature of substances to be their being susceptible of contraries, i.e. capable of movement and change. For Aristotle, it is necessary to posit substance, not as a way of 'overcoming' or 'escaping' flux and change, but precisely in order to account for it, to establish the reality of it.[42]

Of course, as noted earlier, it is the individual substance that moves and changes, not the universal. It is not man who went to the moon (except *per accidens*, as Aristotle would say), but this man. And precisely for this reason, and in this respect, even universal substance is really more a 'suchness,' a *quale*, than a 'this'; it is not separable, and not substance to the highest degree.[43]

At the same time—obviously—Aristotle does not mean that nothing unchangeable is a substance or substance to the highest degree. The unmoved mover is the substance *par excellence*! But it is substance, even to a higher degree than movable substance, precisely because it is a *principle* of motion and even of *substantial* change, generation and corruption. Since 'substance' already connotes a kind of principle for Aristotle, what exists as a principle relative to substances must itself be substance.

By now I hope it is clear that this long discussion of substance and subsistence has not been a mere digression from the question of action, occasioned by the text on 'person.' The conceptual connection between being an individual substance and being a subject of action is extremely tight; as tight, at any rate, as the connection between action and motion. The latter connection is signaled in another text from the *Summa theologiae*, to which I shall often return: 'action, according to the first imposition of the name, conveys an origin of motion.'[44] The separateness which is the proper mark of individual substances is by no

---

42. See *Metaphysics* XII, ch. 1, 1069b2–7.
43. See *Categories* 5, 3b14–22; *Metaphysics* III, ch. 6, 1003a9; VII, ch. 13, 1038b26–28.
44. I, q. 41, a. 1 ad 2. See Ramírez, *De hominis beatitudine*, p. 235.

means unrelated to their being the proper subjects of action. It is virtually the same thing.[45]

3. Parts and Wholes

So, actions have a special connection with individuals. From this, as we have seen, Aquinas draws his desired conclusion: among individual substances, rational ones have a special and more perfect degree of individuality, because they have a special degree of agency. And hence they have that special name, 'person.'

What is of interest to us here, of course, is not so much the term 'person' as the mode of agency that Aquinas attributes to persons. 'They are not merely operated, as other things are, but operate on their own': *non solum aguntur, sicut alia, sed per se agunt*. It is worthwhile spending some time examining this formula. I believe that it captures why, as we saw Aquinas insisting in the *Physics* commentary, action is said 'properly' of agents that have mastery of their acts, free or voluntary agents. In fact, in the *Physics* commentary itself, Thomas immediately goes on to explain himself in almost exactly these same terms: 'what does not have mastery of its act is more something operated [*agitur*] than something that operates.'[46] Moreover, '*non solum aguntur, sicut alia, sed per se agunt*' indicates rather clearly that what he is envisioning is an analogy or proportion of non-voluntary to voluntary action. The analogy is signaled precisely by this, that *agere* is said primarily and without qualification of voluntary agents, as such. When said of others, 'to act' must be qualified or modified somewhat—for instance, by replacing the voice proper to it, the *active* voice, with the passive. Other things *agunt*, to be sure, but less properly; *magis aguntur*.

Yet saying *agunt* of other things is not altogether excluded. This is why, I would suggest, Thomas is careful here to add '*per se*' when saying that rational individuals act. This leaves room for saying that other things act too—only, they do not do so *per se*. He does not mean that action belongs solely to rational beings, as though nothing else had any share in it at all. What supports this reading is that the use of the expression '*per se*' here gives every appearance of being in strict parallel with the statement earlier in the same article, that substances, as opposed to accidents (and all material forms), are individuated *per se*. In that statement, *per se* is clearly *not* taken as opposed to *per accidens*, 'according to an

---

45. If further verification of the Aristotelian credentials of this claim is required, one may cite the way in which, in the *De anima* (e.g. at I, ch. 1, 403a10–16), Aristotle makes the separability of soul depend upon its being *per se* a subject of some sort of operation. For an excellent summary discussion of Aristotle's notion of 'subject' and its relation to form and operation, see Berti, 'Soggetto, anima e identità personale in Aristotele.'

46. Thomas takes the expression '*non solum aguntur, sicut alia, sed per se agunt*' from St John Damascene, *De fide orthodoxa* II, ch. 27, PG 94, 962; see I–II, q. 6, a. 2 obj. 2. He uses it in several places, always to distinguish free agency from agency which is not free. Besides the ones already cited, see, for instance, I, q. 60, a. 1 obj. 2 and reply; *SCG* II, ch. 47, § 1238.

accompaniment'; that would mean that particular accidents (and material forms) are not really particulars at all, but only accompany particulars. Instead, *per se* is taken there as opposed to *per aliud*, 'by dint of something else.' They are truly particulars, but they do not have in themselves the cause or the root of their particularity. Surely *per se* carries this same sense in the phrase *per se agunt*.

The basis of the analogical diversity according to which 'to act' is said of rational and non-rational beings is indicated, then, precisely by the use of the expression *'per se.'* A general principle of Aquinas's metaphysics is that if a feature is possessed in these two ways, *per se* and *per aliud*, then its full, unqualified and principal form is found in the things that have it *per se*. The other things have it only, so to speak, on loan, and hence in secondary fashion, as a mere share parceled out to them by its true owner. Nothing else shares in action in such a way as to have it on its own; and therefore, nothing else has it in its full, unqualified or undiluted form. What we now want to find out is just what is involved in the difference between acting *per se* and acting *per aliud*.

To begin, let us take another look at the text in which Aquinas attributes actions to *supposita* or hypostases. 'Actions are of *supposita* and wholes, but not, properly speaking, of parts and forms, or of powers; for it is not said properly that the hand strikes, but that the man strikes with his hand, nor is it said properly that heat heats, but that fire heats through its heat.'[47] Examining the relation between a hypostasis and its parts, forms and powers will help us to begin to understand the difference between things that operate *'per se'* and things that are merely 'operated.'

Now, we have already seen how St Thomas is willing to attribute subsistence, in a qualified sense, to the parts of substances, whereas subsistence is in no way properly attributed to its accidents (which include its powers); there, indeed, the attribution would be *per accidens*. In that same place—the discussion of the subsistence of the human soul—and on the basis of this attribution of subsistence to the parts, he also distinguishes between the way in which the parts of a substance are related to its *action*, and the way in which its forms and powers are. *In a way*, he says, the parts too are subjects of operation. 'For we say that a man sees by his eye, or touches by his hand, in a different way than that the hot heats by its heat; for heat in no way heats, properly speaking. It can therefore be said that the soul understands, as the eye sees, though it is more properly said that a man understands by his soul.'[48]

Setting aside the difficult question of the soul, the point made here about parts is surely a very plausible one. The parts of a substance, i.e. the subsistent parts, are precisely those 'possessions' of it which, while not actually separate from it, are still separable from it, at least with respect to their matter. (By this I mean that even if

---

47. II–II, q. 58, a. 2. The Latin text is given above, n. 31.

48. *Dicimus enim quod homo videt per oculum, et palpat per manum, aliter quam calidum calefacit per calorem, quia calor nulo modo calefacit proprie loquendo. Potest igitur dici quod anima intelligit sicut oculus videt, sed magis proprie dicitur quod homo intelligat per animam* (I, q. 75, a. 2 ad 2).

an eye cannot survive outside the body, it can still be removed, and at least what was its matter remains.) This very fact shows that they can have some independence of movement. Indeed, it is precisely by *actually* having some independence of movement or function that the parts of animals are usually distinguished, as 'parts,' introducing a certain multiplicity and heterogeneity into the whole. 'Things which are continuous are said to be one, even if they are bent; and they are said to be one to a higher degree if they are not bent; for example, the shin or the thigh is one to a higher degree than the leg, *in view of the fact that the motion of the leg may not be one*.'[49] If we were to refuse any sort of attribution of operations to the parts of animals, insisting that it is only the whole animal that operates, e.g. that sees, then it would be very difficult to explain, for instance, how it is that an animal can see just as well even if its legs are amputated, but not at all if its eyes are removed. It is hardly plausible to say that in the case of the legs, it remains the same (whole?) animal as before, but not so in the case of the eyes; for then, what about the fact that the animal can stand without its eyes, but not without its legs?

So action is attributed to the parts, and not improperly; but it is 'more properly' attributed to the whole. It is the whole that is more unqualifiedly the agent. To understand this, it is now time to introduce the most general and rudimentary formula for 'agent,' as Aquinas understands it. We have already seen that he judges the original sense of 'action' to be 'origin of motion.' The formula for 'agent,' then, is *unde est principium motus*, that from which movement initiates. Not surprisingly, this too comes from Aristotle.[50]

On the basis of this formula, it is not at all difficult to see why a whole substance is more properly an agent than are its parts. The only clarification that might be required is to note that the focus here is not so broad as to cover just anything which somehow functions or moves as a unit and has separable parts, i.e. not just anything that can be called a body (assuming that body is the only kind of substance that has separable parts). The focus is on *natural* bodies, *natural* wholes, wholes whose parts belong to them *per se* or 'by nature.' Aristotle is quite aware that sometimes bodies hold together, move as units, only because they are held together by some other body or bodies: e.g. by string or glue or hooks. But, he is quick to ask, what holds them *and* the string, or glue, or hooks, together? And the string, glue and hooks are bodies too, having magnitude: what holds them together? Eventually something must be found whose parts hold together on their own or by nature.[51] These are principles of all the rest.[52]

---

49. *Metaphysics* V, ch. 6, 1016a10–12 (Apostle translation; my emphasis).

50. On Aristotle's various formulae for 'agent,' the canonical one being 'that from which the primary origin of change or of rest is' (*Physics* II, ch. 3, 194b29–30; 195a22–23), see the treatment by Susan Sauvé Meyer, *Aristotle on Moral Responsibility*, ch. 2, together with her discussion in ch. 6 of the way in which, for Aristotle, precisely the voluntary agent is agent in the most unqualified sense, being the only unqualified origin of actions.

51. See *Metaphysics* VII, ch. 17, 1041b11–32.

52. See *De anima* II, ch. 1, 412a12.

Of course, that a part belongs to its whole 'by nature' need not mean that it cannot exist at all apart from the whole. It means simply that it exists in the whole by an intrinsic principle, that it tends of itself to belong to the whole. Apart from the whole, it is in a violent or unnatural state. The most obvious examples of such parts, of course, are the parts of animals and plants.

It is clear that in the case of such parts, even though they can truly be said to be sources of movement and operation, their wholes are even more so. The reason for this is not simply that the parts exist in the whole and in some way 'belong' to it. This is also true of non-natural wholes, e.g. machines, but in them the whole is precisely *not* a principle of the operations of the parts; rather, the functioning of the whole is nothing but the sum or the net result of the functioning of the parts. If there is any prior principle at work, it is external—the maker or user of the machine.

A better reason for the priority of the whole over the parts, in the case of living things, would be that in many cases, the whole is the source of the *existence* of the parts. An animal does not have eyes or legs from the very moment of its conception, but develops them through its own process of epigenesis. Still, at least the parts of the zygote were there from the start; and yet of these too, the operations are more properly attributed to the whole than to the parts themselves.

The real reason for this is expressed by the ancient term for the parts of living things: organs, which is to say, instruments. The parts spontaneously function according to the exigencies of the whole. They tend to remain in the whole, being distributed in it in a determinate and appropriate manner, and operating in a way conducive to the conservation and self-promotion of the whole. It is precisely this fact—the inner tendency or spontaneity with which the parts serve the whole—which leads to the need for positing a 'form' of the whole distinct from, and prior to, the mere order or structure resulting from the combination of its parts. The whole is not *first* a whole in virtue of that order. In Aristotle's language, of course, that form is the living thing's 'nature' and 'soul.' What the parts of the organic body, and indeed the collection of parts which *is* the organic body, are chiefly instruments *of* is the soul.[53]

In Aquinas's terminology, when one agent is an instrument of another, the latter is called the 'principal' agent. Here then is a first ranking or gradation of agents, *qua* agents, that we may lay down: that of instrumental and principal agents. Let us dwell for a while on this distinction, as St Thomas understands it. As we shall see, it evidently corresponds rather closely to the distinction he has in view in saying that only rational individuals operate on their own, while everything else is merely operated. It will be very helpful in elucidating the primacy that he attributes to rational agents and the order by which he attributes action analogically to other things.

---

53. See *De anima* II, ch. 4, 415b15–21.

C. THE ANALOGY OF 'ACTION'

1. Instrumental Agency

The first thing to note is that an instrument is never something wholly passive or inert. It must genuinely be some kind of principle of action. Otherwise it would be useless. An instrument must have some intrinsic capacity for activity, some ability to contribute to the act which the one using it is seeking to carry out.[54] Recall the phrase we are examining: *non solum aguntur, sicut alia, sed per se agunt*. It is important to note that the term applied to non-rational things is *aguntur*, which I have translated as 'are operated'; perhaps 'are made to act' would also render it. The term is not, for example, *patiuntur*, which is Aquinas's standard way of saying 'are acted upon.' Men who work with machines operate their machines. This certainly does not mean that the machines only have something done to them and do not do anything. The text does not mean to say that non-rational things do not act at all, but that when they act, it is because they are made to do so, by something else.

Still, what makes something an instrument is that it is made to act by something else, the one using it. So although it is not entirely passive, an instrument must be so to some extent. It must be pliant to the one who uses it. This is why, in the phrase under study, the verb expressing the operation of things that do not act on their own is put in the passive voice: *aguntur*. Insofar as something acts in the mode of an instrument, its capacity falls under the control of, or is exercised in the manner determined by, the user.[55]

For this reason, moreover, the full essential account of the action in which the instrument is engaged involves reference to things falling outside the instrument's own contribution, namely, those things that belong to it precisely insofar as it is used by the principal agent.[56] Although these things are accidental to the instrument's proper contribution, they are not accidental to the action in which it is engaged, since it is not by accident that its acting is in accordance with the principal agent's intention. The instrument's proper act and the principal agent's use of it combine to form one action;[57] and the unity is not accidental, but is

---

54. See III, q. 19, arts. 1 and 2; q. 62, a. 1.

55. See III, q. 62, a. 4: *Instrumentum . . . non operatur nisi inquantum est motum a principali agente, quod per se operatur. Et ideo virtus principalis agentis habet permanens et completum esse in natura; virtus autem instrumentalis habet esse transiens ex uno in aliud, et incompletum; sicut et motus est actus imperfectus ab agente in patiens.*

56. See III, q. 19, a. 1: *ilia operatio quae est rei solum secundum quod movetur ab alio, non est alia praeter operationem moventis ipsum: sicut facere scamnum non est seorsum operatio securis ab operatione artificis*.

57. See III, q. 62, a. 1 ad 2: *scindendo enim [securis] facit lectum*. Also III, q. 19, a. 1 ad 5: *concurrunt tamen ambae operationes ad unum operatum secundum quod una natura agit cum communione alterius*.

28 Action and Conduct

comparable to the unity which results from the composition of matter and form. The instrument's proper act is *intrinsically* a part of the act of the one using it.

> Just as in the genus of natural things, a certain whole is composed out of matter and form, as a man out of soul and body, who is one natural being, granted that he has many parts; so also in human acts, the act of an inferior power is material relative to the act of the superior, insofar as the inferior power acts in virtue of the superior moving it; for thus also the act of a first mover is formal relative to the act of an instrument.[58]

In sum, when Aquinas says that what properly acts is a hypostasis and not its parts or powers, the thought is not simply that the parts and powers belong to the hypostasis and that neither they nor their acts are fully independent entities. It is also that their actions are not fully independent *actions*. Their actions are properly understood only as elements in or subordinate contributions to a wider or more far-reaching action, that of the hypostasis itself.[59]

Now, sometimes, this second consideration is applicable even to the actions of things which *are* independent entities and not mere parts or powers of something else. That is, some full-fledged substances act in the manner of instruments. Sometimes they only act under, and as a sort of application of and contribution to, the action of something else. They too are things that are 'merely operated' and do not 'operate on their own.'[60]

To put the point in terms of our earlier discussion of individuality, we might say that not everything that has separate existence *operates* separately. Or more precisely, what is a separate or self-contained subject of operation may not be a separate or self-contained *principle* or *origin* of operation. Its acting or originating movement and operation may in fact be a continuation of, and merely partial contribution to, an operation initiated by something both prior and broader in operational scope. What this order of priority and posteriority consists in will be the concern of the next section. First, however, let us consider some of the original evidence, in the world of nature, that such an order exists.

---

58. *Sicut . . . in genere rerum naturalium, aliquod totum componitur ex materia et forma, ut homo ex anima et corpore, qui est unum ens naturale, licet habeat multitudinem partium; ita etiam in actibus humanis, actus inferioris potentiae materialiter se habet ad actum superioris, inquantum inferior potentia agit in virtute superioris moventis ipsam: sic enim et actus moventis primi formaliter se habet ad actum instrumenti* (I–II, q. 17, a. 4).

59. For Aquinas, even in the action of a merely physical quality, there can be discerned an order toward a further term, set by the substance to which the quality belongs and which the quality serves in the manner of an instrument. *Calor agit ad formam ignis quasi instrumentaliter in virtute formae substantialis* (I, q. 67, a. 3 ad 3). *Corpus agit et ad formam accidentalem, et ad formam substantialem. Qualitas enim activa, ut calor, etsi sit accidens, agit tamen in virtute formae substantialis, sicut eius instrumentum; et ideo potest agere ad formam substantialem; sicut et calor naturalis, inquantum est instrumentum animae, agit ad generationem carnis. Ad accidens vero agit propria virtute* (I, q. 115, a. 1 ad 5).

60. On conjoined and separate instruments, see III, q. 62, a. 5.

One sort of evidence for the merely instrumental character of a thing's operation is that, while not being random, the operation nevertheless exhibits little or no proportion or order *to* the thing itself. Instead, it is carried out according to the exigencies of something else. For instance, we have seen that in Aristotle's view, the physical elements, and inanimate things generally, are, as Donagan puts it, little more than bits of stuff. (The Aristotelian physical elements, or simplest bodies, are earth, water, air and fire.) At the same time, of course, Aristotle sees that even non-living things have some part in the initiation of activity: not their own, to be sure, but that of the things that they are capable of acting upon. They are not 'stuff' purely and simply, since they are differentiable—differentiable with respect to *operation*. They have some degree of substantial form.[61]

And yet, in the case of earth or water or air or fire, there is very little that they can be said to do for their own sake. They show little or no capacity for turning the things outside of them to their advantage, if indeed one can speak intelligibly of 'advantage' or 'need' in their regard.[62] At most, they exhibit some tendency to make other things be like themselves: fire heats other things and sets them on fire, water dissolves, air evaporates, and so forth. But each of the elements rather easily allows itself to be transformed into another. Yet there is considerable regularity, Aristotle finds, in the operations and movements of the elements, beyond their mere tendency to impress their likeness on what they touch. In fact, they evidently form a cyclical system, and each tends to occupy the position relative to the others—its 'natural place'—in which it can most appropriately act and be acted upon, for the maintenance of the cycle. And, he judges, to all appearances the point of this cycle is to provide the necessary environmental and climatic conditions for life.

Living things, even those that lack cognition, the plants, display greater initiative in their activity, and so a higher grade of agency. A sign of this, again, is their greater separateness, which shows up even in their visible shape—the shape being the form of the surface, which is the boundary separating a body from its immediate surroundings. Living things differ from (most) non-living things precisely by *having* shapes that are characteristic of them, i.e. fairly definite and stable. And more importantly, their action upon their surroundings is not limited to their impressing a qualitative likeness. In fact, they do not tend to make the environment just like themselves and merge with it, but rather keep themselves quite distinct; and, in acting upon the environment, they are not 'used up,' but rather appropriate the things around them for their own conservation and development, and even for the formation of other individuals which are both more perfectly like them *and* fully separate from them.

---

61. See the discussion of the relation between form and active power below, Chapter 3, Section C.
62. See Kenny, *The Metaphysics of Mind*, p. 34.

The beasts distinguish themselves even more sharply from what surrounds them than do plants: they move themselves from place to place. Many also have remarkable powers to make both their own parts and other things work to their advantage. Some even live a kind of community life, in which dominant members or leaders can be clearly identified—members which may be said, in a not wholly inappropriate way, to *command* the others.

Still, neither plant nor beast ever quite succeeds in setting itself fully apart as a separate agent, having full initiative. They never altogether stand out from the herd. At least, brutes of the same kind all live the same pattern of life. This is a sign that they retain something of the quality of mere instruments. They are replaceable.

This does not mean simply that whatever one of them can do, others can do too, as though it were a question of possessing some unique power or ability. Abilities and powers are qualities of usefulness. They belong within the instrumental order. To make them the decisive factor in measuring individuality, and to make personhood depend on *this* sort of uniqueness, would be to make 'person' mean 'irreplaceable instrument.' This is plainly not the Thomistic concept of person. In Aquinas's universe, the number of personal beings is immense, yet only one possesses any unique ability. Whatever anything else can do, He can do too.

To say that the beasts are replaceable means above all that they act in the manner of things merely fulfilling some function or role. Its role is not something that the beast takes up or sets aside according to what suits it. What appears to count is only the fulfillment of the role, not the one fulfilling it. In the final analysis, what they are doing is not being done *for them*. It is in rational beings that we first encounter a fully individual way of acting. Rational beings 'have mastery of their acts, and are not only operated, as are other things, but also act on their own.' Only they have the real initiative in acting and live lives that are genuinely their own. A 'history of animals' is always a merely general account of the life of the kind (or perhaps of the transformation of kinds); it is only among rational beings that each individual has a story of his or her own.[63]

---

63. It is certainly no news nowadays that things like newsworthiness, historicity and narrativity are peculiar characteristics of personal individuals; but it may be news that Aquinas was quite aware of the fact, though of course he did not develop it systematically as a philosophical topic. A striking text is found in his discussion of 'person' in the commentary on the *Sentences*: hoc nomen persona significat substantiam particularem, prout subjicitur proprietati quae sonat dignitatem, et similiter prosopon apud graecos; et ideo persona non est nisi in natura intellectuali. Et secundum Boetium, sumptum est nomen personae a personando, eo quod in tragoediis et comoediis recitatores sibi ponebant quamdam larvam ad repraesentandum ilium cujus gesta narrabant decantando. Et inde est quod tractum est in usu ut <u>quodlibet individuum hominis de quo potest talis narratio fieri, persona dicatur</u>; et ex hoc etiam dicitur prosopon in graeco a pro quod est ante, et sopos quod est facies, quia hujusmodi larvas ante facies ponebant (*In I Sent*. d. 23, q. 1, a. 1).

2. Mastery of One's Act as Controlling One's Purpose

On the basis of this rapid survey of the various levels of agency found among natural beings, what seems to emerge as the fundamental difference between agents that act in the manner of instruments and the agents that the instruments serve is that the instruments are ordered to what they serve, and not vice versa. That is, the principal agent is an end relative to its instrument. According to St Thomas, this is what it means to say that the instrument 'belongs' to what it serves: it is ordered to it. 'What is said of someone [or something, *alicuius*] to be "his" [or "its," *suum*] is what is ordered to him [it], as a slave is the master's, and not vice versa.'[64] Similarly, what Aristotle was trying to show, in pointing to the instrumental role played by animal parts relative to the soul, was that the soul is an end or final cause.

This of course is a very interesting consideration, in our present context. For it implies that an agent which does not act merely as an instrument of something else, but acts on his own or *per se*, or with mastery of his act, acts 'for his own sake.' This is how St Thomas continues after the text quoted in the previous paragraph: 'For the free is what is for its own sake [*causa sui*].'[65] In the *Summa contra gentiles*, Thomas goes to considerable length to show that free agents are appropriately treated as beings existing for their own sake, i.e. as beings whose goodness does not belong to them merely for the benefit of something else.[66] However, it is clear that we have not quite gotten at the core of what it is to operate on one's own or *per se*, as opposed to merely 'being operated,' since the difference just noted is a difference in the order of *final* causality, and not precisely in the order of *agent*-causality.

In other places, e.g. in the *Summa contra gentiles* passage just mentioned, St Thomas does use the expression *causa sui* to indicate agent-causality. In this sense, of course, it cannot mean that the agent is 'cause of himself' or 'cause of his own existence,' since nothing is the agent-cause of its own existence. Rather, as Thomas often makes explicit when using the expression in this sense, it can only mean that the agent is cause of his own movement or operation.[67] But this is hardly very illuminating for us. It is difficult to see what 'cause of his own operation' adds to 'operates on his own.' The meaning seems to be exactly the same. We still want to know what being such a cause consists in.

As I said in the Introduction, the present work is not aimed at working out a full analysis of free agency, down to its basic psychological principles, but is

---

64. *Dicitur ... esse suum alicuius, quod ad ipsum ordinatur, sicut servus est domini, et non e converso* (I, q. 21, a. 1 ad 3).
65. *Nam liberum est quod sui causa est.* This expression is taken directly from *Metaphysics* I, ch. 2, 982b26, where it also marks a difference in the order of final causality.
66. *SCG* III, chs. 112–13.
67. See e.g. I, q. 83, a. 1 obj. 3 and reply: *causa sui motus*.

merely preparatory to such an analysis. What I wish to do in what follows is simply to isolate the chief general difference between free and non-free agency, as Aquinas sees it. This in turn will enable us to focus with clarity on what the two modes of agency still have in common, this being the concern of the present investigation. The question, then, is what it means to be a cause of one's act or to act on one's own. As we shall see, ends or final causes do have a great deal to do with the question, after all.

Now, a first answer to the question, and by no means a trivial one, might arise from further consideration of the relation between an instrument and what it is an instrument of. An instrument is useful to something. Conversely, then, an agent who acts on his own operates with his instruments by *using* them. Why not say, then, that acting on one's own consists in *using*? Such an answer has much to recommend it. For instance, the Greek term for 'use' is *chrēsis*, etymologically 'hand-ling' (bringing to mind Aristotle's remark that the hand is the 'instrument of instruments');[68] and Aristotle sometimes uses that term as interchangeable with *praxis*, which is precisely his term for the kind of operation that he considers proper to rational agents. In this vein, from a Thomistic perspective, Ramírez invokes *usus* as synonymous with *actio*, precisely insofar as it 'properly names voluntary operation that is complete and consummated in its genus.'[69]

As this remark by Ramírez suggests, the notion of *usus* is central to a full account of the *efficacy* of human agency;[70] I will dwell on it at some length in Chapter 4. However, as a term for expressing the general notion of 'acting on one's own,' it has the inconvenience of, so to speak, tying the agent down to his instruments. It would be odd if a subject capable of acting on his own could do so *only* through something other than himself, as an instrument usually is, or at best through treating himself as an instrument. In any case, the answer still does not shed much light on the proper difference between a free agent and an instrument, since it simply refers the agent back to the instrument as the one who uses it.

Let us try another answer. Recall the way in which Aquinas signals the difference in the text on 'person.' He puts the verb expressing the action of non-rational things in the passive voice: *aguntur*. Why not say this: that non-rational beings are made to act by something else, whereas rational beings, and only rational beings, *make themselves act*?

This expression, however, does not seem to convey the exact force of *per se agunt*. Had Aquinas wanted to say precisely that rational beings make themselves act, he could have used a reflexive expression, such as *se agunt* or *agunt seipsa*. In

---

68. *De anima* III, ch. 8, 432a1. Cf. Ramírez on the analogical uses of *usus*: *De actibus humanis*, pp. 390–91.

69. *De hominis beatitudine*, p. 235.

70. See ibid.: *iure ergo nomen actionis reservatur proprie usui activo voluntatis, quo active et efficaciter applicat potentias humanas executivas ad opus, eas veluti impellendo ante se; ipsa voluntas seipsam active movet et ducit et ordinat, cum perfecto dominio proprii actus.*

fact, only a few questions earlier in the *Summa theologiae*, he gives a general characterization of living things as things that in one fashion or another have a role in bringing themselves into activity or making themselves act: *se agunt ad motum vel operationem aliquam*.[71] Since he does not think that all living things are rational, he can hardly mean to teach that all non-rational things are *only* made to act by something else, and in no way make themselves act. He must mean that non-rational living things, even if they do make themselves act, only make themselves do what they are made to make themselves do. Not even what they make themselves do is something they do on their own. Aquinas must perceive some sort of difference between *se agere*, or 'making oneself act,' and *agere per se*, which I have rendered 'operate on one's own.'

He explains this difference in a subsequent article on life, I, q. 18, a. 3. His account turns on the fact that life too, like individuality and agency, admits of gradations.

At its lowest level, plant life, 'making itself act' consists merely in initiating some part of the 'execution' of its activity. For instance, by putting forth roots that assimilate nutrients, plants contribute to carrying out the processes of their own growth and reproduction. But they have no activity that contributes to the very direction or formation of their movements. This is not to say that they have no flexibility of movement; but the variations are always an immediate (I stress 'immediate') function of the physical changes produced in them by the surroundings. The path they follow, they are made to follow. Their interaction with the environment elicits no distinct activity in them, as it seems to in the case of animals, controlling the form or path of their movement.

Still, although the beasts in some way form their own movements, they exhibit only a somewhat limited share in self-initiated activity. This is shown by their limited adaptability. For Aquinas, what accounts for this limitation is that they have no hand at all in the formation of the criteria according to which things they sense or imagine appear to them as things to act upon. Even if they do in a way form their own movements, they do not do so in the manner of one who is conforming his movements to some distinctly conceived purpose, some purpose that he himself has adopted and applied to the direction of his movements. Or (in what amounts to the same thing) if, through sensation or imagination, they know some of their immediate purposes, they know nothing precisely in its character as a purpose. They do not arrive through their own effort at the judgment to pursue a certain thing, as though they were able to distinguish between being such a thing and being something to pursue. A given sort of thing merely appears to them as pursuable, or does not so appear, according to their dispositions at the moment and to the context in which it is embedded. This is why they engage in such a limited range of pursuits, and why, if removed from their natural environment, they are utterly at sea.

71. I, q. 18, a. 1.

Evidently, then, it is being a cause of the very conformity of one's act to its purpose, and so of the very fact of acting for that purpose at all, that makes someone the unqualified master of his act and makes his act to be his very own. This requires having distinct grasps of the purpose, on the one hand, and of the resources at one's disposal, on the other, so as to be able to judge the possibility and suitability of acting for it and the order to be followed in doing so. This sort of cognition is proper to intellect, 'to which it belongs to know the proportion between an end and what is for an end, and to order one to the other.'[72] In short, the distinctive note of human agency is the power of ordering one's movements to their end.

What lacks this capacity, even if it makes some contribution to its activity, is not master of its acts.[73] For when something acts for a purpose, the purpose itself is the dominant principle; everything pertaining to the activity is subordinated to it, as far as possible. Hence the act's master is the one who sets its pur-

---

72. I, q. 18, a. 3. See also I–II, q. 6, a. 2.

73. Would it be plausible to extend the meaning of 'freedom' too, in analogical fashion, so as to apply it at least in some qualified way to all living things, insofar as they all are *some* kind of cause of their acts? St Thomas seems prepared to make such an extension. See e.g. SCG II, ch. 48, § 1243: *liberum est quod sui causa est. Quod ergo non est sibi causa agendi, non est liberum in agendo. Quaecumque autem non moventur neque agunt nisi ab aliis mota, non sunt sibi ipsis causa agendi. Sola ergo moventia se ipsa libertatem in agendo habent. Et haec sola iudicio agunt: nam movens seipsum dividitur in movens et motum; movens autem est appetitus ab intellectu vel phantasia aut sensu motus, quorum est iudicare. Horum igitur haec sola libere iudicant quaecumque in iudicando seipsa movent. Nulla autem potentia iudicans seipsam ad iudicandum movet nisi supra actum suum reflectatur: oportet enim, si se ad iudicandum agit, quod suum iudicium cognoscat. Quod quidem solius intellectus est.* <u>*Sunt igitur animalia irrationalia quodammodo liberi quidem motus sive actionis*</u>, *non autem liberi iudicii; inanimata autem, quae solum ab aliis moventur, neque etiam liberae actionis aut motus.*

The concern of this text is with free judgment, and hence it simply leaves out of consideration the realm of animate things that lack judgment. But, returning to the notion of freedom as having control over the end, it does not seem too far-fetched to propose seeing every living thing as a principle upon which an end of movement *somehow* depends. For instance, it is by the beast's own judgment that its motor powers are here and now ordered toward running to catch the prey; where the beast falls short is in the fact that it does not form this judgment through its own comparison between its powers and the situation of the prey, so as to find the 'best' way of pursuing it. And even the plants, although they have no *activity* out of which the form of their movement emerges, nevertheless appear to have a *nature* which is such that the subjection of inanimate materials to it does not simply obliterate the virtualities of those materials, but rather imposes a new or further order upon them. Thus, Aristotle says that *all* natural bodies are instruments of soul (*De anima* II, ch. 4, 415b19). What he seems to mean is not simply that all of the already constituted parts (organs) of a living thing are instruments of it, but that these in turn are composed of all the physical elements (in his sense). The living thing has a principle by which the elements are 'dominated' and their opposed tendencies co-ordinated. Hence Aristotle's emphasis on the fact that plants grow in *all directions*, and to a definite size (*De anima* II, ch. 2, 413a26–31; II, ch. 4, 416a6–18). The physics of this is crude, of course, but the efforts to understand life reductively in terms of non-life can hardly be said to have won the day. For a recent and sophisticated philosophical interpretation of life in terms of freedom, see Hans Jonas, *The Phenomenon of Life*, esp. pp. 64–92.

pose. It is for this reason that Aquinas says that only what has mastery of its acts can be said properly to act. 'To act,' said in the full and most proper sense, means 'to order,' 'to manage' or 'to conduct'; that is, to direct something's acts toward some goal.[74] Things not capable of this are more 'made to act' than 'acting.'[75]

3. Action and Conduct

We are now, at last, in a position to articulate the analogy of action. There are two typical grounds for analogical predication in Aquinas: a relation of likeness and a relation of causality. The latter is clearly excluded in the present case. Obviously man is not called 'agent' because natural things are somehow causes of what he does; and neither is man the cause of natural actions. Even if all other visible things exist for his sake, and *can* be used by him as instruments, obviously not everything they do—indeed, nothing that they do altogether *naturally*—is the effect of such use. Nor does it appear that natural things are given the name 'agents' only once their doings are seen as instrumental to *God's* agency (see below, p. 95). The basis for the analogy, then, is presumably not that the natural agent or its operation is a cause or effect of man or his operation, but that there is a relation of likeness between human and natural things captured by the term 'agent.'

Nor, of course, need it be the case that all natural things are called 'agent' in precisely the same sense either. We have already seen that different natural things resemble human agency in varying degrees. Some merely execute the operation, the form of which is fully naturally determined for them; any differences in what such an agent does between one instance of acting (or not acting) and another are altogether accidental, owing entirely to external forces and conditions. Others not only execute their operation but also play a part in forming it or setting its path, adjusting a predetermined inclination (desire) according to the perceived circumstances, in virtue of an equally predetermined regulative principle ('instinct'). What voluntary agents have, in addition to execution and formation, is the initiation or adoption of the very inclination itself, as a principle of movement, and the formulation of the rule or the criteria by which to judge among the things to be ordered to the object of inclination.

The likeness among all of these 'agents' consists in this: each is, in one way or another, *unde est principium motus*. The execution of a movement, the formation of it, and the ordination of it to an end are all principles of it; and hence the subjects or sources of these operations are all sources of principles of movement. At the same time, these three operations are not to be understood as three forms or kinds, belonging equally to a genus called 'principle of movement.' They do not share equally in what it is to be a principle of movement, since the distinction

---

74. See especially I–II, q. 1, a. 2 ad 1.
75. See also I, q. 22, a. 2 ad 4; I, q. 103, a. 1 ad 1.

between them is precisely a distinction between a principle and what it is principle of. There is priority and posteriority among them with respect to the very thing they have in common. 'Principle of movement' itself is analogical.[76]

This is shown by the fact that the very account of the lower or posterior levels invokes the higher. To execute a movement means that there is given, already, a form of movement, whose execution one initiates; the form is presupposed, and hence too the formation. Likewise, the formation is in accordance with the order to the end. A non-rational being may indeed be something of an origin—but not as original as man.

Since action is attributed to non-rational subjects only by analogy with human action, it would seem desirable to have another term at hand for referring exclusively to human action, human action precisely as human. Aristotle has one: *praxis*.[77] In light of Aquinas's reasons for regarding human action as the chief kind, the best English term seems to be 'conduct.' Conduct is ascribed only to human beings. Only they conduct themselves (and others).

> It is proper to rational nature that it tend toward an end in the manner of one operating or leading [*ducens*] itself toward the end; [tending toward an end belongs] to irrational nature in the manner of one operated or led [*ducta*] by another, whether this be toward an apprehended end, as in the case of brute animals, or toward an end not apprehended, as in the case of things that altogether lack cognition.[78]

---

76. Its primary sense would be the fifth sense for 'principle' given by Aristotle in his philosophical lexicon (*Metaphysics* V, ch. 1, 1013a11): 'that in accordance with whose *choice* that which is in motion moves or that which is changing changes.'

77. Anscombe, 'Action, Intention and "Double Effect,"' p. 13, says that Aristotle's *praxis* is narrower than what is intended by 'human action.' She thinks that for Aristotle, *praxis* 'wouldn't include omissions unless calculated, or sudden impulsive actions.' That is, she takes *praxis* to be something always actually deliberated, and so always something arising from choice; and she wants to say, correctly it seems, that this is not always essential for human action. It is only essential that it be *deliberable*. However, Kenny has shown that this reading of Aristotle is not accurate. 'If [for Aristotle] the origin of conduct [= *praxis*] is purpose [choice, *prohairesis*] does this mean that there cannot be conduct where there is no purpose? Certainly, animals, who lack purposes, have no share in conduct: but in the lives of human beings, is an action disqualified as a *praxis* unless it is the enactment of a *prohairesis*? No: involuntary actions [through ignorance], actions under duress, the actions of the incontinent are all *praxeis* too (e.g. [*Metaphysics*] B, 1144a15–20; C, 1145b12, 1147a2; cf. *EE* II. 11, 1228a14; *NE* 3.2, 1111b13). So: purpose is not the *only arche* of conduct, but it is the *arche par excellence*: the most fully human action is prohairetic action; and no action can be a really good action unless it originates from a good *prohairesis*. Just as there can be *praxis* without *prohairesis* so too there can be *prohairesis* without *praxis*: such is the case with the incontinent man whose *prohairesis* is good but whose conduct is bad (1152a17)' (*Aristotle's Theory of the Will*, pp. 90–91). What this suggests is that conduct itself is analogical.

78. *Proprium est naturae rationalis ut tendat in finem quasi se agens vel ducens ad finem; naturae vero irrationalis, quasi ab alio acta vel ducta, sive in finem apprehensum, sicut bruta animalia, sive in finem non apprehensum, sicut ea quae omnino cognitione carent* (I–II, q. 2, a. 1). Note also the way in which the precise contrast between *per se agit* and *agitur* is glossed by the term *ducitur* in I–II, q. 2, a. 1 ad

Now, these considerations *could* set the stage for a study of the psychological roots of free agency. For instance, picking up on the notion of being a more 'separate' agent, we might try to determine the extent to which the one who orders things to an end is really a 'first,' unable to be seen as acting in sheer continuity with the action of something prior. It is surely not that he absolutely breaks the flow of events, as though acting under no sort of influence at all. (In any case, no matter what happens, it is continuously the case that something is happening.) But perhaps what he does cannot be seen as the mere unfolding of something already existing 'in principle.'[79] Another possible direction which the discussion could take would be in the domain of moral theory. 'Conduct' itself already carries moral connotations. In particular, the consideration that the core of human action consists in the adoption of ends and the ordering of things to them leads toward the idea, fundamental for Aquinas's moral theory, that a distinctive feature of human acts is that they are most properly and formally specified, or distinguished, precisely in terms of ends, i.e. of goods.[80]

However, as already indicated, the focus of the present study is not primarily on questions, whether psychological or moral, proper to the human domain. As I shall explain at length in Chapter 4, one of my principal concerns is precisely to resist a certain tendency to treat the human domain as a separate world, conceptually self-enclosed and incommensurable with the rest. In the rest of this section, I shall merely adduce some general (and I hope less controversial) considerations in favor of looking at action from a high vantage-point, embracing the entire analogical order.

Now, since for Aquinas human action or conduct is the primary kind of action, he would probably have no strong objection to the practice of referring to

---

1: *quando homo per seipsum agit propter finem, cognoscit finem; sed quando ab alio agitur vel ducitur, puta cum agit ad imperium alterius vel cum movetur altero impellente, non est necessarium quod cognoscat finem. Et ita est in creaturis irrationalibus.*

79. To say that he sets the end of his movement means that something becomes an end for him by virtue of his own activity about it. This in turn means that he is the one upon whom depends not only whether to move in one direction or another, but even whether to move at all or to stay at rest (the latter, if the end is already possessed). Hence, even if his own initial activity is caused by some other agent, it does not appear that the movement resulting from that activity can itself have been altogether determined by that other cause; he himself would seem to be the first *proper* cause of his movement, *causa sui actus*. It would be in this sense that he and he alone exists as 'the originator of his actions, as he is of his children' (*Nicomachean Ethics* III, ch. 7, 1113b19; cf. *Eudemian Ethics* II, ch. 6, 1222b15–20). Playing such a role requires a kind of activity which is not itself a movement, since movement is already from contrary to contrary and is initiated by something other than what is moved, but must be a 'perfect' and 'immanent' operation—cognitive and appetitive operation, as we saw earlier. In addition, it must be an activity which is immediately and simultaneously able to effect either one thing or its contrary; this is the consideration which leads Aquinas to attribute mastery of one's acts exclusively to *rational* subjects.

80. See e.g. I, q. 48, a. 1 ad 2: *bonum et malum non sunt differentiae constitutivae nisi in moralibus, quae recipiunt species ex fine.*

the theory of *human* action as the theory of action *simply*, rather than (say) as the theory of conduct. To restrict the term 'action' to human action, for technical convenience, is not necessarily to regard it as inapplicable to non-rational subjects, or implicitly to reject the analogical conception just outlined. It is one thing not to treat the other applications of a term, and something quite different to treat it as though it could have no other.

Still, many action-theorists do treat 'action' in this way, sometimes explicitly; and doing so or not is surely more than a terminological matter. Whatever a theory be called, its purpose is to afford a better understanding of the portion of reality that its name signifies. Granted that the theory of human action may justifiably go simply by the name of the theory of action, it still makes a great deal of difference, for the content of the theory, what the justification consists in. Any such justification must, of course, rest on the thesis that when the term 'action' is attributed to non-rational beings, its sense is altered. But the account of the way in which it is altered will obviously be a function of the understanding not only of rational agency but also of non-rational agency. Even more importantly, if the relation between the term's senses is analogical, then the general notion of action is broader than that of human action, and should be analyzed accordingly; and the study of action as it is found in its secondary instances, non-rational agents, may be of positive assistance in giving an account of its primary instance, human action.

Recall the discussion of *actus* as an example of an analogical term in Aquinas's philosophy. It was suggested that one of the effects of the analogy was to diminish the risk of treating its primary instance as though it were unique or incommensurable with other entities. Some of the essential features of the primary instance of *actus*, which is operation, are also found outside of operation; notably in what Aquinas calls form. In addition, although operation is *actus* to a higher degree than form, it is nevertheless dependent upon and in some way derivative from form whenever an operation and its corresponding form are distinct entities.

Surely the analogical treatment of 'action' has a similar function. Although what 'acts' in the fullest and primary sense is what acts freely, as master of its act, nevertheless the whole substance of action is not exhausted by what is proper to free action. Even when it is free, there is more to it than its being free, and more to it precisely insofar as it is action. Or more precisely, even if freedom implies agency, other notes enter into the concept of agency besides that of freedom; and in fact, a rigorous understanding of freedom does not even seem to be an essential element in the general concept of agency. Surely then the work of giving precision to that concept logically precedes the discussion of the problems proper to free agency.[81]

---

81. In the course of later discussions, a few particular consequences of *not* holding to the analogical conception will also be noted. One concerns the meaning of intention and its role in specifying acts; see Chapter 3, Section E and Chapter 5 *passim*. Another concerns the implications of the question whether that which makes an event an action is its being caused by an act of will; see Chapter 4, Section D.1.

THE ANALOGY OF ACTION 39

Moreover, since free agency is such a difficult thing to analyze accurately, it would surely be helpful, in establishing the nature of agency in general, to draw as far as possible upon the less complex examples afforded by non-voluntary agents. Such a procedure is particularly consistent with Aquinas's outlook, since for him, the very concept of action first enters the human mind out of the experience of purely physical action. I conclude this section with a text, already familiar to us in part, in which he enunciates this point. In the following section, I will enunciate the three 'common' features or accompaniments of action which will be central to the rest of this study: efficacy, finality and 'agent-and-patient.'

> We were first able to conjecture the origin of one thing from another, on the basis of motion; for it was manifest that the removal of something from its disposition, through motion, happened by some cause. And therefore action, according to the first imposition of the name, implies an origin of motion: for just as a motion, insofar as it is in the mobile from something, is called a passion, so the origin of the motion itself, insofar as it [the motion] begins from another and terminates in that which is moved, is called action.[82]

D. COMMON FEATURES OF ACTION

1. Efficacy, Finality and the Agent-Patient Relation

The text just quoted provides a fairly clear basis for presenting the themes upon which the rest of this study will concentrate. First of all, it brings out two aspects or features which, I believe, may be considered to be common to action in all of its instances, across the entire analogical order of agency. These features, which I will explain in a moment, are efficacy and finality. The text also suggests that the notion of action is formed in the setting of the agent-patient relation (or together with the notion of that relation). Attention to this relation is essential for an adequate account of the nature of action. As we shall see in the next chapter, this relation was already found to be problematic by Aristotle, and his problems have much to do with fundamental issues in analytical action-theory.

My eventual aim will be to bring the general considerations of efficacy, finality and the agent-patient relation to bear on the account of action in its primary sense, human or voluntary action. Chapters 2 and 3 will provide the general considerations. Chapter 2 concerns efficacy, and Chapter 3 finality; the agent-patient relation will be a recurring motif in both chapters. Chapter 4 then takes up voluntary agency. The final chapter addresses some of the issues involved in

---

82. *Primo coniicere potuimus originem alicuius ab alio, ex motu; quod enim aliqua res a sua dispositione removeretur per motum, manifestum fuit hoc ab aliqua causa accidere. Et ideo actio, secundum primam nominis impositionem, importat originem motus: sicut enim motus, prout est in mobili ab aliquo, dicitur passio; ita origo ipsius motus, secundum quod incipit ab alio et terminatur in id quod movetur, vocatur actio* (I, q. 41, a. 1 ad 2).

the question of effects brought about *praeter intentionem,* 'outside the intention' of the agent. The inevitability of this question, in anything like a complete account of agency, should become clear as the study proceeds.

To finish this chapter, then, I shall do two things. First, I shall explain briefly what I mean by 'efficacy' and 'finality,' and offer a few observations which suggest that at least they are generally connoted by the *term* 'action.' Arguments will still need to be provided in support of the claim that they do in fact constitute 'common features' of action, belonging to it even at its lowest level, that of merely physical action; I shall postpone this task until Chapter 2 as regards efficacy, and Chapter 3 as regards finality. My concluding discussion in this chapter will serve to indicate, sketchily, some of what is at stake in all of this. It will present a certain set of conceivable objections to the claim that efficacy and finality are intrinsic to action precisely in its *primary* instance—voluntary action—together with evidence that Aquinas, at least, would not be willing to concede them. The fundamental issue will be laid out more fully in Chapter 4.

By 'efficacy' I mean simply a certain sort of causality. Its most manifest form is what Thomas's text spoke of as being a cause of something's 'being removed from its disposition' and placed in another disposition. We might call it 'making something to be so,' or perhaps better, 'bringing about some state of affairs.'[83] In scholastic terminology, it consists in 'reducing something from potency to act.' It corresponds roughly to Aristotle's *poesis* in its broadest sense: not, of course, that of the operation proper to art or craft, but that of the 'generation' of something by virtue of some power.[84]

By 'finality' I mean having an end, tending in a definite direction, carrying an order toward one thing and away from what is opposed to it. The note of being 'away from' something is crucial here. It helps to show that finality should not be thought of as something merely added on to the note of efficacy, as though there could be efficacy without any sort of finality at all. On first reading, Thomas's text may seem not to involve any consideration of a definite goal or an end. But it does speak of action as that by which something is 'removed from' its disposition. The action *opposes* something. It must therefore be possible to formulate, at least negatively, some difference or term at which the action terminates or which the action favors, and which is not merely accidental to the action. There must be some term such that the action's order toward it is constitutive of the action itself.

---

83. Even the form of a thing 'makes' it be so, in a sense—by an analogical extension of 'making' from agent-causality to formal causality. The difference would be that what has a form already is correspondingly 'so,' whereas action begins with the thing's not being so; or at least (if there are any eternal results of action) it begins from something which is other than the thing which it makes to be so, whether this be some other subject or the thing itself not precisely as 'so.'

84. Cf. *Metaphysics* VII, ch. 7, 1032a27–28, b6–17. In this broadest sense, acting is simply what is opposed to being acted upon (*paschein*), and is one of the ultimate genera or categories. It is certainly much broader than the operation of art; a sign of this is Aristotle's giving 'being pleased' and 'being pained' as examples of being acted upon (*Categories* 9, 11b4).

In other words, an action must have some minimal definiteness about it.[85] It possesses a certain asymmetry, an imbalance or proclivity, with respect to the terms of the change enacted through it. And so does the agent, if the agent is conceived precisely as that which the action comes 'from.' If to act is to change something, to make it go from one state or disposition to another, then the agent cannot have exactly the same relation toward the initial state as it has toward the terminal state. Even if there are actions that do not, properly speaking, produce changes, presumably they still carry some note of determining something to some one state or disposition rather than another. Otherwise the agent's presence would simply not 'make any difference.'

It seems unlikely that the full or proper formulation of an agent's tendency or inclination can be merely negative, having only the removal of something as its term. This should come out clearly when we return to finality and its connection with efficacy in Chapter 3.

2. Action 'Versus' Thought

Does the term 'action,' as it is actually used, connote efficacy, and hence (if the previous paragraphs are correct) some minimal degree of finality? Probably many sorts of consideration might be adduced in favor of an affirmative answer. I shall focus on just one. This is the way in which an opposition is typically drawn between action and cognition, or action and thought.

For instance, one man is said to dedicate himself to a life of action, another to a life of thought and contemplation. Connected with this is the opposition between action and speech. People are sometimes blamed for thinking or talking a great deal but not 'doing' anything. Many common sayings rely upon the opposition: 'his bark is worse than his bite'; 'do what I say, not what I do'; and so forth.

Of course, the sense of the opposition can hardly be that action is taken to be something mindless or separate from thought. Men of action are men of decision, which is to say, men who take counsel, plan and judge. We have already seen that for Aquinas, action initiated by thought is in fact the primary kind of action.

Nor is it that the notion of action is restricted to non-linguistic activity or to the kinds of action that dumb animals are also capable of. Taking action often consists precisely in saying something: issuing an order, uttering an insult, accepting a proposal, etc. In certain currents in contemporary philosophy much attention is being given to the ways in which speech can constitute a kind of action, or to 'how we do things with words.'

---

85. This brings the general theory of action into surprisingly close connection with the study of a principle which is frequently, and (from an Aristotelian point of view) quite mistakenly, regarded as 'merely logical': the principle of non-contradiction. For a very forceful presentation of this connection, see Flannery, 'Practical Reason and Concrete Acts.'

What then is the sense of the opposition? Is it not, first of all, that action carries with it the notion of a change or transformation brought about in the action's object? In general, looking at Socrates' nose would surely be less likely to be called an action than, say, punching it. This is why, for instance, action, and not thought, is judged to depend upon power. Power is a 'principle of change in another or in oneself *qua* other.'[86] Similarly, although action is not simply independent from thought, not just any kind of thought has a direct bearing upon action. The thought that bears upon action is 'practical' thought, thought undertaken with a view toward bringing something about or making something to be so. Again, speech is treated as a form of action only insofar as it does something more than merely signify what the speaker is thinking. It needs to produce some kind of change in the hearer or through the hearer, e.g. to teach him something or to persuade him to do something.

The opposition between action and thought also brings to mind the opposition between action and theory, or 'theory and practice.' Normally the juxtaposition of these terms does not refer to the distinction between 'speculative' and 'practical,' but to the distinction between two components or phases of practical reason's approach to action. What it highlights about the meaning of action is that it belongs to the realm of the singular, the concrete. The universal consideration of action, 'theory,' is never enough to provide an adequate guide for it. Theory always wants adjusting and completing according to the situation. Thought bears on the universal, but *actiones in singularibus sunt*. And this is because nothing can be 'brought about' in the domain of the universals. They are intrinsically 'always and everywhere.'

Action and thought are also sometimes opposed in a way that suggests that the term 'action' involves the note of finality, tendency or inclination. Not infrequently, people ask what is the point of speculative thought, the mere exercise of the understanding, not tied in with getting anything *done*. By contrast, the point of 'doing' something, once you understand what the doing consists in, is usually obvious. Or rather, understanding its point virtually *is* understanding what it consists in. (Lest there be any doubt, I do not mean to concede that speculative activity is pointless. The answer to the query would of course be to the effect that some activities do not *have* a point, because they *are* the point. But this means precisely that their point is not something still remaining to be brought about *through* them.)

To be sure, cognition has an *object*; you understand *something*. But an object may not be an effect or an end. Indeed, to understand something is also to understand its contrary and its privation, but of course one thing and its contrary cannot both be the *end* of the very same operation. Because of this, according to Aristotle, even if some kinds or habits of understanding or knowledge constitute

---

86. *Metaphysics* V, ch. 12, 1019a15–20.

principles of action, rational powers, they are by themselves only incomplete principles of action.

They are not actually efficacious just by themselves, because just by themselves they are only imperfectly ordered to a definite end. Medical knowledge exists for the sake of health, but its possessor may use it either to heal or to kill.[87]

3. Action and the Will

This leads to the set of objections I mentioned. Aristotle says that a rational active principle or rational power produces an effect only in virtue of desire or *choice*.[88] The mention of choice, of course, brings us back to the domain of action in the highest sense, human or voluntary or moral action. But is it correct to say that moral action consists in, or at least always involves, bringing something about? Can there not be morality, genuine *conduct*, even in cases in which the subject utterly fails to bring anything about and has merely 'wanted' or 'willed' something? Moreover, does willing even have to be aimed at anything or tend toward anything? Does it have to have an end, or at least any end other than its own goodness?

I will address ('Kantian') questions like these in a detailed way in Chapter 4. They are central to the entire project of this study. Here I only wish to give a summary indication of the fact that at least for Thomas Aquinas, moral action does indeed always involve the agent's bringing something about, at least an 'act of will,' and always involves at least his tending to bring something about in addition to his 'act of will.'

First of all, for Aquinas, an act of will is nothing if not a sort of tendency. By tendency I do not mean merely a state of mind, a wish or feeling or velleity, but rather a disposition upon which real movement toward its object is intrinsically apt to follow.[89] It is a genuine being ordered *toward* something, and *away from* something else. The texts that show this are too numerous to cite. Aquinas *defines* will as a kind of appetite, rational or intellectual appetite, and the very nature of appetite is to be a tendency toward something.

That is, toward something *else*, besides or in addition to itself. 'It is evident that all appetite is for the sake of something. For it is foolish to say that someone desires [*appetat*] for the sake of desiring. For desiring [*appetere*] is a certain movement tending toward something else [*aliud*].'[90]

---

87. See *Metaphysics* IX, ch. 2, 1046b4–24; ch. 5, 1048a8–24.

88. *Metaphysics* IX, ch. 5, 1048a8–24. See also *De anima* III, ch. 9, 433a4–7; ch. 10, 433a23–25; ch. 11, 434a6–12.

89. See I–II, q. 20, a. 4: *non est perfecta voluntas, nisi sit talis quae, opportunitate data, operetur.*

90. *Manifestum est quod omnis appetitus est propter aliquid. Stultum enim est dicere quod aliquis appetat propter appetere. Nam appetere est quidam motus in aliud tendens* (*In III De anima* lect. xv, § 821).

So the will is intrinsically a source of tendency. Need it be an efficacious one? It is all too obvious that in a particular instance, someone may fail to bring about what he wants to bring about. But on the whole, is efficacy something merely incidental to the nature of the will? Let us suppose that by 'will' we mean nothing but that faculty whose disposition determines whether or not a person is fundamentally a 'good' person. If we then ask what it is about this thing called 'will' which makes a person's goodness depend upon it, rather than (say) upon his intellect or his physical strength, Aquinas's answer seems to be its naturally having control over what the person brings about.

> Whoever has a will is called good insofar as he has a good will; for through the will, we use all the things that are in our power. Hence not the man who has a good intellect, but he who has a good will, is called good.[91]

By 'use' he means nothing other than a form of 'moving' something, acting upon it and making it act. 'The will moves the other powers of the soul to their acts; for we use the other powers when we want.'[92]

So, if we ask the general question, concerning the moral order as a whole, about what it is that makes the quality of one's will to be of unique importance, the answer given by St Thomas would appear to be precisely: its efficacy. This also suggests that the will's basic tendency cannot be merely toward its own goodness. Its own goodness depends upon how it tends to move something else.

In such an outlook, the theme of action and passion can hardly be altogether extraneous. In fact, Aquinas brings it in explicitly almost at the very beginning of the *secunda pars* of the *Summa theologiae*, the part concerned with human acts. The issue is whether human acts are specified by ends. He answers affirmatively, by way of considering human acts as movements.

> Each thing receives its species according to an act, and not according to a potency; whence those things which are composed of matter and form are constituted in their species by their own forms. And this is also to be considered in proper[?] movements. For although motion may in a way be distinguished according to action and passion, each of these receives its species from an act: action, indeed, from the act which is the principle of acting; passion, from the act which is the term of movement.... And in both ways, human acts, whether they be considered in the manner of actions, or in the manner of passions,

---

91. *Quilibet habens voluntatem, dicitur bonus inquantum habet bonam voluntatem, quia per voluntatem utimur omnibus quae in nobis sunt. Unde non dicitur bonus homo, qui habet bonum intellectum, sed qui habet bonam voluntatem* (I, q. 5, a. 4 ad 3). See also I, q. 48, a. 6.

92. *Voluntas movet alias potentias animae ad suos actus; utimur enim aliis potentiis cum volumus* (I–II, q. 9, a. 1). See also I–II, q. 56, a. 3: *subiectum vero habitus qui simpliciter dicitur virtus, non potest esse nisi voluntas; vel alia potentia secundum quod est mota a voluntate. Cuius ratio est quia voluntas movet omnes alias potentias quae aliqualiter sunt rationales, ad suos actus . . . et ideo quod homo actu bene agat, contingit ex hoc quod homo habet bonam voluntatem.*

receive their species from an end. For human acts can be considered in both ways, since a man moves himself, and is moved by himself.[93]

Nor is the distinction of moving and being moved applicable to human acts only to the extent that a man uses powers other than his will. The will uses itself too.[94] It moves itself and is moved by itself, chiefly by means of deliberation.[95] So even when someone's will to use his other powers fails or is impeded, there can still be a genuine and genuinely human bringing something about. In fact, a man must bring something about by his own will for there to be human action at all. This is for the very reason that a human act is not just *any* 'act of will.' 'Acts are called human insofar as they proceed from a *deliberated* will.'[96] Such acts already presuppose, and are ultimately brought about by, certain merely natural operations of intellect and will; which is to say, operations that are not free or not rooted in a man's own mastery of his acts. These are *non-voluntary* operations of intellect and will, brought about in him by the author of his nature.[97]

To some readers, all of this may seem fairly clear and straightforward. However, contemporary action-theory has worried a great deal about whether a clear sense can in fact be given to the expression 'act proceeding from the will.' What some of the problems are, and whether Aquinas can deal with them, will be taken up in Chapter 4. There is also a very basic distinction drawn by Thomas under this expression. Its fundamental importance is obvious, but the difficulties of its application are grave. Some of these will be faced in the final chapter (largely by way of preparation provided in Chapter 3, Section E). The distinction is between what proceeds from the will directly and what does so indirectly; for instance, between what a person brings about through exercising his mastery over his acts, and what he brings about through not exercising it.

93. *Unumquodque sortitur speciem secundum actum, et non secundum potentiam; unde ea quae sunt composita ex materia et forma, constituuntur in suis speciebus per proprias formas. Et hoc etiam considerandum est in motibus propriis*[?]. *Cum enim motus quodammodo distinguatur per actionem et passionem, utrumque horum ab actu speciem sortitur, actio quidem ab actu qui est principium agendi; passio vero ab actu qui est terminus motus. Unde calefactio actio nihil aliud est quam motio quaedam a calore procedens, calefactio vero passio nihil aliud est quam motus ad calorem, definitio autem manifestat rationem speciei. Et utroque modo actus humani, sive considerentur per modum actionum, sive per modum passionum, a fine speciem sortiuntur. Utroque enim modo possunt considerari actus humani, eo quod homo movet seipsum, et movetur a seipso* (I–II, q. 1, a. 3). According to the Leonine edition, the term *propriis* in the second sentence of the quotation is found in most manuscripts, but not all. If it does belong there, the sense of it is unclear to me.
94. I–II, q. 16, a. 4 obj. 3.
95. See I–II, q. 9, a. 3.
96. *Actus dicuntur humani, inquantum procedunt a voluntate deliberata* (I–II, q. 1, a. 3).
97. See I–II, q. 9, a. 4; q. 10, a. 1, esp. ad 1; q. 17, a. 5 ad 3. Even the free will of the angels, the pure spirits, presupposes natural operations of intellect and will. With respect to these, Thomas uses a familiar phrase: *magis aguntur quam agunt; nihil enim habet dominium suae naturae* (I, q. 60, a. 1 obj. 2). For in fact, he says, apart from the First Agent, there is nothing in the world which acts in such a fashion that it is in no way at all made to act by something else; yet this does not mean that an angel (or a man) *sic agitur quod non agat, cum habeat liberam voluntatem* (I, q. 60, a. 1 ad 2).

Chapter 2
Agency as Efficacy

INTRODUCTION: ACTION AT ITS LOWEST LEVEL

1. Action and Change

This chapter concerns the common feature of action which I have termed 'efficacy,' together with the action-passion relation. These will be examined mainly in relation to action at its simplest and most elementary form or level, that of merely physical action. This is action considered 'according to the first imposition of the name,' action as an 'origin of motion.' The general question will be simply what it is that an action, so considered, can properly be said to consist in, or where its unity lies. What this question means, and why it is a question, will be explained in the course of the chapter, starting in Section A. First, however, I will introduce some considerations along the lines of the preceding chapter, aimed at bringing out the 'common' character of efficacy.

In the first place, this common character should not be taken *too* broadly. Efficacy does not belong to absolutely everything that exists, because action does not belong to absolutely everything that exists. It does not even belong to everything that has sufficient definiteness to be the subject of scientific inquiry. The standard example of such a thing to which action does not belong is the subject of mathematics. It is something abstract, a subject of science but not a subject of action.[1] Only 'applied' mathematics concerns itself with change and movement. Interestingly, there are several terms whose primary meaning pertains to the field of action, and which are used in an extended sense in mathematics, e.g. 'power,'[2] 'operation,' 'function'; but 'action' is not one of them.

There is another way in which action does not extend to absolutely everything, not even to everything which is somehow involved in movement. This has to do with the fact that at least in elementary cases of action and change, agent and thing changed are separate entities. This means that the thing changed, as such, does not yet fall under the term 'agent.' It would be odd to speak of the 'action' of a rock falling or a nail rusting or a crystal forming. The motions of physical things are not regarded as the actions of those things, but as the actions of

---

1. Recall the discussion of the connection between agency and separateness in Chapter 1. Calling its subject 'abstract' means that mathematics gives separate consideration to things that do not exist separately. Cf. *Summa theologiae* I, q. 5, a. 3 ad 4; *De anima* I, ch. 1, 403a13–16.
2. Cf. *Metaphysics* V, ch. 12, 1019b33.

other things upon them. Falling is thought to be the result of gravitational pull; rusting is the result of the presence of oxidizing agents; and so forth. In other words, the subject of physical motion is merely passive in relation to its motion. Although to be subject to motion is already to be involved in activity, it is not yet to be an agent or a principle of activity. Even if, in the physical world, everything that is acted upon also somehow reacts, this is incidental; the reaction is the source of another change, distinct from the one belonging to the thing reacting.

On the other hand, the 'common' character of efficacy is broader than the expression 'origin of motion' might make it seem. Bringing something about need not always be bringing about a change or bringing something about through change. It might be bringing it about that something does not change, that it stays at rest. Keeping something from moving is certainly an action. This does not seriously affect the formula 'principle of motion,' since rest is nothing but the lack or privation of motion; the principle of a thing and the principle of its privation fall easily under the same general notion. If we want a more general term, to express both change and rest as results of action, we can use 'event.' Donagan argues persuasively that not all events are changes.[3] Socrates' remaining in prison was surely an event, and even an action. He made himself remain there, and resisted attempts to remove him. An action may be the prevention of a change as much as the initiation of one.

Even so, however, action still exists relative to the *changeable*. There is surely no such event as the diagonal's remaining incommensurable, nor, therefore, any agent making it remain so. If there is action about unchangeable things, i.e. if there are things that are at once unchangeable and not merely abstract objects of thought, it must be because something like action belongs to the natural activity of thought itself.[4]

Moreover, within the domain of the changeable, there are grounds for regarding action as more closely connected with change than with remaining the same. Aquinas says that it is change that first makes us suppose an origin or an agent, and this is surely plausible. The mere fact of something's remaining at rest does not make you look for some other thing making it do so, unless you have some reason to think that it might move. On the whole, change is surprising in a way that staying the same is not. That a thing already was in a certain disposition can be enough of an explanation for the fact that it still is. It cannot be a sufficient explanation for the fact that it is no longer.

To be changing (even in the intransitive sense of 'to change') is to be involved in activity; to be remaining the same need not be, even if sometimes it is.[5] And when it is not, neither does it seem to entail an action; perhaps, in some

---

3. Donagan, *Choice*, p. 24.
4. See I, q. 27, a. 1.
5. It is motion, not rest, which Aristotle calls a kind of 'life' of the physical universe: *Physics* VIII, ch. 1, 250b14.

cases, it is not even an event. Socrates' bed remained in the prison while he did. Certainly this does not involve its having done anything. Nor, *prima facie*, did anything else, or anyone, have to make it remain there. This is only *prima facie*, of course; we eventually learn that things like gravity and friction played a role. But would it be natural to call the bed's remaining in the prison an event, without reference either to things like these, or to some reason, based on some kind of potential cause, to expect that it *not* remain in the prison? The term 'event' never wholly loses its sense of 'outcome.' The bed's remaining in the prison deserves to be called an event only if it is seen either as an action or as the outcome of something's *not* acting when there was some reason to expect it to act.

Change, on the other hand, always bespeaks an agent. The law of inertia is sometimes adduced as an objection to the Aristotelian principle that everything moved is moved by something. But this principle was never meant to suggest that at the time when something is in motion, there must be something then moving it; it means merely that the motion must have a source. Indeed, the motion of inert bodies requires an agent even more immediately than do many of the kinds of motion posited in ancient and medieval physics. Whereas an inert body needs an agent acting upon it at the very moment when it begins to be in motion, the natural motions of the older physics were judged to be able to begin without anything acting upon the body at that moment; all that was thought to be necessary at that moment was the removal of external obstacles. The only agent acting upon the body itself was the agent that formed it or gave it the nature from which such motion followed, spontaneously, when nothing impeded it; perhaps long after its generation.[6]

In any case, the law of inertia is not a general law concerning all change; it only concerns change of velocity or direction, saying that there must be a moving force acting throughout such change. It neither affirms nor denies the general thesis that the sheer fact of something's being in motion, e.g. its changing *place*, requires a kind of explanation, a reference to a moving force or agent, which its being at rest does not as such require. In a given case, of course, its being at rest might require this; but only when further considerations are adduced, e.g. that it had previously been moving. But in itself, rest is a mere lack.

2. Action in Non-Living Things

Do all physical things act? Non-living things are in no sense agents of their own activity. But this is not to say that they are so constituted as to be simply inert. For Aquinas, every kind of natural thing, living or not, is constituted in such a way that, at least under certain circumstances, it spontaneously engages in some sort of activity. This is precisely what it means, in his vocabulary, for something to have a 'nature.' Nature is an *intrinsic* principle of activity.

---

6. See Weisheipl, 'The Specter of *Motor Coniunctus* in Medieval Physics,' in *Nature and Motion in the Middle Ages*, pp. 99–120, esp. pp. 118–19; and, in general, essays I–V in *idem*.

Still, to engage in some activity spontaneously, or by nature, is not the same as to make yourself engage in it. It is not the same as to be the activity's agent. An agent is not merely something that has some principle on account of which activity is apt to begin, such as a nature. It is what *gives rise* to such a principle, or *makes* activity begin: *unde est principium motus*. In the case of what engages in some activity purely by nature, the principle has already been implanted. The activity has already been given its start, in the very generation or formation of its subject. Purely natural activity is a mere immediate consequence, a natural result of being a certain kind of thing.[7] Such activity is not something which the subject in any way *initiates*; its belonging to the subject is not the subject's own work. If the subject does not carry it out at once, this is only owing to the presence of external obstacles, not to the fact that the subject itself must first do something which contributes to initiating it. Activity whose existence is the subject's own work is vital activity.

Non-living things, then, do not act on themselves or make themselves act. Why then does Aquinas attribute action to them? Because they do act on other things and make them to be subject to some activity. Moreover, to some extent, they do so in virtue of an intrinsic capacity. This is why it is possible to state, in a general way, specific types of activity that specific types of things are apt to initiate. Fire makes things get hot, water makes them dissolve, air makes them evaporate, acid corrodes, and so forth.

At the same time, nothing can perform its characteristic actions on just any object whatsoever. Each acts on what is able to be acted upon in the corresponding way, i.e. able to be subject to the kind of activity or motion in question. The minimal condition for such ability is being somehow distinct from the agent. This is why Aquinas, following Aristotle, defines 'power,' or the capacity to initiate activity, the capacity for action, as a principle of change in another (or in oneself, but *qua* other).

There are also other limitations on the kind of action that any inanimate thing is apt to perform. For instance, temporal limits: it is always the initiation of a *motion*, that is, a process, undergone by the thing acted upon, toward or away from a certain state. If it is toward a state, then when the state is reached, the action must stop; if it is away from a state, then the action must have had a beginning, before which the thing was still in that state. Also, of course, spatial: the agent will not act upon the corresponding patient until they have been brought into contact with each other; and no merely inanimate thing is the agent of the motion by which it comes into contact with the patient. At most that motion is something that it is naturally apt to undergo.

Yet despite these limitations, what natural inanimate things can do is enough to earn them the name of agents. This is why the analysis of the elements

---

7. For the distinction between an effect of action and a merely 'natural result,' see I, q. 77, a. 6 ad 3, a. 7 ad 1.

of agency, in its general acceptation, may suitably concentrate on merely physical agents. What they have is, as it were, the least common denominator of action. At the same time, the consideration of action in the merely physical order serves to underscore the fact that the study of action cannot get very far without attending to the action-passion relationship. This relationship raises some serious questions about the fundamental unity of an action.

A. THE ACT OF THE AGENT IS IN THE PATIENT

1. *The Aristotelian Formula and its Opponents*

In at least some actions, the agent is one thing, and that of which it is the agent, e.g. a change, belongs to something else. This fact forced Aristotle through a series of reflections on the relation between agent, patient and change, until he arrived at the remarkable formulation 'the actuality of the agent (*qua* agent) is in the patient.' This means that that relative to which the agent is called an agent, namely its action, comes to completion or terminates, not in the agent itself (again, *qua* agent), but in the patient. It is the patient that is changed. The change is called a change insofar as attention is focused simply on its character of bridging the contrary terms that constitute its beginning and its end. It is called a passion insofar as it is seen as received by the patient from an agent. The same change is called an action, insofar as it is seen as initiated by the agent in the patient. Thus the action of the agent, that of which it is called the agent, does not terminate or come to completion in the agent at all, but in the patient. Only if the agent is also the patient is it the subject in which its action terminates.[8]

It is because the action of the agent terminates in the patient that, even when it is a change, it need not involve any change in the agent. If there is any change involved, what is necessarily changed, along the line of the action in question, is the patient. On the other hand, the principle that the act of the agent terminates in the patient does not at all imply that there need be no activity at all to which the agent itself is subject, *qua* agent. It means simply that the activity relative to which the agent may be said to be actually exercising agency, the activity of which it is the agent, is not *per se* an activity in the agent. Indeed, even if action does not always imply change, it does seem to imply activity; if not on the part of what is acted upon, at least on the part of the agent.

If Socrates' staying in prison was an action, there must have been some activity of his by dint of which he did so, say some choice. Otherwise it would not be natural to call it an action, though it might still be true that he was responsible

---

8. See Aristotle, *Physics* III, ch. 3, 202a13–b29. Also *De anima* II, ch. 3, 414a11: 'for the operation of that which is capable of originating change terminates and has its seat in what is changed or altered.' See also *De anima* III, ch. 2, 425b25–426a4.

for it. Not everything of which an agent-cause is the cause, *qua* (potential) agent, is an action or even the result of action. It may be the result of his not acting. But there is no type of agency whose exercise does not presuppose some sort of activity in the agent itself. This is evident by induction.

To say that action always involves activity in the agent, however, is not to say that it is identical with that activity. It hardly could be, if the action comes to completion in the patient, and if the agent is not necessarily the patient; for two acts can hardly be identical if they do not have the same termini. This is an important point in relation to a prominent issue in the analytical philosophy of action: the way in which actions are described, and in particular, to what extent one and the same action admits of several descriptions whose connection with each other is logically contingent. In the discussions of this issue, it is often assumed, or asserted, that an action is something wholly in the agent itself, and that anything outside the agent is at most only the action's effect.

There are strong motives for this assumption. One is simply the fact that many actions do exist wholly in the agent, because it is also the patient. Another is that when an agent acts upon things outside of it, the activity that does belong to the agent itself may also be its action, originating from it. In any case, the agent's *effort* exists in the agent.[9]

Perhaps another motive derives from the tendency to think of action always in terms of human action, or to confuse the common notion of action as 'making something so' with the special sort of 'making something so' which is *conduct*. For conduct *is* primarily in the agent, and the kind of description proper to conduct, moral description, is somewhat independent of its actual external consequences, especially to the extent that these are outside the agent's control.[10]

Yet another, and much more subtle, basis for the assumption that actions exist entirely in their agents is the fact that an action can take on new names by reason of things that happen only subsequently to its accomplishment. (Here lies the connection with the issue of multiple descriptions of the same action.) This fact makes it easy to infer that *everything* that happens subsequently to the movements that take place in the agent itself is something outside its action. But the inference is fallacious.

2. Actions and their Completions

Take the common example: you shot a man yesterday, and he dies of the wound today. It is certainly true that his death is one thing, and your killing

---

9. For a thorough discussion of the 'no further effort' argument and the issues surrounding it, see Bennett, *Events and their Names*, pp. 188–202.

10. This however does not mean that what goes on outside a man cannot also, insofar as it *is* in a certain way the effect of his conduct, be called his conduct, and form an integral part of his action. The grounds for saying that conduct is chiefly in the agent will be discussed in Chapter 4.

him another.¹¹ It is also true that, as Donagan observes, the courts will date the killing yesterday and not today. Yesterday's shooting only *comes to have been* a killing today, when the man dies; but the shooting and the killing are the same action.¹²

But is there warrant for pushing the action back still further, saying that the shooting and killing are in fact identical with your pulling the trigger, your movement of your hand, or something of the sort, and that this becomes a shooting and a killing once the man gets shot and dies? Anscombe, Davidson and Donagan all hold that there is. This is the sense of Davidson's famous line, 'we never do more than move our bodies, the rest is up to nature.'¹³

Donagan presents the idea with typical clarity, using the example of Oedipus's slaying of Laius.¹⁴ He observes that this action can be described in a variety of ways: the slaying of Laius, the slaying of an old man, the slaying of Oedipus's father, the striking of Laius with a stick, and 'certain changes in Oedipus.' The inclusion of this last description is what is of interest at the moment. Donagan insists that these 'changes in Oedipus' (say, some movements of his hand, and so forth) are identical with the action of slaying Laius, indeed are that in which the event which constitutes this action 'consists.'¹⁵ The other descriptions of it are not formed according to its own constitution, but according to its relation to certain results or effects, Laius's being struck and being killed, which themselves are described in terms of various things that are true of Laius.

Similarly, Anscombe distinguishes between the 'completion' and the 'consummation' of an action. The latter evidently means the time at which, or the

---

11. See I–II, q. 73, a. 8 obj. 1: harm is a certain event following upon an act of sin (*nocumentum . . . est quidam eventus consequens actum peccati*). As the corpus of the article indicates, this is true even when the harm is the immediate and proper effect of the act, i.e. when what it *consists* in is a 'harming' (*nocere*).

12. I mean the shooting *of the man* is the same action as the killing of him. If 'shooting' is taken in the sense of merely 'making the gun fire,' then I deny that this is the same as the killing, or even the same as the shooting of the man.

13. 'Agency,' in *Essays on Actions and Events*, p. 59. However, it should be noted that Anscombe, who takes a much less radical line on 'event identity' than does Davidson, does not say that what goes on in the agent is what the action really 'consists' in. Perhaps she does not think there is any such thing (see below, n. 18).

14. *Choice*, pp. 35–38.

15. I say 'the event which constitutes this action' rather than simply 'this action,' because Donagan does want to deny that this event's character as an *action* can be represented in a description that abstracts from all of its exterior effects (ibid., pp. 162–63). But he does not say this because he considers those effects to be somehow intrinsic to the action; if he did, he could not identify the action with the event of the change in Oedipus, since the effects outside of Oedipus are extrinsic to that. Rather, he judges that the very characterization of the event as an action requires reference to something extrinsic; though not, at least immediately, to its effects, but to its cause, which is the agent's intention. It is insofar as the object of the agent's intention includes exterior effects that the description of the action *qua* action requires reference to them.

event by virtue of which, a given description is true of the action. In the case described earlier, the killing is consummated when the man dies, even though it was (in her view) completed when you finished those movements of your own body by which the gun was made to go off. These movements come to have been a killing when the man dies. But, she says, if 'we refer to the time of completion of an act, we usually mean the time by which the agent had completed his activity in the matter.'[16] This is the doubtful assertion—at least, if it is taken to mean (as perhaps Anscombe does *not* mean) that the 'substance' of the action is 'the agent's activity in the matter.'

Although we could stay with the shooting example, suppose we select an example in which there is an even clearer distance between the agent's movements and the other's being acted upon. Say someone poisoned a man's water supply on the day before yesterday (for simplicity, suppose he did so in order that the man die from it), the man drank from it yesterday, and dies today. It is granted that the poisoning of the man is an action identical with the killing of him. But when was this action completed? Surely neither today nor the day before yesterday, but yesterday, when the man drank the poisoned water. For until that moment, the poisoner himself cannot have been sure that 'no more effort' is required to complete his action. He might have discovered, for example, that his victim had planned to have his water-tank drained and cleaned yesterday morning, and that something must be done to delay that. Indeed, even if no such obstacle to his aim appears, he is still in a way continuing to exert effort up until the time that his victim drinks; not physical effort, perhaps, but the effort of vigilance, to see whether anything gets in the way.

The crucial thesis here, which at least Anscombe seems to grant (in seeming to grant that only actions that have the same time of completion can be identical), is the very fact that an action has a time of completion, and therefore a completion, dividing it from things that are outside of and subsequent to it. Granted this, it appears incorrect to say that an action always terminates with the termination of 'the agent's activity in the matter,' meaning by this the acts or movements to which the agent is subject. The argument is as follows.

It is not possible that the *only* true descriptions of an action be descriptions true of it by reason of things extrinsic to it. If it were, how would it be possible to make the very distinction between the action itself and the things extrinsic to it? If someone says that this action came to have been a killing when the man died, he must already have in mind some description according to which he is thinking distinctly of *this* action. The term 'this' is nothing but a pointer toward some already discernible feature. He *may* of course have in mind a description based on other extrinsic items; indeed, he may not know *any* of the action's intrinsic descriptions. But he must judge that it has some. There must be some description according to which the thing that is this action first stands apart from

---

16. 'Under a Description,' p. 216.

the things that are not this action. Call such a description a primitive description of the action.[17]

Furthermore, among the primitive descriptions of a given action, there must be at least one that names a *specific kind* of action. Even if a given action can be sufficiently distinguished by, for example, saying that it was the action of this man at this time (he was only doing one thing at that time), not all of the descriptions by which his action is presented as some specific kind of action can be descriptions that are true of it only by reason of things extrinsic to it. This is shown by the fact that the expression 'an action' is nearly useless as a term for describing or distinguishing. Thus, against authors who reject the thesis that actions are individuals on the grounds that there is no method for counting them, Anscombe acutely observes that actions *of a specific kind*, e.g. kisses or swordthrusts, are certainly countable. An individual action is always an individual of a given kind of action. This suggests that 'an action' is not a term for identifying or describing things. It is not like (say) 'a man' or 'a footstep.' You may notice something, ask what it was, and receive the answer 'a man' or 'a footstep,' but you will not receive the answer 'an action' (nor, for that matter, 'a material object'). But if this is the case, then it is also the case that every action must have some speciesdescription, more definite than 'action,' that is intrinsic to it.[18]

17. Readers familiar with the analytical philosophy of action will be reminded of the concept of 'basic action,' first introduced by Arthur Danto. Originally, this expression designated an action not performed by way of the performance of some other action. Under the influence of the arguments according to which doing one thing by way of doing another may constitute only one action, described in different ways, the concept of basic action has been dropped by many prominent analytical philosophers, in favor of the concept of a basic *description* of an action. This would be a description of an action not relative to some mere effect, but according to its own constitution. I have chosen the term 'primitive description' rather than 'basic description' because I want to deny that what an action consists in can be expressed in a description that abstracts from effects.

18. Oddly, Anscombe simply rejects the question 'If an action can have many descriptions, what is *the* action, which has all these descriptions?,' saying that such a question invokes the old fallacy of 'bare particulars' ('*what* is the subject, which has all these predicates?'). To be sure, this puts distance between her view and the position that what an action 'consists' in is what is in the agent; if anything, this denies that there is anything that it 'consists' in. But surely the sense of the question 'what is *the* action?,' if it is asked sensibly, is not that of a request for something about the action *besides* one of its descriptions. Rather, it is a request for an 'essential' description of the action. This of course is a very problematic notion. But at least some legitimacy is granted to it by the distinction between an action and what is extrinsic to it. This distinction surely makes it possible to put some order among the action's various descriptions. One basis for such order would be the distinction between descriptions that belong to the action by reason of its relation to other things and those that belong to it considered by itself, the latter being in some way prior or primitive. This is not quite to equate the notion of a primitive description with that of an essential one; indeed, in some sense of 'essential,' some of the descriptions of an action based on things extrinsic to it may be more essential to it than some of the ones that are intrinsic to it. The difference can be seen by analogy with material things. The description of Socrates as bald is based on something intrinsic to him, whereas the description of him as the husband of Xanthippe is based on something extrinsic; but neither is essential to him. Nevertheless the distinction between intrinsic and extrinsic descriptions already indicates

This is especially evident if actions have completions. One can speak of a complete or an incomplete action only relative to a definite kind of action, just as only bodies of definite kinds can be called complete or incomplete, according to their kinds. What constitutes the completion of an action also makes it an action of a definite kind. Since its completion is intrinsic to it, some species-description of it must also be intrinsically true of it.

3. The Patient in Intrinsic Descriptions of Actions

But what is it that makes an action to be an action of a definite kind? Is it not precisely the thing whose bringing about *is* the action? An action is an action of heating because it brings about heat. Yet this, the heat brought about, exists in the patient, the thing heated, not the agent. So if an action gets its species from something in the patient, and if not all of its species belong to it by reason of things extrinsic to it, and if in particular it is specified by its term of completion, then the result is the Aristotelian formula 'the actuality (or completion) of the agent (*qua* agent or initiating principle of this action) is in the patient.'

It may be objected, returning to the earlier example, that 'killing' means taking a life, and that it was granted that the killing of the man was completed before he lost his life. But surely the force of the concession is precisely to sharpen the very definition of killing. It must be something like 'inflicting a mortal wound,' or if 'wound' is too specific to embrace the objects of certain kinds of killings (e.g. poisonings or starvings), say 'depriving of necessary vital conditions, with death resulting.' This shows only that the very term of completion of an action, which is always intrinsic to it, can itself be described according to its relation to extrinsic things. What makes the action to be, without qualification, an action of a given kind is always something intrinsic to it. An action whose very completion, *as* a certain kind of action, consists in the bringing about of something extrinsic to it, i.e. something that does not yet exist even when the action is finished, is not that kind of action except in a qualified sense. For instance, if a man loads his gun with the aim of killing someone, it may be said that the loading of the gun finds a certain fulfillment in the killing; but rather than an act of killing, it is only a 'homicidal' act, or something of the sort.

None of the foregoing, of course, is an argument against the general claim that the same action can have several descriptions. But two descriptions can be

---

that looking for the 'fundamental' description of an action, 'what' it is, is not so frivolous as to deserve to be swept aside with the reply 'Take whichever true description of it you prefer' ('Under a Description,' p. 209). As will come out in Section E of this chapter, an action is properly specified, or given its 'what,' in accordance with the intention it embodies. On the other hand, it may readily be granted that *sometimes* there is no straightforward or unqualified answer to the question of an action's species, namely when there is *no* intention that it fully embodies. The clearest example of such action is what is done out of ignorance. See Chapter 5, Section D.3.

descriptions of the same action only if what each is a description of has the same term of completion; and they can hardly do so if they do not terminate in the same subject. The slaying of Laius is identical with the slaying of Oedipus's father, because Laius is identical with Oedipus's father. Likewise, what allows the shooting of the man and the killing of him to be the same action is that both terminate in him. The terminus itself has multiple true descriptions. Being shot *is*, in this case, being killed; having a bullet lodged in one's heart *is* being in a state from which death results. We may even accept a modified version of the criterion used by Anscombe and others to show that the two actions are identical: the shooting is the killing because nothing else has to *be undergone by the one who was shot, from the one who shot him*, in order for it to become true that the one who was shot was killed by the one who shot him.

By contrast, the firing of the gun, as such, terminates in the gun (or perhaps in the bullet), and the poisoning of the water supply, as such, terminates in the water supply. These cannot be identical with the shooting or the poisoning of the man, or with the killing of him. After the gun is fired, something must still be undergone *by the man* from the one who fired the gun, not only in order that it be true that the man was killed by him, but also in order that it be true that he was shot by him. You can have been killed before you die, perhaps; but you can hardly have been killed before you undergo *anything* at the hands of your killer.

At most the firing of the gun can only be a part of the shooting and the killing of the man. There is no reason, in fact, why one action should not have parts that are also actions, just as movements have parts that are also movements. Going to Chicago is hardly the same thing as going to Los Angeles, but part of a going to Los Angeles may consist in a going to Chicago. This however does suggest that an action and its corresponding passion are not simply identical entities. You may begin to kill someone before he begins to be killed by you. Their beginnings do not need to be identical, only their ends.[19]

The question is perhaps rendered more complex by the introduction of cases in which several distinct patients are affected by someone through one and the same movement on his part. Anscombe cites Goldman's example of a man who frightens away a fly, moves his queen, and so forth, all with one movement of his hand. She is certainly right that it is natural to say that he did all of this 'by' one act.[20] Also, sometimes doing one thing 'by' doing another is really only doing one thing, e.g. checkmating by moving your queen.

Now in this sort of case, it may well be acceptable to say that there is only one 'performance' on the man's part. But the term 'performance' has rather

---

19. Thus there is no quarrel with Anscombe's claim that 'passivization often does not produce an equivalent sentence' ('Under a Description,' p. 215). The identity being claimed here is not between an action and its corresponding passion. Rather, the claim is that if two actions are identical, then so are the two corresponding passions.

20. 'Under a Description,' pp. 212–13.

restrictive connotations. For one thing, it suggests something like describing a form or a pattern, as in a dance, so that it is natural to focus exclusively on the agent's own movements. Even when it does not suggest this, it does suggest something intentional, something that the agent 'formed.' In the way in which Goldman's example would be normally understood, it would be odd to say that the man 'performed' an action of frightening away a fly.

Yet even if we grant that in this example there is not only just one performance, but also just one action, it is not at all clear that this action is simply identical with any single one of the things that the man is said to have done. Why *say* that his frightening away the fly is identical with his moving his queen? Would it not be much more natural to say that these are two actions, but two actions that are also distinct parts of one action? They are two insofar as the patients, the fly and the queen, are two; and if it is true that they enter into one action because one act in the agent sufficed to accomplish them both, this truth rests precisely on the fact that *in* falling within the range of the agent's one act, these two patients constitute one composite object of action.[21]

This account is not subject to Donagan's complaint about the 'proliferation' of actions.[22] The claim is not that there are as many actions as there are distinct true action-descriptions. Indeed, in some sense Donagan's own account produces a certain proliferation, if not of actions, then of separate events involved in any action. If the event that the action 'consists in' is entirely in the agent, then whatever happens in the patient is another event altogether. This resembles Aristotle's original trouble. If an action is always in the agent, but at the same time he is an agent of a change which is in the patient, then either the agent is always in fact the agent of two changes (in himself and in the patient), or else what he is the agent of is something other than an action.

Now in the case of the slaying of Laius, Oedipus was, no doubt, the agent not only of the killing of Laius but also of the change in his own state. But this is not always the case. The ice that is cooling my drink is not undergoing any change of which it is the agent; indeed, it is not cooling my drink *by* changing in any way at all, even by melting. At least, such a way of speaking would be difficult to square with saying that it is being melted by the drink. Maybe it is possible to say that there is a kind of non-change event in the ice by which it cools the drink, namely its remaining colder than the drink. But this is not something of which the ice is the agent.

---

21. See I, q. 58, a. 2 (*Utrum angelus simul possit multa intelligere*): *sicut ad unitatem motus requiritur unitas termini, ita ad unitatem operationis requiritur unitas obiecti. Contingit autem aliqua accipi ut plura, et ut unum; sicut partes alicuius continui. Si enim unaquaeque per se accipiatur, plures sunt: unde et non una operatione, nec simul accipiuntur per sensum et intellectum. Alio modo accipiuntur secundum quod sunt unum in toto: et sic simul et una operatione cognoscuntur tam per sensum quam per intellectum, dum totum continuum consideratur.*

22. *Choice*, pp. 26–27.

This is reminiscent of Wittgenstein's famous question: if, from the action of raising one's arm, we subtract the arm's rising, what is left, such that by its presence it makes the rising of the arm to be the action of raising the arm? If 'action' is taken in the broad sense being discussed here, and not in the sense of human action or conduct, hardly anything is left. What is left from the ice's cooling the drink, if the drink's getting cool is taken away? Even if there is some event, there is certainly nothing of which the ice could be called the agent, let alone anything that could be called the 'essence' of its action of cooling the drink.[23]

B. WHAT DO ACTIONS CONSIST IN?

The claim, then, is not that there are as many actions as there are true predications of action-descriptions, but that there are as many actions as there are relations of something acting and something being acted upon. To be a principle of such a relation is in fact part of the very concept of an action. This point merits developing, since it is perhaps the one that comes closest to the heart of the problem of the general identification of an action with what goes on in the agent.

1. *The Importance of the Issue*

The difficulty that Aristotle saw with saying that the action of the agent is in the agent (*qua* agent) arose from his considering the action of an agent to be that which specifies the agent's agency, i.e. that with respect to which the agent is called such and such an agent. What he noted was that in cases in which the agent is an agent of a change, it is never the case that, in acting, the agent itself undergoes the very kind of change that specifies its agency, even if it does undergo some other kind of change. A teacher is called a teacher by being the agent of a process of learning or acquiring knowledge; but in the act of teaching, the teacher cannot be acquiring the very knowledge that he is teaching, even if he also happens to be acquiring other knowledge, and even if he must also be undergoing other kinds of changes (e.g. he must be talking or gesturing). The action of the teacher is in the learner. Naturally Aristotle does not mean to suggest that nothing of the act of teaching is in the teacher. What he found himself bound to embrace and, owing to its paradoxical appearance, to defend was the claim that something of the agent's action resides in a subject other than the agent.

Now as a purely terminological matter, there is obviously nothing wrong with choosing to call the action what goes on in the agent when and insofar as he acts. The point being stressed by those who speak in this way is that very often an action takes on new descriptions without anything further being done by the agent, and that in general the multiplicity of descriptions that are true of an action need not correspond to a multiplicity of activities in the agent. The activity

---

23. See below, Section B.2. On Anscombe's question, see below, Chapter 4, Section D.1.

by which Oedipus moved the stick was identical with the activity by which he slew Laius. But the matter becomes more than terminological when it is said not only that Oedipus slew Laius *by* such and such movements, but also that his slaying Laius was identical with those movements and in fact 'consisted' in them, i.e. has the description of those movements for its 'primitive' or 'essential' description, the description not based merely on its relation to results or effects. This is more than merely terminological because of three implications: that what the action 'consists in' need not be what makes it to be such and such an action; that what it consists in need not be such as to make it an *action* at all; and that no event is an action merely in virtue of what it consists in or what is intrinsic to it.

I will discuss the second and third of these implications in the following two sub-sections. As for the first implication, it is in fact a welcome observation, and need not be dwelt on at length. The idea is simply that some descriptions of an action, although true, may indeed be merely indirect or incidental to it; while others, though not simply incidental, may be in some way merely derivative.[24] However, this general point does not depend on saying that what the action consists in is wholly in the agent. One might wish to say, for example, that Oedipus's killing his father consisted simply in his striking an old man with a stick. It was an accident that in doing this, he was killing his father. What his action consisted in was not what made it a parricide. But this account does make his action to consist in something expressed by a description based on things outside him.

2. Actions as Continuous over Time (Sometimes)

The second implication was that what an action consists in need not be such as to make it an *action* at all. For if performing an action is making something happen or bringing something about, and yet what the action consists in is some activity in the agent, then only if the description of this activity itself shows the agent to have brought something about will it show him to have performed an action. This is an odd result, especially if it is true that the activity or event in an agent by which it brings something about and is an agent need not itself be brought about by the agent, as in the case of the ice cooling the drink. It only seems defensible if an 'action' is taken to be something which is always, under some description, voluntary or intentional or human. For then there is always at least the intention, or the 'trying,' or something of the sort, which the agent brings about in himself. But even then something odd remains.

If every description of an action in terms of an effect is an extrinsic description, then even some of the descriptions based on the activity in the agent himself will be extrinsic. For sometimes even this is something that he brings about by doing something else; e.g. one raises one's arm by contracting certain muscles in

---

24. This is of great interest in relation to what it means to say that an action was or was not, under a given description, voluntary or intentional. This will be discussed in Chapter 5.

the shoulder. This point is well illustrated by A. D. Smith's article, 'Agency and the Essence of Actions.'

Smith accepts the 'identity thesis' (that the same action may admit of several logically contingent true descriptions), and at the same time insists that an action must have a basic[25] and essential description: one which it cannot fail to fulfill except by not having existed at all. As for its non-basic descriptions, these need not be framed in terms of things outside the agent. Rather, any description is non-basic if its fulfillment depends on a condition whose failure to obtain does not imply that the agent has not acted. If an agent does A merely by doing B in the right circumstances, then his doing A is identical with his doing B. On these grounds Smith concludes that each human action is identical with the first impulse, the initiatory act, by which it is exercised, called the 'trying.'[26] If the circumstances (say, the dispositions of your muscles and nerves) are such that when you try to raise your arm, you do, then your trying to raise your arm is identical with your raising it. The difference between someone who successfully raises his arm and someone who tries and fails to do so is not a difference between them *qua* agents. Nor does this imply that actions cannot differ in kind, all being essentially instances of 'trying'; for trying to do one thing is not the same as trying to do another. Thus Smith alters Davidson's formula: 'all we ever do is try.'

Given the starting-points, this reasoning seems sound; yet is not the conclusion odd? It sounds like saying that if, in order to fall into the sea, a rock need only roll off a cliff, then its rolling off the cliff *is* its falling into the sea. Once it rolls off the cliff, its falling into the sea or not depends merely on whether there is something between the cliff and the sea to stop it. Even if something does stop it, it will still have moved, and moved toward the sea, just as someone who tries to raise his arm will still have acted even if the circumstances prevent him from succeeding.

The rejoinder will be that the example of the rock is merely a case of motion, not of 'action.' But in order to make the comparison illicit, it is necessary to deny that actions are the kinds of things that have completions in the way that motions are. The rock's rolling off the cliff is not identical with its falling into the sea, but only a beginning of its doing so. It must be the case that there is no such thing as merely beginning to perform an action, as something distinct from completing it. There is only the distinction between the performance of the action and the occurrence of some effect, relative to which the action takes on a new description. An action must be a simple entity, not divisible into parts that are outside each other. It must be a purely 'spiritual' event.

---

25. See note 17 above.
26. Some authors have quarreled with the use of the term 'try' to express the initiatory moment of an action, since normally someone is said to be trying to do something only when obstacles to its accomplishment are contemplated, in most cases by the agent himself. But Smith's point is clear enough.

Now to be sure, a Thomistic theory of action will have to make room for spiritual events, in particular for those which are called acts of will. Indeed, for Aquinas, the principal element in any human action is an act of will; and if someone performs an act of will, then even if nothing else results, even if there is only the pure 'impulse,' he can already be said to have exercised agency or to have performed an action. But this is not to say that what any human action essentially consists in is always merely an act of will, as though anything else were at most only an extrinsic result.

Even if it is true that when someone raises his arm, all that is necessary is that certain circumstances obtain and that he 'try,' the raising of the arm is not identical with the trying. What makes it tempting to say that they are identical is that obviously the raising of the arm is not another action wholly separate from the trying, and that, if the due circumstances had not obtained, the whole action would consist in the trying, i.e. the trying itself would be a complete (though 'unconsummated') action. These points make one shy away from saying that when it is successful, the trying is only part of the action of raising the arm. If the unsuccessful trying is a whole action, while a successful trying is only part of the action of raising the arm, then one expects to find another whole action or set of actions that forms the other part; and of course there is none. At least, there is none that constitutes a distinct human action. That would require a distinct trying. This would lead to an infinity of tryings for any action.

The fallacy is to assume that because the trying *would* constitute the whole action if it failed, it also constitutes a whole, distinct action even when it succeeds. It is not always the case that if something has parts which can be separated and made to constitute distinct wholes in their own right, then they also constitute distinct wholes even when not separated. In some cases they only become distinct in the act of separation. Unless separated, they are only potentially distinct. The concept of the potentially divisible was first set forth by Aristotle as part of the solution of Zeno's paradoxes concerning motion.

The motion which is the rock's falling into the sea is complete only when the rock has reached the sea. Prior to that, the rock had already been falling, but the movement which is its falling into the sea is not identical with any earlier part of its falling. Nor, of course, does its falling consist in a series of movements, each of which is a complete movement in its own right. This would imply that there is some moment at which something that moves has first moved, an implication which, as Aristotle shows, is incompatible with the very nature of motion. A motion is something continuous or infinitely divisible. If, at a given instant, something has moved, then there is always also some prior instant at which it had already moved. Yet this is possible only because its divisibility is merely potential. Had it actually been divided, had the thing stopped moving, then started up again, there would be two motions, not one; and had it actually been divided into every one of the parts into which it could have been divided, there would have been no motion at all. There is in fact no description of a motion that is 'essential' in Smith's sense, i.e. such that failure of any condition of its fulfillment entails that the subject has not moved at all. In scholastic terms, there is nothing that is a motion *primo et per se*.²⁷

Thus the grounds upon which it would be necessary to regard action as something incomparable with motion make motion itself impossible. If it is reasonable to make actions consist entirely in activity of which the agent is the subject, there at least seems to be no good reason for making them to consist entirely in his initiatory acts. We do at least move our bodies, in the sense that this is what some of our actions consist in. The motion of one's body can be an intrinsic part of one's action of moving it.²⁸

Even on this account, of course, there is a difference between action and motion. The parts into which a motion is potentially divisible are also motions in their own right. They are on an equal footing. The priority of one over another is merely temporal. If the rock falls half the distance to the sea and is stopped, it does not need to back up and fall the first half again before it can fall the second half. But when one raises one's arm, the rising of the arm is part of the action of raising it, and shares in the nature of an action, only insofar as it derives from and is in some way continuous with the act of will by which it is made to rise.²⁹

The rising of the arm is action to a lesser extent than is the act of will that initiates it. The 'continuity' of these parts of the action of raising one's arm, their being united in such a way as to constitute one action and not distinct actions each in its own right, is not quantitative continuity. If anything, it resembles the kind of unity that exists between matter and form in the Aristotelian sense. A man is one substance, composed of body and soul, neither of which is a substance in its own right; and the body is human only in virtue of the soul, while the soul is human in virtue of itself. It is not surprising that the pure acts of the soul should have a similar relation to the acts of the body. For Aquinas, there is something which, for each kind of agent, has the nature of action *primo et per se*; in the case of man, this is a certain act of will. But this does not make that act of will to be a 'basic' action in every case; sometimes the first whole action is something of which the act of will is only a component, albeit the principal one.³⁰

---

27. *Physics* VII, ch. 1, 241b35–243a1.
28. See I–II, q. 72, a. 7 ad 3: *peccatum cordis et oris non distinguuntur a peccato operis, quando simul cum eo coniunguntur; sed prout quodlibet horum per se invenitur. Sicut etiam pars motus non distinguitur a toto motu, quando motus est continuus; sed solum quando motus sistit in medio.*
29. The justification for positing acts of will in the explanation of human actions will be discussed in Chapter 4.
30. This point is in agreement with Candlish ('Inner and Outer Basic Action'), who argues that there need not be any specifiable class of actions (say, acts of will) that are basic. As he suggests, the core of the difficulty here seems to be a certain shying away from *contingency*, i.e. from acknowledging the existence of things that are in fact one though they might have been many. See p. 100: 'basic action theorists have feared that unless there is some independently specifiable class of things I cannot fail to do, there will be nothing that I can succeed in doing.'

3. The Question of Action and Causation

The third implication of the general identification of action with activity in the agent was that there is no event that is an action merely in virtue of what it consists in or what is intrinsic to it. To be sure, every action is said to be an event, so that at least some events are described truly as actions; but on this account, it is only by virtue of its relation to something extrinsic to it that an event gets counted as an action. It is counted as an action insofar as it is seen as that from which something else results in a certain way, as that by which something else, usually some other event, is brought about. The description of the event as an action is never the expression of what it consists in. It is a description of the event as having a certain relation to another event, that of being its cause. The event which is the change in Oedipus is called his killing of Laius insofar as it is seen as the cause of the event which is Laius's dying. The killing is not some third event distinct from the changes in Oedipus and Laius.

Donagan shows the grounds for this position.[31] He gives the example of the event of a pond's remaining calm throughout a given day. On the supposition that 'the pond's being calm invariably moves its oldest inhabitant to take his boat out,' two things follow: the state of the pond on that day was such as to move its oldest inhabitant to go boating, and the oldest inhabitant went boating on that day. Donagan holds that the second consequence is an event altogether distinct from that of the pond's remaining calm, and that the event constituting the first consequence is in fact identical with the pond's remaining calm, though identified by reference to its effect on the oldest inhabitant. There is no distinct event of the oldest inhabitant's having been moved to go boating (by the pond's remaining calm), nor, presumably, of the pond's remaining calm having moved him to do so. The statement that the oldest inhabitant was moved to go boating

> does not narrate an event, but expresses the proposition that a certain event . . . had a cause. Presumably most events, if not all, have causes; but the truth that a given event has a cause is not a truth about a third event distinct from both that event and its cause.[32]

The moving, the 'causing' of the inhabitant's going boating, by the pond's remaining calm is not an event.

Donagan probably does not mean to suggest that the common practice of verbalizing the term 'cause,' by which it is made to seem to refer to an event, indeed to an action, is simply misleading. For, to stay with his example, it could also be said that the *pond* moved or caused the inhabitant to go boating, by its remaining calm; which, for Donagan, is as much of an event as the movements

---

31. *Choice*, pp. 28ff.
32. Ibid., pp. 28–29.

by which Oedipus caused Laius to die. Surely if action-terms express the bringing about of something, then they express instances of causation. So if it is to be granted that actions are events, then there is no reason why some instances of causation should not also be events.[33]

In any case, it does not seem correct, in general, to equate 'causing' with 'being a cause of,' or 'being caused' with 'having a cause'; just as it is incorrect to equate 'fathering' with 'being a father,' or 'being fathered' with 'having a father.' Aquinas distinguishes three relations between agent and patient, all based upon the same causal act, according to different modes of its being. Insofar as the action actually exists, the relation is that of what is acting, the *agens*, to what is being acted upon, the *patiens*. Insofar as the action has already taken place, it generates such relations as that of father and son. Insofar as it is in the power of the agent, it sets up relations such as that of master and slave.[34]

But even if it be granted that some cases of causation are events, there remain the larger claims: that they are not distinct from the event in the agent by which he is the cause, and that they are events of which the event caused in the patient by the agent forms no part at all.

The implicit thought seems to be this. An action-term expresses an event. It also expresses an instance of a certain kind of causation, an agent's bringing something about. But nothing which expresses an instance of causation can express what an event consists in. Therefore no action-term expresses what the event that it expresses consists in.

Something just touched upon casts doubt upon this line of thought. This is the very fact that some events that are causes of other events are not actions. In the case of such events, what they consist in is clearly something other than their causation. But perhaps this is the very reason why they are not actions. However, confirming this suspicion will require a rather lengthy discussion.

C. MOTION AS AN IRREDUCIBLE EVENT

1. *Causation, Relations and Hume*

As noted earlier, Donagan does insist that the nature of an action, in contrast with that of an event, cannot be 'revealed by a basic or minimal description of it, purged of all reference to its effects and circumstances.'[35] His reason, however, is not that actions are events that consist in instances of causation, but that what

---

33. This is not to say that every causation that is an event is an action. The pond's moving the inhabitant to go boating by remaining calm was hardly an action by the pond. If anything, it was the inhabitant's action: his decision, in view of the pond's persistent state, to go boating. Similarly, Laius might be said to have caused Oedipus to kill him, by remaining within striking distance; this need not have been an action on Laius's part. Not all causation is agent-causation.
34. *In III Phys.* lect. i, § 280.
35. *Choice*, pp. 162.

gives events the character of (human) actions is that they themselves have a certain kind of *cause*: the subject's intention. It is only because the identification of the action's cause, and hence the action's own characterization *as* an action, requires reference to effects that those effects are essential to the nature of the action itself.

> For if actions are doings that are self-referentially explained by their doers' intentions, and if, as is readily shown, the only concept a doer often has of what he is doing is in terms of effects he intends, then describing his action without reference to its effects will omit something essential to its character as an action.[36]

So it is still only by reference to something extrinsic that anything is called an action. In short, Donagan makes effects to be part of what an event's 'being an action' consists in, but not part of what the event itself consists in.

Why cannot an event consist in an instance of causation? The answer seems to be that causation is relational. This would explain why the description of an event in causal terms is grouped together with all other descriptions of an event in terms of something extrinsic to the subject to which the event is attributed. All such descriptions are said to express something other than what the event consists in. To be sure, an event may instantiate a causal relation. But the description of it according to which it does so cannot be its primitive description, cannot express what it consists in. No description expressing an entering into a relation can be the primitive description of an event. What an event consists in must be expressed by a non-relational description. The existence of no event yields a relation by logical necessity.

Why is it supposed that no event can consist in something that entails a relation? It is not difficult to suggest an answer: Hume. For Hume, every statement is either an expression of a relation of ideas or an expression of a matter of fact or existence. An event is clearly a matter of fact or existence. But every statement concerning matters of fact or existence can be analyzed into statements concerning 'impressions,' or perhaps more precisely, concerning the objects of impressions. It is difficult to say with precision what Hume means by 'impression,' but at least this much is clear: no impression has a relation for its object. Relational terms are results of operations performed by the mind upon its impressions. Thus every statement about a matter of fact or existence that employs terms signifying relations can be analyzed into statements without such terms. This is as much as to say that no matter of fact or existence can consist in a relation. This does not mean that statements asserting or entailing relations cannot be true. It means that no such statement can express what that which the statement is about consists in, or can present the bare fact, stripped of everything about it that is the mere work of the mind concerning it.

---

36. Ibid., pp. 162.

Anscombe herself seeks to maintain, against Hume, that we do have direct observation of instances of causality.[37] Of course saying this involves departing rather drastically from Hume's account of perception and its relation to reason. This is hardly the place to take up that subject in detail. A few remarks may be in order, however, before going on to consider the being of relations in the domain of action.

Donagan agrees with Anscombe only up to a point. He grants that acquiring the ability to use a natural language, such as English, consists partly in acquiring the ability to interpret observed phenomena as causal transactions of various kinds. But he does not wish to grant that such transactions are simply observed, because, he urges, it is conceivable that one have an alternative interpretative scheme at hand. For instance, instead of a scheme in which the world constitutes a causal system, I might think in terms of a pre-established harmony. In this case, when I observe that 'this paper is dividing into two neat halves and that Johnny is wielding the scissors as it divides,' I would not 'take myself to see . . . that Johnny is cutting the paper with the scissors.'[38]

There is obviously no denying that to learn a language, especially in the way a child does, is to enter into a powerful interpretative scheme. It is also undoubtedly a mistake to think that causality is as much on the face of things as (say) the color red is (the example is Anscombe's). Thus it is much easier to be deceived about whether a given case is an instance of a certain kind of causality than about what Aristotle calls the 'proper sensibles.'

Still, it is not quite clear that the *first* source of the tendency to interpret phenomena causally is an acquired language. At least, abandoning causal notions entirely does not seem quite as easy as using a language in which radically *different* causal nexuses are assumed. The notion of 'pre-*established*' harmony, for instance, invokes a causal concept. Moreover, the risk of error in judging individual cases as instances of a causal concept hardly invalidates the concept; nor does it imply that 'in themselves' the phenomena play no role in the genesis of causal schema, as though they were simply neutral.

Donagan adduces a report by Anscombe of a conversation between her and Wittgenstein, in which she said something like, 'You have to admit that it looks as though at sunset the earth stays still and the sun moves,' and he replied, 'How would it look if the sun stayed still, and the earth rotated?'[39] The point of course is that the sun does stay still (in the respect in question) and the earth does rotate. The desired inference seems to be that it does not in itself 'look' one way or the other, but that only our language disposes us to see it so (and, by our own criteria, to turn out to be mistaken in so doing). But surely one can imagine its *seeming as though* the sun stayed still and the earth rotated, this appearance being different

---

37. 'Causality and Determination,' pp. 136–38.
38. *Choice*, pp. 125.
39. Ibid.

from the way things in fact appear. What if the velocity of the rotation changed very slightly, but suddenly, from time to time, and on each occasion, everyone felt a jolt?

In arguing for the direct observation of causality, Anscombe draws attention to a point surprisingly reminiscent of Thomas's claim about the first imposition of the term 'agent': 'If . . . it must be allowed that we "find" bodies in motion, for example, then what theory of perception can justly disallow the perception of a lot of causality?'[40] It is hardly possible to deny the direct observation of causality and yet to grant the observation of motion. Motion already points in the direction of agent-causality.

2. Motion, Beings of Reason, and Relation

Now, if action is infected with relation, so is motion. In a moment I will try to set forth the way in which Aquinas explains this point. What follows from it is that if no description of an event in terms of causality can present what the event consists in, because it involves relation, then neither can any description of an event as a change or a motion express what the event consists in. No event would consist in a motion. The consideration of the way in which relation is involved in motion will lead us back to the agent-patient relation.

Thomas presents the relational character of motion in the concluding portion of his commentary on Aristotle's argument for the position that the act of the agent is in the patient. His account has, at least on first reading, a remarkably Humean ring to it. He is explaining why, in one respect, motion belongs to the categories of substance, quality, quantity and location (*ubi*), while in another respect, every motion is identical with an action and a passion. I will be dwelling on this text at some length, bit by bit, in the rest of this section and the beginning of the following one. The text begins as follows.

> The definition [*ratio*] of motion is completed [*completur*] not only through what there is of motion in the nature of things, but also through that which reason apprehends. For there is nothing of a motion in the nature of things other than an incomplete act, which is a certain beginning of a complete act in that which is moved; as something of whiteness already begins to exist in that which is being whitened. But in order that this incomplete thing have the definition of motion, it is further necessary that we understand it to be a sort of middle between two terms, of which the preceding is compared to it as potency to act, whence motion is said to be an act; and the subsequent is compared to it as perfect to imperfect or as act to potency, on account of which it is said to be the act of something in potency, as was said above [*In III Phys.* lect. ii, § 285]. Thus if anything, however incomplete, be taken not as tending toward something perfect, then it is called the term of a motion, and will not be a motion according

---

40. 'Under a Description,' p. 137.

to which something is moved; as for instance if something were to begin to be whitened and the alteration were straightway interrupted.[41]

What makes this text sound Humean, of course, is the distinction between what belongs to a motion in the nature of things and what the mind apprehends about it. Thomas is certainly willing to say that the terms or concepts according to which the mind apprehends, judges and reasons about things do not always correspond directly to 'the things themselves,' or express them in just the way they exist outside the mind. Some of what the mind apprehends is the fruit of its own operation. What exists in the things themselves is what Thomas calls a 'real' being; what depends upon the mind's own operation is a 'being of reason,' *ens rationis*.

Moreover, he holds that it is only intellect, and not sense, which is capable of apprehending relations. Relation involves order between things, and intellect alone can grasp order.

However, Thomas does not distinguish real beings from beings of reason in quite the way in which Hume distinguishes matters of fact and experience from relations of ideas. Thomas's distinction does not lead him to make *all* relations into beings of reason. Only reason apprehends relations, but not all of them depend on reason for their status as 'beings.' Explaining this will shed light on the passage about motion just quoted, and also on Thomas's view of the relation between agent and patient.[42]

Now, when Thomas speaks of 'what belongs to a motion in the nature of things,' he is referring simply to what there is, in the being of a motion, that belongs to the order of 'real being,' as opposed to the order of beings of reason. The former is the order of things that are beings *per se*; the latter, that of things that are beings merely *per apprehensionem rationis*. The order of real being, he teaches, is the order of the ten categories.[43] The division according to the categories is a division of things 'outside the soul' and is the proper division of *ens perfectum*. Also falling, partly, within the order of real being is the division of being into being in act and being in potency. Not everything that is divided into act and potency is a real being,[44] but real being, that of the categories, does fall

---

41. *Ratio motus completur non solum per id quod est de motu in rerum natura, sed etiam per id quod ratio apprehendit. De motu enim in rerum natura nihil aliud est quam actus imperfectus, qui est inchoatio quaedam actus perfecti in eo quod movetur: sicut in eo quod dealbatur, iam incipit esse aliquid albedinis. Sed ad hoc quod illud imperfectum habeat rationem motus, requiritur ulterius quod intelligamus ipsum quasi medium inter duo; quorum praecedens comparatur ad ipsum sicut potentia ad actum, unde motus dicitur actus; consequens vero comparatur ad ipsum sicut perfectum ad imperfectum vel actus ad potentiam, propter quod dicitur actus existentis in potentia, ut supra dictum est. Unde quodcumque imperfectum accipiatur ut non in aliud perfectum tendens, dicitur terminus motus et non erit motus secundum quem aliquid moveatur; utpote si aliquid incipiat dealbari, et statim alteratio interrumpatur* (*In III Phys.* lect. v, § 324).
42. In this discussion I am largely following McInerny, *The Logic of Analogy*, pp. 39–45.
43. See *In V Meta.* lect. ix, § 889 (on *Metaphysics* V, ch. 7, 1017a24).
44. Ibid., § 897.

under this division. Being in potency is *ens imperfectum et secundum quid*.[45] Thus, shortly after the passage on motion quoted above, Thomas says: 'with respect to what there is of motion in the nature of things, a motion is placed, by reduction, in that genus which terminates the motion, as the imperfect is reduced to the perfect, as was said above.'[46] There are three genera or categories in which motion can terminate: location (local motion), quantity (increase and decrease) and quality (alteration).

Real beings do not provide the only terms out of which true propositions may be formed. Since the true, too, is one of the senses of 'being,' objects signified by terms which do not signify real beings can take on the name 'beings' to the extent that there can be truth about them. Such, for instance, are negations and privations, e.g. blindness. They are not real beings, since they posit nothing of their own; they do not have essences.[47] They are beings as objects of thought and matter for truth—beings of reason. However, although they are not real beings, they may very well inhere in and be attributed, truly, to real beings. It is a real man who is blind.

Now, besides things like negations and privations, there is also another sort of being of reason, one which is not attributed to things as they are in themselves, but precisely to things as apprehended by reason or as known. These are called 'second intentions,' and are the matter of logic; for instance, species, genus, etc.[48] Animal, for instance, is a genus. But what is called a genus is animal not as it exists in things, but as it is known. Otherwise Lassie would be a genus. Genus is said of animal insofar as animal, over and above its real being, becomes an object of reason. Genus is said of animal insofar as it is a matter of knowledge or science.

Moreover, all of these second intentions express kinds of relation, which is our main concern at present. For instance, 'species' expresses a relation of sameness or unity in definition. It is only in the genus of relation that there can be something *wholly* of reason, something which is neither a real being nor said of real being, and yet matter for truth.[49] So some relations are unquestionably mere beings of reason.

At this point, the topic gets unavoidably complicated. There is a text from the *Quaestiones disputatae de potentia* (q. 7, a. 11), in which Thomas lays out the different sorts of relation in great detail. (So as not to produce more confusion by quoting too many texts, I will simply report the relevant parts of this one.) According to it, relations by no means exist only in the realm of logic. Some are

---

45. Ibid., § 889.

46. *Quantum . . . ad id quod in rerum natura est de motu, motus ponitur per reductionem in illo genere quod terminat motum, sicut imperfectum reducitur ad perfectum, ut supra dictum est.* The reference is to *In III Phys.* lect. i, § 281.

47. Cf. *De ente et essentia* 1.

48. See *In IV Meta.* lect. iv, § 574.

49. See McInerny, *The Logic of Analogy*, p. 40.

real beings. Others are only beings of reason, but nevertheless are attributed to real beings. They are not matters of logic.

A relation of reason consists in some order of things understood. But among orders of this sort, only some are attributed to the things understood *as such*. This is the domain of logic. But other relations of reason, non-logical relations of reason, are attributed to real things. (This is no contradiction; we have already seen how Thomas speaks of attributing beings of reason, such as negations or privations, to real beings.) What makes these relations of reason, rather than real relations, is that the order which they express is not something which the things 'have.' It is not a distinct, positive entity belonging to them, an *ens perfectum*. It is only something which follows, by 'a kind of necessity,' upon our way of understanding them. I will return to this in a moment.

Now in the passage on motion, Thomas clearly means to say that what the definition (*ratio*) of motion involves is partly a real being, and partly a being of reason. The real being places it in the category of quantity, quality or location. The being of reason is clearly a sort of relation. To understand something as a motion, it must be understood as 'a sort of middle between two terms.' We must therefore ask what sort of being of reason this 'betweenness' is. Is it attributed to real things, or is it a merely logical item?

3. The Irreducibility of Motion

The *De potentia* text makes it easy to find the answer. After drawing the distinction between logical and non-logical relations of reason, Thomas further distinguishes four sorts of non-logical relations of reason or relations attributed to real things. The first of these is a relation which follows upon the fact that the intellect sometimes treats things which are not beings after the fashion of beings. (This is not false, since the intellect is conscious that this is merely a way of treating things.) The example he gives is of the mind's taking two future things, or one present and one future thing, and understanding one with an order to the other, saying that the one is *before* the other. The future is not a real being (yet); but we must treat it after the fashion of real beings precisely in order to put things in certain relations to it. For instance, when Heidegger says that time comes out of the future, he is ranging the future under the present tense of the verb 'come,' treating it after the fashion of a really existing being. The same sort of treatment is involved in speaking of a 'time-line' or of time as a 'dimension.'

It is this sort of relation of reason which is evidently at work in the case of motion. A thing's being in motion, at a given moment, consists partly in its having an imperfect act, and partly in its being considered as between two terms, one past and one future. It is only by understanding a thing in this relation that it can be understood as in motion. This is what must be added in order to complete the notion of motion, over and above the notion of incomplete act.

We might note that even the notion of incomplete act involves a certain *comparison*, and hence a kind of relation. For instance, the tepid is understood as imperfectly hot, by comparison with two things: something not hot at all, and something just plain hot. By comparison with the former, the tepid is in act or perfect; by comparison with the latter, it is imperfect. Such a comparison, however, may very well be between three really existing things—a *real* relation[50]—and it may not involve any motion at all. For there to be motion, it is necessary that there be an order in the thing moved, *from* its own being less perfect or in relative potency *to* its being even more perfect or further actualized.

> The imperfect act of heat in the heatable is itself a motion; not, indeed, according to what it merely is in act, but insofar as, already being in act, it has an order toward further act; for if the order toward further act were taken away, then the act itself, however incomplete it be, would be the term of a motion and not a motion; as occurs when something is partially heated. The order toward further act, however, belongs to that which is in potency to it. Likewise, if the incomplete act be considered only as ordered toward further act, according to which it has the character of potency, it does not have the character of a motion, but of a principle of motion; for just as a heating can begin from what is cold, so too it can begin from what is tepid.[51]

However, a motion's order between something past and something future cannot be simply a matter of temporal priority and posteriority, its being after one thing and before another. Something tepid may previously have been cool, and may later be hot, and yet perhaps at present it is not being moved or being heated at all. Coming after a state of relative potency and before a state of relative actuality is not enough to constitute something a motion; it may be precisely a pause in a motion, breaking it into two motions. If the motion is one, it is because it enjoys a certain unity, in the form of continuity, with its terms. The motion continues only so long as there remains the 'order toward further act' in the thing moved.

In other words, the thing's having been previously in a state of relative potency, and its subsequently being in a state of relative act, cannot be merely accidental to it, insofar as it is being *moved* from one state to the other. The 'being in potency' of the earlier stages of the motion must be the very potentiality which those stages provide *for* the later stages; and the being in act of the later stages

---

50. See I, q. 13, a. 7.

51. *Ipse igitur actus imperfectus caloris in calefactibili existens, est motus: non quidem secundum id quod actu tantum est, sed secundum quod iam in actu existens habet ordinem in ulteriorem actum; quia si tolleretur ordo ad ulteriorem actum, ipse actus quantumcumque imperfectus, esset terminus motus et non motus, sicut accidit cum aliquid semiplene calefit. Ordo autem ad ulteriorem actum competit existenti in potentia ad ipsum. Et similiter, si actus imperfectus consideretur tantum ut in ordine ad ulteriorem actum, secundum quod habet rationem potentiae, non habet rationem motus, sed principii motus: potest enim incipere calefactio sicut a frigido, ita et a tepido* (In III Phys. lect. ii, § 285).

must be the actuality *of* the earlier potentiality. The being in act which is proper to motion *depends* on the prior being in potency, and the being in potency which is proper to it *depends* on the subsequent being in act. Something may be tepid without having previously been cool, or subsequently hot, but something is being heated only *if* it was previously cooler, and will subsequently be hotter.

> Thus imperfect act has the being of motion, insofar as it compares with further act as potency, and insofar as it compares with something more imperfect as act. Hence it [motion] is neither the potency of something existing in potency nor the act of something existing in act, but it is the act of something existing in potency: such that by the fact that it is called 'act,' there is designated an order of it to an anterior potency, and by the fact that it is called 'of something existing in potency,' there is designated an order of it to a further act.[52]

To put it another way, the actuality of what is in motion, as such, is not merely the actuality of a potential which it then has. For instance, what is now actually hot also now has a capacity to be hot, but the actuality of this capacity is not a motion; it is simply being hot. The actuality of what is in motion must be preceded by its potency. For in fact every motion is potentially divisible into parts, one after another; and the previous ones make the subsequent ones possible. Everything in motion at the present moment was in motion previously.[53] And the being in potency belonging to what is in motion is not merely the potentiality for something which it can have but does not. It is precisely the potentiality for something which it does not yet have but will, namely, further motion. For if it will not have any further motion, then it has already stopped. Through its motion, what is moved is continuously both eliminating and perfecting its own potentiality for that very motion. As long as the motion exists, it is incomplete, and when it is fully actualized, it ceases.

In short, although the relation which is involved in completing the definition of motion is a relation of reason, it is attributed to the motion as it is in itself, not merely as it is in our knowledge. An imperfect act which does not have that order cannot be a motion. Unless such an order is attributed to it, it cannot be understood as the act of something mobile *qua* mobile, the very exercise of its mobility. A motion is a different mode of imperfect act from one which is not a motion. The difference is not in degree or kind. Being heated does not mean being hotter than what is not being heated. The difference between what is being heated, and what is only tepid but not being heated, is that being heated is tend-

---

52. Sic igitur actus imperfectus habet rationem motus, et secundum quod comparatur ad ulteriorem actum ut potentia, et secundum quod comparatur ad aliquid imperfectius ut actus. Unde neque est potentia existentis in potentia, neque est actus existentis in actu, sed est actus existentis in potentia: ut per id quod dicitur actus, designetur ordo eius ad anteriorem potentiam, et per id quod dicitur in potentia existentis, designetur ordo eius ad ulteriorem actum (*In III Phys.* lect. ii, § 285).

53. Cf. *Physics* VI, ch. 5, 236a14–28.

ing toward being hotter and, indeed, toward being heated further. The difference from what is only at the start of being heated is that what is being heated has already been heated, and, indeed, has already been *being* heated. The definition of motion means: the actuality of what is still in potency to *that very actuality*. No actuality except motion has this character.

D. ACTIONS AS EVENTS THAT CONSIST IN CAUSATIONS

1. *The Real Relation of Movement to Mover*

A motion, then, is an irreducible kind of event. It cannot be made to consist in something that is not a motion. To describe some event as a motion is to describe it relative to its terms; but a motion is precisely a kind of event to which some relation to terms is intrinsic. What seems to be the decisive feature in this regard is its continuity between its terms.[54] It is conceivable that something pass from a state of potency to a state of actuality by a series of discrete steps; but none of those steps will be a motion from the first state to the last, and there will in fact be no such motion. It is impossible to analyze the continuous, if it is really continuous, into the discrete.

Of course the terms of a motion are extrinsic to each other. So are all the states of the thing moved at different points of the motion (meaning by 'states of the thing moved' just the form belonging to it in the genus of its motion, e.g. how hot it is). Yet the terms, and any intermediate states, are also, in a certain way, united, by the motion itself. For the terms of a motion are no more separable from the motion than the boundaries of a body are separable from the body; and by hypothesis, the motion is one. So describing an event as a motion is describing it relative to its terms; but the terms, and the intermediate states as well, are not extrinsic to the event. Some events consist in motions.

Nevertheless, we should not forget that St Thomas says that relations of reason, even if they are attributed to real things, are not relations that the real thing 'has.' This is precisely to say that they are not real beings. In the case of motion, the relation with the motion's terms cannot be a real relation, because the terms themselves are not real, i.e. are not real while the motion is. The order to the terms is attributed to the motion, and in this way it is made intelligible as motion; but the order itself is not a real being.

This is a difficult doctrine to grasp. Drawing out two of its corollaries may help to clarify it. These two implications will bring us back to the consideration of action and passion.

---

54. See Waterlow, *Nature, Change and Agency in Aristotle's Physics*, p. 197, citing *Physics* V, ch. 4, 227b20. Naturally the 'continuity' required for a motion to be one may differ for different kinds of motion. We do not say that a man has discontinued the writing of a book just because he has gone to lunch.

The first corollary is that motion itself, in itself, is something only imperfectly intelligible. To be fully understood, reference must be made to terms extrinsic to it. This is along the lines of the way in which, according to Aristotle, a motion as a whole is properly specified or defined: by the terms that constitute its proper beginning and end. 'The whence and the whither give the species.'[55]

But understanding a motion involves more than specifying it. This is because a motion is always a motion of something; it has a subject. A motion is one motion only to the extent that it is the motion of one and the same thing, and of a thing capable of such a motion. Understanding a motion also involves understanding its belonging to its subject.

This leads to the second corollary of Thomas's doctrine that the order involved in motion is not a real relation. What prevents the relation from being real is that it is between terms which do not co-exist, either with each other or with the movement. Why is it that the terms of the relation involved in motion never co-exist? Because they are contraries. Put most generally, they are being in potency and being in act with respect to the same form or disposition. Now, it is precisely this, the contrariety of the terms, which implies a *subject* of the movement, distinct from either of the terms. Otherwise the unity of the movement is unintelligible.[56] Perhaps the only known feature of this subject is that it is something capable of the movement, but such a something is necessary. There must be something whose continuous sameness provides the continuity in the motion, its continuously *being a motion*.

Now, the subject of movement, precisely as such, is what is capable of undergoing the movement. But its being capable of undergoing the movement requires its being (according to the very same capacity) capable of existing under either of the movement's terms. The subject must be capable of existing in act, and capable of existing in potency.

This in fact implies, as well, that in itself the subject must be capable of being moved and capable of not being moved. Its being moved is something *contingent*, able to be or not to be. Indeed, during the first part of its movement, it is *not* subject to the second part of the movement (and vice versa). More generally, if motion is something continuous, then it is potentially divisible; it could be interrupted, or at least there is nothing in the motion itself that prevents its interruption.

To repeat, the focus is on the subject precisely as moved and capable of being moved, not as having any other feature. The subject's capacity for the movement

---

55. *Nicomachean Ethics* X, ch. 3, 1174b4.

56. Thus Anscombe, against the Humean claim that we do not 'find' causality, says: 'when we consider what we are allowed to say we do "find", we have the right to turn the tables on Hume, and say that neither do we perceive bodies, such as billiard balls, approaching one another. When we "consider the matter with the utmost attention", we find only an impression of travel made by the successive positions of a round white patch in our visual fields . . . etc.' ('Causality and Determination,' p. 137).

cannot itself consist in an order toward either of the terms of the movement; even if it has such an order, that does not show it capable of the movement. For it cannot consist in an order to *both* terms; there can be no such thing. The terms are contrary to each other, and exclude each other. An order which is an order toward both would destroy itself. So, again focusing on the thing precisely as moved, its being subject to either of the motion's terms, and indeed its being subject to the motion, is something *accidental* to the thing, not belonging to it *per se* or, in Thomas's words, 'in its own nature.'[57]

Once again, the focus is on the thing *as moved*. If there are things which are moved 'by nature,' it can only be because they have a *composite* nature: not only a capacity to be moved, but also something, necessarily distinct from that capacity, which serves as a principle ordering them toward their motions.

Motion is accidental, something that merely 'happens' to what is moved, precisely *qua* moved. And this means that understanding the motion's belonging to the thing is not possible if we attend only to the motion and to the thing itself, *qua* moved. As in the case of the motion itself, we must look to something extrinsic in order to complete the account. In this case, what we are looking to are not the terms by which to define the motion, but the origin of it. Recall that now-familiar passage about the notion of action: 'it was manifest that the removal of something from its disposition, through motion, happened [*accidere*] by some cause.'[58]

This brings us, at last, to the conclusion of Aquinas's discussion of motion in relation to the categories. What is real in the motion itself, we have seen, belongs to quantity or quality or location.

> But with respect to that which reason apprehends about motion, namely its being a certain middle between two terms, the note of cause and effect is already implied; for the reduction of something from potency to act is not except by some agent-cause. And in this respect motion belongs to the category of action and of passion; for these two categories are taken according to the notes of agent-cause and effect.[59]

Now, if action and passion are categories, then they must be 'real beings.' Of course, they are accidents. No substance just is an action or a passion. These are said of substances, in the way all accidents are, by way of some sort of denomination.[60] But, as opposed to 'intrinsic' accidents, such as color, the denomina-

---

57. Cf. I, q. 28, a. 1, corp. and ad 3.
58. I, q. 41, a. 1, ad 2.
59. *Sed quantum ad id quod ratio apprehendit circa motum, scilicet esse medium quoddam inter duos terminos, sic iam implicatur ratio causae et effectus: nam reduci aliquid de potentia in actum, non est nisi ab aliqua causa agente. Et secundum hoc motus pertinet ad praedicamentum actionis et passionis: haec enim duo praedicamenta accipiuntur secundum rationem causae agentis et effectus* (*In III Phys.* lect. v, § 324).
60. Ibid., § 322; cf. *Categories* 1.

tions by action and passion are from 'something extrinsic.'⁶¹ They are taken 'according to the notes of agent-cause and effect.'

The conclusion is that these, action and passion, intrinsically involve relation, and *real* relation. The real relation is the dependence of an effect upon its cause.⁶² In contrast to the relation of a motion to past and future, this relation cannot be to something that is not a real being. Much less can it be a logical relation. For the effect's dependence upon its cause is its *existing* thanks to the cause.⁶³

2. *The Continuity of Action between Agent and Patient*

Now, in arguing for the irreducibility of motion as a type of event, despite its involving a relation (and a mere relation of reason at that), I stressed the continuity of motion between its terms. My eventual aim is to argue for the irreducibility of action. If action rests upon a *real* relation, then its irreducibility would seem to follow *a fortiori* from that of motion. But as a way of confirming this conclusion, it would seem possible also to isolate a kind of continuity, analogous to that of motion, belonging to action. The continuity I mean here is not continuity over time. What I mean is that there appears to be a kind of bridge or bond between what goes on in the agent and what goes on in the patient; and this, I would suggest, is the action itself. Agent and patient are certainly extrinsic to each other. But they are not extrinsic to the action.

> It is not unfitting that the act of one thing be in another, because [for example] the teaching is the act of the teacher, but nevertheless tending from him toward another *continuously and without any interruption*; whence the same act is 'of this one,' that is, of the agent, as that from which; and it is nonetheless in the patient, as received in it. But it would be unfitting if the act of one were in another in the very way in which it is its [the former's] act.⁶⁴

This account has several implications. First, it is a mistake to conceive of the agent's action as simply distinct from the patient's passion. They are the same act, taken now as from the agent, now as received by the patient; just as if someone travels from Chicago to Los Angeles, his trip from Chicago is the same as his trip to Los Angeles. This in turn means that the action is *not* the *cause* of the passion, at least not its agent-cause. Rather, it is that *by* which, formally, the agent is cause of something in the patient. It is what sets up the relation between the

---

61. *In III Phys.* lect. v, § 322. It is because things are denominated action and passion by something extrinsic that there is no contradiction in saying that motion involves only the categories of quantity, quality and location, and then saying that a motion is an action or a passion. What is intrinsic to a motion is only something in the category of quantity, quality or location.
62. Cf. *De pot.* q. 7, a. 10.
63. See below, p. 81.
64. *In III Phys.* lect. v, § 316; my emphasis. See *Physics* V, ch. 4, 227b20.

agent and the patient. So it is true that describing some being as an *agent* is describing it by reference to something extrinsic; thus Aquinas says that when a term is *predicated* of a subject according to action or passion, the predication is always by a kind of extrinsic denomination.

> Granted that a motion is one, the categories that are with respect to motion are two, insofar as the predicamental denominations are taken from diverse extrinsic things. For one thing is the agent, from which, as from something extrinsic, is taken the category of passion, by way of denomination; another is the patient, by which the agent is denominated.[65]

Hence the description of something as an *agent* cannot be a description expressing what *it* consists in.

But, as opposed to what it is predicated of, what the action-predicate *signifies*, namely an action, need not itself be something that is being signified through extrinsic denomination. Otherwise either there would be an infinite regress, or at least *something* must be acknowledged to serve, of itself, as a principle of a relation, i.e. as that by which the subjects of the relation are united in the relation. For the action is that through which the agent comes to be able to be denominated by reference to the patient. If it plays this role only through itself being signified by extrinsic denomination, then there must be something *else* through which it is set in relation to that by which it is denominated. There must be something which, itself one, embraces both of the terms of the relation (though not necessarily in the same way).[66]

But if this principle of unity were to embrace the terms only according to the way they are understood, and not in themselves, then not only would there be nothing that *consists* in an action, but also there would be nothing that could be truly *called* an action. Recall the case of motion. The fact that something is now in one state, now in another, is not enough to justify saying that it has been the subject of a motion from one to the other. Not even its having been in intermediate states in the mean time is enough to justify this. None of these facts entails any act that is essentially *from* one state *to* the other. That by which the terms of a motion are united must be *in* the thing moved, if it is to constitute a motion. Likewise, the fact that the occurrence of some event in one thing is followed, even immediately, by the occurrence of another event in something else, even

---

65. *In III Phys.* lect. v, § 322.

66. See Brentano, *The Psychology of Aristotle*, p. 43: 'From these two causes [efficient and final] results the effect itself, which consists in this: the affected object now receives in actuality the form it had contained potentially; for the effect is in the affected object, not in the agent, at least not in the agent as such. But that which had the capacity to be affected is actually affected by the very same thing through which that which had the capacity for action became actually active. One and the same actuality is received by the passive capacity and also actualizes the corresponding active thing; by being the affection of the one it belongs at the same time to the other as effect.'

something contiguous with it, is not enough to justify saying that the one is, by virtue of the event in it, the agent of the event in the other. Calling it the agent means that the event in the other comes *from* it somehow, and that it did something *to* the other. As Anscombe observes, this note of coming 'from,' this derivativeness, is at the very core of the notion of causality.[67] So, to assert that an action exists wholly in the agent is not only to deny that there is any event that consists in an action; it is also to deny the existence of any genuinely causal relation according to which an event may be truly *called* an action.[68]

Some events must consist in actions, and belong both to the agent and to the patient; and even if action entails an event that is wholly in the agent and an event that is wholly in the patient, nevertheless these cannot be wholly extrinsic to the action itself, but must constitute its starting-point and its terminus.[69]

3. The Irreducibility of Action

Let there be no misunderstanding about the conclusion just reached. The claim is not that, for instance, when a knife slices an orange, there is one event in the knife, say its downward movement; another event in the orange, its dividing into two orange-halves; and a third event which is the slicing, or which, by coming between the other two, makes the three of them to constitute a slicing, this third event consisting in the 'production' of the orange's dividing by the knife's downward movement. This would lead to absurd questions, e.g. how long did it take for the dividing of the orange to be produced by the knife's moving down? One can, however, ask how long it took for the orange-halves to be produced by the knife.

The claim is simply that the slicing cannot consist solely in the knife's downward movement. It cannot consist in anything to which the orange's dividing is merely extrinsic. The term 'slicing' does not add a reference to any further, separate event alongside these two. Instead, it represents the two of them as ordered elements of a single event. Relative to this event, the description of either of them alone is merely abstract.[70] The order between them must be in the event itself. The relation of agent and patient between the knife and the orange follows upon this order. To say that the description of something as an action, i.e. as

---

67. 'Causality and Determination,' p. 136.

68. It might be remarked that even if Hume were right that our only basis for *judging* one thing to be the cause of another is the regular occurrence of the succession of one upon the other in spatio-temporal continuity, this is still not what we *mean* by calling one the cause of the other. We mean that the other derives from it.

69. See I–II, q. 1, a. 3 ad 1: *finis non est omnino aliquid extrinsecum ab actu; quia comparatur ad actum ut principium vel terminus; et hoc ipsum est de ratione actus, ut scilicet sit ab aliquo, quantum ad actionem, et ut sit ad aliquid, quantum ad passionem.*

70. See Waterlow, *Nature, Change and Agency in Aristotle's Physics*, p. 200; also *Summa theologiae* I–II, q. 72, a. 7 ad 3, quoted above, n. 28.

entailing some agent-patient relation, is always a function of merely extrinsic considerations is to eviscerate the relation. If events always consisted solely in 'changes or persistences in states of continuing individual objects,'[71] then no event would be an action. In general, action-description must be an irreducible form of event-description.

The argument just presented somewhat resembles Donagan's own argument against Geach's claim that 'events are logical constructions out of people and things.'[72] Donagan holds that definite descriptions of events cannot be reduced to descriptions of the objects in or to which the events occur, because one of the properties of events is to relate the things to which they occur to time. Things that are not events are not *per se* related to time. If they have a relation to time, not merely in virtue of the way the mind considers them but in themselves or 'really,' then they must have in themselves something which is related to time *per se*; and such a thing is an event.

This is not to say that I subscribe fully to the position for which Donagan is arguing here. Perhaps there is a middle ground between it and Geach's position. I merely wish to say that, just as not everything that one might say about people or things is such that *any* event-notion at all can be drawn from it, and hence event-notions do show that being people and things is not all there is to people and things; so too, not everything that one might say about events is such that *any* action-notion can be drawn from it.[73]

Similarly, mere changes or persistences are not sufficient bases for the kind of relation that notions of action entail. A relation to time is not a causal relation, but one based on a comparison between the thing timed and the motion against

---

71. Donagan, *Choice*, p. 38.
72. Ibid., p. 32; the quotation is from Geach, *Logic Matters*, p. 313.
73. None of this, I think, contradicts Geach; when he says that events are logical constructions out of people and things, he obviously means people and things that are acting, moving, etc. It seems to me that Geach may be going too far, and that events may very well have a certain reality of their own. Donagan's position, however, is more radical: it is that propositions referring to individual events cannot successfully be reformulated into propositions in which the only individuals referred to are substances. I am not convinced of this. Of course Donagan is right that in order to bring the substances into relation with *individual times* (e.g. dates), individual events are needed; but this supports his position only on the assumption that the times themselves are irreducible. His example is: 'The battle of Ramillies was fought in 1706.' This, he says, can *apparently* be transformed into 'In 1706, once and only once, some armies joined battle at Ramillies'; but this is only apparent, since the 'in' indicates a relation, and that relation can only be of the battle to the date. But, I reply, what if we eliminate the date? 'After 1706 years had passed since Jesus Christ was (in the opinion of those who made the calendar) born, and before 1707 years had passed since then, some armies joined battle at Ramillies.' I do not wish to deny that there are individual events (or, for that matter, individual colors, or relations, or sizes), but only that they are irreducible. In terms of predication this would mean that whatever modifies events also modifies their subjects, which are substances; and the reverse is not the case. If Socrates ran slowly, then Socrates was slow (in running); but if Socrates is both bald and dashing from prison, it follows neither that he is dashing baldly nor that he is dashingly bald.

which it is timed, a relation to a measure.[74] Relations of comparison may be 'real' and not merely 'of reason,' i.e. may be based on what belongs to the compared things in themselves, not just in the mind's consideration of them; but nevertheless the comparison itself, i.e. the very combination of the compared things from which the relation follows, is a work of the mind. By contrast, to assert a causal relation between two things is to assert a combination belonging to them in themselves, not just in the mind; for it is to say that the one comes from, *exists* in virtue of, the other. For things so related, not only does something in them *specify* the relation, as is sometimes the case in relations of comparison, but also something in them must *give rise* to the relation.

Of course, if the activity of the agent, *qua* agent, is in the patient, *qua* patient, then there is a sense in which Anscombe is right: the time of completion of an action *is* the time of completion of the agent's activity in the matter. Aristotle's point is precisely that 'the agent's activity in the matter' is not confined to what goes on *in* the agent. The activity in the patient, *qua* patient, is not only the patient's activity, but *also* the agent's. This may be paradoxical; but is it any more paradoxical than causality itself? To assert a causal relation is to assert some kind of belonging or pertaining of what is the effect to what is the cause. An effect is said to be 'due to,' 'owing to' the cause, to exist 'thanks to' the cause, and so forth. This cannot be unless the subject of the effect has been in some way united to the cause, communicates with it, so that the two of them somehow constitute a single unit of operation. Yet the nature of the union is not such as to obliterate the distinction between them; rather, it depends on the distinction, because their respective roles in the production of the effect are asymmetrical.

E. AGENT AND PATIENT IN THE SPECIFICATION OF ACTION

The final considerations will serve as an introduction to the next chapter, on finality. These may be ranged under three headings, arising from the thesis that the act of an agent terminates in what is acted upon. First, we need to address the relation between an action and the activity in the agent himself; then, the relation between the action and what goes on in the patient. Discussion of this will necessarily bring up the notion of an agent's intention. The final question, then, concerns the need to consider the patient, or the action-passion relationship, not only in the account of action, but also in the account of intention.

1. Action and the Activity in the Agent

Now, if an agent's action is not necessarily identical with the activity or movements in the agent himself, not even with the activity by which he immediately (without any further activity in him) accomplishes that action, what *is* the

---

74. Cf. *In III Phys.* lect. v, § 322.

relation between the activity in the agent and his action? As Davidson insists, it cannot be that his activity causes him to accomplish the action.[75] You did not cause yourself to kill someone by moving your finger. The reflexive formulation implies that it is through having some effect *on you* that your moving your finger resulted in another's death. Yet it would be altogether natural to say that you killed the man 'by' moving your finger, and 'by' surely suggests some sort of causality.[76] In this case the causality is that of a means or an instrument, whose causality, relative to the action of the principal agent, Aquinas assimilates to material causality.[77]

Not every cause of something is a cause of its very beginning or a cause upon which everything about it depends. Parts are sometimes causes, in a certain way, of the things of which they are parts, though of course they are not causes of themselves; and the means of accomplishing certain actions can be parts of the actions of which they are the means. Nor is every cause wholly outside that of which it is the cause. Indeed, in some cases what is designated as a cause is identical ('in subject') with what it is the cause of. Anscombe's example is that of the President of the United States, who is Commander in Chief 'by' being President. Similarly, in the case of killing someone by means of shooting him, the causality is material. It consists in constituting the potential for something. What enables the action to be a killing is that it is a shooting.

Not everyone agrees with this account. Carr, for instance, rejects the 'identity thesis' (the same action may admit of several logically contingent true descriptions) precisely on the grounds that a means cannot be identical with what it is the means of.[78] His argument is that if they were identical, then deliberation would be impossible. You may have decided to undertake some action, without yet having hit upon the way to go about it; so, how can the way that you eventually take be identical with the action originally intended? Actions get their names from their objects, and insofar as their objects are distinct entities, so are they.

Carr helps himself by the example he chooses: replenishing a water supply by operating a pump. I would agree that these are distinct actions, because their objects are distinct entities. The object of an agent's action is nothing other than the patient,[79] and the pump is not the same thing as the water supply. But sometimes the distinction between the objects from which diverse descriptions of actions are derived is not a distinction between diverse entities or subjects, but only between diverse descriptions of the same subject. The man shot is the same as the man killed.

---

75. 'Agency,' in *Essays*, pp. 56ff. See also Anscombe, *Intention*, pp. 37–47.
76. The 'by-locution' is given exhaustive analysis by Bennett in *Events and their Names*, pp. 213–31; see also *The Act Itself*, ch. 2.
77. See e.g. I-II, q. 17, a. 4; q. 18, a. 6.
78. Practical Inference and the Identity of Actions.'
79. See I-II, q. 18, a. 2 ad 3.

This is enough to allow deliberation. The movement of deliberation need not be from one subject to another. It may be only from one thought about a subject, or one description of it, to another. All that Carr shows is that to shoot is not the same kind of thing as to kill, which no one ever denied. Indeed, it is part of the point that Anscombe, Donagan and the others are aiming to establish: *even though* shooting and killing are not, and cannot be, one *kind*, they may nevertheless be one in subject (one 'individual'). What I have tried to show is simply that an action cannot necessarily be identified with what goes on in the agent when he acts.

On the other hand, it would be rash to say that the activity in the agent is always a means of his action, even when the completion of the action is outside of him. For 'means' carries the note of a middle, uniting the beginning and the end. But at least some of the agent's activity must constitute the very *start* of the action; something is called his action precisely insofar as it takes its start from him. Actions accomplished with an instrument begin with the agent's initial application of the instrument, whose own act is a means to the action's fulfillment. In order to act upon anything with the instrument, he must first act upon the instrument. (This may itself be done through an instrument, but that cannot go on indefinitely.) This only underscores the doctrine that the act of the agent is in the patient. For an instrument is passive relative to the principal agent. It is *made* to act, and its act *is* an act of the principal agent as well. We have already noted how Aquinas considers that the acts of a principal agent and his instrument combine to form one action, which is the action of both.[80]

The fact that the act of an instrument, *qua* instrument, is also the act of the principal agent also serves to explain how it is possible for an agent to be truly said to act upon something with which he is not in immediate contact. We have claimed that when someone kills a man by shooting him, this action terminates with the man's being shot, which is in him and not in the shooter. But at no time during this action have the two of them come into contact. The only thing that has touched the one who is shot is the bullet. How then can the one who is shot be said to be the object of the shooter's action, that which is 'thrown over against' and configures the action? The answer is that what the bullet does *is* the shooter's action. Insofar as he *uses* the gun and the bullet, the shooter not only adjusts their operations in conformity with his own aim; he also *appropriates* their operations. *He* has penetrated the victim's body; not, of course, with his own body, but with the bullet. It is the motion of the bullet itself that establishes the 'communication' between the two, in its role as a 'means' of the action. The means unites the extremes.[81]

---

80. Donagan, *The Theory of Morality*, pp. 46–47, puts the point well: 'A man may act either in his own person, or by his agents, or partly in his own person and partly by his agents.'

81. See Wittgenstein, *Philosophical Investigations*, § 626: when I touch something with a stick, I feel something hard and rough *over* there (*ich fühle dort etwas Hartes, Rauhes*).

2. The Patient as a Source of Action-Descriptions

Now, if the action of the agent is in the patient, then is everything that takes place in the patient, in continuity with the agent's acting upon it, equally fit to serve as that by which the action is described?

At least on the face of it, the answer seems no. It is frequently the case, for instance, that the use of something yields results in addition to that for which it is used. Not everything that an instrument does when set to work by the principal agent constitutes the whole or even a part of the agent's use of it. This is only a particular instance of the general fact that what takes place in the patient, when acted upon, often includes many things not entailed by what would properly be regarded as the agent's handling or treatment of it. But it would seem that, in some way, a description of an action that expresses the agent's use or treatment of the thing acted upon is a more proper description than one that does not.

On the other hand, it may still be the whole instrument, and the whole patient, which is engaged by the agent. The whole patient is the object of the agent, and, as Aquinas says, the agent is denominated by the patient. For this reason, everything that the instrument does, through being set to work by the agent, and everything that happens to the patient, resulting in continuity with the agent's acting upon it, may serve somehow to describe the action. Thus the fact that the action of the agent is in the patient is at least one of the reasons why the same action may admit of several logically contingent descriptions. As Donagan notes, it would be strange if the mere introduction of other facts or truths always sufficed to yield another event or action. Further conditions on the part of the same patient may yield new descriptions of an action; but they can hardly yield new actions.

Perhaps it should also be granted that not even the addition of new patients, other things in which something is made to happen when the agent acts, always adds another action on the part of that agent, even if sometimes his action is denominated by those results. For instance, if I knock you down, and as you fall your head strikes a lamp and breaks it, then in some way I have made the lamp break; but my doing so need not be another action of mine besides my knocking you down, although it *is* another action—of yours (or, of your head's). This need not be another action of mine because it need not be true that I have broken the lamp, even if I am a cause of its breaking. I may have made *you* break it. Only if I knocked you down *in order* to break the lamp would it be proper to say that I broke it, for then I have, as it were, appropriated your (head's) action, used you (or it) as an instrument. Not every instance of causing something to happen is an action. Thus the lamp's breaking does not confer a new action-name on what I did or constitute it another *kind* of action. This will be explained in a moment.

Of course the fact that the act of the agent is in the patient is not the only reason why the same action may admit of many logically contingent descriptions; nor is it the only reason why the same action may constitute many kinds or forms of action. It is important to note that not every description of an action expresses a kind of action. For instance, someone's action of stealing a car may also be described as 'the action that landed him in jail,' but this is not another kind of action. This example also suffices to show that the multiple descriptions of an action do not all derive from a multiplicity of conditions in the patient. However, an action that constitutes an instance of many kinds of action need not do so *only* because of the condition of the patient. The various kinds of action that it instantiates may all fall within the intention of the agent, so that the agent himself has a hand in making it to be all those kinds of action. If you shoot someone in order to kill him, then granted that your action is a killing only if he dies, you can be said not only to have made him die, but also to have made your action be one of making someone die and of killing someone.

However, perhaps it *is* because the action of the agent is in the patient that it might not, under some descriptions which express kinds of action, be an object of the agent's intention. By 'intention' here, I do not mean solely a certain 'interior act of the will,' belonging only to rational agents; I mean simply the tendency, the order toward something, according to which an agent, any agent, acts. What belongs to the agent, insofar as he first exercises agency, cannot serve as a principle of features of his action that fall outside of his intention. This is because, as I shall try to explain in the next chapter, one first exercises agency in beginning to execute some intention. What can serve as such a principle is only the patient, or else some instrument, which is but a secondary principle of an action and acts only because the principal agent has already acted upon it, and so already exercised agency. So if what the action consisted in remained entirely in the agent, *qua* agent, it could not instantiate any kind of action not embraced by the agent's intention. This of course does not mean that it could not have results that fall outside of his intention. But the descriptions conferred upon it, relative to those results, would not express kinds of actions; they would only be descriptions of the form 'the action from which such and such resulted.' For, *ex hypothesi*, such results would be extrinsic to the action and not directly traceable to anything intrinsic to it. What makes an action to be an action of a given kind must be something intrinsic to it, or at least something directly derived from what is intrinsic to it, i.e. something toward which it somehow 'tends.'[82]

These points help to show in what way the descriptions that express an agent's use or treatment of what he acts upon are more fundamental descriptions of his action than those that do not. What constitutes a use of an instrument, or a treatment of a patient, is limited to what is an object of the agent's intention,

---

82. Thus the description of someone's stealing a car as 'the action that landed him in jail' at least *suggests* a certain kind of action, namely a crime; but this, or at least the risk of it, is already expressed in the description 'stealing a car.' In some way, going to jail cannot be *wholly* outside the car thief's intention. See below, Chapter 5.

something his agency is directed toward. Anything else is merely an 'indirect' result, a 'side-effect.'[83]

But even though an action-description derived from one of its side-effects is true, it is a description that belongs to the action only in virtue of the patient, not of the agent. It is true, but what makes it true is not what first makes the action to be an action. It only, so to speak, happens to be true. It does not express what the action is *per se*, i.e. just as initiated by the agent. Not every true description of an action, even one which expresses a kind of action, is a specification of it as an action, i.e. an *explanatory* description, expressing 'what' it is.[84] For not all such descriptions are true of it in virtue of what it gets from the agent. What enables it to be called an action is precisely that it comes from the agent, so it must be specified in terms of what it gets from the agent.

Putting these points in Thomas's language may help to clarify them. For Aquinas, what makes an action to be an action of a certain kind is its object. He also calls the object the 'matter' of the action, that 'around which' (*circa quam*) the action is formed. This is the patient. The patient, however, can be considered in various ways—as something having precisely the capacity for what the agent intends, or as something having some other characteristic—and, under each of these considerations, as not yet acted upon or as acted upon. Properly speaking, it is as acted upon that the patient makes the action be of a certain kind. This means, among other things, as subject to an effect derived from the agent. But not every effect introduced into the patient by the agent is something intended by the agent; and even an effect intended by the agent may be described in terms of characteristics of the patient other than its proper capacity for that effect, and so in terms that may in some way place it outside the agent's intention. Yet only what is intended by the agent is an object of the action *per se*, that is, in virtue of the action itself *qua* action, *qua* initiated by the agent. Only what is intended by the agent enters into the 'form' or 'substance' of his action, or 'specifies' it, in Aquinas's sense.

---

83. It makes no difference whether or not the instrument, or the patient, is something outside the agent. Granted that the agent's intention is in some way the first intrinsic principle of his action, side-effects may be expected whenever the execution of the intention presupposes other principles not wholly derived from the intention itself, i.e. whenever the intention is not identical with the power or the possibility. The power of the instrument to contribute to the agent's aim, and the patient's capacity to be acted upon, seldom exhaust them.

84. Anscombe's rejection of the question, '*what* was the action that has all those descriptions?' has already been noted (above, n. 18). But, also as noted earlier, it was Anscombe herself who observed that for the most part, the natural answer to the question 'what' someone is doing will be a statement of something he is (or seems to be) doing intentionally. The specifying role of intention is also at least suggested by Davidson's thesis that even if not all descriptions of an action are descriptions under which it is intentional, it is an action only if it has some description under which it is intentional.

> An operation receives its species and name from its *per se* object, not from what is an object *per accidens*. But in things that are for an end, it is something that is intended which is called *per se*; whereas what is outside intention is called *per accidens*.[85]

Even more explicit, though highly compressed, is a text in which Thomas explains the way in which sins are specified by their objects. What lies behind the explanation is that objects are called *materia circa quam*, functioning rather like 'matter,' and that matter seems to play only a weak role in specification. Thomas says, in effect, that the *materia circa quam* cannot be regarded in just any way whatsoever; it must be considered precisely as an end, i.e. as falling under the agent's intention. The text is also interesting because its final portion lines up with my use of 'intention' to cover active tendencies generally, not just certain acts of will.

> Objects, according as they are compared to exterior acts, have the nature of matter about which. But according as they are compared to the interior act of the will, they have the nature of ends; and it is on this account that they give the act its species. Though indeed, according as they are matter about which, they have the nature of termini, from which motions are specified, as is said in the fifth book of the *Physics* and the tenth book of the *Ethics*; but nevertheless, even the termini of motion give the species to motions insofar as they have the nature of an end.[86]

3. *The Patient, Intention and Action-Specification*

At this point one may well ask: if it is the agent's intention that determines the action's species, why bring the patient into consideration at all? Two answers, which probably amount to the same thing, suggest themselves. The first is that even if the agent's intention determines the action's species, the intention is not the action. The patient must be brought into consideration simply because the action does not exist without it. The action is in the patient. Taken as existing somehow apart from the action, the intention can at most determine only what sort of action the agent will perform, *if* it acts and acts successfully. Its doing so requires both the intention and the patient. Without the patient, there is simply

---

85. *Operatio recipit speciem et nomen a per se obiecto, non autem ab obiecto per accidens. In his autem quae sunt ad finem, per se dicitur aliquod quod est intentum; per accidens autem quod est praeter intentionem* (II–II, q. 59, a. 2). See also *In II Phys.* lect. viii, § 214; *VII Meta.* lect. vi, § 1382; *In XI Meta.* lect. viii, § 2269, 2284.

86. *Obiecta, secundum quod comparantur ad actus exteriores, habent rationem materiae circa quam; sed secundum quod comparantur ad actum interiorem voluntatis, habent rationem finium, et ex hoc habent quod dent speciem actui. Quamvis etiam secundum quod sunt materia circa quam, habeant rationem terminorum, a quibus motus specificantur, ut dicitur in V Phys. et in X Eth.; sed tamen etiam termini motus dant speciem motibus, inquantum habent rationem finis* (I–II, q. 72, a. 3 ad 2). The expression 'exterior acts' in the text refers to acts of powers moved by the will and executing its inclination. The references are to *Physics* V, ch. 1, 224b8; *Nicomachean Ethics* X, ch. 4, 1174b4.

no action; without reference to the intention, it is impossible to judge the action finished or unfinished, accomplished or failed. But it is because the action is in the patient that it *may* be either, and action taken simply is accomplished action.

The second answer is that the patient itself is in a way an object of the agent's intention. 'The object, even though it be the matter around which an act is formed [*terminatur*], nevertheless has the nature of an end, insofar as the intention of the agent bears upon it';[87] and, again, it is insofar as something is an end that it specifies action.[88]

The point is not restricted to human action. Even the act of a merely physical agent is specified by the agent's tendency, and since a physical agent can exercise its typical action only upon the kinds of things capable of being so acted upon, the full description of its tendency must include some reference to those things. This also shows that it is not merely as already acted upon and actually subject to the intended effect that the patient falls under the agent's intention. It does so as something capable of being so acted upon. In technical terms, this means that, properly speaking, what an agent intends, and enacts, is not solely the form to be realized in the matter acted upon, nor of course the matter itself alone, but the composite.

Of course, for Thomas as for Aristotle, it is not the matter but the form which gives the species to a thing; and similarly with an action. But this does not mean that the matter and its dispositions are merely accidental to the thing. In things composed of matter and form, the matter too, up to a point, enters into the full definition of the thing. It does so to the extent that it is proportioned to the form. In so doing, it also adds certain secondary—but not accidental—determinations to the thing, e.g. necessary qualitative predispositions, the distinction and distribution of the thing's parts, etc. In the case of actions, what gives the species is the end. What functions as matter are the things that are for the end. Presupposed to the action is not only the agent's intention, but also any instruments with which he acts, and that upon which he acts; and entering into the action itself are the parts or stages of its execution, together with the determinations or qualifications deriving from the proportionate contributions of the instruments, and from the proportionate capacity, to receive the action, in what is acted upon. To be sure, it is difficult to give general criteria for judging how far the things that are involved in an action for an end are really essential to the action, i.e. are proportioned to the end and fall within the definition, as matter; it is difficult to give rules for 'what is included in a means to an end.' I shall return to this topic in Chapter 3, Section E and Chapter 5.

These answers to the question, 'Why consider the patient?' probably amount to the same thing, because the intention determining an action's species is an intention *to act*. Of course, an intention to act may exist without

---

87. I–II, q. 73, a. 3 ad 1.
88. See also I–II, q. 1, a. 3.

the action intended; but it is still an intention that the action exist, a tendency toward the action's actual accomplishment. But this requires the thing acted upon.

However, the intention that determines an action's species is not just a general intention 'to act.' It is an intention to act according to just that species of action, an intention whose object is the term constituting the very completion of the action, the intention which (to use Anscombe's expression) the action embodies. Yet, assuming that the term is integral to the action itself, and that intentions are specified by their objects, this seems to mean that the action itself specifies the intention!

In fact, it does mean just that; but this does not make the account circular. For the intention does not determine the action's species in the sense that it is the object of the action. It does so in the sense that of all the true descriptions of the action, the one expressing its *species* is the one corresponding to the intention that the action (*per se*) fulfills; the one representing the action as an end of the agent's. This is because to call it an action is to look at it precisely as deriving from the agent. For that reason, its species, as an action, must correspond to that by reason of which the agent gives rise to it; and this is the feature according to which it is an end for the agent.[89]

What I am here calling the end that specifies an action is what the scholastics call the *finis operis*. This is opposed to the *finis operantis*, which refers to that which the agent aims at *for its own sake*, that in which the agent's desire comes to rest. This may be extrinsic to a given action performed for the sake of it; an action may be desired and intended only as a means to something else.[90]

Sometimes, of course, the *finis operis* and the *finis operantis* coincide. But it is important to note that in the scholastic usage, the *finis operis*, even when distinct from the *finis operantis*, is *also* an end of the agent's: not in the sense of something desired for its own sake, but in the sense of something the agent is aimed at.[91] This deserves mention in part because some contemporary authors

---

89. The full resolution of the 'circle' of specification between the intention that an action fulfills and the action itself depends upon the distinction between the action as something toward which the agent is ordered, i.e. as 'existing' only in the agent's order toward it, and the action as actually performed. In the case of voluntary agents, this is the distinction between the action as preconceived by reason, and its execution under reason's command. See below, Chapter 4, Section D.2, and Chapter 5, n. 75.

90. This does not mean that the *finis operantis* does not in some way qualify every action performed for its sake; but it sometimes does so in some way other than as determining the action's species. See I–II, q. 7, a. 3 obj. 3 and reply; q. 7, a. 4 obj. 2 and reply; q. 18, a. 4; *De malo* q. 2, a. 4 ad 9. For further discussion, texts and references, see Finnis, 'Object and Intention,' pp. 10–14.

91. This is implicit in Aquinas's assertion that '*finis operis semper* reducitur *ad finem operantis*' (*In II Sent.* d. 1, q. 2, a. 1). For other references to the distinction, see: *In II Sent.* d. I, q. 2, a. 4; *In IV Sent.* d. 16, q. 3, a. 1, qqa. 2, 3; *De malo* q. 2, a. 4 ad 9; *Summa theologiae* II–II, q. 141, a. 6 ad 1. See below, pp. 97–98.

use these terms to express a different distinction,[92] but also because it helps to explain why a distinctive role, that of specifying, is assigned to the description taken from the action's (proper) end. The end enjoys a special role in explaining the agent's actually engaging in the action.

Indeed, saying that the agent's intention specifies his action means that it has a particularly strong relation to the action. Its relation is stronger than that of something that the action fulfills or embodies; it is even stronger than that of something which determines the proper description of the action *qua* action. The species of an action, as opposed to any of its other descriptions, is what the action primarily is, i.e. the first description according to which it is a distinct whole action (an individual action). This means the description without which none of its other descriptions would be descriptions of something that is one and whole, and few would be true descriptions of anything. To draw an analogy with individual things, the species of Socrates is 'human being.' The unity and wholeness of Socrates was that of a human being. When the portion of stuff that was Socrates stopped being a human being, most of the other descriptions that were true of it up to then (including its being Socrates) also stopped being true; and those that did remain true were no longer descriptions of something unqualifiedly one and whole.

The claim then is that the intention that an action fulfills is related to the action as Socrates' soul was to Socrates.[93] It is a cause of the action: of the fact that it is an action, of its unity, of its very existence. It determines the action's 'substance.' This means that an action exists only because it is an end of the agent's, or, that every agent acts because of some end. This has been taken for granted throughout the foregoing discussion, in the form of the thesis that one first exercises agency in beginning to execute some intention. This thesis wants clarification.

To repeat, the term 'intention' is used here, not in the narrow sense of a certain act of will, but in the sense of something common to all agents, voluntary or not: the sense of tendency or aim. But even supposing this broad sense, the thesis wants justification. Its defense will serve as the bridge between the consideration of action as something common to all substances and action in the sense of human action; for, as we saw in Chapter 1, the essential difference between them is the manner in which the agent is related to the tendency that his or its action embodies.

---

92. For example, Spaemann (*Glück und Wohlwollen*, p. 19) uses them to distinguish between the end which a given *kind* of action, taken generally, exists to promote, and the end for which some individual agent might actually engage in an action of that kind. Understood in this way, it is not necessarily the case that the *finis operis* can be 'reduced' to the *finis operantis* (see preceding note).

93. However, it can happen that an action does not fulfill *any* intention perfectly; see below, Chapter 5, Section D.3.

Chapter 3
Agent-Causality and Finality

As indicated at the end of the last chapter, the purpose of this one is to explore the basis of the principle that a subject first exercises agency in beginning to execute some aim or inclination; or, in Aquinas's terms, that every agent acts primarily on account of (its inclination toward) some end. In other words, the aim is to determine the basis of the connection between efficacy in action and finality. The exploration will proceed by way of an analysis of the principal elements required for being constituted an agent, so as to show the dominance of the element of aim or inclination. However, an agent's efficacy is not altogether limited to its effecting the object of its inclination. The chapter's final section will therefore address the way in which effects or results that fall outside an agent's inclination may still be attributed to its agency. The discussion is still at the level of the 'common features' of action, action as something shared in, to different degrees, by both rational and non-rational subjects.

A. FINALITY AS A COMMON FEATURE OF ACTION

1. Omne agens agit propter finem

The notion of finality as a common feature of action was presented in Chapter 1. In these introductory considerations, I will first present the notion again, from a slightly different vantage-point and with reference to some texts from Aquinas. Then, by way of a brief comparison between some views proposed by Charles Taylor and those of Aquinas, I shall try to indicate something of what it means to say that finality is present in all action, even merely physical action. The whole chapter is in fact concerned with establishing this point; in a contemporary setting, it is the issue of finality which is most likely to raise doubts about the propriety of the analogy between rational and non-rational agency which is being proposed here.

Now, as we saw in Chapter 1, what shows that a non-voluntary agent does not act on its own—is not a *per se agens*—is that it does not set the purpose of its act. It acts by dint of another, because it is another that orders it to its end. Yet this means precisely that the non-voluntary agent does *have* a purpose. The difference is not in the possession or lack of purpose, but in the mode of possessing it. For Aquinas, everything that is in any way an agent, and insofar as it is an agent, whether or not it is master of its acts and an agent in the full and proper sense, acts for an end.

He defends this thesis in one of the very articles in which he claims that only rational agents set their own purposes.

For if an agent were not determined to some effect, it would not do this rather than that; so, in order that it produce a determinate effect, it is necessary that it be determined to something definite [*certum*], which amounts to an end.¹

As this text shows, the principle that every agent acts for an end is intrinsic to Aquinas's understanding of the very meaning of 'to act.' Whether or not the agent is master of its act, it must be aimed at something if it is to act at all. It must at least be aimed at the act itself; and since every act is something definite, its aim must also be definite. Every act is itself in some way an end.

This does not mean, however, that every subject of activity is aimed toward its activity. It means that nothing is the agent of the activity to which it is subject unless it is somehow aimed toward it. If something is subject to an activity, not out of any inclination, but out of sheer compulsion, or merely at random, then it will not have made any contribution to it. Hence it will not be an agent of it.

In other words, what the principle really means for us to notice is a certain criterion for judging something to be an agent or not.² If a subject is not somehow determined or inclined toward something, at least toward its very act, i.e. if it is simply neutral or indifferent to performing it or not, or to performing it or some other, then it cannot really be the act's agent. Being the act's agent means being its source, that from which the act takes its start. To be an agent is to be *unde est principium motus*.

But not being master of its act, or lacking 'management capacity,' does not necessarily prevent something from contributing to the achievement of some definite result; and this not merely indirectly,³ but as in some way aimed toward it. Lack of mastery does not wholly preclude being some kind of source or principle of one's act. It only precludes being the source of one's very aim toward the act. That source, which is the act's principal agent, must be outside. This is why Aquinas says, in the same article, that 'the whole of irrational nature is compared to God as an instrument to the principal agent.'⁴

---

1. *Si enim agens non esset determinatum ad aliquem effectum, non magis ageret hoc quam illud; ad hoc ergo quod determinatum effectum producat, necesse est quod determinetur ad aliquid certum, quod habet rationem finis* (Summa theologiae I–II, q. 1, a. 2). It may be noted that the terms *determinatum* and *determinetur* in this passage carry no connotation of 'determinism,' i.e. of the view that it was always impossible for the agent to do otherwise. It simply means that, at the time of acting, the agent is aimed at something, or has an end, a *terminus*.

2. See Ramírez, *De hominis beatitudine*, pp. 285–91, on the analytical character of the principle that every agent acts for an end. Cf. Anscombe, 'Embryos and Final Causes,' p. 301: 'what is indifferent between just any outcomes does not *produce* one rather than the other.'

3. See below, Section E.

4. So viewed, irrational things may be called agents, not only by an analogy of likeness with rational agents, but also by one based on their being made to act by one. The two analogies are closely connected; Aquinas in fact deduces their character as instruments from their very lack of mastery over their acts. See *SCG* III, ch. 112, § 2856.

Only rational beings are more than instruments in the management of the universe. They are not merely individuals but also persons.[5] But from a Thomistic standpoint, to deny purpose in the acts of non-rational subjects would be to deny not only the existence of non-rational persons, but also the existence of non-rational agents. Efficacy cannot be entirely divorced from finality. The aim of this chapter will be to offer a more rigorous account of the existence of this connection, by isolating the principles required for it in the constitution of an agent, and indicating the qualifications that must be placed upon it.

2. The Two Senses of 'Intention' and Teleology in 'Uniform' Acts

Some further clarification of the notion of final causality and of the principle that all (direct) agents act for an end may be afforded by comparing the preceding account with the discussion of teleological explanation offered by Charles Taylor in his book *The Explanation of Behaviour*.

Taylor's chief concern in the first part of the book is to show the validity of teleological explanation, or to show that it cannot be reduced to physical or mechanical explanation, i.e. explanation on the Humean model. It is a distinct form of explanation, with its own empirical criteria. The most general condition for the applicability of teleological explanation is that the object to be explained generally appear or be produced just in proportion as it is conducive to something else. When such a situation obtains, it is evident that the object exists in some way precisely on account of its conduciveness to the end.

Taylor easily rebuts two common objections to teleological explanation.[6] To the observation that failures in the process toward a goal cannot be explained teleologically but only mechanically, he simply replies that this objection depends on a failure to distinguish between necessary and sufficient conditions. Teleological explanation does not wholly exclude mechanical, but rather adds a further condition for the appearance of the thing to be explained: its conduciveness to an end. The operation of a mechanism may be enough to explain the absence of the phenomenon or the failure of the process, but this is no proof that the presence of the phenomenon is adequately explained in mechanical terms.

The other objection is that the functioning of machines can be explained in purely mechanical terms; hence there is no reason why apparently teleological systems in nature cannot be explained similarly. To this Taylor replies by looking to the very origin of the machine itself, human thought. The operation of a machine is not sufficiently explained by the action of its physical components. Their composition itself must also be explained. Taylor argues that the production of machines is an imitation of teleological systems first observed in nature.

5. See I, q. 29, a. 3 ad 2.
6. *The Explanation of Behaviour*, pp. 17–25.

At the same time, Taylor insists on avoiding the supposition of any sort of invisible entity, i.e. of 'volitions' for teleological explanation in general.[7] To attribute causality to the term or result of a process is not to posit some further entity acting to direct the process toward that result. It is merely to observe the conditions under which the elements of the process normally appear, and to posit characteristics of the subject that correspond to its capacity for undergoing the process under such conditions; in particular, the characteristic of 'tendency.'

This is not fundamentally different from Aquinas's account. As we shall see, what Aquinas calls 'form,' 'power' and 'appetite' are not, in general, acts or operations exercised by their subject. Aquinas does of course posit spiritual acts and volitions, but teleological activity is broader than what these are meant to explain.[8] It is also true that St Thomas holds that teleological activity in irrational beings cannot be fully *explained* without appeal to a guiding intelligence. To grasp something as acting because of an end is implicitly to grasp it as acting 'intelligently.'[9] But only implicitly. The causality of an end is not the same thing as the causality of a mind directing something toward an end, which is agent-causality. One may posit the one without yet drawing the conclusion about the other. Witness Aristotle's *Physics*.

It is of the utmost importance to see that the notion of final causality, or of something that acts from an intention or an aim, is not the same as the notion of something that acts by actively *aiming* something (itself or another). Aquinas distinguishes two senses of 'intention,' active and passive.

> 'Intention' means to tend toward another, as the word itself expresses. But both the action of a mover and the motion of something mobile tend toward some-

---

7. See esp. pp. 30ff.

8. See below, Chapter 4, Section D. Of course, neither Aquinas's 'form' nor Taylor's 'tendency' are strictly 'sensible' objects. Tendency cannot be grasped without grasping its *relation* to its object; it is an 'intentional' entity.

9. Thus Aquinas characterizes nature, in the sense of the form of a natural thing, as a certain *ratio* of the 'divine art' instilled in things: *patet quod natura nihil est aliud quam ratio cuiusdam artis, scilicet divinae, indita rebus, qua ipsae res moventur ad finem determinatum; sicut si artifex factor navis posset lignis tribuere, quod ex seipsis moverentur ad navis formam inducendam* (*In II Phys.* lect. xiv, § 268). The last part of this quotation shows that, Heidegger notwithstanding, this characterization is not a denaturing of nature, a confusion of natural things with human artifacts. On the contrary, it is an extremely concise way of expressing the essential difference between divine and human 'products.' The human mind cannot introduce the very *ratio* of its art into its artifacts. Forms induced by merely human art yield no tendency in their subjects to form other things accordingly, nor even to persist in their possession of such forms. The stability of artifacts is wholly a function of the materials of which they are composed. The thought is that, *up to a point*, the presence of a natural form in a natural thing functions in a way comparable to the presence of the form of an artifact, *not* in the artifact itself, but in the reason of the artificer. It serves as a principle of forming something else. The difference is that it is not present in the natural thing in such a way that the thing itself can adjust its own movements according to the relation between the end and the circumstances in which it finds itself. That is the privilege of intellect.

thing. But this, that the motion of something mobile tends toward something, proceeds from the action of the mover. Hence intention belongs first and foremost to that which moves toward an end.... Therefore, insofar as something moved toward an end by another is said to intend an end, in this way nature is said to intend an end, being something moved to its end by God, as an arrow by an archer. And in this way too the brute animals intend an end, insofar as they are moved by natural instinct toward something. In the other way, to intend an end belongs to a mover; namely, insofar as it orders the motion of something, either of itself or of another, toward an end. This belongs only to reason. Hence the brutes do not intend an end in this way, which is to intend in the proper and chief way, as has been said.[10]

In terms familiar to readers of Anscombe's *Intention*, this means that the applicability of the question 'why?' is not restricted to the domain of voluntary agents. If it marks off actions initiated by some distinct act of intending or aiming on the part of the agent, this will only be within the sphere of things done by human beings; perhaps a human being, as a whole, is only aimed toward things that he aims himself toward.[11] But as Anscombe insists repeatedly, the mere notion of an intentional act does not entail any act of intending, either as a causal antecedent or in any other way, on the part of the agent. As something attributed to acts, 'intentional' does not mean 'caused by an act of intention.' It refers to the *manner* in which the act proceeds from the agent: directly, as something toward which the agent is directed or aimed.

However, for Aquinas, final causality is even broader than Taylor's account makes it seem. It is broader in the sense that it need not be restricted to complex or multiform processes, processes involving a multiplicity of distinct steps or stages, wherein one step is explained by its conduciveness to another. Taylor's restriction of teleology in this way is connected with his tending to confine it to the domain of life, and specifically to things that act to satisfy some need, to fill some lack, to bring themselves from an incomplete to a complete state.[12] Obviously in the case of acting to satisfy a need, there is an intermediate step between the original state and the attainment of the end, namely the action itself. If the action itself were the end, it could not constitute an instance of acting to satisfy a need; for to the extent that something is capable of acting, to that extent it is not something lacking, but something full or complete. Acting to satisfy a need is always applying the perfection that one already enjoys to the acquisition of some further perfection. It is acting in order to be acted upon, giving in order to get.[13]

---

10. I–II, q. 12, arts. 1, 5.
11. That is, the proper 'natural tendency' of a human agent is toward aiming himself toward his acts. See Makin, 'Aquinas, Natural Tendencies and Natural Kinds.'
12. See his article, 'Explaining Action,' p. 88.
13. See below, Section C.2.

But sometimes the accomplishment of the action *is* the attainment of the agent's end, or is all that the agent is aimed toward. This is the case when the end is simply the expression, the outward promotion, of the agent's perfection. Even in the simplest cases of (direct) action, of 'like generating like,' Taylor's stipulation for the applicability of teleological explanation is verified. Only, what is being explained is not some event or action defined in terms of anything other than the end itself. It is an action whose own defining term is the end in question. The end is not some other action of the agent's; it is simply the term of its one action. What shows that it has the character of an end is a phenomenon which I shall discuss in more detail below: this is that the action is not only something to which the agent is proportioned, something conformed to the agent, but also something which the agent shows a stronger tendency to accomplish the more capable it is of accomplishing it. It is both unlikely to be accomplished by something that is not proportioned to it or that it is not conformed to, and likely to be accomplished by something that is. Its tendency to appear is a function of its correspondence to the agent's own form or perfection.

This is not to say that the action and its end are in no way distinct. If they were not, then the end could hardly be a cause or an explanation of the action. The action's term need not be the same thing as the action itself, even when the action is uniform; for its uniformity may be that of a *motion*. The very form of the motion derives from its proper term and end.

3. Ends and Goods

It will have been noted that none of the discussion up to now has involved the use of the notion 'good.' Taylor's reference to 'need' does seem to have some connection with the notion of good, but I have been at pains to make finality even broader than the satisfaction of an agent's need. This is in line with the discussion of instrumental and inanimate agency in Chapter 1.[14] If what such agents enact satisfies a need, it is not *their* need. Even if it turns out that every end is some sort of good, and every good some sort of end, nonetheless 'end' and 'good' do not carry exactly the same meaning.[15] An end is that to which something is ordered or directed and which brings it to completion. A good is an object of appetite or desire. But not every 'being ordered' is a desire; sometimes it is only the effect of a desire. A paintbrush has no desire for the painting. What 'good' adds to 'end,' when attributed to something, is an *explanation* of its being an end. An action is ordered to such-and-such *because* such-and-such is good.

---

14. See above, pp. 28–29.
15. Note, for instance, that Aquinas clearly distinguishes the principle 'every agent acts for an end' from the principle 'every agent acts for a good': *SCG* III, chs. 2 and 3.

However, since Aquinas often uses terms like 'desire,' 'appetite' and 'inclination' to cover *any* 'being ordered,' in an agent, to something,[16] it will help to put the same point in another, more precise way. I am using 'end' here merely in the sense of that to which some motion or action is ordered, i.e. *finis operis*. This is distinguished from things that may be brought about or result from an agent's action in some sort of accidental fashion, mere side-effects. But in another sense, of course, 'end' is distinguished from 'means,' and means are things done, not accidentally, but 'in order' to reach the end. Here 'end' signifies *finis operantis*, something not merely sought or aimed at, but something aimed at *for its own sake* or on its own account; a means is something aimed at for the sake of something else. In this sense, the means too are things to which the agent is ordered, and are not accidental results; in the other sense of 'end,' *finis operis*, they can be seen as 'intermediate' ends.[17] Conversely, desire can be not only of a *finis operantis* but also of means; both ends and means are called 'good.'

The distinction which I am trying to draw, then, is this. The primary and *proper* object of desire is a *finis operantis*, not a means; the means are desired because the end is. But for a given action, its *proper* object may only be a *finis operis*; the term to which it is immediately ordered and in which it finds its proper completion may only be a means, may not be desirable on its own account. And it is sometimes possible to judge (e.g. by Taylor's method) that an action is ordered to something, that it embodies a genuine tendency toward the thing and that the thing is not merely a side-effect, without yet seeing what the *good* of such a thing is. You can see the *fact* of the order without yet understanding the reason for it; you still want to know *why* the thing is an end. And this reason (assuming there is one) may be either the fact that the thing itself is a *finis operantis*, or the fact that it is conducive to one. Moreover, since it is possible that one agent will act under the impulse and direction of another, it may very well be that the subordinate agent will have no desire at all for the end which the principal agent primarily desires.[18]

Consequently, if we want to follow Aquinas and call the subordinate agent's 'being ordered' to the term of its own action (its *finis operis*) a 'desire' or 'appetite,'

---

16. Cf. e.g. *De ver.* q. 22, a. 1.
17. See I–II, q. 12, arts. 2 and 3.
18. None of this is meant to suggest that the principle 'every agent acts for a good' can be saved only by extending 'good' to cover means or instrumental goods. We saw in Chapter 1 how an instrument, if it is to be of any use, must have some proper efficacy of its own, rooted in its own nature. This means that it must have some measure of being and perfection of its own, and an inclination to operate in conformity with that perfection, according to the principle that *omne agens agit sibi simile* (see below, p. 105). Every perfection is something desirable for its own sake or on its own account, even if it is only a finite perfection, still leaving much to be desired, and so fit to be ordered toward something beyond itself as well. Thus the proper object of such a being's inclination, although it is desirable for its own sake, does not absolutely coincide with the *finis operantis* of the agent using it; at most, the one is only a partial likeness of the other. See I, q. 5, arts. 1 and 3; q. 6, a. 1.

then we shall need to be sure to understand this as a merely derivative and secondary sort of desire. It has the character of a desire for a means, resulting from the principal agent's desire for a *finis operantis* and from his own judgment of the proportion between it and his *finis operantis*. This too follows Aquinas.[19]

One final remark. As I mentioned in Chapter 1, I do not wish here to enter into the discussion of 'perfect' operations, operations which are not motions and which are themselves ends (*finis operis*). However, this sort of operation may raise a doubt about the common applicability of teleological explanation, a doubt not resolved in the discussion of Aquinas and Taylor. Such operations are not only uniform but also simple or indivisible. In their case, the proper or immediate end (*finis operis*) is the operation itself. Hence the end cannot *explain* the operation. Nevertheless, it can have a genuinely explanatory function. It does not explain itself, perhaps, and it may not explain any other operation in the agent, but it can very well explain elements in the agent's *constitution* or *state:* a form, a power, a desire.

Such elements are in fact essential, for Aquinas, to the very explanation of efficacy itself. This is because, for him, there is such a thing as the efficacy of an *agent*, as something distinct from and irreducible to the efficacy of some operation or event *in* the agent. As we shall see, this notion of 'agent' causality is intimately involved in the question of finality.

B. THE ORIGIN OF THE NOTION OF A CAUSE

It is well known that in the philosophy of Thomas Aquinas, as in that of Aristotle, the notion of 'a cause' is a very broad one. Its breadth goes even beyond the fact that many different kinds of things can be causes. It is causality itself that comes in many different kinds. Best known is the fourfold division of causality into formal, material, moving or efficient, and final. This division is in fact itself a subdivision of causes; it falls under *per se* or direct causes, which are distinguished from indirect causes. Again, the four *per se* causes can be further subdivided. Many other distinctions could also be mentioned. Some of them go back to Aristotle; others, to those philosophers who are so famous, or infamous, for their love of distinctions, the scholastics.

It is also well known that Descartes, not solely on account of his distaste for scholasticism (much more on account of his love for mathematics), sought to eliminate final causes from the science of nature. The focus was to be on efficient or moving causality (understood, of course, in such a way as not to *depend*, as it did for the Aristotelians, on final causality). This is henceforth 'causality' pure and simple. Descartes' influence in this matter was powerful. It was heavily present in the setting in which Hume undertook his famous critique of the rationality of the notion of causality, the influence of which is still very powerful, and very pertinent to the present topic. For the notion of 'agent' causality, and the related one

---

19. See I–II, q. 25, a. 1; I, q. 6, a. 1 ad 2; I, q. 60, a. 1; I, q. 103, a. 1 ad 1 and ad 3.

of active 'power,' are highly controversial in contemporary action-theory, and at least part of the controversy can surely be traced back to the influence of Hume.

Up to now, in presenting the notion of finality, I have for the most part avoided the expression 'final *cause*,' but of course this is what is under discussion. Also, as I indicated, Aquinas's doctrine of final causality is closely connected with a notion of agent causality, as well as with a notion of active power. Given the contemporary setting and its background, making Thomas's doctrine intelligible would seem to require our going all the way back to the meaning of the term 'cause' and to the question of how the very notion of a cause enters the human mind. This will be a recurring theme in this chapter. I shall begin with a brief consideration of Hume's account of causality and of what might be said about this account from a Thomistic viewpoint. Fortunately, we do not have to look far for a text that can help us to bring the Humean and Thomistic positions into contact with each other. Thomas's text on the imposition of the term 'action' is quite well suited to the task. I quote it again, so that we may have it before us.

> We were first able to conjecture the origin of one thing from another, on the basis of motion; for it was manifest that the removal of something from its disposition, through motion, happened by some cause. And therefore action, according to the first imposition of the name, implies an origin of motion.

1. Humean and Thomistic Causality

It is not necessary to rehearse Hume's whole account of causality here. It suffices to note two elements. First, he denies the mind's capacity to discern any inner basis, in what is called an agent or a cause, for its giving rise to what is judged to be its effect.[20] That is, the mind has no impression of active 'power.' Secondly, he makes the formation of the concept of cause to be the result of the experience of particular cases of causality; and this experience consists in the repeated observation of the succession of one thing upon another. This experience gives rise to the mind's coming to expect the one when it perceives the other.[21]

The implication of the second thesis is that if, faced with some phenomenon, the mind goes looking for a cause of it, in advance of experience, this can only be

---

20. Hume's fullest treatment of causality is in *A Treatise of Human Nature*, book I, part III. Elements of the doctrine, tersely formulated, figure in the discussion of the will later in the *Treatise*. For instance, on the present point, book II, part III, § 1, p. 182: 'in no single instance the ultimate connexion of any objects is discoverable, either by our senses or reason, and . . . we can never penetrate so far into the essence and construction of bodies, as to perceive the principle, on which their mutual influence depends.'

21. 'If objects had not a uniform and regular conjunction with each other, we should never arrive at any idea of cause and effect; and even after all, the necessity, which enters into that idea, is nothing but a determination of the mind to pass from one object to its usual attendant, and infer the existence of one from that of the other' (ibid.).

because the mind is already accustomed to finding that things have causes. The mind comes to expect to find, for any given phenomenon, some other phenomenon upon which the first could be expected to follow. The criterion of discovery is simply the regularity of the succession. Moreover, the critique of the notion of active power means that this criterion is a sufficient one for judging one thing to be the cause of another. There is no need to find something having the adequate 'power' to produce it, as though power consisted in something other than the mere fact of being the prior term in a regular succession.[22]

By contrast, Thomas's text on the first imposition of 'action' shows that for him, certain phenomena, for instance that of motion, are intrinsically of such a character as to make the mind go looking for a cause. This corresponds to the primitive sense of 'cause' (*aitia*), which is not 'that from which something can be expected to result,' but rather 'that which answers the question why something is or is not so,' i.e. 'that on account of which.' Even if the judgment of particular instances of causality requires experience (in Hume's sense of 'experience'), the formation of the concept of a cause does not; for asking why does not. Certain phenomena are intrinsically apt to make you ask why. Asking why does not presuppose the concept of a cause. It is the source of that concept.

Of course, 'why' itself can have various senses, not all of which are requests for the identification of an agent. But evidently for Aquinas, the most elementary phenomenon that is apt to make one ask why in the sense of 'from what source' or 'by what agent' is physical change or movement.[23]

What is it about movement that makes the mind look for an agent, an initiator? It is that movement is always the movement of some thing, and consists in the thing's either acquiring something which it previously did not have, or losing something which it previously had; e.g. its surroundings. In either case, the thing itself, considered precisely as being in movement, i.e. as existing between the two terms of having and not having some feature, cannot possibly be a sufficient explanation of the event.

---

22. 'Here then are two particulars, which we are to consider as essential to necessity, *viz*. the constant *union* and the *inference* of the mind; and wherever we discover these we must acknowledge a necessity. As the actions of matter have no necessity, but what is derived from these circumstances, and it is not by any insight into the essence of bodies we discover their connection, the absence of this insight, while the union and inference remain, will never, in any case, remove the necessity' (*Treatise*, p. 182).

23. Is there such a thing as motion, or even change, in Hume's philosophy? As Aristotle shows pretty well definitively, the existence of change requires entities that are essentially and irreducibly composite, i.e. whose components are at once really distinct and yet incapable of existing on their own. What is changed is always both the same and not the same as it was before it was changed; but it is not possible that the enduring substrate exist apart from *any* of its differences, nor that the differences exist apart from any substrate. But Hume's theory of knowledge entails a kind of atomism that tends to exclude such entities. On this point, see Charles Taylor, *The Explanation of Behaviour*, pp. 10–17. On the substrate or subject, see above, p. 75.

If, at the start of the movement, the thing moved were sufficient of itself to have what it gets through the movement, then it would already have it and would not need to get it; and if it were fully determined at the start not to have what it eventually loses, then it would already be without it. As discussed in the previous chapter, motion is in some way 'accidental' to the thing moved, as such. So something other than the thing in movement, or at least some feature of the thing itself besides what is intrinsic to its being in movement, must be involved in explaining the movement. Put loosely, movement always seems to have the appearance either of a getting something or of a losing something. In either case, it is natural for the mind to look for the giver or the taker.

This does not mean that there always is one—at least, not one of the type at first expected. As Anscombe insists in another context, the question 'why?' may sometimes turn out not to be applicable.[24] Still, what she means is that it is not always applicable in a certain special sense. The sense she was studying was that of a request for the explanation of an *intentional* action, which generally seems to boil down to the question of what good the agent saw in what he did. It may be that the action (as described in the question) was simply not intentional; in which case, even if the agent saw some good in it, his so doing contributes nothing to its explanation. Its explanation cannot be in terms of things proper to human agency, at least to the human agency of the person under examination. The question 'why?,' in these cases, springs from a mistaken interpretation of the explanandum. Yet the inapplicability of 'why?' in this special sense does not mean that what is asked about needs no explanation at all. It means that a different kind of explanation applies, that a different kind of agency is involved, from the one first conjectured.

Similarly, to say that not every case of getting something need involve a giver means that it need not involve a giver in the sense originally sought: something that gives, something that sends forth the thing gotten. Perhaps in fact the cause of the getting was something that was taking some other item away, some item whose loss carries with it the gain of the item originally noticed. So the agent is only indirectly a 'giver.' Likewise, a thing might lose some item, not because anything is taking it away, but because something is giving it some other item, one which can only be gotten by losing the other. Or, the cause may be something neither working on giving anything to the thing moved, nor working on taking anything away from it; it may be something that is acting on some other object altogether, yet in such a way that the movement originally noticed accompanies that action.

At this point, it may be objected that whereas at first we seemed to be discussing the question of active power, the subject of direct and indirect agency pertains to aim or finality, not to power. But, at least in Aquinas's thought, the two are much more closely connected than it is sometimes supposed that they are, especially in the case of merely physical agents. What a physical agent has

---

24. See *Intention*, beginning at § 5 (p. 9).

the power to do, it *will* do, unless something else stops it. However, the question of the basis for the connection between the two may be postponed briefly; for the present, we can make do with a less charged notion of direct agency. The basic distinction to take note of is between an agent that is *proportioned* to its effect and one that is not.

2. Direct and Indirect Causes

The distinction between direct and indirect agency is of the first importance for grasping Aquinas's doctrine of agency. As regards Hume, it means that Aquinas is ready to grant that it is *sometimes* true that there is no inner basis or power in the agent corresponding to the effect attributed to it. It may merely *happen* to have that effect. An accidental connection between cause and effect, in this sense, may even obtain in the case of a true *general* causal statement. That is, it may not be a case of chance causality. Aquinas's concept of indirect, non-casual agency will be explored more closely later in this chapter. Here the point is simply to suggest that at least some of the force of Hume's reductive criticism of the notion of power comes from treating power as something supposed to be an essential or universal condition for agent-causality. St Thomas does not suppose this; his notion of power cannot be swept aside on the basis of a general analysis of causality. Power is not an element of agency in every sort of case.

It is so only in the *primary* sort of case. To grant that direct agency is not the only kind is not to say that what the mind originally 'conjectured,' in supposing a cause for (say) some motion, was not a direct agent. In fact, if it is true that the sheer observation of motion, not accompanied by experiences of regular successions, suffices to give rise to the notion of a cause or an agent, then the original meaning of 'agent' must be 'direct agent,' and the notion of indirect agency will be derivative from it. That is, if the phenomenon of motion induces the mind to form at once the notion of an origin, then the kind of thing that it will naturally 'conjecture,' as the motion's origin, will be something to which the motion is configured or conformed; something which, as it were, enjoys the paternity of the motion. When it is found that there is no origin of this sort, that the motion arose only indirectly from something, this indirect origin may still be given the name of agent, but only in a weaker sense: it serves to supply the answer to the question 'why?,' but the answer imports a lesser degree of explanatory force or intelligibility than what was at first sought.[25]

This is along the line of a suggestion made in the previous chapter:[26] even if Hume were right that our only basis for *judging* one thing to be the cause of another is the regular occurrence of the succession of one upon the other in

---

25. See *In I Post. an.* lect. iv, § 38: what is a cause to the highest degree, the 'proper' cause, 'should be' proportioned to the effect.

26. See above, Chapter 2, n. 68.

spatio-temporal continuity, this would still not be an account of what we *mean* by calling one the cause of the other. We mean primarily that the other derives from it, comes out of it, in such a way that knowing the cause contributes to a fuller *understanding* of the effect, to knowing why it exists.

A Humean cause does not really perform that function, or at most it does so only in an indirect way. If calling one thing the cause of another is merely identifying it as the prior term in a law-like or regularly observed relation of spatio-temporal sequence, then the effect's 'proceeding' from the cause means no more than that its following upon the cause is something foreseeable, something that generally obtains. On this account of causality, a cause constitutes the explanation of something only in a very qualified way. What the cause really explains is not so much the effect in itself as one's expectation of the effect before it appears, and one's lack of surprise at it once it has appeared. There is no real warrant for saying that the cause 'makes' the effect appear or that it possesses its own power to yield the effect.

Moreover, the presence of the cause serves to explain the effect only insofar as one invokes the relevant causal law or rule. It is the rule itself that has the main explanatory role. The explanation of the effect does not consist simply in adducing the cause; it also requires adducing the causal rule, enabling the effect to be seen as an instance or an application of that rule. Knowing the thing that is the cause is not enough to enable you to say why the effect exists; you need to know both the thing that is the cause and the causal rule.[27]

By itself, though, the causal rule is not an explanation of anything either. A statement of the form 'y if and only if x' does not explain the existence of y; it only asserts that x and y go together. But x does not explain y in the sense of making the existence of y more intelligible, i.e. of presenting y in union with something which *does not per se require the same kind of explanation as y itself does*. This is the distinctive feature of (direct) agents in Aquinas's sense: they are not symmetrical with, do not belong to the same order as, their proper effects. For example, the proper explanation for something's becoming hot, precisely its *becoming* hot, would be something that already *was* hot and *not* merely becoming so. The phenomenon of becoming hot wants an explanation in a way that being hot does not. For this very reason, the explanation of something's becoming hot, by the presence of something already hot, is immediate. There is no need of a general rule stating a connection between instances of hot things and instances of things being heated.[28] Indeed, there may be no such rule, or it may suffer a

---

27. It does not matter whether the mind's conception of a causal relation between phenomena is incidental to the phenomena themselves, as it is for Hume, or whether the very conditions of the appearance of phenomena as such, space and time, already point toward the conception of causal relations among them, as for Kant. The issue between Hume and Kant here has to do only with the truth-status or scientific value of causal laws. It does not concern the meaning of such laws.

28. See Taylor, *The Explanation of Behaviour*, p. 45, on the fact that explanation by reference to an agent may precede the knowledge of any law.

host of exceptions. The fact that a fire in the hearth sometimes fails to warm the room (there may be a draft) hardly proves that when the room does get warm, the fire in the hearth was not the source.[29]

To repeat, Aquinas does not hold that such explanations are always to be found. A particular case of becoming hot, for instance, may turn out to be no more than the mere accompaniment of undergoing some other process or of being acted upon in some other way. It may not derive from the action of any already hot thing. But this means precisely that the effect has no *proper* explanation; its explanation can only be in terms of general rules of accompaniment. Still, such rules themselves are capable of receiving an explanation, in terms of some principle that accounts for the connection between the companion items, although such a principle may not be an agent. Thomas in fact offers some discussion of principles upon which to explain indirect agency. This will be treated in Section E.

C. ACTIVE POWER

1. Action as Forming

For Aquinas, then, the simplest instance of an exercise of agency is giving something;[30] and the agency itself, or the power to act, consists in nothing other than *having* that thing, of which the giving constitutes the action. This is what it means to say that every agent acts insofar as it is 'in act.' It gives insofar as it has the thing given. Its being in act, or having the thing, *is* its power.[31]

On this account, there is nothing mysterious at all, in general terms at least, about the power binding agent and patient together. Looking for an agent is looking for what had power to produce a movement in something, and this simply means looking for the original depository of the wealth or the 'substance' whose parceling out is the movement. 'To act is nothing other than to communicate that through which the agent is in act, insofar as it is possible.'[32] The principle guiding the search is that you cannot get something from nothing.

Here it should be remarked that Aquinas does not conceive of physical action literally as a 'giving' or 'handing over' of the feature taken on by the thing

---

29. On the difficulties created by things like interference and prevention for the Humean understanding of causal laws as expressions of invariable successions, rather than *tendencies*, see Geach, *Aquinas*, pp. 101–04. Interference and prevention, or things related to them such as obstacles, are central to Thomas's conception of 'indirect' agent-causality; see Section E.

30. The action of an agent that directly takes something away is properly understood as a case of giving something *to itself* (or to some third party). Strictly speaking, only living things are capable of that. On acting as 'giving' in Aristotle, see Waterlow, *Nature, Change and Agency in Aristotle's Physics*, p. 244.

31. See *De pot.* q. 1, a. 1.

32. *Agere nihil aliud est quam communicare illud per quod agens est actu, secundum quod est possibile* (*De pot.* q. 2, a. 1).

acted upon. What is 'given' is a form, not a thing, and the 'giving' of form does not consist in handing it over, but in forming something according to it. 'A natural agent is not something handing over its own form to another subject, but reducing the subject which undergoes [the action] from potency to act.'[33] The action does not consist in the agent's letting go of something and leaving it in the patient, but in its bringing the patient into conformity with itself.[34] Despite possible first appearances, this is true even in the case of reproduction; indeed it is most true in this case. Obviously in reproduction, something literally 'comes from' the parent plant or parent animals; what comes from them is a whole new subject, the offspring. But the principal action in reproduction is not the mere sending forth of the seed or the parturition (in any case, this latter action is simply giving the offspring a new place or environment). The principal action in reproduction consists in forming something *into* the offspring. This formation takes place *within* the parent body or bodies. Aristotle in fact thought, wrongly, that what the parents formed into the offspring was residual food, food never actually made into an organic part of the parents; but the point still holds. If it is first assimilated, then it is certainly transformed.

Far from an occult and superfluous entity, duly extracted by Ockham's razor, power then is something that the agent may well bear on its very face. Correspondingly, the identification of a direct agent of a change consists simply in the discovery of something to which the thing changed has been conformed, something of which the thing has come to bear the stamp. This is the sense of the common Thomistic dictum that every agent enacts its like: *omne agens agit sibi simile*.[35] Plainly this dictum is more an expression of what he means by 'agent,' in its principal sense (direct agent), than something that happens to be observed of things already identified as agents. But of course, he certainly wants to claim that agents can be observed to exist. Some of them are bodies.[36]

At this point one may want to ask, what about instruments? Are they not also direct agents, even of the effects with respect to which they are merely 'instrumental'? Yet in this respect, is the effect not something conformed only to

---

33. *Agens enim naturale non est traducens propriam formam in alterum subiectum, sed reducens subiectum quod patitur de potentia in actum* (SCG III, 69 § 2458).

34. See Waterlow, *Nature, Change and Agency*, p. 164. Obviously, not all form is 'power.' Or at least, it is not power in all of the modes in which it may be possessed. The form given to marble by a sculptor does not constitute any new power in the marble. However, it does constitute a certain power in the mode in which it exists in the sculptor, namely as an idea.

35. *In VII Meta.* lect. vii, § 1443. The characterization of power as capacity to effect a likeness of oneself is made explicitly in I, q. 5, a. 4.

36. See I, q. 115, a. 1. In this article he also says that 'to act, which is nothing other than to make something to be in act, is *per se* proper to what is in act, insofar as it is act; *whence* every agent enacts something like itself.' (*Agere autem, quod nihil est aliud quam facere aliquid actu, est per se proprium actus inquantum est actus; unde et omne agens agit sibi simile.*)

the principal agent, the one using the instrument? Not quite. So long as it is actually being used by the agent, the instrument itself is also being moved or acted upon by him, and it is only to this extent that it is a direct agent of what he intends; but to the same extent, there is necessarily some kind of proportion between the instrument's movements and what the principal agent intends. Proportion is partial communication in form.

Of course this is a rather weak way of possessing form.[37] But then, an instrumental agent is an agent only in a rather weak sense. It would be more correct to say that insofar as it is a cause of what the principal agent intends, it is not wholly distinct from the principal agent. It is such a cause insofar as it is in the power of the principal agent or is appropriated by him. To the extent that it is something distinct, with its own power, to that extent its proper effect, i.e. that to which it is proportioned according to its own nature, is also distinct from that of the principal agent. The principal agent is, to this extent, incidental to it. Hence what we may call the 'substance' of its action cannot consist in the production of the effect intended by the principal agent. Rather, it is presupposed by the principal agent, as that which renders the instrument useful. If the instrument's action may nevertheless be *specified* according to the intention of the principal agent, this is only up to a point. What corresponds to the agent's intention is the species of action that the instrument's use constitutes. This does not belong to the instrument considered as a distinct agent in its own right; it is not the 'proper' species of the instrument's act, but a species in which that act merely shares, by having been initiated and modified by the chief agent.[38]

2. The 'Logical Connection' between Cause and Effect

The Thomistic conception of the relation between an agent-cause and its effect is in a way exactly the reverse of Hume's. First, as indicated earlier, an agent and that of which it is the agent are not, so to speak, ontological equals. The agent is more self-sufficient than what is enacted, with respect to the possession of the form of the thing enacted. It may be true that what the agent enacts comes to be its equal, as in procreation; but at the very moment when equality is reached, the action ceases.

Secondly, it would at least be very misleading to describe the relation between agent and effect as 'logically contingent.'[39] Of course agent and effect must be distinct, so that each must have some description which is not true of the other. Normally each will also have some description that is neither true of

---

37. See III, q. 62, a. 4, corp. and ad 2.
38. See I-II, q. 1, a. 3 ad 3; q. 18, a. 6 ad 2; a. 7, esp. ad 1.
39. On the logical connection between cause and effect in Aristotle's account of animal movement, see Nussbaum, 'The "Common Explanation" of Animal Motion,' esp. pp. 139ff., and *The Fragility of Goodness*, pp. 276–82.

the other nor even implies a reference to it.[40] Nevertheless the note of 'proportion,' the conformity of the effect to the agent, means that understanding the causal relation between them consists precisely in seeing a *kind* of logical unity between them.[41] This unity is more than the mere fact of likeness or the sharing in a common description. The likeness is in fact the basis of the causal relation. To know the effect *is* to know something about the cause, even before anything is identified as the cause. The form of the effect in fact serves as the principal criterion for the identification of the cause. The causal relation consists in this, that some description is true of the effect because it is true of the cause, and to a higher degree.

Moreover, and perhaps most in contrast with Hume's doctrine, the 'logical connection' between cause and effect in Aquinas is even compatible with the effect's following upon the cause contingently. The existence of the cause does not always necessitate the existence of the effect. It hardly ever does so 'logically,' and it seldom does so as a matter of 'fact and experience.' For Aquinas, an agent-cause produces its effect of necessity only if it is 'sufficient and not impeded.'[42] Yet the cause and the effect are logically connected in this sense, that it is possible that, even without any experience of a regular succession of one upon the other, the mere knowledge of the thing that is the effect can make you expect to find something like the thing that turns out to have been the cause. The mere knowledge of the thing that is the cause can also make you expect, or at least not be surprised at, the appearance of something like the effect. This last point will become clearer when we finally reach the discussion of finality; the basic thought there is that it is not surprising to find that a thing acts to promote the good proper to it.[43]

40. I say 'normally' because there are at least two exceptions. Both are outside the physical order. One is creation. There is nothing in the creature that does not, if analyzed, reveal the hand of the creator. Still, it remains true that the nature of the creator does not require the existence of the creature. The other exception is the procession of persons in the Trinity. The distinctions between the persons are all based on the processional relations. But the absence of non-relational distinctions between them is connected with the fact that they belong to the same order; and precisely because they do, Aquinas is inclined to refrain from saying that the Father is the 'cause' of the Son. See I, q. 33, a. 1.
41. See Taylor, *The Explanation of Behaviour*, pp. 11ff. In general, teleological explanation consists in saying that something comes about because it is 'conducive' to something; but 'conduciveness to' is a relation, a kind of logical connection.
42. I–II, q. 75, a. 1 ad 2.
43. Obviously the 'logical connection' here is not sheer 'logical necessity.' But it is a noteworthy difference between Aquinas's conception of the causal relation and Hume's. It means something like an 'intrinsic' connection. One of the striking features of Aquinas's (and Aristotle's) notion of causality is that there can be an intrinsic connection between cause and effect, and yet the effect may follow on the cause in a contingent way. The proper term for this way of following is not 'casual' or 'by chance,' but 'natural.' It is not surprising to find in Aquinas an analogous domain of pieces of reasoning or of logical connections, in which a conclusion validly derived from true premises is generally true but sometimes false.

108   *Action and Conduct*

In view of the passage quoted in the preceding paragraph, this is probably the place to glance at Aquinas's notion of a 'sufficient' cause. Anscombe's remarks on the term are exceedingly apt.

> Now 'sufficient condition' is a term of art whose users may therefore lay down its meaning as they please. So they are in their rights to rule out the query: 'May not the sufficient conditions of an event be present, and the event yet not take place?' For 'sufficient condition' is so used that if the sufficient conditions for *X* are there, *X* occurs. But at the same time, the phrase cozens the understanding into not noticing an assumption. For 'sufficient condition' sounds like: 'enough.' And one certainly *can* ask: 'May there not be *enough* to have made something happen—and yet it not have happened?'[44]

In Aquinas, the 'sufficient cause' of something is precisely what is 'enough' to cause it; and one may not only ask Anscombe's last question, but also receive an affirmative answer. What follows is the whole of I–II, q. 75, a. 1 ad 2, which is given in reply to an objection based on the thesis that a cause is 'that upon which something else follows of necessity.'

> If that definition of a cause is to be verified universally, it will have to be understood to be about a sufficient and unimpeded cause. For it happens that one thing is the sufficient cause of another, and nevertheless the effect does not result of necessity, on account of some impediment intervening. Otherwise it would follow that all things happen of necessity, as is clear from the sixth book of the *Metaphysics*.[45]

This text is interesting both because it shows Aquinas to be quite free of the (for Anscombe, troublesome) assumption that causation implies necessity, and also because of its implicit suggestion that the term 'cause,' taken without qualification, does *not* mean 'a sufficient and unimpeded cause.' Within the domain of 'moving' causes (recall that there are three other sorts of direct causality for Aquinas), it seems to mean simply a sufficient cause, a cause proportioned to the effect, a principal cause. (This also shows another difference from Hume: for Aquinas, one and the same effect may have several causes, even several moving causes.)

3. *The Irreducibility of Power*

It should be evident that the causality of an agent, so conceived, cannot be reduced to the causality of events or to 'occurrent' causes (causes that consist in

---

44. 'Causality and Determination,' p. 135. Here I do not consider what she herself may intend by 'sufficient cause.'
45. See *In VI Meta.* lect. iii, § 1192–93. See also *De malo* q. 6 a. 1. obj. 15 and reply.

occurrences or events).⁴⁶ That is, as Donagan puts it,⁴⁷ not all causal relations are between events. An agent is not only an antecedent condition for the occurrence of some event; it is also, and even primarily, a determinant of the constitution or form of something. This is not to deny that in some, or perhaps all, cases of action, the agent cannot produce its characteristic effect without itself being, or having been, the subject of some event or occurrence. It means that at least in some cases, the relevant event in the agent is not something proportioned to the effect.

Sometimes the needed event is merely a removal of obstacles to the action; e.g. a fire can burn a piece of wood only once it has been brought into contact with the wood. On the other hand, there may be an event in the agent to which the effect is conformed, for instance the event by which the agent acquired its power. But even in this case, the event, *qua* singular event, may not be something fully proportioned to what follows from it. It may not be true that the agent has to undergo the same sort of event again each time it produces its effect. The result of the one event of acquiring its power may be an indefinite number of actions. The existence of this sort of case was in fact one of Aristotle's chief motives for regarding power as something distinct, not reducible either to the event of its acquisition or to the event of its exercise.⁴⁸ It is also what Aristotle means by speaking of an agent as a kind of *principle*, that is, an origin, an irreducible (though not necessarily in every respect uncaused) starting-point.⁴⁹

However, it must be granted that at least within the domain of merely physical agents, there is hardly any distinction between the agent's power and its nature. Donagan, though, goes so far as to suggest that it is really only necessary to posit power, as an explanatory principle irreducible to events, in the case of agents that exercise their powers or not at will, i.e. free agents, agents that have their acts 'in their power.'⁵⁰ His thought seems to be that only in this case is it clearly impossible to formulate laws of nature that explain events as the outcome of other events. But on the above account of the meaning of power, this is not really to the point. Even if it is possible to formulate such laws of nature, they do not provide the same *kind* of explanation as that provided by reference to power. They only explain an event by showing it as an instance of the apodosis of a conditional proposition, which itself merely *asserts* a connection between kinds of

---

46. Davidson ('Agency') in fact denies that being an agent implies being a cause of one's action, evidently because he thinks of causality exclusively in terms of occurrent causality. For he thinks that being a cause of one's action means doing something else by which it is brought about; and of course an agent is not always a cause of his action in this way.
47. *Choice*, p. 167.
48. See *Metaphysics* IX, ch. 3, 1046b28–1047a29; cf. Waterlow, *Nature, Change and Agency in Aristotle's Physics*, pp. 186f.
49. See *Eudemian Ethics* II, ch. 6, 1222b16: 'all substances are naturally starting-points of a sort, *which is why each one can actually generate many things of the same sort*' (trans. Michael Woods; my emphasis).
50. *Choice*, pp. 165–70.

events. Causal laws do not purport to explain events by reference to something whose giving rise to them is *self*-explanatory.⁵¹

On the other hand, again in contrast to Donagan's position, an event's being caused by a power does not rule out its *also* being caused (in a different way) by another event, *even* in the case of free agents. There is no reason why 'the ultimate [i.e. undeliberated] elicited acts of will and intellect by which choices and hence actions are caused' should not, in a way, be 'in turn caused by events that are neither acts of [the same person's] will nor acts of [his] intellect.'⁵² There must be at least the event of the agent's being endowed with intellect and will, and also the event of his being presented with an object that he can understand and take an appetitive attitude toward.⁵³ What freedom rules out is only that the causality of an action by some prior event be an instance of a *law* of nature, such that the occurrence of the event under determinate conditions entails a unique action as its result. Donagan himself acknowledges that 'events may be causally related without their relation being an instance of a law of nature.'⁵⁴

D. ACTION, INCLINATION AND CAUSALITY

1. *The Reasons for Positing Inclination*

We may now turn to the question of inclination. Although up to now we have succeeded in prescinding from it, inclination is an essential component of the notion of agency. This is because the mere notion of power, as just set forth, does not quite suffice to merit something the name of agent. What it leaves out is any note of impulse or thrust. To have power is, so to speak, to be only a depository. Power explains where the feature gotten by the recipient, the thing acted upon, came from; but it does not explain how it got there. Only if the subject of the power 'put' it there was he the agent.

---

51. Moreover, it will still be necessary to distinguish power and nature, at least wherever one and the same subject is capable of a variety of actions that can be exercised or modified independently of one another, and so cannot be reduced to a single formula. Rational or voluntary agents are not the only ones of this sort. Most living things show such a capacity. Indeed, although properly speaking a 'faculty' is something belonging only to living things, a faculty is a species of quality, and even in inanimate things it is necessary to distinguish between their natures and their active qualities, even when the activity for which they are naturally apt can be reduced to a single formula. This distinction is necessary because it is necessary to distinguish between the existence of these things, which they have through their natures, and their activity, the absence of which does not necessarily imply that they no longer exist. The nature then is an actuality, the active quality a potentiality. (See I, q. 77, a. 1.) The term 'faculty' is reserved for living things, it seems, because it connotes something useful to its possessor, and it is in living things that one first finds something like 'use'; a living thing is an 'organism.'

52. Donagan, *Choice*, p. 165.
53. See I–II, q. 9, arts. 4 and 6; q. 17, a. 5 ad 3.
54. *Choice*, p. 165.

Consider the Aristotelian account of how physical action comes about: by the sheer fact that the agent and patient are in contact, or that the patient is in the presence of the agent.[55] This may be true, but it can hardly be accounted for merely by the fact that such an agent has the power of acting in such a way upon such a patient. At most this explains only the fact that *if* any action takes place there, it will be an action of such a sort. It only explains the action's direction or specification. But why need there be any action at all? It is this that the notions of inclination, finality and appetite aim to explain.

As before, this does not mean that it is always necessary to posit inclination or appetite as some distinct quality of the agent; for Aristotle, as for Donagan, it is only in the case of rational agents, who have contrary operations simultaneously in their power, that there must be a capacity for appetite that is not wholly reducible to the agent's specific active powers. The thought here is that even if power and appetite are functions of one and the same principle, the term 'power' is insufficient to characterize it as a complete principle of action.

As noted earlier, to say that an agent acts for an end means, first, that an act is something definite, and that its origin, the agent, has a correspondingly definite order toward it. It means there must be a reason why the agent did this rather than that. Since what makes something definite is form, the equation of acting with acting for an end means that acting is roughly the same as 'forming.'[56]

But it also means more. It even means more than that every agent acts toward a good. Indeed, this hardly adds any new information. The definite, the formed, is always, insofar as it is definite, something good. This is because goodness is convertible with perfection, which is to say, fullness or wealth, as opposed to defect, privation or penury. The good is 'positive' and not 'negative.' But the definite is always something positive. Negation merely *removes* something definite from the subject. It never, by itself, attributes anything definite to it. It leaves the subject indefinite. To the extent that something is indefinite, it cannot have the quality of an object apt to be that toward which something is aimed or inclined, the quality of something good.[57]

These explanations of the principle of finality serve only to give a more detailed statement of *what* it is that an agent acts for. That is, they are still in the order of the specification or the direction of action. The agent's definiteness accounts merely for why it does this rather than that; its having power accounts merely for the fact that something else comes to be conformed to it or is influenced by it, receives an 'influx' from it. But these are not, by themselves, sufficient to explain the very fact that the agent actually engages in action. They only explain why it can act, and what sort of act it will engage in, if it engages in any. If it actually engages in action, this can only be because it has some appetite or

---

55. *Metaphysics* IX, ch. 5, 1048a4; *Physics* III, ch. 2, 202a11.
56. I–II, q. 21, a. 1 ad 2: *operatur enim natura aliquid formando*.
57. See *In IX Eth*. lect. xi, § 1903–04.

inclination to do so. That is, there must be some tipping of the balance between its not acting and its acting. This was Aquinas's point in his argument that every agent acts on account of a determination toward some end. But what is the explanation of this imbalance, this proclivity in favor of acting? Why does the agent not simply remain 'in potency'?

Sometimes, of course, the answer is that it is set to work by something else. It bends under the force of another agent. It actually acts toward the end for which its form enables it to act only because it is made to do so by something else; as when a sharp piece of metal actually cuts wood only because the woodcutter makes it do so. But this is not always the case. Sometimes, its very possession of a certain form is sufficient to incline it to act and to form something else accordingly. Once it possesses the form, no further agent is needed in order to set it to work. It has its own impulse to set to work. The only external requirement is the absence of impediments. The edge of an axe is not a form of this sort. The forms that are of this sort are what Aquinas calls natures. It is of like *natures* that the dictum 'like generates like' holds.

The basis for the claim that in some cases things tend spontaneously, by reason of what they are, to act is not merely that sometimes things are observed to act without any other observable agent making them do so. The claim is not that there is no agent directly responsible for the action of natural things (*qua* natural). Indeed, for Aquinas, there must be such an agent; it is precisely that which formed or generated the natural thing itself. The action which the natural thing engages in, once it has its form, is in the very same 'direction,' so to speak, as that of the action by which it was itself formed.

The crucial observation, however, is that sometimes things are *most* apt to act, not while they are being acted upon or formed by something else, but precisely when *that* action has *finished*, i.e. when they have been fully formed and released from the other's influence. For instance, when fire is made to act upon something flammable, the latter is most apt to heat other things, in its turn, when the action of the fire upon it is finished, when it has been set afire itself. Also, in such cases, if the action of the agent is interrupted by some external impediment, it will start up again spontaneously when the impediment is removed. Another illustration of this idea, from modern physics, would be that bodies are heavier the closer they are toward the term of their gravitational movement, i.e. to the surface of that toward which they fall. This sort of phenomenon is interesting precisely because it does *not* always obtain. For example, when a projectile is thrown, the force with which it strikes another body is greatest at the *beginning* of its movement, not at the end; and if it is stopped, it has no abiding tendency to start up again.

In short, the precise translation of *omne agens agit propter finem* would be 'every agent acts,' not just for or toward, but also 'because of an end.' The end is not only a principle of the act's specification, but also a principle of its exercise. The identification of the agent's end makes it possible to say not only that if the agent acts, it will act for this, but also that it is acting because it is acting for this. In other words, it means not only that the agent acts for a good, but also that what it acts for, it acts for because it is good. It acts because of an inclination toward that which it enacts, and 'good' means 'object of inclination.'[58] The principle means that goodness is an irreducible element in the account of action.

The conclusion, then, is that in the case of natural agents, the role of form as a principle of action is not exhausted in its making the agent to be something definite (to which some definite action or effect corresponds) nor its constituting the agent's power, the wealth whose giving forth constitutes its action. The possession of the form according to which they act is *itself* a source of their inclination to act. The inclination is intrinsic to them. It does not consist merely in their subjection to some other agent. In these cases, not only does the agent act because of some inclination, but also it is *inclined* to act because of the very *object* of its inclination, insofar as that object is somehow present to it. The more perfectly it is present, the more intensely is the agent inclined to act in favor of it. In a purely natural agent, the object of its inclination is identical with the form making it what it is.[59]

It should be stressed that the object does not incline it in the manner of an agent acting upon it; rather, it has a kind of causality of its own, the kind invoked when something is explained by the fact that it is good or better.[60] It does not

---

58. The judgment that what the thing acts for is something good does not depend on having grasped the inclination toward it existing in the thing itself. Likewise, the (virtually identical) judgment that the thing itself is good does not depend on grasping its inclination to remain itself. 'Good' means a potential object of inclination, and evidently for Aquinas we first apprehend things as good by apprehending them as potential objects of *our own* inclination, i.e. as things we might desire or love; it is the inclination that proceeds from understanding that is inclination in the primary sense. (See I, q. 16, a. 4 ad 2.) But all natures, or things having natures, have some lovability about them; for all have a certain form and beauty. (See I–II, q. 27, a. 2; II–II, q. 145, a. 2, and St Augustine, *De natura boni, passim*.) It is for these reasons that the explanation according to final causality comes 'naturally' to us. It would be surprising to find that things did *not* have some inclination to promote the goods found in them.

59. See Brentano, *The Psychology of Aristotle*, pp. 42–43: 'A principle frequently enunciated by Aristotle is that whatever comes into being, comes from something synonymous with it [from a namesake]. This principle holds for both art and nature. . . . In another version Aristotle expresses this by saying that like things are generated by like, and elsewhere that in the particular case potentiality precedes, while absolutely speaking actuality precedes. A second law of activity is that each activity proceeds from a striving. . . . This striving must be envisaged as the proximate origin of the effect. It is brought about by that similarity due to which, as we have said, that which is to be wrought preexists in that which acts. Like has a tendency toward like; thus we have to acknowledge that that likeness is also a principle, indeed a prior principle of becoming. The efficient cause moves only if it is moved by the effect, insofar as the latter preexists as a likeness in the agent, i.e. insofar as it is moved by a purpose.'

60. On final causality as a different *kind* of causality from 'efficient' causality, see Taylor, *The Explanation of Behaviour*, pp. 6–7, 15ff.; also de Finance, *Essai sur l'agir humain*, p. 106: '*si le bien ne meut que par l'influence physique de sa représentation sur le vouloir, sa causalité propre est, qu'on le veuille ou non, aussi complètement éliminée que dans l'Ethique* [of Spinoza].'

take the place of agent-causality; rather, it explains the causality of the agent itself. It is the cause of the agent's very causality.⁶¹

This causality can be characterized further only by way of metaphor. For example, we may say that the presence of a good 'elicits' inclination toward it. Form is a principle of action, not only as making the agent definite and empowering it to act, but also as eliciting its very inclination to act. The point is that without invoking this kind of causality, it is not always possible to give a full explanation of an agent's acting. When Aquinas argues that 'good' contains the note of final cause, he means 'cause' strictly: something really prior to, more fundamental than, that of which it is the cause. In his terminology, 'good' means *neither* merely 'what is actually desired' *nor* merely 'what ought to be desired,' but 'what is apt to elicit desire' (and action in fulfillment of desire).

2. Action as More Giving than Getting

What is more, the thesis that every agent acts for its own good, or in the maintenance and promotion of its own form, also shows that the principle of finality does not always mean that an agent acts to *get* some good, or acts out of need. Rather, to the very extent that it is an agent, it already possesses the good on account of which it acts. Indeed, if the end for which an agent acts is precisely a share in its *own* form, then every agent acts for its *own* good; and its first inclination toward *this* good is not expressed in its outward action at all, but in its own remaining what it is, its persisting.⁶² To say that when it acts, it acts for its own good means that it acts to give, to promote the good that it already enjoys. Power is wealth, not penury. If an agent only acts, only gives or provides, in order to receive, then it is an imperfect, not fully formed agent.⁶³ It is once the agent receives what it needs and is made perfect, is fully formed, that it is able to act to the highest degree, to give of itself most unrestrictedly.

Still, it is probably more natural to think of finality in terms of need than in terms of liberality or generosity. Two reasons may be offered. One is that human beings mostly find themselves in a state of need, and act out of need. The other

---

61. See *In V Meta.* lect. ii, § 775.

62. See I, q. 59, a. 2: *videmus in corporibus naturalibus quod inclinatio quae est ad esse rei, non est per aliquid superadditum essentiae, sed per materiam, quae appetit esse antequam illud habeat, et per formam, quae tenet rem in esse postquam fuerit. Sed . . . inclinatio . . . ad faciendum sibi simile est per qualitates activas.*

63. See I, q. 44, a. 4: 'every agent acts for an end; otherwise, from the action of an agent, this would follow no more than that, except by chance. But the end of the agent and of the patient, insofar as they are such, is the same, though in different ways; for it is one and the same thing that the agent intends to impress, and that the patient intends to receive. Yet there are certain agents that at once act and are acted upon, which are imperfect agents; and it belongs to these that, in acting, they also intend to acquire something.' See also ad 1: 'to act on account of neediness belongs only to an imperfect agent, which is apt to act and to be acted upon.' On the general importance of the idea that the ultimate goal of acting, or that action in its fullest instances, is pure giving, see Polo, 'Tener y dar.'

is that in nature too, the existence of finality is most strikingly apparent in things that act to satisfy needs, that is, in living things. Almost without exception, living things are not complete or fully formed, are not mature, from the first moment of their existence. Much of their vital activity consists in bringing themselves to completion or in maintaining their integrity.

Nevertheless, what things are objects of need? That is, for what are things needed? Is it not always for the protection or the completion of a good already possessed? Moreover, the chief criterion for the maturity or completion of a living thing is precisely its capacity to generate another of the same kind. Were it not for such a capacity, the self-movement of living things would not be an unambiguous sign of superiority over inanimate things, since it would be entirely a function of their neediness. But in fact the satisfaction of their needs is itself ordered toward their giving of themselves, and doing so in a more perfect way than do inanimate things—'reproducing' themselves.

Before looking at a text from St Thomas which is especially relevant to the present discussion, let us back up for a moment, and consider what the consideration of action in natural things, even at the level of inanimate things, reveals about action generally. Negatively, it reveals that being an agent does not always require being something that makes itself act. An inanimate thing does not make itself act at all. It does not establish any end for which it acts. The only end toward which it is intrinsically inclined is the form making it to be what it is, and it does not make itself to be what it is. If it is aimed toward any further end, this is only under the force of some other agent. It does not contribute, by any operation of its own, either to the singular guise in which its end appears in any of its instances, or to the adoption of the path by which the end is reached. These are entirely functions of the object upon which it acts and of the circumstances permitting it to be brought into contact with the object. It does not even contribute to the execution of its action by giving rise to any movement by which it is brought into contact with the object. Self-movement is not a minimal condition for action.

Positively, the consideration of the action of inanimate things reveals three essential principles of agency, and three corresponding dimensions of active efficacy. The first is form, by which the agent is constituted as something definite, a being. To this corresponds the determinateness of the action, its having a definite term, an end. The second is power, or the capacity to bring something into conformity with the agent, consisting in the agent's already being perfect or relatively self-sufficient in the relevant respect. To this corresponds the bond of dependence between the effect and the agent, the effect's being a communication of some feature from the agent to the thing acted upon. The third is inclination, the agent's tending actually to adhere to its perfection, and to give and promote it in others as far as it can; to this corresponds the goodness of its effect.

> Since 'good' is 'that which all desire,' and this has the note of an end, it is clear that 'good' carries with it the note of an end. But nonetheless the notion of good

presupposes the notion of efficient cause and the notion of formal cause. For we see that what comes first in causing is last in the thing caused; for fire first heats, before it induces the form of fire, even though the heat in the fire follows upon its substantial form. Now in causing, what comes first is a good and an end, which moves the efficient cause; second, the action of the efficient cause, moving toward a form; and third comes the form. Hence it must be vice versa in what is caused, such that what is first is form itself, through which it [what is caused] is a being; second, there may be considered in it its effective power, according to which it is perfect in its being (for each thing is perfect when it can make its like, as the Philosopher says in the fourth book of *On Weather*); and third comes the note of good, through which, in the being, the perfection is poured forth.[64]

This text is extremely dense, but it is obviously of great importance, not just as regards inclination, but as regards the whole question of our notion of causality; so I shall hazard a few observations about it.[65] First I shall simply gloss it briefly, and then, in the next sub-section, I shall address an interesting difficulty that it raises for us.

Aquinas is here concerned mainly to show that *although* 'good' has the note of final cause, and although the final cause is the cause of the causality of the other kinds of cause,[66] *nevertheless* final causality is not the first kind of causality understood by the human mind. This is in accordance with Aristotle's dictum that what we first understand is not always what is first in the nature of things. It is also in accordance with Aquinas's view that the order of understanding in the human mind is in a way parallel to the order of generation in physical things.[67]

Now, the notions governing the account—being, perfect and good—are among the very most general notions to be found, not only in the human mind, but also in reality. They belong among what Aquinas calls the proper effects of

---

64. *Cum bonum sit quod omnia appetunt, hoc autem habet rationem finis; manifestum est quod bonum rationem finis importat. Sed tamen ratio boni praesupponit rationem causae efficientis, et rationem causae formalis. Videmus enim quod id quod est primum in causando, ultimum est in causato, ignis enim primo calefacit quam formam ignis inducat, cum tamen calor in igne consequatur formam substantialem. In causando autem, primum invenitur bonum et finis, qui movet efficientem; secundo, actio efficiens, movens ad formam; tertio advenit forma. Unde e converso esse oportet in causato, quod primum sit ipsa forma, per quam est ens; secundo consideratur in ea virtus effectiva, secundum quod est perfectum in esse (quia unumquodque tunc perfectum est, quando potest sibi simile facere, ut dicit Philosophus in IV Meteor.); tertio consequitur ratio boni, per quam in ente perfectio fundatur* (I, q. 5, a. 4).

65. For a magisterial discussion of St Thomas's understanding of causality, and its relation to Hume's in light of this text, see Lawrence Dewan, 'Saint Thomas and the Principle of Causality.'

66. The final cause is the cause of the causality, not only of the agent-cause, but also of the formal cause, in everything that has a formal cause; for every such thing is something *formed*, and hence the causality of its form derives from the agent forming it, whose causality in turn derives from the inclination toward the end. The form in something formed is that toward which it was generated, its 'what it was to be,' *quod quid erat esse*.

67. See e.g. I, q. 85, a. 6; a. 3 ad 1; *In I Politicorum*, proem.

the highest and most universal cause of all things, God.[68] Moreover, the first things understood by the human mind are not this highest cause itself, but its effects. Or, in what amounts to the same thing, God is first conceived by the human mind precisely *as* a cause, i.e. in accordance with his explanatory role in relation to something *else*. It is something else that is first grasped *in itself*. This is why Aquinas makes the order of these terms in the human mind correspond to the order in which they belong to something *caused*. First something is brought into existence, in a determinate nature; then it comes to the maturity or perfection corresponding to its nature; then it tends to communicate or give forth what it can of its perfection. Clearly what is envisioned as the subject of this process is substance.

At the same time, what he is attending to is the order according to which the thing caused is made to be *like* its cause, and like it precisely in its character as a cause.[69] This is why the order among these terms in the mind corresponds to the order among the kinds of causes that the mind grasps, the causal roles that it perceives to be played by a substance. Again, it is substance to which causality is primarily attributed. The first of these roles is its causality in relation to *itself*, its having in itself a principle of its own being and subsistence, which is its form. Then comes its causality of something *else*, its communicating a share in its form, through power; power is a principle of change in something *qua* other. Finally, the substance's actual exercise of its power is explained by its having the relation to the perfection of its form that is expressed by saying that this perfection is its good. This relation is that of appetite or inclination.

3. Formal Causality and Agency

Supposing that the drift of the passage from I, q. 5, a. 4 is sufficiently clear, the order that it assigns to the notions of the causes may very well generate some surprise. Particularly striking is the priority, in understanding, of formal causality over agent- or efficient causality. At least since Hume, it has been common to regard efficient causality, not just as the first kind of causality, but indeed as the only kind. But even staying within an Aristotelian perspective, granting the doctrine of the 'four causes,' there might be reasons for assigning priority, at least in our understanding, to efficient causality. For instance, the very way in which we speak about 'causes' seems to arise from the notion of efficient causality. The term for the correlate of a cause is 'effect,' which of course derives from *efficere*. Again, even in discussing one of the other kinds of causes, it is common to use terms of action. The very use of 'cause' as a *verb* assimilates it to action. Thomas himself

---

68. Cf. I–II, q. 66, a. 5 ad 4: *cognoscere . . . rationem entis et non entis, et totius et partis, et aliorum quae consequuntur principia indemonstrabilia, pertinet ad sapientiam: quia ens commune est proprius effectus causae altissimae, scilicet Dei.*

69. See I, q. 103, a. 4.

often says that form 'gives' being to matter, that the final cause 'moves' the agent, and so forth. This does not mean that he is confused; he is of course using these terms analogically. Yet it does suggest not only that 'cause' itself is analogical, but also that the primary analogate is efficient cause. Forms and ends would be called causes only in an extended sense, by virtue of some relation to efficient causes.

Other considerations also suggest this. Form and end might well be said to fall short of the name 'cause' in its most proper sense. For instance, essential to the notion of cause is that cause and effect are distinct. But a thing and its own form are only distinct up to a point or in a qualified way; they are not separate subjects or even in separate subjects. Or, in the case of final causality, the *priority* of the cause over its effect, which seems to be another essential note of causality, is only qualified; a final cause, a goal, need not be prior in *existence* to what it causes, but only prior in understanding or in intention.[70] Not even the form in a thing (the individual form *in* it, *this* whiteness or this humanity or this soul) is prior to the thing in *time*. So it might be quite plausible to say that forms and ends are called causes simply on account of possessing some feature in common with efficient causes, e.g. the feature of being that upon which something somehow depends. A thing's being moved depends on the mover; similarly, a thing's existence depends on its own form, and the mover's tending to move depends on its end.[71]

How is it, then, that Thomas can assign priority to formal causality in our understanding of causality?

First of all, we should note that it would be a mistake to see our familiar text on the imposition of the term 'action' as contradicting the thesis that formal causality is prior in our understanding. That text is not about the first imposition of the term 'cause,' but about that of 'action.' To be sure, it does say that it was manifest that motion 'happened by some cause.' But of course the cause by which something 'happens' (*accidit*) cannot be a formal cause. Nor is formal causality even a case of an 'origin of one thing from another.' The formal cause is not an *origin* of its effect; it does not *give rise* to its effect at all. It is one in being with its effect.

Now, even granting primacy to the moving cause, as regards what we signify by the name 'cause,' this does not mean that the moving cause has primacy as regards our understanding of the *content* of its causal role. Thomas can very well hold that we first grasp the causal role of *form*—even if it is only later that we come to call this a 'causal' role. This in fact squares perfectly with the text on the

---

70. To complete the list of causes, we might note that the material cause, too, falls short, especially with respect to what it is a cause *of*. A cause is a cause of the *being* of something (see below, Chapter 5, n. 77); but matter is, in itself, only a cause of being in potency, not being in act, which is a more primary meaning of 'being.'

71. Thus the fact that the final cause is the cause of the causality of the moving cause need not mean that it has priority in meriting the name 'cause' or is more properly 'a cause.' As McInerny observes (*The Logic of Analogy*, pp. 132–33), the fact that medicine is a cause of health in animals does not mean that it is more properly called 'healthy.'

imposition of the name 'action.' For, according to that text, prior to understanding action, it is necessary to apprehend movement. And in apprehending movement, the causal role of form is already grasped, even if it is not yet *called* a cause.

To grasp a change is to grasp something changed; and this is to grasp something as being first 'thus,' and then 'so' (or at least 'not thus'). The thing is distinguished from its being 'so' and from its being 'thus' or 'not so.' Subject and contrary forms, or subject, form and privation, are principles of change, and precisely *intrinsic* principles; the very apprehension of change, having a notion of what change is, involves some sort of apprehension of these principles.[72] So grasping the 'gist' of formal causality would be prior to grasping that of agent-causality, even if it is agent-causality that first gets the name 'causality.'

Against this answer, however, it might be objected that the formal cause discussed in the passage in I, q. 5, a. 4 is evidently not just any form in a thing, but its substantial form, the form 'through which it is a being.' Effective power, for instance, is also a kind of form, a quality (the example in the passage is heat); but here power is said to enter the picture only later on, after the form that plays the role of formal cause. But surely it is possible to grasp movement, and hence to conceive of a moving cause, prior to having a notion of substantial form, is it not? The first changes that the mind apprehends are not substantial changes; it is only later on that the mind comes to distinguish between substantial form and its 'subject,' the underlying principle of substantial change, which is prime matter. Thomas says this explicitly in one of his accounts of the history of philosophical progress toward the notion of a cause of the whole of being.[73]

A quick reply to this objection would be that while it is true that I, q. 5, a. 4 focuses on substantial form, it is also true that the agent-causality focused on in that text is not just any agent-causality, but precisely the causality of a generator, an agent with power to effect another *substance* of the same kind. The example (which assumes the ancient physics, according to which fire is a substance) is a fire igniting another fire. Apprehending the fire's power to ignite presupposes some grasp of the substantial form of fire. So we might try to save Thomas's posi-

---

72. This also indicates that it is not as a request for these principles—subject and form—that one originally asks 'why' a movement occurs. These principles are already known. But even though they are grasped as principles of the movement, one immediately perceives that the movement is not yet fully intelligible, not fully explained; it is not self-explanatory. (Cf. Aquinas, *De principiis naturae*, Leonine edn., vol. 47, p. 41, § 3, ll. 1–5: *patet tria esse naturae principia, scilicet materia, forma et privatio; sed hec non sunt sufficientia ad generationem. Quod enim est in potentia non potest se reducere ad actum.*) It is in relation to change that one first looks outside the thing itself for a cause. However, this need not mean that a moving cause is the first kind of cause that the mind seeks. There is also a question properly expressing a search for the form, namely 'what?'; such a question is *in fact* a kind of 'why,' namely 'why—in accordance with what form—is this such-and-such a unity?,' e.g. 'why are these materials a house?' (Cf. *Metaphysics* VII, ch. 17, 1041a10–34.) And surely the mind's very first effort (which is spontaneous, not self-directed by way of a question) bears on grasping the principle of unity *in* what is presented to it. The search for a mover is the search for a *further* principle.

73. I, q. 44, a. 2.

tion by making the general priority of form over agency a matter of proportionality. That is, we might say that the grasp of a form is essential to the grasp of a change with respect to that form, and precedes the notion of an agent capable of initiating that sort of change. When it is a case of accidental change, the form too is accidental; when the change is substantial, so is the form.

Nonetheless, I suspect that Thomas wants to give more than proportional priority to the grasp of the causality of substantial form. I say this for two reasons. First, note that our objection is based on a strict, highly sophisticated notion of 'substantial form,' substantial form as nothing but substantial *actuality*, clearly distinguished from prime matter, understood as nothing but substantial potentiality. (The 'less sophisticated' notion is that of substantial quiddity or whatness. I shall return to this in a moment.) Together with this, note also that what Thomas is presenting in I, q. 5, a. 4 is the priority of substantial form over effective *power*, where power is likewise clearly distinguished from substance and substantial form. This distinction is no less sophisticated than the other. Even if it is true that we only need to notice accidental changes in order to form the notion of an action or an agent, noticing this hardly suffices for drawing the distinction, *in* the agent, between the principle making it be what it is and the principle upon which its action immediately follows. Understanding the heat in the fire as something that is distinct from and 'follows' on its substantial form, as the text says, is hardly a mere result of noticing that something has been heated, looking for what heated it, and discovering a fire. And of course, distinguishing the heat from the substantial form implies grasping the substantial form.

To be sure, 'an action' and 'an agent' need not be taken in such a sophisticated sense, according to which active power is sharply distinguished from substantial form. So—the objector might continue—does grasping the *fire* as an agent of heating—never mind its distinct 'active power'—require a grasp of substantial form? Can we not have a concrete notion of agency, the notion of something's being powerful and a source initiating change in another, e.g. of fire as a heating agent, without going into the metaphysics of power as a quality?[74] This leads to my second reason for suspecting that Thomas wants to attribute absolute priority to the grasp of the causality of substantial form. Certainly we can have a

---

74. Obviously it is not necessary to grasp the fire's heat as something distinct from the fire in order to understand that fire heats or 'has the power' to heat; to say that fire 'has the power' to heat means, in the first instance, that *this* fire is heating *because it is fire*. Or again, this morphine will put you to sleep because morphine puts people to sleep. This is really to say something. If you say, 'that lecture put me to sleep,' one may very well ask whether it was because you were sleepy (just about anything short of a heavy-metal rock concert would have put you to sleep), or because the lecture was a boring, soporific one. To ask why morphine *generally* puts people to sleep, and to answer that it has a soporific power, is indeed to say nothing more than that it puts people to sleep; the question is asking for what its power consists in. It is in order to answer this that you must distinguish between morphine's various qualities (and so between the many qualities and the one substance of morphine), in order to find the quality or qualities that have a bearing on its putting people to sleep.

concrete notion of agency; but we can also have a concrete notion of substance and substantial being, prior to the distinction between substantial form and prime matter.

The text of I, q. 5, a. 4 says nothing about matter. This is quite striking, given that it is about the different kinds of causes. The omission of matter can hardly have been a mere oversight. Rather, I suggest, its references to substantial *form* should in fact be taken to be references to quiddity or 'whatness,' i.e. to what Aquinas calls the 'form of the whole' (*forma totius*),[75] e.g. humanity. Some grasp of this sort of form is involved in even the most elementary understanding of substance.[76] What is first called a substance, or that to which substantial being is first attributed, is always a definite 'what,' something of a certain kind or species. The notion of the species includes its matter. It is only later on, when substantial change is acknowledged, that a distinct notion of prime matter is formed, together with the more sophisticated notion of substantial form as a part of the substance, something composed with matter to constitute the quiddity or the form of the whole.[77]

Yet the notion of the quiddity of a substance is already a *causal* notion. For the quiddity is the *essence* of a substance. The essence is that which the substance is in virtue of itself, the *ratio* according to which it is first and unqualifiedly a being, '*per quam est ens*.' A substance depends on its quiddity, even in formula— as it does *not* depend on its accidents.

Taken in the sense of quiddity or whatness, the grasp of substantial form retains priority over that of agency, even in the concrete sense of agency. First of all, as we have noted more than once, it is presupposed in the very grasp of movement and change, even accidental change. The reason why accidental change is more evident than substantial change is precisely that its *subject* is more evident, being something actual, of a definite kind, and something separate, subsisting in its kind throughout the gain or loss of an accidental disposition. Hence the *composite* character of the subject-form relation is more evident in the case of accidental form; for the subject is already something definite, and can be given separate consideration much more easily than can the pure potentiality which is matter. The composite character is displayed most manifestly, of course, precisely through the change; it is the change that involves something quite *accidental* to the substance. And as Fr Dewan explains,[78] for Thomas it is precisely the composite character of the efficient cause's effect which shows the need for, the

---

75. *Humanitas significatur ut forma quaedam, et dicitur quod est forma totius, non quidem quasi superaddita partibus essentialibus, scilicet formae et materiae, sicut forma domus superaddritur partibus integralibus eius, sed magis est forma, quae est totum scilicet formam complectens et materiam* (De ente et essentia 1).

76. See Dewan, 'St Thomas and the Principle of Causality,' pp. 61–62.

77. On the grasp of matter as merely secondary and posterior in the causal understanding of a being, see Dewan, 'St Thomas Aquinas against Metaphysical Materialism,' esp. pp. 428–34.

78. 'St Thomas and the Principle of Causality,' esp. pp. 56–71.

dependence upon, that cause. The composition is what provides the efficient cause with its proportionate object, the object relative to which it is understood *as* efficient cause. To understand something as a composite is to understand it as at once a unity and (since the components *might* be separated) as a not fully self-explanatory unity, a *unified* unity, a dependent unity. Without the prior grasp of the subject-form composition in the effect, efficient causality is unintelligible . . . just as Hume says it is. It is only the grasp of the connections *in* a perceived event that gives a foothold for grasping that event's connection with another.

Of course, the substantial form of the *subject* of movement is the substantial form of what is moved or acted upon, not of the agent; whereas in I, q. 5, a. 4 Thomas appears to see a need for grasping the substantial form of the *agent* before its agency can be grasped. But in this respect, too, substantial form, i.e. quiddity, does indeed retain priority over agency.

For one thing, the original grasp of agency, as Thomas presents it in the text on the imposition of 'action,' is the grasp of the 'origin of one thing *from another*.' An agent, too, is first conceived as a separate entity, a substance in act. Moreover, along the lines of our earlier discussion, what makes movement or change so manifestly dependent on something else, so clearly lacking in self-sufficiency, is its merely accidental status with respect to its subject. In looking for an agent, one is implicitly looking for something upon which the change follows, not merely *per accidens*, but *per se*; one is looking for something 'ontologically superior,' relatively self-explanatory, in the relevant respect. For instance, fire is grasped in its role as a heating agent because it is understood, first of all, as something that is hot *per se*, on its own. Once this is grasped, one goes on to consider its relation to other things, to regard it as having power over them, able to influence them and make them like itself. And then, finally, one considers why the thing would in fact 'go out of its way,' emerge from its self-containedness and actually communicate something of itself to another, in the way that it can, and did. If a reason for this can be found in the thing itself, it is that the perfection thus poured forth is something good.

E. DIRECT AND INDIRECT AGENCY

In this section I shall go back to a distinction drawn in Section B of this chapter, between direct and indirect causes, and turn our attention to Aquinas's understanding of indirect causes. Doing so will give a more complete picture of his notion of agency, and will serve to flesh out my earlier remarks about Thomistic and Humean causality.

1. Intention and Mechanical Causality

The thesis that agency is first exercised in beginning to execute some intention, which really means nothing more than that every agent acts for an end, will have reminded some readers of Davidson's thesis that an event is an action if and only if there is some description of it according to which it is intentional.[79] Davidson's consideration is restricted to human action; but it seems valid also as applied to action in the broader sense, taking 'intention,' of course, in the broad sense of tendency.[80] The present claim is that every action is in some respect directly intentional. It also goes beyond Davidson, in holding that the feature(s) according to which an action is intentional is more fundamental in the explanation of the action's existence than any of its other features. Aquinas expresses this claim by saying that 'we are said *per se*, and not *per accidens*, to do those things that we intend to do.'[81] This means that if we are said to do something that we do not intend to do, it is only because this in some way accompanies something we do intend to do. It may, for instance, be an accompanying feature of what we intend to do. What belongs to something *per accidens* is secondary and subordinate to what belongs to it *per se*.[82]

According to the foregoing account, to say that a subject first exercises agency in beginning to execute some aim or intention means something very definite. It means that every agent acts primarily on account of (an inclination toward) some end pertaining to the agent's own good. Whatever else it enacts, it enacts in function of its acting to promote a good, the kind of good proper to it. Thus the aim or intention attributed to the agent, as the chief inner causal principle of its action, is more than a mere tendency to yield some definite result, more than a conformity to a rule connecting it in a general way with something that follows upon it. It adds the further notes of a proportion between the agent and the result, and of goodness or inclination as explaining the agent's actual tendency to promote what is proportioned to it.[83]

But none of this is meant to deny the existence of regular results that have no direct basis in the agent's form or good. That is, there is no denying the existence of 'mechanical' causality. Nor is it necessary to place mechanical causality wholly outside the sphere of agency. Actions having effects or results, or simply features, that are incidental to the cause's own form or good may still be counted as instances of action or agency.

This is particularly clear if it is possible to apply teleological explanation to acts of which even non-living things are capable. The distinction between events

---

79. 'Agency,' in *Essays*, p. 46. See also Donagan, *Choice*, pp. 86–87.

80. See Makin, 'Aquinas, Natural Tendencies and Natural Kinds': for anything, to be active presupposes doing something from a tendency.

81. *In V Eth*. lect. xiii, § 1036. See also II–II, q. 59, a. 2.

82. See I–II, q. 10, a. 1: *in omnibus . . . ea quae non per se insunt, reducuntur in aliquid quod per se inest, sicut in principium.*

83. Obviously not every instance of direct agency consists in the full achievement of the agent's inclination or intention. But the agent must do something in the direction of its inclination. See I–II, q. 21, a. 1 ad 2: *in peccato . . . naturae, deficit quidem actus a fine ultimo, qui est perfectio generati; non tamen deficit a quocumque fine proximo; operatur enim natura aliquid formando.*

that are explainable by agents whose acting is itself explainable teleologically, and events that are only explainable in mechanical terms, cannot correspond directly to a distinction of things or subjects of which some, e.g. living things, are agents, and others, e.g. non-living things, are merely physical or mechanical causes. It must be simply a distinction of modes in which one thing gives rise to or causes another: modes which we have termed 'direct' and 'indirect.' Both modes of causality may very well belong to one and the same subject (though not, of course, with respect to one and the same effect).

For example, it may be that in engaging in the sort of action toward which it is inclined, an agent also gives rise to other events or results having no intrinsic conformity to the agent. It just happens to be the case that the production of the agent's direct effect carries these other effects with it. In that case it will be the agent of these effects in an indirect way. Such indirect effects may even follow with a certain necessity or as a general rule.

Perhaps such efficacy may be considered as an exercise of agency only to the extent that it is in function of direct agency. Still, at least to the extent that indirect effects or side-effects accompany a given sort of action as a general rule, or according to some sort of tendency, a full account of such action must, it seems, include reference to them. This is analogous to the need to include not only form but also matter in the full account of a physical subject. This analogy also suggests that a full account of the agent's very *inclination* should in some way make reference to the results that generally accompany its exercise, even if they fall outside its proper object; just as a full account of the form of a physical subject must include not only its proper effect, which is to determine the species, but also the matter and its dispositions, to the extent that the efficacy of the form requires it. In short, it would be wrong to treat all indirect effects as merely incidental to the agent's inclination or intention. There is such a thing as indirect intention. However, in this section, I shall concentrate mainly on indirect agency. Indirect intention is a more complicated matter, and the interest of it is primarily in relation to human or voluntary action, the action of agents having some power over their own intentions or tendencies. I shall take it up in Chapter 5.

To avoid misunderstanding, it should be stressed at once that the thesis that an agent first exercises agency in beginning to execute some intention or inclination does not mean that every instance of mechanical causality must always be accompanied by the production of some effect toward which the cause was inclined. The reason why it does not mean this is that not every mechanical cause is an agent or an action *at all*. Only if it is an instance of agency does it presuppose something done out of inclination. To be an agent is to be an origin, a starting-point, a (relatively) *self*-explanatory antecedent. The exercise of agency does not exist apart from some result to which the agent is proportioned; but its production of this result may also yield other, non-intended results, and it may sometimes be termed the agent of them also, to a lesser degree. They may be explained as accompaniments of something explainable teleologically. But examples of 'moving' causes that are not agents of their effects at all are plentiful. One is Donagan's example of the tranquil pond, which causes the zone's eldest inhabitant to go boating. To be what is called a 'catalyst' is to be a cause of this sort. The collapse of a bridge caused by a defect in its structure is another example.

This note of caution serves to obviate the impression of an exaggerated claim concerning the connection between agency and mechanical causality. It is also important in a positive way. It helps to *establish* a certain kind of indirect effect that may be attributed to an agent, considered in its very quality of an agent. This is the sort of effect attributed to it by reason of its not acting. We will return to this presently.

2. Causality per removens prohibens

A moment ago I said that indirect effects may result from their causes with a certain necessity or as a general rule, according to a sort of tendency. Aquinas is very clear on this point. The most extensive (though still incomplete) presentation of his doctrine of indirect moving causes is found in his commentary on the *Metaphysics*.

> Something can be called a cause *per accidens* of something else in two ways. In one way, on the part of the cause; that is, because that which accompanies the cause is called a cause *per accidens*, as if 'a white' were to be called cause of a house. In the other way, on the part of the effect; that is, such that something be called a cause *per accidens* of some other thing which itself accompanies that which is a *per se* effect.
> This, in fact, can be in three ways. In one way, because it has a necessary order to the effect, as the removal of an impediment has a necessary order to the effect. Hence the *removens prohibens* is called a mover *per accidens*; and this, whether the accident in question be a contrary, such as choler, which inhibits chilling, whence scammony is said to chill *per accidens*, not because it causes chillness but because it removes the impediment to chillness, which is contrary to it, namely choler; or whether the accident not be even a contrary, as a column impedes the movement of a stone, whence the remover of the column is said *per accidens* to move the stone resting on it. In another way, when the accident has an order to the effect, yet not a necessary one, nor for the most part, but rarely, such as the discovery of a treasure upon digging in the ground. And in this way luck and chance are called causes *per accidens*. In the third way, when they have no order, except perhaps according to opinion; as if someone were to say that he was the cause of an earthquake because the earthquake happened while he was entering the house.[84]

---

84. *Aliquid potest dici causa per accidens alterius dupliciter. Uno modo ex parte causae; quia scilicet illud quod accidit causae, dicitur causa per accidens, sicut si album dicatur causa domus. Alio modo ex parte effectus; ut scilicet aliquid dicatur causa per accidens alicuius, quod accidit ei quod est effectus per se. Quod quidem potest esse tripliciter. Uno modo, quia habet ordinem necessarium ad effectum, sicut remotio imped-*

First, let me gloss the text. After drawing the general distinction between direct (*per se*) and indirect (*per accidens*) moving causes, he subdivides the latter into things that accompany a direct cause of something, and causes whose direct effects are accompanied by something. He further subdivides the latter into chance causes, causes 'according to opinion' (specious causes) and the kind that interests us here. This he describes as causes that have a necessary or general (*ut in pluribus*) order toward the effect in question. The note of necessity or general validity is what distinguishes this sort of causality from chance causality. The order between a cause and a chance effect obtains rarely or seldom (*ut in paucioribus*).[85] An example of a type of non-casual, indirect cause is that of causes *per removens prohibens*, things that cause something by removing an obstacle to it.

Developing the notion of causes *per removens prohibens*, he notes that the obstacle being removed may or may not be the strict contrary of the effect. For instance, in the theory of bodily humors, choler was held to be produced by bile, and was the contrary of the chillness and torpor attributed to phlegm; so that the purgative called scammony, by reducing bile, would cause chillness, but only indirectly—not by producing phlegm.[86] On the other hand, a column impedes the fall of a stone resting upon it, and what removes the column indirectly causes the stone to fall; but the (perfect) contrary of its falling would be its rising, not its being at rest.[87]

On the basis of other texts in Aquinas, a few observations and additions may be made to this account of non-casual, indirect moving causality. The first derives from his insisting in numerous places that direct agency is not restricted to what the agent primarily intends, i.e. to the ultimate or complete expression and satisfaction of its power and inclination. Not only the end, but also the things brought about because of their conduciveness to the end, are direct objects of action. This

---

iment habet ordinem necessarium ad effectum. Unde removens prohibens dicitur movens per accidens; sive illud accidens sit contrarium, sicut cholera prohibet frigiditatem, unde scamonaea dicitur infrigidare per accidens, non quia causet frigiditatem sed quia tollit impedimentum frigiditatis, quod est ei contrarium, scilicet choleram: sive etiam si non sit contrarium, sicut columna impedit motum lapidis, unde removens columnam dicitur per accidens movere lapidem superpositum. Alio modo, quando accidens habet ordinem ad effectum, non tamen necessarium, nec ut in pluribus, sed ut in paucioribus, sicut inventio thesauri ad fossionem in terra. Et hoc modo fortuna et casus dicuntur causae per accidens. Tertio, quando nullum ordinem habent, nisi forte secundum existimationem; sicut si aliquis dicat se esse causam terraemotus, quia eo intrante domum accidit terraemotus (*In V Meta*. lect. iii, § 789).

85. As Boyle points out, although most of Aquinas's uses of the expression *praeter intentionem* to denote indirect effects of action concern things brought about fortuitously, the two notions are not identical ('*Praeter intentionem* in Aquinas,' pp. 658–59). Boyle cites a passage from *SCG* III, ch. 6, § 1902: *sciendum est quod non omne quod est praeter intentionem oportet esse fortuitum vel casuale. . . . Si enim quod est praeter intentionem sit consequens ad id quod est intentum vel semper vel frequenter. . . , non erit fortuitum nec casuale; esset autem casuale si sequeretur ut in paucioribus.*

86. The example is a bit obscure, but clearer ones are at hand; for instance, some 'coolant' systems are actually systems for removing sources or bodies of heat.

87. Cf. *In VIII Phys*. lect. viii, § 1035.

implies that the expression *removens prohibens* is not meant to cover cases in which an agent achieves its own goal precisely by clearing away obstacles to it. The participle *prohibens* should be rendered by some expression such as 'the thing that obstructs'; or even better, 'the thing that happens to obstruct.' The agent must be acting on the *prohibens* by reason of something else about it, other than its being a *prohibens*. It must fall under the agent's intention according to some other description. Likewise, there is no reason why what the agent is fundamentally about should be the 'removal' of the *prohibens*. What the 'removal' of it is *from*, i.e. that with respect to which its motion is a removal, is the place or state in which it constitutes an obstacle; but the action of the agent on the *prohibens* may only happen to constitute such a removal. If, in the earlier example, what removes the column is aiming to make the stone fall, it is not a merely indirect cause of the fall.[88]

Secondly, it is clear that for Aquinas, causes *per removens prohibens* are not the only sort of non-casual, indirect moving causes, i.e. causes whose proper effect is necessarily or generally accompanied by something else. The reason why he cites causes *per removens prohibens* seems to be that these constitute the clearest example. The relation between cause and effect in this type of causality is the *most* 'indirect.' In other words, the *logical* connection between cause and effect, the proportion between them, is minimal. It is achieved via a sort of double negation. The cause causes the effect, not by a straightforward production of it, nor by making a positive but partial contribution to it, but only by removing what prevents it. It 'impedes the impediment.'

A general point implicit in the preceding paragraph should be brought out. This is that if this sort of causality is not chance causality, then there must exist *some* sort or some degree of logical connection or proportion between cause and effect. Knowledge of the cause must, so to speak, remove some of the surprise at the occurrence of the effect, help make the effect expectable. That a man is digging a hole in a certain place does not in the least make you expect a treasure to be uncovered. Likewise, saying that this treasure was found because a man dug a hole just above it does not remove the surprise, but only relocates it; you are surprised that he dug the hole on the very spot of the treasure. Most places where one might dig a hole do not hold treasures. But it is not surprising that displacing a column results in the falling of a stone, since columns usually have stones, or some heavy object, resting on them. Both of these are cases of causality *per removens prohibens*; but only the latter is non-casual.

What makes causality of this sort indirect, then, is not always the utter lack of proportion between cause and effect; sometimes it is only the lack of direct or full proportion. It is something other than an immediate conformity or likeness

---

88. This point enables us to observe again that the same thing may have more than one direct cause, or even more than one direct moving cause. What it cannot have is more than one *principal* cause, one chief direct moving cause. The principal cause of the stone's falling is still whatever causes it to be heavy.

between them. The effect is not the very object of the inclination in virtue of which the cause acts.⁸⁹ Some other term or terms must be introduced to establish the proportion. In the case of causes *per removens prohibens*, the mediating term is the very thing that the cause *is* properly acting upon. This same thing, prior to the action of the cause, is also an obstacle to something else.

3. Absent Causes and Effects

What is it to be an obstacle? It is to be a cause of the *non*-occurrence of something. Aquinas sometimes calls the very act of obstructing something indirect causality, even when it is not performed for the sake of making way for something else, and even apart from the consideration of *any* further, positive results. Thus he says that when fire, by burning, consumes air, the corruption of the air is an indirect effect.⁹⁰ The fire is an obstacle to the air's remaining air. It would make little sense to say that the consumption of the air clears the way for the burning, since it is by the burning itself that it is consumed.

Now, an obstacle is something whose presence or action renders something else impossible or difficult, and hence whose absence or inaction renders it possible or less difficult, or at least less impossible (there may still be other obstacles). This brings to mind Aristotle's remark that the same thing, by its presence or absence, is sometimes the cause of opposite effects.⁹¹ The causality that belongs to something by reason of its absence is, for St Thomas, another sort of indirect, non-casual causality.

That the causality of an obstacle, whether by its presence or by its absence, is not direct causality is obvious: if it is by *not* being there that one thing causes another to be there, or by being there that it causes the other not to be, the full basis of the causality can hardly be conformity between the two things.⁹² The

---

89. Here one might object, what difference would an 'inclination' toward the effect make, since it is brought about all the same? But this sort of objection mistakes the causal role of inclination. It is not another agent-cause, and certainly not another event, adding further effects. What it is meant to explain is the agent's very causality, the *fact* of which has already been established. The point is that in order to justify saying that the agent had an inclination toward the effect, the agent must do more to promote the effect than merely remove a particular obstacle to it. To use Aquinas's example, if the doctor were aiming to produce chillness, he would probably do something to stimulate the production of phlegm directly; and at the very least, he would limit himself to administering scammony only after deliberating and judging that reducing the bile would suffice. So it is still true of something that he does, namely his deliberation, that it is aimed toward something beyond merely reducing the bile.

90. I, q. 49, a. 1; see also I–II, q. 75, a. 2.

91. *Physics* II, ch. 3, 195a11–14; see VIII, ch. 1, 251a28–34.

92. I say the *full* basis, because conformity or likeness may well be a partial basis for opposition; e.g. between competitors. If they were not striving for the same goal, they would not compete. But saying that they have something in common, namely a striving for the same goal, is not sufficient for explaining the opposition between them. You must add that the goal is *not* something they can *possess* in common. By itself the likeness between them is a source of union. Competitors in a given field certainly tend toward solidarity when the interests of the field as a whole are at stake.

proportion between them cannot be direct. Rather, it is an inverse proportion. Here the term establishing the proportion is not some intermediate effect between the cause and the effect in question, but the very subject of the effect in question, e.g. the stone resting on the column. Its nature is such that in the presence of the cause, e.g. the column, it tends not to possess the effect; and in the absence of the cause, it tends to possess it.

The point of the 'sometimes' in Aristotle's remark on things that cause by their absence seems to be that *if* something is a cause by virtue of being absent, what it is a cause of is the opposite of what it causes through its presence. The mere fact that if something were present, the opposite of something actually taking place would have occurred, does not entail that its absence is a cause of what is actually taking place. Otherwise any given occurrence would have innumerable causes. For instance, in order to give a full explanation of my presently sitting in this chair, I should have to mention the facts that the building had not collapsed, that the sun had not exploded, and so on indefinitely. This would be absurd.[93]

Things that are absent are mentioned in the explanation of some occurrence only when there was some reason to expect them to be present and, by their presence, to prevent the occurrence or to yield an opposite occurrence. That is, they are mentioned only when they 'should' have been present, in some sense of 'should.' It need not be in the sense that the absence is an evil for the thing. You might have expected something to be there, not because it was good and suitable for it to be there, but because it usually is, or because it had been there a moment before, or because someone said it would be, etc.

Since the absence of something explains an occurrence only when there was some reason to expect it to be present, mentioning it in the explanation of the occurrence gives rise to a need to explain the absence itself. This may or may not consist in making reference to some agent, saying that the thing was removed or prevented from being there *by* something. It may consist simply in showing that the expectation was unfounded; e.g. the person who told you that it would be there was mistaken. On the other hand, if the expectation was well founded, then the thing must have actually been removed or prevented from being there, which requires an agent.[94] Thus the indirect causality belonging to something by reason

---

93. See Anscombe, 'On Brute Facts,' p. 23. Perhaps this is one of the reasons why Aquinas does not conceive of a 'sufficient' cause in such a way that it *cannot* be impeded from producing its effect. If, in enumerating the causes of some effect, it were necessary to name all the conceivable impediments that were *absent*, the job would be impossible. So would reasonable prediction and conclusive deliberation. It would be an infinite task to enumerate all of the conceivable obstacles to something foreseen, so as to state why they are expected to be absent; for most of them, the only reason is the excellent one that there is no reason to expect them to be present. Likewise, it would be impossible to design a plan to overcome every conceivable obstacle to one's goal. (See I–II, q. 14, a. 6 ad 2.)

94. See I, q. 49, a. 1; I–II, q. 75, a. 1. Again, the basis for the expectation may be nothing more than the fact that the thing had been present earlier. Recall our discussion of the original grounds for conjecturing the existence of a cause or an origin. The removal of something from its prior disposi-

of its absence seems to presuppose the existence of an indirect cause that is present and acts *per removens prohibens*.[95]

Perhaps it is not even wholly precise to say that the thing that was absent 'caused' the effect. The verb at least suggests that the thing was some sort of origin of the effect, hence a cause by reason of its presence or its action. Better to say simply that the effect occurred because of its absence. What may be said to have 'caused' the effect is the remover. Still, of course, what removed the thing may have been the thing itself; and to this extent it may be said to have 'caused' the effect, *per removens prohibens*.[96]

In similar fashion, a thing is said to cause something else *not* to happen or not to exist only when there was some reason to expect it to happen or exist. The fact that I had no time to train for the last Olympic games was not a cause of my not winning a gold medal there; for I would not have had the slightest chance to qualify, let alone to win, even if I had time to do nothing but train.

Now, it was suggested that the absence of something enters into the explanation of some occurrence only when the thing 'should' have been present, but that this may or may not be in the sense that the absence is bad for it. Nevertheless, this does seem to be the only sense of 'should' that *entails* that its absence, or causing its absence, is *not* a mere *chance* cause of the resulting occurrence. (To repeat, sometimes causality *per removens prohibens* is chance causality.)

Suppose that there is a genuine reason to expect the thing to be present, but the reason is something other than the thing's own inclination to be there. If the thing has no tendency of its own to be there, then relative to it, its being there and preventing the occurrence would be by chance; and hence its absence would not be by chance. This in turn means that it may be only by chance that what removes it or prevents it from being there causes the occurrence. (Of course, it may still not be by chance, if what was intended in the removal or prevention was the very occurrence.) It is only when it is against the thing's own inclination, only when the thing itself is inclined to prevent the occurrence, that the removal or prevention is necessarily not a mere chance cause of the occurrence. That is to say, it is only when the thing is *per se* expectable to be there that the removal of

---

tion begs for an explanation. The very fact of its being in that disposition yields some expectation that it will remain so.

95. See I–II, q. 72, a. 6: *semper enim in rebus negatio fundatur super aliqua affirmatione, quae est quodammodo causa eius;* and q. 75, a. 1: *Negationis autem alicuius potest duplex causa assignari. Primo quidem, defectus causae, id est ipsius causae negatio, est causa negationis secundum seipsam: ad remotionem enim causae sequitur remotio effectus. . . . Alio modo, causa affirmationis ad quam sequitur negatio, est per accidens causa negationis consequentis: sicut ignis, causando calorem ex principali intentione, consequenter causat privationem frigiditatis. Quorum primum potest sufficere ad simplicem negationem. Sed cum inordinatio peccati, et quodlibet malum, non sit simplex negatio, sed privatio eius quod quid natum est et debet habere; necesse est quod talis inordinatio habeat causam agentem per accidens; quod enim natum est inesse et debet, nunquam abesset nisi propter causam aliquam impedientem.*

96. See I–II, q. 6, a. 3, together with I–II, q. 71, a. 5.

it is always a non-casual cause of what results from its not being there. But what is contrary to something's inclination is an evil for it. In short, to act upon something in such a way that it is stopped from impeding some result is, necessarily, to cause the result not by chance, if the thing is *per se* an obstacle to the result, an enemy of it; when this is not the case, such action may or may not be a chance cause of the result.

The same point seems to hold as regards merely causing something not to be present or not to occur. If what is prevented from being present, or from yielding some occurrence, has no inclination to do so, the action performed upon it by which it is prevented may be only a chance cause of its absence or of the non-occurrence. It may be only the consideration of something altogether incidental to the action that gives rise to the expectation of the thing's presence or to the expectation of the occurrence.

As I said, I shall return to the direct/indirect distinction in Chapter 5, after having examined the general question of the causality of the will, in Chapter 4. The will, for Thomas, is essentially a kind of appetitive capacity, and a capacity of originating one's own appetitive dispositions, inclinations and intentions. Yet its causality extends in some way even beyond what falls directly under one's intention. The bearing of the foregoing general account of indirect agency upon the question of the agency of the will is signaled by the following text.

> That is called 'voluntary' which is by the will [*a voluntate*]. But something is said to be 'by something' in two ways. In one way, directly; namely, what proceeds from something insofar as it [the 'something'] is an agent, as in heating by heat. In the other way, indirectly, from the very fact that it does not act; as the sinking of a ship is said to be 'by the steersman,' insofar as he leaves off steering. But it must be known that what follows upon a lack of action is not always reduced to the agent, as to a cause, by reason of the fact that he does not act; but only then, when he can and should act. For if the steersman could not steer the ship, or if the steering of the ship were not entrusted to him, the sinking of the ship, which would happen for lack of a steersman, would not be imputed to him. Therefore, because the will, by willing and acting, can impede that which is a not-willing and a not-acting, and sometimes it should; that which is a not-willing and a not-acting is sometimes imputed to it, as though existing by it.[97]

---

97. *Voluntarium dicitur quod est a voluntate. Ab aliquo autem dicitur esse aliquid dupliciter. Uno modo, directe, quod scilicet procedit ab aliquo inquantum est agens, sicut calefactio a calore. Alio modo, indirecte, ex hoc ipso quod non agit, sicut submersio navis dicitur esse a gubernatore, inquantum desistit a gubernando. Sed sciendum quod non semper id quod sequitur ad defectum actionis, reducitur sicut in causam in agens, ex eo quod non agit; sed solum tunc cum potest et debet agere. Si enim gubernator non posset navem dirigere, vel non esset ei commissa gubernatio navis, non imputaretur ei navis submersio, quae per absentiam gubernatoris contingeret. Quia igitur voluntas, volendo et agendo, potest impedire hoc quod est non velle et non agere, et aliquando debet; hoc quod est non velle et non agere imputatur ei, quasi ab ipsa existens* (I–II, q. 6, a. 3). See below, pp. 216–17.

Chapter 4
The Agency of the Will

It hardly seems necessary to undertake to demonstrate the existence of things voluntary. In its most elementary sense, the voluntary is simply what someone does or brings about because he wants to. It is by no means an easy matter to state with full precision what it is to want something, or what it means to say that some action or result came about 'because' someone wanted it; there are also several borderline cases, that is, actions and events of which it is not easy to say whether they are voluntary or not. But as just formulated, the notion of the voluntary is sufficiently precise for making perfectly unexceptionable judgments about the voluntariness of a wide range of phenomena, and it is so readily accessible to normal intelligence and so thoroughly embedded in ordinary human affairs that it would be hard to understand what someone who seemed genuinely to deny its existence could have in mind. Its existence is too obvious to allow for any real proof. Anyone who was genuinely to question it would find the answer in the question's own asking. As Augustine says, I ought not to reply to you when you ask something unless you want to know what you ask, and ask because you want to know.[1]

The difficulties surrounding voluntary action do not begin with the question of its existence. They begin with the questions of its nature and properties. The common intelligibility of the notion of a thing by no means excludes considerable vagueness or imprecision as to what it properly consists in. Many of the questions about the voluntary are classic issues in the history of philosophy.

The general aim of this chapter is to arrive at a more precise account of the nature of the voluntary. The first two sections will be devoted to giving some precision to the position that, as the above formula implies, the notion of the voluntary refers mainly to a certain sort of action and effect of action, or to what someone does or brings about in a certain way, namely, in the manner of someone who wants something. That is, 'voluntary,' in its chief sense, invokes a certain type of agent-causality. Another way to say this is that the domain of things capable of being voluntary is nearly the same as the domain of things able to be in a man's power to do or to bring about. This judgment will need only a slight qualification, based on the possibility of suffering or undergoing things voluntarily.

---

1. St Augustine, *De libero arbitrio* I, ch. 12, § 25.

From a certain point of view, this thesis may seem so obvious as hardly to merit a protracted discussion. However, there are strong reasons for dwelling upon it. Examples of such reasons have been sketched in Chapter 1, Section D.3, and I shall give a fuller presentation of them here. Doing so will serve to show that what is at stake is not just the meaning of a certain term. Rather, in saying that 'voluntary' refers primarily to actions and effects, what is meant is that what is called 'wanting' is itself above all a causal disposition, a disposition toward action, *even though* not everything a man wants is something he can cause or do, or even thinks he can cause or do. That is, what is really at stake is the intrinsic connection between 'will' and action. A quotation from Aquinas will serve to show what this means.

> The will is a medium between the intellect and exterior activity; for the intellect proposes the will's object to it, and the will itself causes the exterior action. Hence the beginning of the motion of the will is considered on the side of the intellect, which apprehends something universally as good; but the termination, or the completion, of the act of the will is considered according to its order toward activity, through which one tends toward the attainment of a thing; for the motion of the will is from the soul to things. And therefore the completion of the act of the will is looked at in relation to that which is something good for someone to do.[2]

After indicating the importance of this point in Section A, I will proceed with the defense of the thesis that the domain of things capable of being voluntary is very nearly the same as the domain of things capable of being in a man's power to do or to bring about. This will be carried out chiefly through an analysis of the very notions of 'wanting' and 'the wanted,' to show that wanting is chiefly a disposition to cause something. This is along the lines of Aquinas's assertion that the completion of the act of the will exists in relation to something to be done by the one willing. Section B covers this aspect of the question. The rest of the chapter will be devoted to delineating some of the more fundamental principles involved in articulating and explaining voluntary efficacy. Particular attention will be given to the reasons for distinguishing between acts of will and acts of intellect, and to the way in which human action is explained by acts of will, especially the act of will called 'use.' These concerns are motivated mostly by certain issues and tendencies in the analytical philosophy of action, which will be set forth in the course of the discussion.

---

2. *Voluntas media est inter intellectum et exteriorem operationem; nam intellectus proponit voluntati suum obiectum, et ipsa voluntas causat exteriorem actionem. Sic igitur principium motus voluntatis consideratur ex parte intellectus, qui apprehendit aliquid ut bonum in universali; sed terminatio seu perfectio actus voluntis attenditur secundum ordinem ad operationem, per quam aliquis tendit ad consecutionem rei; nam motus voluntatis est ab anima ad rem. Et ideo perfectio actus voluntatis attenditur secundum hoc quod est aliquid bonum alicui ad agendum* (Summa theologiae I–II, q. 13, a. 5 ad 1).

A. AUTONOMY OR AGENCY?

1. The Concern with the Source of the Will's Object

The significance of the question which heads this section, 'autonomy or agency?,' arises from the consideration of certain features common to much of modern ethical speculation, features which are at least potentially misleading. Especially since Kant, the study of ethics and of human conduct has concentrated heavily on the question of the object of the will and how it gets presented, or in other words, how something comes to appear to us as good or 'willable.' In particular, the concern has been to establish the role of reason in the constitution of the will's object. Since the will is nothing other than the rational appetite, the appetite that takes its object from among things grasped by reason, a common way to pose this issue is in terms of the autonomy of the voluntary agent.

The question would be whether it belongs to reason itself to determine or to measure the application of the will to its object, and if so, how; or whether instead, reason is only as it were the line of communication between the will and its object, making their union possible but contributing no criteria of its own to the determination of the 'willability' of things or to the discrimination between what is and what is not to be willed, i.e. between good and evil. In the latter case, the ordering of the will to its object would not proceed chiefly according to principles corresponding to the very nature of the voluntary agent *qua* voluntary, i.e. *qua* rational. It would follow laws drawn from something foreign to the nature or to the order of reason, and so would be 'heteronomous.' In the former case, the order of reason itself would in some way constitute the will's principal object, and whatever else might rightly fall under the will's movement would do so only insofar as it is according to reason.

The question of the autonomy of the voluntary agent often takes the form of the question of the existence of conditions of possible or suitable objects of will which hold for 'any possible rational being.' What is sought are the regulative principles governing voluntary action considered simply as rational, in abstraction from any other attributes or conditions that might pertain to the voluntary subject besides rationality. The question of the autonomy of reason, which at first seems to mean only the question of the existence of principles of voluntary conduct that are connatural or proportioned to the nature of reason, thus becomes the question of the existence of practical dictates of 'pure' reason, reason treated as though independent, as though determined only by itself, not by any 'object.'

If not altogether misconceived, this way of framing the question can be at any rate quite misleading, at least if it is correct to say that the voluntary essentially involves a relation to an agent-cause. The danger being signaled here is not that of giving insufficient weight to the role of non-rational factors in the constitution of human values.³ Rather, the danger is of an undue separation between the order of values itself and the order of action, and above all a neglect of the dependence of the former on the latter. This danger arises from the exclusive focus on one aspect of voluntary action, that of its specification, i.e. the determination of the will's object. Or more precisely, it arises from the exclusive focus on only one aspect of the will's relation to its object, namely, the mediating role of reason in the genesis of that relation. The actual, 'efficacious' exercise of voluntary action may easily come to be looked upon as nothing more than the 'positing' of the will's object. The conditions of its exercise may, in the end, be treated as more or less incidental to the original constitution of the will's object. This is certainly what happens when the question of reason's role in the determination of the will's object is framed in terms of the question of the practical dictates of 'pure' reason.

The difficulty with this kind of treatment is that, to the extent that the actual exercise of voluntary action is regarded as incidental to the constitution of the will's object, the very reasons for originally postulating the existence of 'will' are in fact nearly lost sight of. 'Will,' taken in the sense of a faculty, primarily names the root of the capacity for voluntary agency. Let us take it for granted here that voluntary agency is the kind of agency proper to rational beings. Now, perhaps the *possibility* of will is sufficiently secured by disclosing a 'law of reason': if reason finds such a law in itself, this must be because there is nothing in the nature of reason that prevents it from being a cause. The law is there just in case it actually exercises any causality. But being a mere form of action, no law is sufficient by itself to secure such exercise. It is legitimate to posit the actual existence of will only because the rational subject really can and does act through reason, or act voluntarily.⁴

Now, at least in the case of the rational agent that is man, the capacity for action is not co-extensive with the range of his reason, nor even with the potential range of his will. Reason is capable of apprehending an untold number of things which a man is in no position to bring about, or in fact to do anything about at all, through action; it is even capable of apprehending many things of

---

3. This is the complaint of Scheler and others about Kant's ethics. It will not be assessed here, except to note with agreement Donagan's insistence that the Kantian ethic is not so 'formal' as to allow for any 'content' whatsoever (*The Theory of Morality*, p. 13). The efforts to show the 'emptiness' of Kant's moral law are usually rather hasty. Anscombe, for instance ('Modern Moral Philosophy,' p. 68), attributes the rigor of his doctrine on lying entirely to his upbringing, saying that he was simply unable to conceive of the possibility of describing a lie as anything other than just a lie. But surely Kant's thought is that even if your maxim is not simply 'Tell a lie!' but (say) 'Tell a lie of this sort in these sorts of circumstances!' even *that* cannot be raised to a universal law without contradiction. (However, no doubt Kant's upbringing does show up in the *gravity* that he attributes universally to lying.)

Regarding the following line of argument, see the criticisms of the views of both Kant and Scheler that are offered by K. Wojtyła in 'Il problema della volontà nell'analisi dell'atto etico.'

4. This of course does not by itself imply that reason and will must be really distinct; Kant, for instance, holds that they are not. But there is no justification for attributing will to the rational subject, even if doing so only means giving (practical) reason the name of will, except insofar as the subject really does act somehow through reason.

this sort as somehow good or potentially 'willable.' A man needs something more than reason and will in order actually to exercise any agency. He needs power. The point being urged here is that this need redounds upon the very kinds of objects which he is actually able to will fully. This is because, in line with the reasons for positing its existence in the first place, willing is nothing other than a certain way of initiating the exercise of action.

What the examination of action from the point of view of 'any possible rational agent' might make one overlook, then, is that the very specification of action, or the very application of the will to its object, the very 'willing' of anything, already requires power: not merely in the sense that in order to will a man needs a capacity for willing, but also in the sense that he needs to see the object of his will as something he has the power to do something about, *precisely in order to be able to will it*. In other words, to will always is, or at least always involves, the will to do something; and the will to do something always requires the belief that one actually has available the power needed to carry it out. In short, willing is inseparable from hope. The question 'what may I hope?' precedes the question 'what should I do?' Duty depends upon possibility, not to mention necessity, just as action does.

2. The Will as its Own Principal Object

'Pure' reason could be regarded as practical only if an entirely different concept of the will were held. It would require that, as Kant in fact holds, the very possession of will be intrinsically sufficient to secure the power needed for the kind of action or the kind of life which reason judges worthy of itself. This is to say that what is by nature the primary object of the will, the primary willable object and the only 'unqualified good,' is not some activity distinct from willing; it is the good will itself. It means that to will to live well is, *formally*, to live well.

That is, it does not mean merely that the humanly good life is the natural result of the humanly good will, as Aristotle claimed in the *Nicomachean Ethics*. Nor does it mean merely that the supernaturally good life is the divinely ordained, infallible reward of the supernaturally good will, as Aquinas believed. On either of these positions, the object of the good will is still something other than its own goodness, and before it can be willed, the possibility of attaining it must first be ascertained. Then the thesis that willing well 'is' living well would mean: reality is so ordered that the good will is liable to be satisfied, whereas the bad will is liable to be frustrated. But what it means for Kant is that willing to live well consists above all in this: willing to will well. The will is by nature more about itself than about anything else. The first precept of his moral law is not only a dictate about what to will, as is, for instance, the dictate to love God. Kant's first precept proposes the (good) will itself as the object to be willed.

'Living well' is taken here in the sense of living rightly or according to reason. Often, of course, especially in the setting of Aristotelian ethics, it is taken as meaning pretty much the same thing as happiness. That Kant refuses to make happiness the measure of moral rectitude is too well known to require much discussion. If one can still speak of happiness as 'living well' or as the 'good life' in the Kantian system, it is only because of the nearly complete equivocity of 'good' that runs throughout that system. In general, for Kant, 'good' means apt to be willed; but this divides sharply into what is *intrinsically* willable or willable without qualification, and what is willable only in virtue of the existence of a desire, which it satisfies, in the voluntary subject. *How it is possible* that the will can be determined to objects in virtue of their mere suitability to desire, or how the will can be conditioned by desire, seems to remain mysterious. At any rate, it has nothing to do with the essential constitution of the will. That is, Kant's conception of desire is wholly naturalistic. Happiness, however, is nothing but the full and permanent satisfaction of desire. It is true that happiness is in a way something proper to rational beings, these alone having the capacity to reflect on their desire and to desire an absolutely unrestricted and perpetual satisfaction.[5] But it does not constitute the good life of the voluntary subject *qua* voluntary, or the object of the good will.

To be more exact, Kant's thought is that the good will, as such, does not really *have* an object. What makes it good is precisely that its act is determined without reference to an object. Its act is nothing but the affirmation or the glorification of its own freedom, taken both negatively, as the quality of being independent of objects, and positively, as the quality of being one's own end.

To say this is to overturn the very notion of the voluntary; for it is to overturn the very notion of action or agency. It is to make the practical order independent of the sphere of objective, exterior acts (i.e. acts of powers other than the will) and effects. It is to deny that action, and therefore also willing, consists principally in the establishment or the exercise of a certain relation of union between the agent and some *other*, some object. It is to postulate a form of voluntary activity or of willing which does not necessarily consist in initiating anything or bringing anything about, or at least clinging to or resting in something, other than the willing itself.

Does this mean that in the Kantian conception, the causal character of the will is entirely abandoned? Yet Kant calls the will a causal faculty, and extends its causality beyond the production of pure acts of willing. So its causal character is not simply abandoned; but it is rendered secondary and incidental to the 'essence' of the will.[6] This is true even as regards pure acts of willing. *Some* of these may

---

5. That the morally good man deserves to be happy, of course, is what provides the basis for the conclusion that there 'must be' a God. So, moral goodness 'must' get you happiness, in the life that 'must be' to come; but that is not what makes it moral goodness. By the same token, neither in this life nor in the next does happiness *consist* in one's union with the principle of moral goodness.

6. Kant says that will is a faculty *either* of producing objects according to a representation *or* of determining itself to such actuation, whether or not the physical power at hand is sufficient. (*Critique*

be caused by the will as by an agent acting upon or producing something. These are the acts of will that bear upon some object. Such acts may even be acts befitting a good will, insofar as what is willed in the object is the particular form taken by the moral law, as applied to such an object. The good will may, as it were, apply itself to the willing of particular forms of moral rectitude. Nevertheless its principal act, the willing of the law in itself, is something the will 'causes' only negatively, in the sense that no other agent is its cause; and this act is simply identical with the will's proper end, the good will itself.

This last point makes the Kantian conception of will in general differ even from Aquinas's understanding of the *divine* will. For St Thomas, even if the divine will is in reality identical with the divine goodness, not everything belonging to the divine goodness is expressed by the term 'will,' nor even by 'divine' or 'holy' will. Because they are conceptually distinct, Aquinas sees nothing illogical in speaking of God's will as a kind of causal disposition with respect to his possession of his goodness: not of course that he produces any good in himself by an act of will, but that, in the manner of one who has will, he tends to *rest* in his good,[7] and to pour it forth according to the measure of his wisdom. I will return to this point in Section A.4.

3. Will and Appetite

Kant's view, of course, is that it is only according to the idea of an autonomous will that philosophy can disclose a practical order which is proportioned or connatural to reason, or can make intelligible a form of agency which is not subordinated to merely physical or sensuous nature. Nothing presented to the will or to practical reason from without, nothing that is first of all a matter of speculative consideration and only subsequently a possible matter of action, is commensurate to practical reason's own inner potential. No mere object is a sufficient determinant of it. It must be its own determinant.

There is a text in Aquinas's commentary on the *Metaphysics* which draws a distinction reminiscent of Kant, and which also brings out clearly the difference between the two perspectives.

> What is sought in accordance with concupiscence [sense-appetite] seems good because it is desired.... But what is sought by the intellectual appetite is desired because it seems good on its own account.[8]

---

of Practical Reason, introduction.) It is as though an adequate basis for the will's operation were provided by the mere consideration of what one *would* do *if* one had the power. The 'pure' will functions 'as if' it were a cause—in the subjunctive mode, so to speak. For Thomas, this would be to say that its operations are nothing but *velleitates* (see below, p. 147).

7. See I, q. 19, a. 1.

8. *Quod appetitur secundum concupiscentiam videtur bonum eo quod desideratur.... Sed illud quod appetitur appetitu intellectuali desideratur quia videtur bonum secundum se* (*In XII Meta*. lect. vii, § 2522).

What this has in common with Kant is the distinction between what is judged good because it is already desired and what is judged good on its own account. But for St Thomas, the result of the latter judgment is *also* a desire. For him, 'good' in either case still *means* 'desirable.' He is so far from conceiving desire as a cause of heteronomy for the will that he holds will itself to be the primary sort of desire.[9] As we saw in Chapter 1, desire, for Thomas, is always for the sake of something else besides itself. 'It is foolish to say that someone desires [*appetat*] for the sake of desiring.'[10]

Owing to their apparent similarity, it is also instructive to compare Kant's doctrine of the good will with that of St Augustine's *De libero arbitrio*.[11] For Augustine, a good will is a will to live rightly. To live rightly is to live according to the eternal law, which is the law by which it is just that all things be perfectly ordered. Now, one of the principles of order emanating from the eternal law concerns the nature of happiness. Happiness is possession of the perfect good. One feature of the perfect good, whatever it is, must be utter stability and incorruptibility. This means that once possessed, it cannot be lost unwillingly. Another principle of the eternal law, therefore, is that nothing should be loved, or taken as one's highest good, which can be lost against one's will. But a good will is a will in conformity with the eternal law; hence what is loved with a good will cannot be lost unwillingly. Therefore, the man with a good will is a happy man. Thus the only really decisive factor for the possession of happiness is the disposition of one's will. The good will is the good man's most prized possession.

To say that the good will is the good man's most prized possession sounds like saying that the good will is the only, or at least the chief, unqualified good. To say that the principal object of the good will cannot be lost unwillingly also suggests this. But Augustine manifestly does not mean that the good will is its own chief object, or that the good man wants a good will for the sake of nothing but itself.[12] He means simply that of all corruptible things, the only one upon which one's happiness depends is the one which depends entirely on one's will, because it *is* one's will. This is the 'decisive' factor because it is the one contingent factor. But the *dominant* factor in happiness, and the principal object of a good will, is precisely something that is not contingent, hence something other than the will's own goodness. It is one thing to say that the good will's object cannot be lost except willingly, and quite another to say that it is its own object. The former retains the distinction between the will and its object, and *presupposes* belief in the possibility of perfect happiness.[13]

9. Ibid.
10. See above, p. 43. See also I–II, q. 1, a. 1 ad 2.
11. I, chs. 13–15.
12. See ibid., II, ch. 18, § 47 to ch. 20, § 54. Cf. I–II, q. 3, a. 4 obj. 5 and reply.
13. See I–II, q. 3, a. 2 ad 4.

Why does Kant refuse to make the goodness of the will consist in the very *way* in which it seeks happiness or the *kind* of happiness it seeks? Is it not ultimately because he regards happiness as essentially selfish? Happiness is unmixed and continuous satisfaction of desire; and the satisfaction of desire is joy. But the object of joy is, for Kant, always something in oneself (the objective, empirical self). He has no notion of rejoicing or being happy 'at' something other. Even if he grants the existence of certain intellectual or spiritual objects of joy, his conception of the structure of joy, and hence of happiness, is in Thomas's terms essentially sensual.[14] There is no joy, for instance, in the contemplation of the moral law. This is because if it is not other than the will, it is certainly other than the objective ego. It can be an object of humiliation and reverence, but not delight.

This conception of the moral order and of moral goodness is commonly regarded as extremely demanding or difficult to fulfill. At least from Aquinas's point of view, it is not merely difficult, but altogether impossible, 'logically' impossible. For him, the will cannot possibly have itself for its principal object. It certainly can have itself for its object, but only secondarily, or only to the extent that it has already willed something else.[15] Its first act is one of love, a 'passion,' and this necessarily takes the form either of desire or of joy, according as the object loved is absent or present. The will is intrinsically a faculty of *appetite*, the rational appetite.

I stress the nature of love as a 'passion,' because it is this that shows the difference from Kant. Kant reasonably regards all appetite as a *moved* mover, involving a passive dimension. But, as already noted, he also regards it as something foreign to the intrinsic nature of the will. For this reason, any operation of the will that is determined by mere objects of appetite is necessarily 'heteronomous,' not only in the sense that the object willed is something other than the will, but also, and most importantly, in the sense that it pertains to an order that is foreign to the will or not connatural to it or proportioned to it. Passion connotes the working of cause and effect, and this belongs solely to the physical and 'anthropological' orders. The will's proper domain is simply incommensurate with the domain of things that are 'generated' and that have a proper 'destination,' determined by their generator. In *this* sense, the 'natural' has no place in the constitution of the pure will, though of course one may speak of the 'nature' of the will in a merely logical sense. For Aquinas, by contrast, even insofar as man is a voluntary subject, he is acted upon before he acts; and the due measure of his will must be established accordingly.[16]

---

14. See I–II, q. 4, a. 2 ad 2. On how the contemporary polarity of 'egoism' and 'altruism,' deriving from Kant, is fundamentally misconceived, see Veatch, 'Is Kant the Gray Eminence of Contemporary Ethical Theory?'

15. See I–II, q. 1, a. 1 ad 2: *impossibile est quod primum appetibile, quod est finis, sit ipsum velle.*

16. See I–II, q. 10, a. 1; q. 9, a. 6; q. 91, a. 2. This difference between Kant's practical doctrine and Aquinas's would seem to be more clear-cut than anything brought to light by the so-called

4. Will and Activity

This is obviously not the place to undertake a global assessment of Kant's moral doctrine. Such an assessment would need to include major features of his doctrine of speculative reason as well. In these final paragraphs of this section, I wish merely to draw out one last point of comparison, of a theological character, so as to complete my chief purpose in referring to his teaching. This purpose is simply to indicate that it is not at all trivial to maintain that voluntariness pertains chiefly to objects of a certain kind of agent-causality, and that this presupposes, as a matter of principle, powers of bringing things about, 'physical' powers if you like. To subscribe to this position is to say that by its very nature voluntary action, and therefore also the will, presupposes and depends upon other things besides the will itself. It is to say that voluntary activity is inserted within a larger order of things, not only as a matter of fact but also as a matter of principle. In particular, it is to say that the will's existing under the conditions of a determinate nature, human nature in the case of man's will, is quite 'natural' to it.

Now, if Aquinas can maintain an intrinsic connection between 'passion' and morality, and yet is not compelled to take the path followed by Hume, that of frankly denying that the moral order is something proportioned to reason, this is in part because he simply denies Kant's principle that the only unqualified good is the good will. Needless to say, Aquinas does consider the good will to be an 'unqualified good,' or, in his language, to be a noble good; but it is not the primary noble good. The primary noble goods are God and beatitude, and these are precisely what constitute the will's primary natural objects of love, desire and joy.[17] That he can do this, of course, rests on his judging it possible to establish the existence of these objects in a strictly theoretical way, i.e. as matters of fact, not just as things that 'must be.' As already indicated, this in turn rests precisely on his thinking it possible to place even the rational subject itself, as such, within an order of cause and effect; which of course Kant disallows.[18]

---

deontological/teleological distinction. Kant is perfectly happy to explain his moral doctrine in terms of finality; the good will (or practical reason, or the moral law, or the rational agent *qua* rational) is its own end. The issue between him and Aquinas is whether or not the intrinsic end of the will is something outside the good will, hence outside practical reason itself. See I–II, q. 3, a. 5.

17. See II–II, q. 145, a. 1 ad 2. Wojtyła, 'Il ruolo dirigente,' aptly describes the role that Kant ascribes to reason in human action as merely 'defensive.' The rational 'good' cannot attract, it can only set a boundary not to be transgressed.

18. In making these observations, I am taking issue with Donagan's claims that 'Kant's moral theory can be detached from the transcendental idealism by which he offered to show how natural science is possible' and that 'when it is thus detached, the theory of action it incorporates can be seen as what it is: a revival of the traditional pre-Humean one' (*Choice*, p. 140). The transcendental idealism has a twofold function: to show, against Hume, how natural science, as a science of necessary relations of cause and effect, is possible *even though* (as Hume persuaded him) metaphysics, as a science with substantive content, is impossible; and to establish, against Hume's doctrine that all agent-

This however is not to say that Kant is unable to distinguish between intrinsically different 'kinds' of will. For instance, he insists on a fundamental diversity between the human and the divine will. The human will is capable of being alienated from its own goodness; it has that contingency which struck Augustine so forcefully. Even when it is good, it is not holy.[19] The divine will, however, of course is holy. Moreover, one might even attempt to frame a Kantian answer to the concerns I have raised, by appeal to Thomas's own understanding of God's will.

Aquinas, too, considers God's will to be intrinsically indefectible. Moreover, properly speaking, God's will does not have an 'object' really distinct from itself. What God primarily wills is his own goodness; but he, his goodness, and his will are in reality one and the same thing. This is why God not only cannot possibly will badly, but also cannot possibly act badly.

> In us, in whom power and essence are something other than will and intellect, and intellect other than wisdom, and will other than justice, there can be something in our power which cannot be in a just will or in a wise intellect. But in God, power and essence and will and intellect and wisdom and justice are the same. Hence nothing can be in the divine power which cannot be in his just will or in his wise intellect.[20]

So might we not say, in a formula at least approaching Kant's, that what is good without qualification is primarily God's will, and secondarily a will conformed to his? Aquinas certainly makes the goodness of the human will depend upon its conformity with God's.[21] So is it not still 'will' which is the only unqualified good?

Now, first of all, in the place in which Aquinas makes conformity with God's will a condition for any will's goodness, what he says he means is that it

---

causality (even man's) is necessitated, the *possibility* of free agency. But the concept of free agency whose possibility is established on this basis is anything but a revival of the traditional one, and how it could be detached from the transcendental idealism is very difficult to imagine. And literally everything in Kant's moral theory depends upon *that* concept. To put it another way, Kant's concept of free agency is not only one according to which the existence of free agency can be sufficiently secured *within* the practical order; it is also one according to which the existence of free agency needs no *explanation*. If it needed an explanation, it would need metaphysics. But even if, in doctrines in which it does need an explanation, the explanation of it falls outside the domain of moral theory, i.e. is a speculative matter, the very fact that it can require an explanation shows that it is conceived in a very different way; and the differences have consequences for moral theory that are anything but trivial.

19. *Critique of Practical Reason*, I.i.7, second scholium; II.ii.4.

20. *In nobis, in quibus est aliud potentia et essentia a voluntate et intellectu, et iterum intellectus aliud a sapientia, et voluntas aliud a iustitia, potest esse aliquid in potentia, quod non potest esse in voluntate iusta, vel in intellectu sapiente. Sed in Deo est idem potentia et essentia et voluntas et intellectus et sapientia et iustitia. Unde nihil potest esse in potentia divina, quod non possit esse in voluntate iusta ipsius, et in intellectu sapiente eius* (I, q. 25, a. 5 ad 1).

21. I–II, q. 19, arts. 9–10.

must will the good that God wills. This of course is primarily God's own goodness. And this good, Thomas says in that same place, is 'compared to the divine will as its proper object.'[22] The divine will and the divine goodness are not really distinct; but we still think and speak of them in this fashion. They are distinct 'in reason,' and this distinction has a genuine basis in God. For God's reality exceeds what is captured in any one term we may attribute to him. In order to deal (somewhat) with this 'excess,' which affects all our language and thought about God, it is necessary to use a multiplicity of distinct notions. Thus, even if God's goodness is identical with his good will, not an object of it, there is nevertheless more to it, 'really,' than what is captured by us in the expression 'God's will.' That God's goodness and his will are identical does not imply that his goodness consists entirely, or even primarily, in what is signified by 'goodness of will.'

Moreover, there is also another distinction which, in God, is only one of reason: the distinction between his will and the *operation*, the activity, which he wills. This is indicated by the quotation given above, in which God's will is identified with his power. The distinction between interior acts and exterior acts does not exist in God. (Exterior acts are not the same as acts *ad extra*; they are commanded acts, normally acts of powers other than the will, moved by the will, *in* the willing subject.) This means that 'efficacy' has not at all been rendered 'incidental' to the will; on the contrary, it means that the scope of the object of God's will is necessarily *identical* with the scope of his efficacy. Such a situation can hardly be captured by what *we* understand by 'will.'

In short, for Aquinas, the primary 'good without qualification' *includes* good will, but is not comprehended by this notion. And, since what *we* understand by will is something ordered to and satisfied by something other than itself, neither is the notion of will the most adequate one for expressing that good. 'Beatitude' would do better, but in the present context it might be said to beg the question.[23] But also better than 'will,' I think, for expressing the substance of the divine good would be the notion of divine *life*.[24]

These considerations should give at least some indication of why, for Thomas, the created will only makes sense within an order of moving and being moved. The creature's fullest union with God's goodness does not consist for-

---

22. *Hoc autem bonum . . . comparatur ad voluntatem divinam ut obiectum proprium eius* (I–II, q. 19, a. 9). Cf. I, q. 5, a. 4 ad 3.

23. Kant in fact defines 'beatitude' as the freedom *from* all appetites or inclinations; it involves only a kind of negative 'joy,' that of pure independence (Cf. *Critique of Practical Reason*, II.ii.2.) It would, so to speak, eliminate the 'need' for what he calls 'happiness.' Thomas often uses the two terms more or less interchangeably. If *felicitas* is not strictly synonymous with *beatitudo* for him, it at least expresses a likeness of beatitude. (Cf. I, q. 26, a. 1 obj. 2; I–II, q. 2, a. 2 obj. 1; I, q. 4, a. 1 obj. 3; q. 4, a. 5 obj. 4; q. 4, a. 7.) More importantly, he understands beatitude as the perfect *satisfaction* of (intellectual) appetite, not the elimination of it (I–II, q. 1, a. 7; q. 2, a. 7; q. 3, a. 1; q. 5, a. 8; etc.).

24. Taking life, of course, not in the sense of the *existence* of a living thing, but in the sense of vital activity: see I–II, q. 3, a. 2 ad 1. Cf. *Metaphysics* IX, ch. 8, 1050b1: happiness is a kind of life.

mally in willing what God wills. That of course is the required disposition; strikingly, Aquinas compares it to *matter* and to an *instrument*.[25] But what the fullest union consists in is sharing in God's life, communicating in God's activity. The highest good then is utter fullness of activity, 'eternal life.'

Finally, it would seem to be precisely this conception of true happiness (in contrast to sensual 'happiness') as primarily an activity, and only secondarily as the subject's enjoyment of it, which allows Aquinas to regard happiness as both intrinsically capable of being shared and intrinsically tending to share itself, *diffusivum sui*. It is anything but egocentric. Correspondingly, the good disposition of the created will, the root of its conformity with God's, consists in charity, which Aquinas conceives as a form of *friendship*, one 'founded on a certain communication,' according as God 'communicates his beatitude to us.'[26] This friendship, like any other, is rooted in mutual knowledge—a knowledge which, on the creature's side at least, possesses a 'speculative' core, since it does not *produce* the friend but simply contemplates him. And, perhaps most significantly for us, this friendship also constitutes a kind of 'power.' I close this section with Aquinas's assertion of this point.

> Just as nature does not leave man lacking in necessary things, even though it did not give him weapons and coverings as it did to other animals, because it gave him reason and hands, by which he could obtain these for himself; in the same way, it does not leave him lacking in necessary things, even though it did not give him any principle by which he could obtain beatitude; for this was impossible. But it gave him free decision, by which he might be converted to God, who would make him blessed. For the things we can do through friends, we can in some way do ourselves, as is said in the third book of the *Ethics*.[27]

B. WANTING AS A CAUSAL DISPOSITION

Before looking at the difficulties with the position that voluntariness is primarily a characteristic of actions and effects, a pair of preliminary observations are in order. The first is that to say that voluntariness is primarily a characteristic of actions and effects is not to say that the voluntary is restricted to positive effects. It also covers omissions or cases of 'not acting,' insofar as these are also owing to someone's wanting something. Just as we say that someone did this or

---

25. I–II, q. 4, a. 4.
26. II–II, q. 23, a. 1.
27. *Sicut natura non deficit homini in necessariis, quamvis non dederit sibi arma et tegumenta sicut aliis animalibus quia dedit ei rationem et manus, quibus possit haec sibi conquirere; ita nec deficit homini in necessariis, quamvis non daret sibi aliquod principium quo posset beatitudinem consequi; hoc enim erat impossibile. Sed dedit ei liberum arbitrium, quo possit converti ad Deum, qui eum faceret beatum. Quae enim per amicos possumus, per nos aliqualiter possumus, ut dicitur in III Ethic.* (I–II, q. 5, a. 5 ad 1; the reference is to *Nicomachean Ethics* III, ch. 5, 1112b27.)

that because he wanted to, so also we say that he did not do something because he did not want to. His not doing it consists in his refraining from doing it, and, as Donagan and Anscombe urge, this itself is already a sort of action. Still, 'not to do something' can be voluntary only because 'to do something' can be. The negative effects of which something is capable depend on the positive effects of which it is capable, just as what a thing is not depends on what it is.

It is also worth noting at the start that the English expression 'he does not want to' contains a certain ambiguity: it can mean either 'he wants not to' or 'it is not true that he wants to.' Only in the former case does the expression convey a determinate state of wanting, the state of what used to be called 'nilling' something. It is also usually in this sense that 'not wanting to' is spoken of as the cause of something. The mere absence of a determinate will about something gives a man a non-fortuitous causal role with respect to it only in very special cases, cases probably not contemplated in (though not excluded by) the ordinary consideration of the term 'voluntary.' At the same time, even in these cases, to the extent that the thing is somehow voluntary in relation to the man, he is also somehow a cause of it; and the ascription of voluntariness is still relative to his capacity for wanting and not wanting, willing and nilling.

In relation to the general notion of 'wanting,' at least two doubts may be raised about the position that the voluntary is chiefly what someone does or effects. The consideration of these, in the rest of this section and in the following one, will help define the position more sharply.

1. The Wanted and the Possible

The first is that someone may very well want or not want (nill) something which he is in no position to bring about (or prevent). Wanting seems to be a disposition that can bear equally on what someone can and cannot bring about. But if so, why should the voluntary be restricted to what someone can bring about? The easy reply would be that this is merely a peculiarity of the term 'voluntary.' In that case the position under scrutiny would have little more than linguistic interest. But does not the connection between the voluntary and what someone can bring about correspond, in fact, to something in the very nature of what is called 'wanting'? Is it really true that wanting is a disposition that can bear *equally* on what a person (thinks he) can and cannot bring about?

Even if wanting is not completely restricted to things which are to be brought about directly by the one who wants them, saying that he wants them still seems to connote at least a disposition to act 'toward' or 'in favor of' them. Thus, in the case of something which it is physically or morally impossible for someone to bring about, to say that he wants it must mean that he would bring it about if he could. It would be at least very difficult to understand what someone might mean in saying that he wants something which he himself considers to be in his power, if at the same time he takes no steps to bring it about. He could not really be 'wanting' it in the full sense. His disposition toward it must be only what Aquinas calls a *velleitas* (from the Latin *vellet*); i.e. it must be such that he merely 'would want' it if some condition were otherwise. *Velleitas* corresponds to one of the meanings of the English 'wish,' as when one says that he wishes that he did not have to take some medicine, or that some disaster had not happened, or that he could fly.

In fact, for Aquinas, one of the conditions vitiating the genuine want for something, turning it into a mere wish, is that the wanting subject consider it to be impossible to come about. Such a consideration simply suppresses the capacity to want the thing fully. This is because it suppresses the capacity to move toward it.[28]

In this regard it is noteworthy that in most of the English translations of the passage in which Aristotle argues that *prohairesis* (choice) cannot be the same as *boulesis* because *boulesis* can be of impossible things, for instance immortality, the term *boulesis* is rendered 'wish.' It is as though the translators felt uncomfortable with speaking of 'wanting' impossible things; and rightly so. Yet Aristotle also argues that whereas *prohairesis* is only of things done for the sake of an end, *boulesis* can also be of the end; and at least in most instances, a person's attitude toward the end for which he is choosing and acting is hardly well described as a mere wish. 'Wish' tends to connote a lack of seriousness, mere fancy, or in any case an attitude not immediately bearing on one's actual choices and actions.

Aquinas, having before him the term *voluntas* as the translation of *boulesis*, solves the problem differently. His interpretation is that while both *electio* (*prohairesis*) and *voluntas* are of the good, *voluntas* can bear on the good taken 'absolutely,' whereas *electio* is only of goods regarded as in one's power to bring about. By this he seems to mean that *voluntas* can be of things considered in abstraction from their real possibility, things not yet determinately judged to be possible or impossible. For instance, so long as someone thinks only of what immortality is, he may somehow want it; but once he considers that it is impossible, his want turns into a mere wish.[29]

To be sure, nothing prevents someone from considering something as *somehow* possible, though not possible for *him* to bring about. In this case, he can still genuinely want it. But even in this case, must his wanting it not mean that he would have contributed to producing it if possible and necessary; that he does nothing to prevent it; and that he is inclined to conserve it and cultivate it, or at least to think about it or pay attention to it and to praise it, or honor it, or glorify it, as the case may be? All of these acts *are* voluntary in the sense of 'from' the will; and it would seem to be only by reference to a disposition for such acts that an object of this sort, one which a man has no hand in causing to come about, might nevertheless be called voluntary with respect to him.

---

28. I–II, q. 13, a. 5 ad 1; see also *De malo* q. 16, a. 3 ad 9.
29. *In III Eth.* lect. v, § 443–44; see Charles Taylor, *The Explanation of Behaviour*, p. 61.

It might be objected that this account fails to do justice to the anxiety or frustration that a man may suffer in the face of the impossibility of something he judges desirable; for instance, not to die. The claim that he cannot really be wanting such a thing seems contrary to human psychology. If he did not really want it, why his frustration?

In fact this objection really supports the position that genuine wanting is always a disposition to act in favor of the thing wanted. What the objection brings to light is that, as suggested by Aquinas's reading of the passage on *boulesis* of impossible things, the simple or absolute consideration of something is distinct from the consideration of whether and how it might actually come about. The simple consideration of something is already sufficient to make wanting it possible; and precisely because wanting it is an inclination toward its realization, the wanting of it naturally leads to the investigation of whether and how it might come about. This investigation is a kind of preparation for movement toward it. The frustration produced by the discovery of its impossibility is nothing other than the 'forced' interruption of that preparation. Moreover, nothing prevents the mind from subsequently returning to the simple consideration of the thing, in abstraction from its real possibility or impossibility, and so repeating the process just described; hence the man's frustration may be a more or less enduring condition. The point is merely that so *long as* he considers the object to be impossible, he 'must' stop wanting it, because it can no longer seem wantable to him, something toward which he might tend.

Indeed, if he was able to start wanting it at all, this is only because one of the meanings of 'possible' is 'conceivable.' To the extent that something is merely the object of simple consideration, to that extent it still seems possible, or at least does not seem impossible, i.e. there is no determinate judgment as to its possibility or impossibility; and only for that reason can it also seem wantable. There is no such thing as wanting hot cold soup, though of course one may want hot soup and at the same time also want cold soup.

2. Wanting and the Involuntary

A more serious and more instructive objection to the position that the (apparently) impossible cannot be fully wanted arises from the notion of the involuntary. The involuntary is what comes about against someone's will. So it presupposes a want for something, at least the want that the thing which comes about involuntarily not come about. Now surely it is possible for someone to foresee or expect that something is going to happen against his will. His expectation may well be altogether certain. Likewise, it is obviously possible for someone to be aware that something contrary to his will is presently occurring or has already occurred. But both the certain expectation of something's occurring, and the awareness of its presently occurring or having occurred, seem to entail the belief that its not occurring is no longer possible. Yet if it is impossible to want what one considers to be impossible, then this belief will make it impossible to want the thing not to occur; and without the want that it not occur, its occurring cannot rightly be called involuntary.

The proper reply to this objection would seem to be simply that it must involve a somewhat imprecise notion of the involuntary. To be sure, the involuntariness of some occurrence must imply that it is an occurrence, or at least the *sort* of occurrence, which someone *previously* wanted not to occur. But to say that the involuntary is what happens against one's will can hardly mean that one must continue to want it not to happen even after becoming certain that it will happen or has happened. In the face of the occurrence of something a man wanted not to occur, his reaction always takes some form which implies that he is no longer able to go on wanting it not to occur. His reaction may be sadness, which is a kind of shrinking of vital activity and cessation of movement, produced by the deprivation of his object. It may be resignation, a sort of readjustment of his plans, expectations and wants that involves at least a reluctant acquiescence to the thing previously not wanted, a coming to terms with it. It may be anger, which although *almost* a continuation of his will for the thing not to occur, is not quite that; rather, it is a will for something else that compensates or vindicates him for the thing's occurrence.

Of course, each of these reactions also implies that the man retains some sort of dislike for or repugnance toward the thing. This repugnance was the root of his previously wanting the thing not to happen. It is surely a consideration of this sort that leads Aquinas to be careful to say that there can be no *perfect* wanting of the impossible. There can certainly be some sort of appetitive disposition toward it, a disposition which may well have significant consequences, as we have just seen. But in describing the imperfect appetite for the impossible as a *velleitas*, St Thomas clearly wants to stress that appetitive dispositions, even imperfect ones, always contain the note of tendency, movement or action; for the object of a *velleitas* is what one 'would' want, and what one 'would' want is what one would try to get or bring about. In Anscombe's well-known words, 'the primitive sign of wanting is "trying to get."'[30] What makes *velleitas* a merely imperfect disposition is precisely that no movement or action is apt to follow upon it.

Although what has been said is sufficient to remove the objection based on the notion of the involuntary, there is a further consideration that can be drawn from the notion of the involuntary which also serves to indicate that unqualified wanting can only be of possible things. This is the consideration that involuntariness belongs properly only to things which are by nature able to be or not to be, contingent things.

The term 'involuntary' surely means something more specific than whatever one 'wishes' or 'would want' not to occur. Otherwise more things would be called

---

30. *Intention*, p. 68.

involuntary than actually are. For instance, although someone may wish to have been born in another time or place, or with a different hereditary endowment, no one calls the circumstances of a person's birth involuntary. Similarly, Aristotle holds that growing old and dying cannot rightly be termed involuntary—nor, for that matter, voluntary.[31]

He certainly does not mean by this that a man is always indifferent to growing old and dying. Rather, at least part of what he means must be that it makes sense to apply the term 'involuntary' only to things which a man might at some time have genuinely wanted not to come about. Since things like the conditions of one's birth and the natural process of aging are already determined to come about before a man can acquire any appetitive disposition toward them at all, they cannot properly be called voluntary or involuntary. What is involuntary must be the sort of thing which by nature, and also at some time relative to the one to whom it happens involuntarily, is possible not to happen. It must only *become* impossible not to happen, owing to the emergence of some special condition which is itself contingent.

This would explain why Aquinas, for whom the relation between the wanted and the voluntary is, if anything, even closer than it is for Aristotle, can agree that death from old age is not involuntary, and yet have said earlier that it is possible to want to be immortal. There is never a time when it is really possible for a man to be immortal. His capacity to want this derives merely from the possibility of considering it in abstraction from its real possibility or impossibility. In this case the frustration of his will does not come about through any change in the condition of the thing wanted, but only through a change in his own consideration of it. Hence his being mortal cannot properly be called involuntary.

We might say that being 'against' someone's will requires that he be genuinely prepared to try to avoid it. It needs to have some real resistance to run up against. The discovery that death is impossible to avoid simply prevents a man from becoming fully prepared to try to avoid it or even to look for a way to avoid it. The reason why growing old and dying cannot be involuntary, Aquinas explains, is that the involuntary falls within the class of things that are by nature in our power; they become involuntary when they cease to be in our power through violence, that is, contrary to nature.

More will be said about the restrictions on the use of the term 'involuntary' in the next sub-section.

---

31. *Nicomachean Ethics* V, ch. 8, 1135a34. He must mean precisely dying of old age; obviously violent and early death can be involuntary—and voluntary. For a very strong argument in favor of regarding 'voluntary' and 'involuntary' as good translations of Aristotle's *hekousion* and *akousion*, see Meyer, *Aristotle on Moral Responsibility*, pp. 9–14.

3. Voluntary Action and Voluntary Passion

The second difficulty with the position that the voluntary is chiefly what someone does or effects is that not only what someone does, but also what is done to him, is often spoken of as voluntary relative to him. Not only actions but also passions, and therefore also states, qualities, dispositions, etc. can somehow be voluntary. They can be undergone or possessed 'willingly.' Such things obviously play a significant role in human life.

It is in view of these things that up to now the voluntary has been described as only 'chiefly' what someone does or brings about voluntarily. Not all voluntary things fit neatly within this description. Nevertheless, it still seems possible to say that the voluntariness of something always implies some sort of causality on the part of the one relative to whom the thing is voluntary, even if it is not the kind of causality according to which one would say that he 'did' it or that he 'brought it about.' This point can be established by way of returning to the notion of the involuntary and considering what the involuntary and the voluntary have in common.

We have already seen that of things which do not come about voluntarily, only some can be called involuntary. Not even all of the things which a man finds repugnant or which he 'would' avoid if he could are involuntary. To be involuntary it must at least be contingent, both in itself and relative to the person in question. This removes things that happen by necessity, and things that happen by nature, from the domain of the involuntary. It also removes things that can *only* happen by luck or fortune relative to the person in question, such as being born wealthy or poor. There is no such thing as trying to bring these things about (for oneself) or avoid them; hence they cannot be spoken of as happening 'against' one's efforts and one's will.

But even the restriction of the involuntary to contingent things seems to leave the domain too broad. There are things which are genuinely able to happen or not to happen and which a man may actually want not to happen, but which, when they do happen, are nevertheless not called involuntary with respect to him. For instance, a soccer fan may want a certain team to win the World Cup, but it would be very strange to describe the team's loss as involuntary *with respect to the fan*. It would only be called involuntary with respect to the team itself.

The use of the term 'voluntary' corresponds directly to these restrictions on the involuntary. No one calls being born wealthy voluntary. The victory of the fan's team would not be called voluntary with respect to him. The range of the voluntary is more restricted than the range of things which a person might genuinely want.

What is the significant difference here? The example of the soccer fan might suggest that it depends on whether the event happens *to* the person himself. It is not the fan who wins or loses, but the team. But this suggestion is contradicted by the Aristotelian position that growing old and dying cannot be called voluntary. These obviously affect the person himself.

The real solution would seem to be something suggested by the fact that Aristotle says that things like growing old and dying are not only not *involuntary* but also not *voluntary*. This seems odd at first, since normally no one would be tempted to think that someone grew old and died of old age voluntarily, because this is normally not something that people want. But what Aristotle seems to mean is that even if someone did want it, it could not be called voluntary. Why not? Is it not because this is just not the sort of thing about which a man's will can make any difference? Even if he (or anyone else, for that matter) wants it, his wanting it can contribute nothing to its coming about, any more than his not wanting it can contribute to avoiding it. By contrast, it is normally possible to take steps both to bring about and to avoid deaths by other causes. This does not mean that the efforts will always succeed. But it does mean that it makes sense to ask whether such deaths are voluntary or involuntary.

In other words, both the voluntary and the involuntary only concern those sorts of things about which a man's will *can* make a difference, at least generally speaking or in principle. Something comes about involuntarily only when it is also the kind of thing that might come about voluntarily. Those sorts of things are voluntary or involuntary which, under normal circumstances, it is in a man's own power to do something about. Naturally, to say that a thing is in a man's power to do something about does not mean that he enjoys full control over it. If he enjoyed full control over it, it could never come about involuntarily, since that implies that at some point he has lost control over it. But it also implies that it came about 'despite' him, and this means that his attitude toward it is not always altogether negligible as regards its coming about or not.

> Many of the things that are not in our power are not involuntary; for there are many natural things that we do and undergo knowingly, for instance, grow old or die, of which nevertheless none is voluntary or involuntary; for each of these [the voluntary and the involuntary] is with respect to the things that are apt to be in our power. But if it happens, through violence, that one of these things [apt to be in our power] not be in our power, then it is called involuntary.[32]

---

32. *Multa quae non sunt in nobis non sunt involuntaria; multa enim sunt naturalia quae et operamur et patimur scientes, puta senescere vel mori; quorum tamen nullum est voluntarium vel involuntarium, quia utrumque eorum est circa ea quae sunt nata in nobis esse. Si autem accidat per violentiam quod aliquid eorum non sit in nobis, tunc dicitur involuntarium* (*In V Eth.* lect. xiii, § 1037). The Leonine editor conjectures the insertion of *non* after *ea quae*, apparently thinking that *utrumque eorum* refers back to *senescere vel mori*. But, besides contradicting the entire manuscript tradition, this obscures the sense of the rest of the passage. Kenny (*Aristotle's Theory of the Will*, pp. 8–12) offers a reading of the *Eudemian Ethics* II, ch. 6 according to which Aristotle would be making a distinction between things 'in our power to do or not,' these being voluntary, and things only 'in our power to do' but not 'in our power not to do'; these would be natural. ('In our power' translates *eph' hemin*, or Aquinas's *in nobis*; another rendering might be 'up to us.') Kenny supports this by appeal to *Nicomachean Ethics* V, ch. 8, 1135a34 (which, on independent and quite strong grounds, he thinks originally went together with the *Eudemian Ethics*); this is the passage Aquinas is commenting on in the above quotation. Aristotle

Now if it is true in general that the voluntary and the involuntary concern things which a man can generally do something about, then it is true not only of things which a man does but also of things which a man suffers. Not everything a man undergoes can reasonably be termed voluntary or involuntary. Not even everything he undergoes gladly or with sorrow can be so termed. Of course, it need not be the kind of thing that he himself can do or bring about; there are some things which it is possible to undergo only by the action of someone else, for instance to receive a gift. But it must be the kind of thing that he can try to avoid undergoing, just as voluntary and involuntary actions must be the kinds of things that one can try to do. For instance, if it is possible to kill a man by accident *and* involuntarily, it is also possible to kill a man by trying.

In particular, to suffer something *voluntarily* implies at least that it was in your power to try to avoid suffering it, and that you did not exercise this power. That is, you must have consented to it;[33] and consent is relative to what is in your power.[34] So even if it is not something that you 'did,' it is still called voluntary only relative to something you could have done, namely, the action you might have undertaken in order to avoid it. Granted, since you did not undertake that action, this is a genuine instance of something voluntary which is not the effect of what someone positively does. But this seems only to bring to light a peculiar feature of the voluntary, one already noted by Aristotle: if it is possible to do

---

says there that the involuntary is 'what is done in ignorance, or though not done in ignorance is not in the agent's power, or is done under compulsion.' Aristotle then adds an explanatory remark: 'for many natural processes too we knowingly perform or undergo, none of which is either voluntary or involuntary; e.g. growing old or dying.' Kenny judges that this remark is a gloss on 'or though not done in ignorance is not in the agent's power,' as though to say growing old and dying are not involuntary, because they are in our power (though not voluntary, since not in our power to do or not). This reading makes Kenny draw a very strained distinction between two senses of 'cause' in the *Eudemian Ethics* passage; it also puts the text quoted in direct contradiction with *Nicomachean Ethics* III, ch. 4, 1113b7–8. Kenny justifies it by saying that if Aristotle thought that growing old and dying were not in our power, then they would be involuntary according to the definition given in the text quoted. But his reading makes the addition 'or is done under compulsion' in that text completely superfluous; for what is done under compulsion is certainly not in our power, and if Aristotle thinks that natural processes are in our power, then what is done under compulsion is the only thing not in our power. So the text would mean 'the involuntary is what is done in ignorance, or though not in ignorance is not in the agent's power, or is not in the agent's power.' Aquinas's reading, which seems to be much more natural, takes 'or is done under compulsion' as a *correction* to 'is not in our power,' i.e. as meaning 'or rather, is done under compulsion.' This makes the ensuing remark aimed at explaining why this correction was necessary. We cannot identify the involuntary with what is not in our power, because natural processes are not in our power, and yet they are neither voluntary nor involuntary. Then 'in our power' would mean, as usual, 'under our control,' 'up to us.' For a similar account of Aristotle's view, see Meyer, *Aristotle on Moral Responsibility*, appendix II: ' "Up to Us" and the Internal Origin,' pp. 185–89.

33. See I–II, q. 6, a. 6 ad 1; q. 6, a. 5 ad 2.

34. I–II, q. 15, a. 3: *consensus nominat applicationem appetitivi motus ad aliquid praeexistens in potestate applicantis*.

something voluntarily, then it is also possible not to do it, voluntarily. Besides, we have already included 'not acting' within the domain of things that are voluntary in the sense of being 'because of' a man's wanting something.[35] It is still attributed to him relative to his having the nature of an agent. In short, passion undergone voluntarily is not passion to the fullest degree; it retains something of the nature of action.

> Action, according to the very notion of it, proceeds from the agent; whereas passion, according to its proper notion, is from another; whence the same thing, in the same respect, cannot be agent and patient, as it says in the third and eighth books of the *Physics*. But the proper principle of acting in men is the will. And therefore, properly and *per se* a man does that which he does wanting to; and contrarily, a man properly suffers that which he suffers apart from [*praeter*] his will. For insofar as he is willing, a principle is from him, and therefore, insofar as he is so, he is more agent than patient.[36]

It seems reasonable to maintain, then, that the term 'voluntary' applies primarily to objects of action and movement. Normally it refers to things of which the voluntary subject is the principal agent. But even when it refers to something whose principal cause is something else, e.g. to what someone suffers voluntarily, it still tends to present the thing as the object or term of some type of action or movement initiated voluntarily, and at least as something which was in one's power to try to avoid and which one did not try to avoid precisely because one wanted it or something connected with it. Voluntariness, then, always involves a relation to a certain kind of agent-cause, even if not always to one that has positively exercised its causal power.[37]

4. *The Voluntary, Conduct and Consent*

One final observation before going on to the next section. We have been taking it for granted here that voluntariness, in the proper sense, is something exclusively human; a human act, or piece of conduct, and a voluntary act are the same. But some interpreters, for instance Anscombe, maintain that Aristotle's

---

35. See I, q. 41, a. 2 on 'from the will' vs. 'with the will.' Aquinas denies that what happens merely 'with' or 'according to' someone's will, in no way depending upon it (at least negatively, as a thing he could willingly prevent), is properly called voluntary.

36. *Actio, de sui ratione, procedit ab agente; passio autem, secundum propriam rationem, est ab alio, unde non potest esse idem, secundum idem, agens et patiens, ut dicitur in III et VIII Physic. Principium autem proprium agendi in hominibus est voluntas. Et ideo illud proprie et per se homo facit quod volens facit, et e contrario illud proprie homo patitur quod praeter voluntatem suam patitur; quia inquantum est volens, principium est ex ipso, et ideo, inquantum est huiusmodi, magis est agens quam patiens* (II–II, q. 59, a. 3).

37. By a different route, Kenny arrives at what seems to be the same conclusion: 'the form of description "A is bringing it about that p" is the fundamental one for the description of voluntary human action' (*Action, Emotion and Will*, p. 183).

'voluntary' (*hekousion*) is not convertible with 'conduct' or *praxis*, since Aristotle in the *Nicomachean Ethics* says that babies and beasts 'share in' the voluntary.[38] If it were not for this, it would be fairly easy to identify his 'voluntary' with 'human action' or 'conduct,' *praxis*. As noted earlier, it is no objection to this identification that he says in the same place that since the voluntary is not always deliberated, it is not the same as the chosen; for although the primary sort of *praxis* is something deliberated and chosen, secondary forms of it need not be.[39]

Aquinas handles the remark about beasts and babies by taking 'share in' very strictly: what babies and beasts have is an imperfect degree of the voluntary.[40] But whatever Aristotle's reason might be for attributing the voluntary to babies and beasts, it does not follow that he thinks that for a person having (as we say) the use of reason, what he does can be voluntary without being what we call a human act. For one thing, Aristotle makes voluntariness a sufficient condition for praise and blame.[41] He also makes a condition for voluntariness one's having the thing 'in one's power.'[42] But having something in one's power is the same thing as having the possibility of deliberating and exercising choice about it.[43] For Aquinas, this suffices for making an act voluntary and a piece of human action.[44]

However, as indicated in the passage quoted at the end of the previous chapter, Aquinas also extends voluntariness to things other than what a man does, things other than someone's positive acts. Things a man does not do, when he could and should do them, and things resulting from a man's not doing what would prevent them, when he could and should have done that, are also voluntary. Aristotle would no doubt have agreed with this; but there appears to be something lacking in his technical vocabulary to account for it, namely, a term for 'consent' (a Stoic notion).

This lack comes out in Aristotle's explanation of what is involuntary in the sense of forced or violent. The violent, he says, is that whose moving principle is outside, with the one who suffers it contributing nothing.[45] Without the notion of consent, it is very difficult to give an accurate statement of what it must mean for the one who suffers to 'contribute' something. Aristotle is mainly concerned to ensure that things done out of desire of an external good, or out of fear of an external danger, be excluded from the domain of the involuntary. But in fact it is not necessary that the subject make any positive outward or 'physical' contribution at all, in order for what he undergoes to be undergone voluntarily and so not

---

38. III, ch. 4, 1111b9. See Anscombe, 'Action, Intention and "Double Effect," ' p. 13.
39. See above, Chapter 1, n. 77.
40. I–II, q. 6, a. 2.
41. *Nicomachean Ethics* III, ch. 1, 1109b27.
42. Ibid., III. ch. 7, 1113b22, 27; 1114b19.
43. Ibid., III. ch. 5, 1112a31; 1113a8; ch. 7, 1113b4.
44. See I, q. 49, a. 1 ad 3; I–II, q. 6, a. 3 ad 3; q. 71, a. 5 ad 3; q. 74, a. 7 ad 2, 3, 4; q. 109, a. 8.
45. *Nicomachean Ethics* III, ch. 1, 1109b35, 1110b2.

by violence. Perhaps no such contribution was necessary.[46] On the other hand, neither is it proof that he underwent it voluntarily, that he did *not* do anything positive outwardly to *prevent* it, even if he knew of it; for he may also have known that there was nothing he could do to prevent it, and so he did not even bother to try. Perhaps it is necessary that he have at least looked for a way to prevent it; he must have been disposed to prevent it if he could. But to be disposed *not* to prevent something is to consent to it.[47]

The point is important, because for Aquinas, merely consenting to something, letting it happen, can be conduct and proof of one's character to the highest degree. This not only holds for bad conduct; in fact, if one's bad conduct consists solely in consenting to something that one should not consent to, without any positive striving for it, then (though it may be what Thomas calls a mortal sin) such conduct is less bad, and less a sign of a vicious character, than in the contrary case. But there are also cases of things that a man should consent to, though he should not in any way strive for them; and in such cases his consent may be both exceedingly good conduct and proof of the highest degree of character. For instance, Aquinas judges that, *ceteris paribus*, tolerating takes more fortitude than attacking, and that the most perfect sign of charity is martyrdom.[48] In fact, consent would appear to be one of the better terms for expressing the minimal condition for voluntariness generally. At least, Aquinas is willing to let it stand as the distinguishing mark of the voluntary. 'Actions are called voluntary from the fact that we consent to them.'[49]

C. THE DISTINCTION OF UNDERSTANDING AND WILLING

1. 'Acts' of Will and Propositional Attitudes

Now, none of what has been said depends strictly upon a claim that to be voluntary is to be an event which is preceded and caused by a certain other event

---

46. Kenny (*Aristotle's Theory of the Will*, pp. 29–30) shows both the lack of clarity in Aristotle's account and the grounds for saying that Aristotle would agree with Aquinas's position. 'Without . . . positive contribution on the part of an agent it seems that something forced might fail to be involuntary in other ways: perhaps the agent fails to resist when he could; or, though he can do nothing to prevent the episode, he may be pleased when it happens. A man carried by strong winds to the port of his choice may be forced there, but not unwillingly so. In the light of what Aristotle later says about taking pleasure in actions performed in error (1110b20) he should perhaps regard such cases as not involuntary.'

47. Thus in his commentary, Aquinas judges it necessary to clarify Aristotle's definition of the violent by explicitly excluding any merely interior act of the will: *Non omne tamen cuius principium est extra est violentum, sed solum quod ita est a principio extrinseco, quod appetitus interior non concurrit in idem. Et hoc est quod dicit, quod oportet tale violentum esse in quo nihil conferat, scilicet per proprium appetitum, homo* (*In III Eth.* lect. i, § 387). He does not use the term 'consent,' but *concurrit* amounts to the same.

48. II–II, q. 123, a. 6; q. 124, a. 3.

49. I–II, q. 15, a. 4 ad 2.

called an 'act of will.' It would be sufficient to think of 'willing' as a certain kind of intentional disposition, that is, a certain way of being related and ordered, or inclined, toward something; namely, through the knowledge of it or belief about it. To say that a man was a voluntary cause of something is not to assert the occurrence in him of some act of will that caused it. Rather, it is to specify the nature of the causal relation or order between *him* and what he caused, the manner in which what he caused arose from him. The discussion of 'acts' of will belongs to the *explanation* of that order, not to the identification of it.

A great deal of the literature on action-theory, in analytical philosophy, has concerned the existence and explanatory value of 'acts of will.' It is not necessary to rehearse the entire history of this discussion here, but a few remarks are in order.[50] Much of the early controversy centered on the question of how you know you have such acts. Ryle, Wittgenstein and Anscombe all showed cogently that they certainly cannot consist in, or be known in the manner of, Humean 'impressions.'[51] This was not regarded as fatal to their existence (except by Humeans). Why it was not will be addressed in a moment.

Another part of the controversy concerned the difficulty of incorporating such acts into the Humean doctrine of causation as the instantiation of a causal law. Here the camp remains divided, even among those who grant the existence of acts of will. Some of those who hold to such a doctrine think that such acts can be incorporated into it, in one way or another; others deny that they can, and maintain that they have no place in the 'causal' explanation of events, but belong to a distinct order of discourse: that of reasons, motives, character and so forth. Still others simply deny that causal explanation is always explanation by appeal to causal laws. I have already expressed my agreement with this last view, and will take it for granted here.

As just mentioned, the fact that acts of will cannot be assimilated to Humean impressions, or in general to 'events' in the inner flow of consciousness or to perceptible mental 'states,' has not led to a universal refusal among analytical philosophers to acknowledge such acts. This is simply because many of them deny that everything in our mental life is an impression or a sensation, or reducible to one. Russell's notion of 'propositional attitudes' has been particularly influential here. A propositional attitude is an attitude taken by a subject toward

---

50. A good account of it, up to the date of the article, is given by MacIntyre in 'The Antecedents of Action.' Much of the following discussion is drawn from Donagan's *Choice*. See also Arregui, 'Wittgenstein on Voluntary Actions.'

51. Hume in fact defines the will as 'the internal impression we feel and are conscious of, when we knowingly give rise to any new motion of our body, or new perception of our mind' (*A Treatise on Human Nature*, book II, part III, sect, i, p. 181). Thus the attacks are directed against a conception of acts of will as internal events that merely accompany acts 'knowingly given rise to,' as though it were the presence of such events, rather than the very fact of being 'knowingly given rise to,' that makes such acts to be voluntary. 'Giacchè la volontà come oggetto dell'esperienza si manifesta appunto nell'esperienza dell'«io» proprio, come una causa dell'azione . . . non può comunque essere identificata con l'impressione che accompagna il suscitarsi delle azioni' (Wojtyła, 'Il ruolo dirigente,' p. 99).

an object whose proper mode of being presented to him is in a proposition. That such attitudes cannot be reduced to impressions or sensations is shown by the fact that their objects cannot be. For it is proper to a proposition to present itself as true, and truth cannot be sensed, but only understood. The same therefore holds for attitudes towards objects expressed in propositions.

Many of those who hold that there are acts of will defend their view by maintaining that propositional attitudes may be divided into cognitive and appetitive, or into ways of apprehending (or failing to apprehend) the truth of a proposition and ways of being inclined toward or away from its truth. The various forms that the latter may take are the various types of possible acts of will.

Now, propositional attitudes are essentially attitudes toward the truth or falsity of the propositions expressing their objects. To believe, for example, is to accept some proposition as true. Hence conceiving acts of will as propositional attitudes makes their immediate objects to be the contents of propositions, not 'real things.' Nonetheless, this is not thought to deprive them of a real causal role. For even if propositions are not 'things,' they are about things, though not always present or actually existing things. To be inclined toward the truth of a proposition entails being inclined toward making what it expresses be the case. Thus the core of Donagan's theory of human action is that 'actions are doings, explained by their doers' taking attitudes to propositions about them.'[52]

Aquinas's notion of the object of wanting, we may observe, bears some resemblance to this. For in his view too, wanting bears on 'things' only via a medium.

> Since every inclination follows upon some form, natural appetite follows upon a form existing in nature; whereas the sensitive appetite, and also the intellectual or rational appetite, which is called wanting, follows upon an apprehended form. Therefore, just as that toward which natural appetite tends is a good existing in the thing, so that toward which animal or voluntary appetite tends is an apprehended good.[53]

An objection and reply in this article show that he regards the scope of wanting to be as broad as that of thought.

> [Objection] Good and being are convertible. But wanting is not only of beings, but also of non-beings; for we sometimes want not to walk and not to speak. We also sometimes want future things, which are not beings in act. So wanting is not only of the good.[54]

---

52. *Choice*, p. 20.

53. *Cum omnis inclinatio consequatur aliquam formam, appetitus naturalis consequitur formam in natura existentem, appetitus autem sensitivus, vel etiam intellectivus seu rationalis, qui dicitur voluntas, sequitur formam apprehensam. Sicut igitur id in quod tendit appetitus naturalis, est bonum existens in re; ita id in quod tendit appetitus animalis vel voluntarius, est bonum apprehensum* (I–II, q. 8, a. 1).

54. *Bonum et ens convertuntur. Sed voluntas non solum est entium, sed etiam non entium, volumus enim quandoque non ambulare et non loqui. Volumus etiam interdum quaedam futura, quae non sunt entia in actu. Ergo voluntas non tantum est boni* (I–II, q. 8, a. 1 obj. 3).

[Reply] That which is not a being in the nature of things is taken as a being in reason; whence negations and privations are called beings of reason. In this way too, future things, insofar as they are apprehended, are beings. So, insofar as they are beings of this sort, they are apprehended under the aspect of good; and it is thus that wanting tends toward them.[55]

The will can bear on anything capable of having some being through the intellect's apprehension, anything about which there can be truth or falsity.

However, the nature of the mediacy according to which the will bears upon 'real things,' for Aquinas, is not entirely the same as that which obtains in the doctrine of will as a propositional attitude. The importance of this difference will become more and more apparent as we proceed. For Aquinas, the will is brought to bear on things by way of a medium, the intellect's apprehension; but this does not mean that the will bears on things only remotely, by bearing first and immediately on the intellect's apprehension. The doctrine that the will is a propositional attitude, on the other hand, makes something pertaining to the apprehension itself to be the principal object of the will.

The will's proper object is what Aquinas calls the good. But the good, he says, is 'in things'; whereas truth, the proper object of understanding, is in the mind. To say that truth is the proper object of understanding, then, is to say that what is primarily and most properly intelligible is something in the mind.

> This therefore is what is understood primarily and through itself: that which the intellect conceives within itself about the thing understood, whether that [conception] be a definition or a proposition. . . . And what is thus conceived by the intellect is called an interior word.[56]

By contrast, although what is wanted is always something understood, i.e. something gets wanted only through getting understood, nevertheless what is primarily and most properly wantable is *not* something pertaining to its existence in the mind or belonging to it *qua* the content of a proposition. That is, although wanting (say) for something to happen is also wanting that the proposition asserting its happening be true, what is primarily wantable is that it happen. That the proposition be true is wantable only as a consequence. This is what it means to say that the proper object of the will, the good, is 'in things.'

Aquinas's reason for saying this is precisely that he conceives wanting as a disposition of agent-causality. What it is primarily about is therefore what it pri-

---

55. *Illud quod non est ens in rerum natura, accipitur ut ens in ratione, unde negationes et privationes dicuntur entia rationis. Per quem etiam modum futura, prout apprehenduntur, sunt entia. Inquantum igitur sunt huiusmodi entia, apprehenduntur sub ratione boni, et sic voluntas in ea tendit* (I–II, q. 8, a. 1 ad 3).

56. *Hoc ergo est primo et per se intellectum, quod intellectus in seipso concipit de re intellecta, sive illud sit definitio, sive enuntiatio. . . . Hoc autem sic ab intellectu conceptum dicitur verbum interius* (De pot. q. 9, a. 5). See also I, q. 16, arts. 1–2.

marily tends to effect. But its primary effect cannot possibly be the truth of a proposition. An agent can make a proposition true only remotely, by making things to be as the proposition states them to be. (To be sure, the truth of a proposition does have a cause, namely, its subject's being as it asserts;[57] but this is not an *agent*-cause.)

Anscombe proposes a type of truth, which she calls 'practical truth,' that would make it in some way true to say that what the will primarily bears upon is truth. Practical truth is the truth pertaining to practical knowledge; and the truth pertaining to practical knowledge is not a feature of the knowledge, but of what the knowledge is knowledge of.[58] It is the action that is true or false, in this sense, by conforming or not conforming to what the agent had in mind (assuming that what he had in mind was truly good). But this is no objection to Aquinas, since this sort of truth is not the truth of a proposition.[59]

2. The Assimilation of Willing to Understanding

The practice of speaking of willing as a type of propositional attitude, then, at least gives the impression of a notable *assimilation* of willing to understanding. This impression can be corroborated. For instance, it is a striking feature of Anscombe's account of intention, in *Intention*, that it is very difficult to say what she might take to be the *difference* between intention and 'practical knowledge.' She gives no very clear indication as to what intention might add to the apprehension of the plan embodied by an intentional action.[60]

In saying this about Anscombe's *Intention*, I do not wish to suggest that she positively favors the kind of assimilation of willing to understanding that I am trying to signal. On the contrary, she gives every indication of opposing it; she does so, in part, precisely by insisting on the great difference between speculative and practical knowledge. Her stress on the intimate connection between intention and practical knowledge is an extremely important correction to the (Humean) view according to which an 'act of will' is merely another 'impression,' accompanying cognition (which is conceived on the speculative model) and providing the causal link to action. And in fact, she positively rejects what seems to me to be another sign of the tendency toward the assimilation. This is the importance given to the question of how acts of will are properly expressed in *speech*.[61]

---

57. See I, q. 16, a. 8 ad 4: *sessio Socratis, quae est causa veritatis huius propositionis, 'Socrates sedet.'*
58. *Intention*, p. 57; 'Thought and Action in Aristotle,' pp. 76–77.
59. Aquinas allows using the term 'truth' in this way, but it is not what *he* means by 'practical truth.'
60. See also her 'Will and Emotion,' p. 107: 'a positive act of mine is voluntary, not because it is accompanied or preceded by an act of will, but because it is done by me either for its own sake or for the sake of something else. This new dimension of "What for?" enters into the description of the act and belongs to the *intelligence* of the agent' (my emphasis).
61. See Donagan, *Choice*, pp. 141–45. Indeed, at least in Donagan's account (p. 141), this question arises directly from the characterization of acts of will as propositional attitudes. The

This question is not how one can speak about such acts. The answer to that would be simple: by giving names to them, by instituting conventional signs for them. The question is in what way linguistic utterances might *constitute* expressions of them, or serve as 'natural' signs of them. The question may or may not be reasonable; Anscombe refers it to Wittgenstein, but she herself evidently thinks it based on a misunderstanding.[62] In any case, the importance given to it is a sign that it is thought that what acts of will are primarily about is what finds its proper expression or manifestation in speech, namely, truth and falsehood.

Thus, one favored answer to the question is along the very lines of Anscombe's account of the difference between the kinds of truth pertaining to speculative and practical knowledge. This answer is that the expression of appetitive attitudes resides in utterances whose 'direction of fit' with the world, or with 'things,' is the reverse of that which belongs to expressions of cognitive attitudes.[63] Utterances that are materially the same may possess either 'direction of fit.' For instance, the same utterance may express either an expectation (a cognitive attitude) or an intention (an appetitive attitude). It expresses an expectation if the speaker takes it as something to be measured against the way things turn out; it expresses an intention if the speaker takes it as something against which the way things turn out is to be measured. In other words, in expressions of cognitive attitudes, what is true or false is the expression itself, according as it does or does not fit the thing; in expressions of appetitive attitudes, what is true or false is the thing, according as it does or does not fit the expression. Once again, it is difficult to see, on this account, what difference there might be between an intention and (say) an idea for something, a plan.

Yet another sign of the assimilation is the difficulty that is felt to be posed by an objection which argues that appetitive attitudes, considered as really distinct from cognitive ones, are merely superfluous. The objection is that everything they are meant to account for can be accounted for by cognitive attitudes of a particular sort, to wit, cognitive attitudes about what is *good*. On this view, for instance, wanting something is not really anything distinct from believing that it is good for you.

---

question is, if they are propositional attitudes, what is the way of expressing propositions that corresponds to them?

62. 'Intention appears to be something that we can express, but which brutes (which e.g. do not give orders) can *have*, though lacking any distinct expression of intention. For a cat's movements in stalking a bird are hardly to be called an expression of intention. One might as well call a car's stalling the *expression* of its being about to stop. Intention is unlike emotion in this respect, that the expression of it is purely conventional; we might say "linguistic," if we will allow certain bodily movements with a conventional meaning to be included in language. Wittgenstein seems to me to have gone wrong in speaking of the "natural expression of an intention" (*Philosophical Investigations*, § 647)' (*Intention*, § 2, p. 5).

63. See Donagan, *Choice*, pp. 144–45.

Donagan shows the typical way of addressing this difficulty,[64] which is by appeal to special cases in which an action explained by a belief about what is good cannot be *sufficiently* explained by it, i.e. cannot be reduced to it. The phenomenon of incontinence is a case often adduced. Here it is thought necessary to posit something like 'will,' distinct from both reason and passion, in order to explain how it is that one and the same subject, in whom reason and passion are in conflict, can follow now one, now the other. However, Davidson, who denies a real distinction between appetitive and cognitive attitudes, has argued convincingly that even in incontinent action, the agent is acting under a (temporary) belief that what he is doing is best; that is, he is acting for a reason.[65] Donagan, who accepts this argument, adduces a different case, which he borrows from Bratman. This is the case of 'Buridan's Ass' decisions, i.e. decisions between alternatives neither of which is *intrinsically* preferable to the other; decisions that we might call purely 'arbitrary' (though etymologically, 'arbitrary' *means* 'a matter of decision'). His use of this case to refute Davidson is weak,[66] but the point here is a more general one. It concerns what this way of arguing for the existence of 'acts of will' shows about how such acts are conceived.

It shows that what is deemed necessary, in order to establish appetitive intellectual attitudes as really distinct from cognitive ones, is to demonstrate that cognitive attitudes are insufficient in a very specific way: in providing the *objects* of

---

64. *Choice*, pp. 146–56.

65. See 'How is Weakness of the Will Possible?,' *Essays*, pp. 21–42. His argument is not so far removed from Aquinas's position as it is often taken to be (by Davidson himself, for instance). It is based on two distinctions: (1) between a belief that something is best, 'all things considered,' and a belief that it is best relative to a particular goal (say, that of satisfying some passion); and (2) between 'all-out' beliefs and *prima facie* or 'as far as it goes' beliefs. The former is a distinction between a rational and a sub-rational belief about what is good, i.e. a belief based on rational principles of judgment and one based on sub-rational principles; the latter is a distinction between what you believe without qualification and what you merely acknowledge to be believable from a particular vantage-point, whether or not that vantage-point is *yours*. What one acts upon is always an *all-out* belief about what is best; but this may or may not coincide with what one believes to be best from the *particular* vantage-point of 'all things considered.' If it does not, then one's action is a case of incontinence.

66. His argument is based on the fact that, as Davidson acknowledges, a decision between alternatives whose intrinsic values are equal is arrived at only by adopting some extrinsic grounds. For Donagan, this means that such a decision is not reducible to a belief that the one decided upon is all-out better than the other (see previous note). But this is a misapplication of the concept of 'all-out beliefs.' What one acts upon, for Davidson, is not a belief that one's action is all-out best, but an all-out belief that it is best; that is, 'all-out' is not part of the predicate in the proposition believed, but a way of believing it. So Davidson's point is that in 'Buridan's Ass' cases, as there is no way to form an 'all-out' belief that one alternative is better than the other on the basis of the alternatives themselves, you adopt an extrinsic basis for doing so, say flipping a coin. If you cannot find a point of view from which one alternative is better, then you make one; and by adopting it, you form an all-out belief that one alternative is better. Aquinas is in complete agreement with this; he does not think that 'Buridan's Ass' cases serve to show that there is anything in a choice which is not in the judgment on which it depends (see I–II, q. 13, a. 6 obj. 3 and reply).

appetitive ones, or in providing the principle by which human actions are specified. Incontinence is adduced to show that sometimes we want things without believing that they are good; Buridan's Ass is adduced to show that sometimes we choose things without thinking that they are preferable. If, as is apparently the case, such attempts to demonstrate this are unsuccessful, then it is thought that there is no ground for a real distinction between the two sorts of attitudes; appetitive ones will be only a special set of cognitive ones. But what this implies is that, whether the distinction is affirmed or denied, it is taken for granted that the general nature of the *relation* established by the attitude, between its subject and its object, is the same for both types of attitude.

In other words, it is assumed that the distinction between the two, if it exists, must be shown by the irreducibility of the object of one to the object of the other. If something forms the object of one just in proportion as it also forms the object of the other, e.g. if you want something just in proportion as you think it to be good for you, then the two attitudes, wanting it and thinking it good for you, cannot be really distinct. This conclusion would not be drawn unless it were assumed that the two attitudes constitute the same kind of relation to something, or make something to be an 'object' of the mind in the same way. It makes no sense to posit two relations of the same kind, in the same subject, to the same object. And the reason why those that lose out, or get reduced to the other sort, are appetitive attitudes is that the kind of relation involved is in fact the kind proper to cognition: the relation of fit or conformity or correspondence.

3. How Aquinas Distinguishes Will and Intellect

Now, this is not at all how Aquinas conceives of the distinction between intellectual and volitional acts. For him, the distinction is generic, not specific. That is, it is *not* that they constitute fundamentally the same sort of relation, but apply to different things (or more precisely, different aspects of things). That is how, for example, the various powers of sense-cognition are distinguished, and how intellectual cognitive power is distinguished from sensitive. Rather, intellectual and volitional acts constitute fundamentally diverse types of relation. This is why they remain distinct even though they bear on the same thing, and even though one presupposes and is proportioned to the other.

Thus, in the course of enumerating the genera of powers of the soul, and after distinguishing the vegetative powers, which bear only upon the living thing's own body, from vital powers that also bear upon external things, St Thomas goes on to draw further general distinctions among the latter.

> Since it is necessary for one engaged in some activity to be in some way conjoined to the object with which his activity is concerned, it is necessary that an extrinsic thing, which is the object of an activity of the soul, be compared to the soul in a twofold way. In one way, according as it is apt to be conjoined to the

soul and to exist in the soul through its likeness. . . . And in the other way, according as the soul itself is inclined and tends toward the exterior thing.⁶⁷

The first sort of relation between the soul and things, he explains, includes two sorts of powers, the sensitive and the intellectual; these are distinguished according to the lesser or greater universality of their object, i.e. according to the extent of their capacity to become like other things. We may call these the 'assimilative' powers. The second includes appetitive and motor powers; these are distinguished according to the distinction between (1) the exterior thing considered as a goal, i.e. an object of intention, which initiates the motion toward it, and (2) the exterior thing considered as that in which the motion or operation initiated by the intention actually terminates. We may call these the 'tending' powers.⁶⁸

The fundamental basis for positing a real distinction between intellect and will, then, is for Aquinas the real distinction between the knowing or willing subject and the object of his knowing or willing. The soul is one thing, its object another. The duality of soul and object generates a duality of forms of operational relations: from the object to the soul, and from the soul to the object. There is an order between these relations: the one according to which the soul first operates about the object is the one by which the object is first in the soul, i.e. the relation of knowing. Intellect is 'closer to the essence' of the soul than is will.⁶⁹ If any sign is needed to show that knowing bears on things in a simpler, more uniform way, more purely according to the 'being of the soul' and less conditioned by the 'being of the things,' it would be this: to understand a thing is also to understand its contrary, whereas to want a thing is the contrary of wanting its contrary.

This is the reason he gives for the real distinction between intellect and will in angels; and the reason why they are *not* distinct in God is that his knowing and willing are *not* exercised through any conjunction with something that extends outside him.⁷⁰

On the other hand, Aquinas holds that even in God, really distinct relations are established through his understanding himself and his loving himself. Aquinas's description of the difference between the establishments of these relations, i.e. between the processions in the Godhead, follows his account of the general difference between the relations of intellect and will to their objects. This shows that even when he makes an intellect and a will to be really one and the

---

67. *Cum autem operans oporteat aliquo modo coniungi suo obiecto circa quod operatur, necesse est extrinsecam rem, quae est obiectum operationis animae, secundum duplicem rationem ad animam comparari. Uno modo, secundum quod nata est animae coniungi et in anima esse per suam similitudinem. . . . Alio vero modo, secundum quod ipsa anima inclinatur et tendit in rem exteriorem* (I, q. 78, a. 1).

68. See also I, q. 79, a. 1 ad 2: what he distinguishes the intellect from are the will and the sensitive appetite taken *together*.

69. See Dewan, 'The Real Distinction between Intellect and Will,' pp. 582–83.

70. I, q. 59, arts. 1 and 2.

same principle, Aquinas does not do so by *reducing* the activity of this principle to what is proper to intellect.

> This is the difference between understanding and willing, that understanding comes to be in act through the fact that the thing understood is in the understanding according to its likeness; but willing comes to be in act, not through the fact that some likeness of the thing willed is in the will, but from the fact that the will has a certain inclination to the thing willed. Therefore the procession which is in accordance with the nature of understanding is according to the nature of a likeness. . . . But the procession which is according to the nature of the will is not according to the nature of a likeness, but rather according to the nature of something impelling and moving toward something.[71]

In Aquinas's doctrine, then, the proper basis for the distinction between intellect and will in man is not, as is sometimes suggested, man's peccability. To be sure, this is a sign of the distinction; for it is a sign that the rule of man's conduct, his proper end, is something outside him, hence something from which he can deviate, even when he knows it.[72] But the proper basis for the distinction is just the fact that his object is outside him.

Neither does the basis for the distinction lie in the fact that the will must be assigned some role in determining its object or in establishing the principle by which human action is specified. Aquinas certainly grants it some such role; but it is never that of an *additional* source of objects or specificatory principles, outside or apart from those given by the intellect. Rather, the will plays a role in the determination of its object precisely by playing a role in the process by which the intellect itself comes to provide it with an object. It does this in two ways: by

---

71. I, q. 27, a. 4.

72. See I, q. 63, a. 1. Still, from a Thomistic standpoint, making incontinence the crucial phenomenon for distinguishing will from intellect must be an odd procedure, or at least roundabout. It is like trying to prove the existence of bodily strength from cases of muscle atrophy. Incontinence is 'weakness of will.' Much stronger evidence for will is provided by strength of will, continence. I will try to explain this here in a merely summary way (cf. II–II, qq. 155 and 156). The continent and incontinent man have two things in common: a belief that some sort of pleasant thing ought to be avoided, and a passion inclining them to pursue something of that sort. What incontinence shows is that the belief, by itself, is not enough to make them avoid the thing. But incontinence does not require will, over and above the passion, in order to incline them to pursue the thing; the passion itself does that quite adequately. Rather, it is continence that involves the exercise of will, over and above the *belief*, inclining the subject to consider the belief, to apply it to the judgment of the case at hand, and to remain firm in abiding by it, all in the face of the solicitation of the passion. Will is involved in incontinence only indirectly, by its failing to act when it could and should, its failing to take or keep the rational initiative. (Thomas speaks of a kind of 'negligence of spirit': II–II, q. 155, a. 1 ad 3.) It lets passion get the upper hand and dominate the subject's outlook. (This means, of course, that *he* lets it dominate. To be sure, this 'letting' may be seen as a kind of consent; but not even this need be a positive 'act' of will. It may only be a lack, a failure to *refuse* consent: cf. I–II, q. 15, a. 4 ad 3.) Then, at most, will comes into play in slavish fashion, in choosing whatever the passion's satisfaction requires.

being a moving principle of the intellect's own act,[73] and by being an *object* of understanding, one whose disposition is itself a potential criterion of the judgment of one's suitable good.[74] But assigning it these roles presupposes the distinction between it and intellect.

Even less is the basis for the distinction to be looked for in the freedom of the will. Aquinas is unwavering in his insistence that the reason why the will is free is the very fact that it takes its object from the intellect, whose *judgment* in matters of action leaves various possibilities open.[75] Besides, he denies the distinction in God, and yet attributes to him the maximum of freedom.[76] What the freedom of the will indicates is not its distinction from the intellect, but its distinction from the sensitive appetite.

In the light of our earlier discussions of the union of agent and patient in action, and of the 'real' nature of the relation of effect to cause in agent-causality, it is not surprising to find that the analytical thinkers under study have difficulty in maintaining a distinct role for acts of will in the explanation of human action. Consciously or not, they show a marked tendency to think of acts of will on the model of mental *words*. These are the 'mental acts' most readily acknowledged by these philosophers. Nor, it should perhaps be added, only by them. Acts of will are rather slippery items.

> In the divinity, there are two processions, one in the mode of intellect, which is the procession of the word, and the other in the mode of will, which is the procession of love. And because the former is better known to us, fairly adequate

---

73. See I, q. 82, a. 4; I–II, q. 9, a. 1.
74. See Rodriguez Luño, *La scelta etica*, pp. 73–77.
75. I, q. 83, arts. 1, 3. The reason for this is that matters of action are singulars, whereas the proper object of the intellect is universal. (See *SCG* II, ch. 48, §§ 1244–46.) The universal serves as a principle of comparison, a means of measuring one thing against another. But when the things compared are singular, and sometimes even when they are universal, it can happen that both 'measure up' *and* that neither is a clear winner; both fulfill the criteria equally well, or each falls short in some feature which the other satisfies. In this case, if taking one excludes taking the other, such that saying 'yes' to one is saying 'no' to the other, i.e. such that it is a decision, then it is a free decision, a decision that is simply 'up to you.' You refuse one thing when all conditions needed for your accepting it are present, and you accept the other when all conditions needed for your refusing it are present. But the will is precisely the appetitive faculty that bears upon its object according to the intellect's apprehension. Hence not everything it moves toward is something it is bound to move toward; and sometimes it moves toward something when all conditions needed for not moving toward it are present, and vice versa. The will moves toward one thing *despite* a sufficient attraction toward something excluding it; this is a choice, a taking one thing in the face of another, a preference. This is not at all to say that the choice is not informed by a judgment. The chooser must have formed a judgment declaring the preferability of what he chose. Only, he may have also formed a judgment declaring the preferability of the alternative he rejected. Nor are these two separate judgments; it is one judgment, declaring one alternative preferable in some respect, and the other preferable in another respect.
76. See I, q. 18, a. 3; q. 19, a. 10; q. 25, a. 5. On the greater degree of freedom belonging to impeccable wills, see I, q. 62, a. 8 ad 3.

names have been found to signify the things that can be considered in it. But it is not so with the procession of the will. Whence we use certain circumlocutions to signify the person so proceeding. . . . Nevertheless it is necessary to give each procession similar consideration. For just as from the fact that someone understands some thing, there arises in the one understanding a certain intellectual conception of the thing understood, which is called a word; so from the fact that someone loves some thing, there arises a certain impression, so to speak, of the thing loved in the affection of the lover; in accordance with which the beloved is said to be in the lover, as a thing understood is in the one understanding. . . . But terms have not been adopted that indicate the relation of the impression or affection of the thing loved, which arises in the lover from the fact that he loves, to its principle, or vice versa.[77]

That the mind's act of will tends to hide from view is perhaps what is to be expected, if it is true that the proper object of the will, in contrast with that of the intellect, is 'in things' rather than in the mind itself. The mental 'word' is both the proper enactment and the proper object of the intellect; its very nature is that of something apt to be thought of. But the proper enactment of the will, its 'affection' or 'impulse,' is something other than the will's chief object. It tends to come forth while the mind is attending to something else, because it comes forth through the mind's tending toward something else.

D. THE TWOFOLD RELATION OF THE WILL TO ITS OBJECT

How then does Aquinas conceive the causal role of acts of will in human action? In the context of the present study, answering this question requires first that we dispel a typical objection to the hypothesis of 'acts of will' or 'volitions' in the explanation of human action. Doing so will lead us to the consideration of Aquinas's notion of 'use,' a rather neglected one in the studies on his psychology of action. It will be suggested that this notion brings together most of the salient features of his conception of the will's causality.

1. Interior Acts of Will and Exterior Acts

The objection is raised against the proposition that the essential difference between an event that is an action and one that is not is that the former is caused by a certain prior event, called an act of will. It is not difficult to show the absurdity of such a proposition, as has been done repeatedly, in different ways. Melden, for instance, argues that it leads to an infinite regress, since volitions are actions too.[78] Others point out that an act of will can bear upon, and be the cause of, some event, and yet the event is not an action;[79] hence even if acts of will are

---

77. I, q. 37, a. 1.
78. *Free Action*, ch. 5.
79. Cf. Donagan, *Choice*, pp. 88–89.

causes of actions, being caused by acts of will cannot be what properly distinguishes actions from other events. In general, what is extrinsic to something cannot constitute the chief essential difference between it and something else; if some events are essentially actions, as I have been at pains to show in Chapter 2, then the difference between them and events that are not actions cannot be merely their causal dependence upon some other event.

So, if the only reason for positing acts of will is to establish a difference between actions and other events, and yet doing so fails to establish a satisfactory difference, then, as some have concluded, there is simply no reason for positing such acts. Indeed, there will be *no* essential difference between actions and other events, *qua* events, i.e. qua *effects*. That is, the kind of explanation proper to actions, as opposed to events, will not be *causal* explanation, explanation in terms of what makes them come about. Actions will belong to another order of discourse altogether: that of reasons, justifications, etc.[80]

However, this way of approaching the question of acts of will is vitiated at its very roots. It introduces the question at the wrong point. What acts of will are meant properly to explain, if they explain anything, is *human* action. But the foregoing objection is directed against acts of will as providing the proper explanation of action in its more *general* sense, what we have spoken of earlier as 'bringing something about' or 'making something so,' efficacy. Consider the example commonly adduced in this matter, which comes (with some modification) from Wittgenstein.[81] What does the notion of raising one's arm, which is the notion of an action, add to that of one's arm's rising, which is not? To be sure, the notion of raising one's arm is the notion of an action; but it is not the notion of a human action. Of course raising one's arm *can* be a human action, just as the rising of one's arm *can* be a raising of it. But it need not be. Calling something a raising of one's arm does not yet amount to calling it a human action. The point is utterly obvious. Raising one's arm is something that can be done by sleepers, babies, lunatics and monkeys, none of whom is capable of a human act. Raising one's arm is not essentially a human action, not essentially conduct.

In St Thomas's language, when raising one's arm *is* a piece of conduct, it is not 'essentially' so, but 'by participation,' by sharing in what is essentially conduct. To be conduct in this way is to be what he calls an 'exterior act.' This is an action exercised by some faculty or member other than, but under the command of, the will. Considered for what is essential or intrinsic to it, such an action is

---

80. See MacIntyre, 'The Antecedents of Action,' pp. 201–03.
81. Wittgenstein's question (*Philosophical Investigations*, § 621) was, 'what remains when, from the fact that I raise my arm, I take away the fact that my arm rises?' This is followed by another question, put in double parentheses, evidently to show that it is meant to bring out the absurdity of the view against which the first question was directed: 'Is my will the kinaesthetic sensations?' His argument is against treating 'willing' as a Humean impression, an 'inner state,' another 'fact' alongside (say) that of my arm's rising.

merely 'physical' (in the broad sense, taking imaginations, thoughts and so forth as physical acts). What is essentially a human act or a piece of conduct is a deliberate (or deliberable) 'elicited' act of will.

Now certainly, if a 'physical' action can share in the nature of conduct, this is because it can be caused by that which is essentially conduct. So, acts of will must play a causal role in some instances of such acts as raising one's arm. We may therefore say that some physical actions, or some actions exercised by powers other than the will, are pieces of conduct, and some are not; and that what makes the difference is whether or not they are caused (directly!) by an act of will. But this is not to state the essential difference between *events* that are pieces of conduct and events that are not; it cannot do so, since it concerns only participated or secondary instances of conduct, and therefore only *partial* instances of conduct. What is conduct primarily is an elicited act of will, and what constitutes a single *complete* piece of conduct is the composite of the act of will and the exterior act that the act of will is the principle of. It is precisely because the 'physical' act is conduct only in a secondary way that it does not constitute a distinct, whole piece of conduct in its own right.[82]

I shall not attempt to give a strict general definition of 'act of will,' as Thomas understands it. As Kenny says, not all 'acts' of will are to be understood as actions or doings.[83] 'Act' here merely means the correlate of a faculty or power; 'will' means the faculty of rational appetite. An act of will is something for which the rational appetite is a power. By itself, this is probably not very illuminating. By way of a general characterization, perhaps we can say simply that an act of will is something by which, formally, its subject possesses a 'volitional relation' to something. A volitional relation would be a kind of appetitive relation, and a kind of rational appetitive relation. Thomas's well-known 'scheme' of acts of will, laid out in I–II, qq. 9–17, seems to be just this: an attempt to distinguish and set in order the chief general forms of volitional relation. I do not mean to go through this scheme systematically here,[84] but only to glean considerations which may shed light on how Thomas understands the will's causality (which, too, is a kind of relation).

The most general distinction which Thomas draws among acts of will is between 'interior' and 'exterior' acts. It is of the utmost importance to be clear as to what he means by these terms. It should be obvious that the distinction has nothing to do with what only the agent himself knows versus what can be observed 'externally.' But at least two other misunderstandings are possible. One shows up in Donagan.[85] Aquinas identifies interior acts with 'elicited' ones; and

---

82. See I–II, q. 20, a. 3 ad 3.
83. See below, n. 111.
84. For a very helpful overview of the scheme, its historical background, and interpretations of it, see Westberg, *Right Practical Reason*, part III, pp. 119–83.
85. *Choice*, pp. 157, 161; 'Thomas Aquinas on Human Action,' p. 650.

since he describes these as acts that are from the will immediately,[86] Donagan takes them to be the same as spontaneous acts. For this reason, Donagan also sometimes speaks of certain acts of intellect as 'elicited,' i.e. as emerging from it spontaneously.

Now, one *can* speak of elicited acts of the intellect; one can also speak of elicited acts of the sensitive or motor faculties.[87] But 'elicited' is a relative term, not an absolute one. That is, an act is spoken of as elicited, or not, relative to some power to which it is attributed. The very same act may be elicited from one power, and commanded by another.[88] 'Elicited' means exercised by that power immediately. But 'immediately' does not mean 'spontaneously'; it means 'not by means of some power subject to it.' That is, it means 'proximately.' An elicited act of some power is one exercised by it as by that act's immediate source. So, for instance, it is simply not true that 'no elicited act of intellect can be commanded [by the will].'[89] Neither is it true that the only elicited acts of the will are those that are not deliberated.[90]

Perhaps another way to express the distinction is to say that an 'interior' act is something which *essentially* constitutes a volitional relation with something; if it constitutes any other sort of relation as well, it does so in virtue of its volitional element. Such acts are intention, choice, consent, and so forth. An exterior act also constitutes a volitional relation, but it does so in virtue of constituting some other relation; that is, it merely mediates a volitional relation, and somehow shares in the relation that it mediates. For instance, my sitting down may be a voluntary act, an exterior act; through it, my being seated is related to my will (i.e. to me *qua* capable of volitional relations) as its (my) effect. But it establishes this relation only through being an act of muscles, nerves and so forth, i.e. through being the very sitting down that I wanted to perform. (Thus, the relation established through the sitting down depends on the relation of 'wanting to sit down'; the latter is prior, in order of dependence. But we are talking about relations, not events; there need be no prior event called 'wanting to sit down.')

The other possible misunderstanding concerning interior or elicited acts of will is to think that they always consist in acts which not only originate immediately from the will but also terminate 'in' the will, never in any power subject to the will; or in other words, to think that *per se* they *only* constitute volitional relations, and never *per se* constitute any other sort of relation as well, i.e. any relation involving some other power in addition to the will. As I shall try to show in a

---

86. I–II, q. 6, proem.

87. One can also speak, perhaps somewhat loosely, of commanded acts of intellect, where 'commanded' means exercised by a power which in some way participates in the action of the 'commanding' one. Speech, for instance, might be termed a commanded act of intellect.

88. Or even by the same power, insofar as it can reflect on itself and make itself act. See I–II, q. 17, arts. 5 and 6.

89. Donagan, 'Thomas Aquinas on Human Action,' p. 650.

90. Donagan, *Choice*, p. 157.

moment, Aquinas does not think that all acts originating immediately from the will terminate in the will. The term 'interior' is the source of this potential confusion. It sounds as though it refers to where the act terminates, to the act's remaining enclosed within its subject. To be sure, for Thomas, all elicited acts remain 'enclosed' within the human agent; what proceeds immediately from his will is something in him. But then, *some* of the will's commanded or 'exterior' acts also remain enclosed in the agent, e.g. in his intellect. So it would be better to stay with the terms 'elicited' and 'commanded' acts. Even here there is some overlapping, since the will can also command itself; but the will's act is called 'commanded' insofar as it is seen as proceeding mediately from the will, by way of intellect.[91]

The reason why it is so important to be clear on this point, for our present purposes, is as follows. According to Thomistic theory, acts of will play a causal role relative to the 'physical' component of human action. At some point, this requires the existence of an act or a moment in which the 'volitional' and 'physical' orders are unified. This means there must be an act that is *at once* an elicited act of the will, i.e. exercised by it immediately, *and* a physical act, i.e. immediate also to the physical agency involved.[92] This is both necessary and possible, according to the general scheme of agent-causality laid down in Chapter 2: the same act is at once immediately 'of' the agent, as its action, and 'of' the patient, as what it undergoes.

But it terminates 'in' the patient. In accordance with this principle, then, there must be some elicited act of will that does not remain solely *in* the will, but extends to that upon which it acts or that which it moves. There must be an act that is at once an immediately voluntary action and a physical passion. This, I believe, is the act which Thomas places last in his list of interior or elicited acts of will, the act called *usus*, 'use.' He characterizes it as the application of something to some operation.[93]

The application of something to some operation terminates in the thing so applied. Thus, Thomas says that 'the user's use is conjoined with the act of that which he uses; for someone is not using a stick until he is in some way operating with the stick.'[94] Of course, to be precise, it is necessary to distinguish between

---

91. I–II, q. 17, a. 5.

92. It is only to simplify the discussion, of course, that we speak of acts exercised *by* the will or some physical power; properly speaking, it is the man who exercises them, but according to diverse capacities.

93. I–II, q. 16, a. 1. The very location of the question on use shows that Aquinas considers it to be an elicited act. But if it were an act terminating in the will, then it would be unintelligible how he could say that it *follows* upon command (I–II, q. 17, a. 3). To say that it terminates in the will would be to say that it pertains to the process by which the agent comes to be determined toward some action. But command *presupposes* a complete determination toward action. Use pertains to the execution of the command; and this belongs to the *executive* powers, insofar as these are *subject to* the action of the will.

94. I–II, q. 17, a. 3.

the user's action upon the thing used, which is his application of it to some operation, and that operation itself, which is an action performed by the thing used *in virtue* of having been applied by the user. That is, in accordance with our earlier observations about instrumental agency, there is in fact a twofold operation pertaining to the thing used: a passion, i.e. its being acted upon by the user, and the consequent action exercised by it. *This*, in turn, will terminate in that which is the *instrument's* patient (if the instrument's operation is a transitive one), e.g. what is struck by the stick.[95]

2. Use as the Interior Act of the Will Qua Agency

In previous sections we observed a notable tendency among the analytic philosophers toward assimilating acts of will to acts of understanding, toward conceiving of them as acts that 'terminate in the soul' of the act's subject. This goes along with their tendency to assimilate the relation between agency and its effects to that of knowledge and its objects, a tendency which came to light in the course of discussing the fact that the agent's action is *in* that upon which it acts (whereas knowledge is not in the thing known). In rather striking consistency with these tendencies, Donagan, who is one of the few writers on Aquinas's theory of human action even to pay attention to the subject of 'use,' thinks Aquinas mistaken in making it something distinct from the act of choice.[96] I shall now lay out Thomas's notion of use in greater detail and try to address Donagan's criticism.[97]

In the article on use which Donagan criticizes, I–II, q. 16, a. 4, Aquinas lays down a twofold relation between the will and what is willed. One relation, he

---

95. Thus the later scholastics distinguish between use in the active sense, referring to the action of using something, and use in the passive sense, referring to the operation performed by the thing used. This distinction is latent in Aquinas's observations that 'the operation to which we apply something is called its use, as riding is the use of a horse, and striking the use of a stick' (I–II, q. 16, a. 1), and that, on the other hand, 'the motion by which the will moves toward executing precedes the execution of the work itself' (I–II, q. 16, a. 4 ad 1). It is the latter, the 'motion toward executing,' which is the will's elicited act of use, 'active' use. The distinction helps to resolve a potential objection to saying that use is an interior or elicited act of the will. The objection is that according to Aquinas, the interior acts of the will cannot be produced or impeded by force (I–II, q. 6, a. 4); but obviously one's use of something, even one's own powers and members, can be so impeded (a. 5). The core of the reply is that you can always give a 'push' to the other powers, undertake to use them, *start* moving them toward execution (active use); that is, you can if you want to, and only if you want to. Only, they can sometimes resist, or fail to be moved in the direction of the push (passive use). As before, this does not mean that active use and successful passive use constitute two fully distinct acts; they are one act, but an act capable of being interrupted or cut short. Of course, it may also happen that you are incapable of wanting to use your powers, e.g. because you think that you have lost control over them; but this is not prevention by *force*.

96. 'Thomas Aquinas on Human Action,' p. 652.

97. For further discussion, see Brock, 'What is the Use of *Usus* in Aquinas's Psychology of Action?'

says, is according to a certain way of existing that the thing willed has in the one who wills it. He calls this a certain proportion or order of the one willing to the thing willed. This sometimes goes by the name of 'intentional' existence. The other is what he describes as tending toward 'really' possessing the thing willed. He regards such a tendency as the natural complement of the first relation between the will and its object. To will something is to will to have it. But to 'have' it in the manner constituted by the first relation between the will and its object is to have it only imperfectly. To will something not yet really had is in a way to have it, but it is not fully to have it in the way that willing it disposes one to have it. If the proportion established between the one willing and the thing willed does not result in this tending toward really having the thing willed, the reason can only be that the proportion itself is merely imperfect; as seen earlier in this chapter, it cannot be a full act of willing, but only a *velleitas*.[98]

In this respect, Aquinas holds, willing and understanding differ. To understand also involves an intentional existence of the thing understood in the understanding subject, a proportion between the subject and what is understood. But the act of understanding is brought to its proper completion, not in any tending toward the object to which it is proportioned, but in the conception and judgment of it.[99] These leave the 'distance' between subject and object altogether intact.[100] Although both willing and understanding are acts concerning things having a certain intentional existence in the soul of the subject of those acts, understanding is an act that terminates in the soul, whereas willing terminates in the thing itself.[101] This of course means that the 'intentional existence' of the

---

98. See I–II, q. 13, a. 5 ad 1; also I–II, q. 20, a. 4: *non est perfecta voluntas, nisi sit talis quae, opportunitate data, operetur*.
99. It is only if this proportion is *imperfect* that the act of understanding might, *of itself*, be said to give rise to a tending toward really possessing the thing understood; it might do so insofar as such possession makes it possible to investigate the thing more thoroughly and so to understand it better, i.e. insofar as really possessing the thing gives greater access to its intentional existence in the understanding subject. If the *only* thing desirable about what we understand were the understanding of it, then there would be no reason to posit an intellectual appetite distinct from the intrinsic tendency of the intellect itself; see I, q. 78, a. 1 ad 3.
100. See I–II, q. 15, a. 1 ad 3: 'to assent [which is to execute a judgment] is as though "to sense toward another," and so connotes a certain distance from that which is assented to. But to consent is "to sense with," and so connotes a certain conjunction with that which is consented to. And therefore the will, to which it belongs to tend toward the thing itself, is more properly said to consent; but the intellect, whose operation is not according to motion toward the thing, but rather the contrary . . . is more properly said to assent.'
101. This is why Aquinas judges that, in general, or attending solely to the nature of the acts in question, understanding is a more 'noble' operation than willing (I, q. 82, a. 3). It is more independent or self-sufficient. Indeed, willing something depends upon understanding something, but not vice versa. The 'formal nature' of the intellect's object, i.e. the determination through which any of its objects is *constituted* its object, belongs to the object *as* existing in the understanding subject. But this very fact, that the act of understanding is in general more noble than the act of willing, is the reason why, relative to a given thing understood and willed, the act of willing it may be more

object in the soul, or the proportion established in the soul to the object, is itself not the same in understanding as in willing.[102]

To continue with I–II, q. 16, a. 4, after Thomas distinguishes the two relations of the will to its object, he recalls that the object of the will is itself twofold: an end and what is ordered to an end, a means. The two relations of the will to its object are found both in the will for the end and in the will for the means. To make matters even more complicated, he also indicates that more than one act of will pertains to *each* relation of the will to its object, both when the object is the end and when the object is the means. Thus, he says that choice is the *last* act pertaining to the *first* relation of the will to the means, 'for there is completed the proportion of the will, such that it completely wills' the means. In the preceding question, in fact, he had posited another act bearing on the means and prior to choice (and so obviously still in the first relation), namely consent. But both consent and choice, as such, terminate in the will of the chooser, establishing a proportion between it and some means.

Use, he holds, is concerned with the same kind of willable object as choice, namely with what is *ad finem*, and most precisely, with action;[103] but, he says, it constitutes an instance of the second relation of the will to its object, the tending toward obtaining the thing willed. Hence it is clear that use comes after choice. One first deliberates, then chooses to do something, and then applies himself to doing it.[104] Use reaches beyond the proportion of the will to its object. It belongs within the order of the object's actual realization.

Before addressing Donagan's objection, we might consider how these distinctions apply in the case of the will for the end. Thomas does not lay this out

---

noble than the act of understanding it. If the thing itself is even more noble than the soul, then granted that understanding it is a more noble relation of the soul to it than is willing it, willing it ennobles the soul more than does understanding it, since willing it is closer to the 'real' union between it and the soul. The very fact that the willing is subsequent to the understanding shows that the willing is closer to the complete or perfect ennobling of the soul.

102. See below, Section E. 1.

103. I–II, q. 13, a. 4. This is an important point. It means that the act of use does not constitute the willing of *some other* object besides that which was chosen; it does not establish any new order of the subject toward something to be done. It is strictly the mere initiation of the exercise or the execution of the order established in the act of choice. This is why use adds no further moral qualification to a choice, if the choice is full-fledged (see I–II, q. 20, a. 4).

104. See *Nicomachean Ethics* III, ch. 3, 1112b21–27: 'For the person who deliberates seems to inquire and analyze in the way described as though he were analyzing a geometrical construction ... and what is last in the order of inquiry is first in the order of generation. And if we come on an impossibility, we give up the search, e.g. if we need money and this cannot be got; but if a thing appears possible we try to do it' (Ross translation). The verb that Ross translates by 'try to do it' is *encheirousi*, 'put one's hand to it.' As mentioned earlier, the Greek term for 'use' (*chrēsis*) comes from this verb, and Aristotle frequently uses that term as interchangeable with *praxis*. The text just quoted has a clear connection with Aristotle's much-discussed remark that the conclusion of deliberation *is* an action (*praxis*); see Anscombe, 'Thought and Action in Aristotle,' p. 73.

explicitly here, but it should not be too difficult to do so. According to his scheme, there are three acts of the will about the end: simple willing or wanting (*simplex velle*),[105] intention and enjoyment. Of these, only wanting appears to belong to the first relation, the proportion of the will to its object. Wanting regards the end 'absolutely' or as understood to be a kind of good,[106] while intention and enjoyment both bear on the end's real attainment. Intention involves moving or tending to the attainment of the end, while enjoyment is resting in the end already attained.[107]

We may suppose that 'simple wanting' refers to an act of will which completes the first relation to the end, just as choice was said to be the act of will about the means which completes the first relation of the will to the means. Thomas does not devote a question to any incomplete act of the will in its first relation to the end, but he does draw the distinction, as we have already seen; an incomplete wanting is a *velleitas*.[108]

I would also draw attention to two points regarding these acts about the end, which suggest parallel points regarding the acts about the means. The first point is that simple wanting, the complete act of the will pertaining to its first relation to the end, is at the same time the principle initiating the second relation, the tendency toward really having the end. 'By the fact that the will wants the end, it moves itself to willing the things that are ordered to the end,'[109] while intention already involves some willing of things that are ordered to the end.[110] Similarly, choice, which completes the first relation to the means, is surely the principle initiating the second relation to the means, while use already involves the actual execution of the means; 'for someone is not using a stick until he is in some way operating with the stick.'

105. I shall henceforth use 'willing' as a generic term covering all the acts of will.
106. I–II, q. 12, a. 1 ad 4; I–II, q. 13, a. 5 ad 1.
107. I–II, q. 12, a. 1 and a. 2 ad 3.
108. To this it might be objected that in the passage where Aquinas distinguishes *velleitas* from wanting as incomplete from complete acts of will (I–II, q. 13, a. 5 ad 1), the difference turns on the possibility or impossibility of the object. If it is judged to be impossible, the willing can only be a *velleitas*. The objection is that, on the standard account of the Thomistic 'scheme of human acts' (see e.g. Bourke, *Ethics*, p. 59), the judgment of possibility is said to come after *simplex velle*, and provides the cognitive basis for intention. However, it is important to remember the distinction between what someone judges to be possible to come about and what he judges to be in *his* power to bring about. The latter judgment is not required for a complete act of wanting; only the former is. The fact that I can do nothing to help the Cubs win the World Series does not mean that I cannot fully want them to win; I fully want them to win, although I 'would want' (*vellem*) them to lose if they were playing against the White Sox (a *velleitas*). Of course, I cannot *choose* that the Cubs win the World Series, nor can I intend it. But it is only after someone judges that something is possible in itself that, wanting it, he goes on to consider whether he himself can do anything to bring it about. If he thinks he can—which does not require that he have determined exactly *how* he might bring it about—*then* he can intend it.
109. I–II, q. 9, a. 3.
110. I–II, q. 12, a. 4.

The other point is that, as regards the will's second relation to the end, intention and enjoyment may themselves be distinguished as incomplete and complete. Intention is a movement toward the end; enjoyment is resting in it. Similarly, I would suggest, use must be regarded as an incomplete act in the second relation to the means. Use is the application of the executive power to the execution of the action which is the means. Using always implies that execution is taking place—'he is in some way operating with the stick'—but it does not imply that the execution is complete.

Of course, the execution itself is an exterior act, an act of some power moved by the will, not an interior or elicited act proceeding immediately from the will. There is no elicited act of the will about the means which corresponds to the complete act of the will in its second relation to the end, i.e. to enjoyment. This is because, considering the will's activity as a whole, *everything* done about the means is something incomplete. There is no resting in the means; the will does not tend to the means in order to rest in it, but in order to move through it to the end. The will moves toward the means until it really and completely brings the means about, but it does not take satisfaction in the means (*qua* means, of course). It strives on toward the end. However, use and enjoyment do have this in common (and in distinction from the other elicited acts): they always exist together with the real existence of their objects, which are operations of some other power. Just as one is not using until something is being done with the thing used, so one is not taking enjoyment in some activity until the activity is being performed. For this reason, I would suggest, while the other elicited acts, the other forms of essentially volitional relation, might be regarded more as states or dispositions,[111] use and enjoyment must be regarded as genuine actions or doings. No one answers the question 'what are you doing?' with 'I am wanting an ice cream' or 'I am intending to go to the store';[112] but one may very well answer it with 'I am using the telephone' or 'I am enjoying a novel.'[113]

---

111. See Kenny, *Aquinas on Mind*, pp. 83–88; cf. his *Action, Emotion and Will*, pp. 183–86.

112. You might answer 'I am choosing a tie,' but this does not make choice itself an action or a doing; the doing here is deliberation. Choosing a tie consists in deliberating between ties, as to which one to take. While choosing a tie, you have not yet made the choice. To have made a choice is to have a preference; you cannot answer 'I am preferring a tie.'

113. 'Enjoyment' (*fruitio*) is not the same thing as 'joy' (*gaudium*) or 'delight' (*delectatio*), though it involves these. It is not a merely passive state, but connotes an active (though immobile) adherence to the object of enjoyment. Kenny, *Action, Emotion and Will*, p. 183, says that 'to enjoy' is not a 'static' verb (one expressing a state), but rather an 'activity' verb, distinguished from static verbs by its having a continuous tense. At the same time, he distinguishes 'activity' verbs from 'performance' verbs, the latter expressing some kind of 'bringing about' of something. All performance verbs have imperatives, and all performances have a purpose. Only some activity verbs and activities share these features, namely those which can be redescribed as 'attempting to bring it about that p'; e.g. listening is attempting to hear (bringing it about that one hear). In view of the features of imperative and purpose, he judges, quite plausibly, that 'the form of description "A is bringing it about that p" is the fundamental one for the description of voluntary human action.' However, Kenny insists that 'to enjoy,'

Now, Donagan misreads Aquinas on the nature of the 'second relation' of the will to its object. It is an instructive misreading. He thinks that the second relation of the will to its object is always, as in the case of enjoyment, one that *results* from 'really having' the object. It is on this basis that he thinks Aquinas wrong to distinguish use from choice; for the use of some power is an act *directed toward* that power's exercise, i.e. toward the actual performance of an action, and can therefore hardly *presuppose* the exercise of the power, or at least the complete exercise. Donagan therefore concludes that use must pertain to the *first* relation of the will to its object, and that it must be identical with choice, since choice is the ultimate determination of this sort of relation of the will to an action.

As we have seen, however, Aquinas's distinction between choice and use is between two sorts of acts, *both* of which are causes, not results, of the actual exercise of one's power or the 'really having' of an action. The first one, choice, establishes the agent's 'proportion' to it. The second one is his moving toward its accomplishment, and this is his using the power or applying it to the chosen operation. There is no elicited act about the chosen operation that results from the completion of that operation; in this Donagan is right. But instead of ranging use under the first relation of the will to its object, and identifying it with choice, it is in fact much more plausible to see choice itself as the starting-point of the second relation, and use as its first result.

What is instructive about Donagan's misreading is that it shows the strength with which he holds the views on causality that we have previously identified. He wants the mere 'proportion' between an agent and his action to do all the work of constituting the agent as its cause, and does so to such an extent that he cannot even imagine that Aquinas thinks it necessary to identify a further moment of 'tendency' or 'impetus.'[114]

---

while an activity verb, has no imperative, and that enjoying is not for a purpose. So, it cannot be brought under 'bringing it about that *p*.' Evidently this means that it is not, properly speaking, a human *action*. Are Kenny's claims about it true? As regards imperatives, surely you might say to someone going to the movies, 'enjoy yourself!' (Contrast 'be delighted!') Also, though of course one does not enjoy something for a purpose (this squares with Thomas, for whom enjoyment is only of a 'last' end: I–II, q. 11, a. 3), perhaps enjoying necessarily *involves* doing something for a purpose. Augustine says, '*omnis qui fruitur, utitur*' (*De trinitate* X, ch. 11, § 17, PL 42, 982; quoted by Thomas in I–II, q. 16 a, 3 obj. 1). Enjoying is enjoying something. If the something is a 'thing,' e.g. a novel, the enjoyment of it is by way of some activity about it, e.g. reading it. If the something is an activity, e.g. reading, the enjoyment of it derives in some way from what it is about, e.g. the novel (cf. I–II, q. 16, a. 3). So the enjoyment involves some kind of active application of a power to an operation, some kind of 'bringing it about that. . .' (Cf. I–II, q. 1, a. 1 ad 2.) At any rate, it is striking that Thomas associates 'perfect' enjoyment, the kind proper to rational agents, with the power of 'free command' (I–II, q. 11, a. 2).

114. See I–II, q. 16, a. 1 obj. 2. Kenny, in his own effort to get at the core of the will's causality, to find a 'volition' which is an action, finishes by appeal to the notion of 'command' (*Action, Emotion and Will*, pp. 238–39), though he admits that this is only a metaphor. (He develops the 'Imperative Theory of the Will' in much more detail in *Will, Freedom and Power*, ch. 3.) Commanding is indeed

However, there is something which Donagan says in his account of the causality of choice which is both persuasive and, I believe, at least very much like something which must be stressed about the causality involved in use. This is the causality's reflexive character. What Donagan says is that the human agent chooses not only his doing, but also its being explained by his choice, as well as the manner in which it is to be explained by it.[115] Something similar to this must be posited in the case of use. It is not simply that in 'applying a power to an operation' one is always applying a part of *himself* (since even when we apply other things, we first apply ourselves to them). It is that in applying the power to an operation, he is simultaneously, and knowingly, applying his power *over* that power to an operation, namely the operation of using that power. His power *over* that power is a power of his will; it is precisely his power to use the other power. If he did not have this, his use of the other power would not constitute a genuine control of it, a constant readjustment of its operation in accordance with the choice or with the pre-conceived form of operation which is to be executed.[116]

The will, then, must have its own power in its power, or be able to use itself.[117] And so the application of its own power of using to a use cannot be a separate act, prior to the use; this would lead to an infinite regress in the will's use of itself. In causing one of his powers to act, the human agent is simultaneously causing himself to do so.

---

a kind of action, and it is probably the one most expressive of the will's role of *dominant* causal power. Still, for Thomas at least, command is an elicited act of intellect, not of will (I–II, q. 17, a. 1); it arises out of the will's *use* of intellect to impel toward action (I–II, q. 17, a. 3 obj. 3). (Intellect impels toward action in the manner of one *ordering* toward action.) Of course, to the extent that a given act of use constitutes the (beginning of) the fulfillment of a command, it must follow upon that command; and the will's use of reason to issue a command can itself be seen as the fulfillment of a command to do so (I–II, q. 17, a. 3, corp. and ad 3). Perhaps then *every* human act of use, including every voluntary use of reason to issue a command, is preceded by a command of reason. But this would necessarily lead back to commands issued by reason, not freely but naturally. The dimension of impulse would belong to these natural commands only to the extent that intellect is moved naturally—again, not freely—by will itself. (On natural, as opposed to free, movements or inclinations of will, see I–II, q. 10, a. 1, esp. ad 1.) For instance, Thomas says that there is in man a natural inclination to act virtuously, and that according to this, everyone's reason *naturally dictates* to him that he act virtuously (I–II, q. 94, a. 3; cf. I–II, q. 51, a. 1). But if the dictate is natural, then although it proceeds from intellect and will, these are not yet functioning in the capacity of a *dominus sui actus*, one who is 'in command.' The natural operations of intellect and will arise out of the use or application of these powers by the Author of Nature (cf. I, q. 60, a. 1; I, q. 105, arts. 3–5). Thus even the first, natural commands in human reason would still proceed from a use or application of man's will and intellect, though not from *his* use or application of them. The volitional relation which is an action is use.

115. *Choice*, pp. 87–93.

116. See I–II, q. 16, a. 2 ad 2: use involves the understanding of the order between the power used and the operation for which it is used. The point is illustrated by an example used (for a different purpose) by Anscombe: that of someone who applies extra force to the dial of a telephone, because it is a bit jammed ('The Causation of Action,' p. 180).

117. See I–II, q. 16, a. 4, obj. 3 and reply.

3. Use and Choice

Now at this point, one might very well be inclined to ask: if another act is what is going to constitute the agent's tendency toward his action, then why even posit the first act or the first relation of the will to its object, e.g. choice? Is the agent not already 'proportioned' to the thing, i.e. in possession of its form, through *understanding* it? What is the difference between these two ways in which a person is 'proportioned' to something or in which something 'exists in the soul' of someone?

Evidently the difference lies precisely in whether or not the thing 'exists in the soul' in a way that constitutes an *immediate* or *per se* principle of tending toward 'really' having it. This is what it is to exist in the soul *per modum amoris*. To understand something is to be proportioned to it in the manner of 'having a likeness of it,' and in such a way as to be apt to *conceive* a representation of it and judge the truth of one's conception by it; whereas to love something, although it presupposes having some sort of likeness of it, consists in a different way of being proportioned to it: that of something apt to move toward it and *receive* it.[118] Loving something is not forming another concept of it, over and above the concept upon which the love depends. Loving something is, so to speak, embracing the idea of it, becoming one who *lives* by it. It is upon this sort of 'proportion' that the tendency toward really possessing the object naturally follows. We might say that the proportion established in understanding is that of a representation to what it represents, whereas the proportion of willing is that of a need to what is needed.

That understanding and loving are not really the same sort of 'having a likeness of something' is readily shown: you may hate something that you understand, and hate it more the more you understand it. Nor is it any objection to this that one loves something just in proportion as one understands it to be *good*; for the difference between understanding what something is and understanding it to be good is not *per se* any further assimilation of it, any further degree of intellectual possession of its form. What it adds is only an application of the understanding of the thing to the judgment of its appetibility or lovability. Thus the very fact that it is one thing to understand something, and another to judge it good, is proof that understanding it and loving it are not the same. Loving something depends on judging it good, but understanding something can be without any judgment that it is good.[119]

But even if the distinction between understanding and wanting is sound, why distinguish between wanting and 'tending toward really having the thing'? The difference that Aquinas has in mind here cannot be merely between a want for something conceived in general terms and a want whose object is sufficiently concrete, and proportioned to the subject's actual circumstances, to serve as a princi-

---

118. See I, q. 27, a. 4 ad 2.
119. See I–II, q. 9, a. 1 ad 2.

ple of action. That is, it cannot be the difference between *simplex velle* and choice. To be sure, choice may be said to belong within the process of tending toward having the object of a *simplex velle*. But what Aquinas is talking about are distinct relations between the will and the *same* object. In any case, his very point is to distinguish between the choice of some action and the 'tending to accomplish it.' But if the object of a given choice is sufficiently definite, such that no more deliberation is necessary, what place is left for any further appetitive act prior to the action itself, especially in the case of an action to be performed at once?

The answer has already been indicated: there is no place left for a further act terminating *in the appetite itself*. That is, there is no place left for a further formation or determination of the appetite, a further process undergone by it toward its being proportioned to an object. In the appetite itself, there only remains place for the exercise of its causal power. This exercise terminates in that which the power is power *over*. Use does not terminate in the appetite (except incidentally, when what is being used is the appetite itself). It terminates in the power being used. Let us see why this exercise cannot be identical with the choice.

Between the formation of the choice to perform some action and the completion of the performance, the power by which the action is to be performed must take on a definite inclination or tendency to perform it. It cannot have that tendency already; otherwise it would act spontaneously, not as an instrument of the will. At the same time, we may recall the twofold sense of 'intention,' active and passive.[120] In its active sense, it belongs to the will; in its passive sense, it belongs to an executive power. But, in accordance with the nature of the distinction between action and passion generally, these are really *one and the same tendency*. The will's aiming a power toward some action, and the power's being aimed toward some action by the will, are the same aim, seen now as emerging from the will and terminating in the power, now as belonging to the power and coming from the will.

Now, assuming that a power is unimpeded in its operation, its actual reception of a tendency will be altogether simultaneous with its beginning to operate. If it is operating as something used by an agent, its tendency must belong to it in virtue of its subjection to the agent's will. Yet the tendency in the power operating cannot be identical with the choice for that operation. What shows that it cannot is that the choice can be complete before the power even begins to operate or has any tendency to operate. Indeed, the choice *must* be complete beforehand, if it is truly a choice that has *that* operation by *that* power for its object.

An example from Wittgenstein supports the phenomenological accuracy of this account.[121] Suppose I decide at 3:00 to ring a bell at 5:00, and this decision gets carried out. Which is the more proper description of one of the things that happen when the bell rings: 'my arm makes this movement' or 'I raise my arm'?

---

120. See above, pp. 94–95.
121. *Philosophical Investigations*, § 627.

Surely the latter. At 5:00, it is *neither* the case that I must make a new choice to ring the bell at 5:00 (though I could) *nor* the case that my arm and other parts just 'go off' automatically like an alarm clock. I am still in control. Certainly between 3:00 and 5:00 I do not feel any sort of pressure or urge in my arm to ring the bell; or even if I do, it is still I who 'release' the pressure, at 5:00. It is at 5:00 that *I* start using my arm to ring the bell. Precisely because the movement of the arm exists in virtue of being (part of) the object of my choice to ring the bell, that movement cannot constitute a 'going off' of the arm; what 'goes off' is *me*, by virtue of my will, and 'in' my arm.[122]

As is clear from the earlier discussion of use, what Aquinas means by the 'tendency toward really possessing the thing wanted' is not something *separate* from the movement whose completion is the possession of the thing. (In the case of a tendency toward an action, the 'possession of the thing' is the accomplishment of the action.) It exists *together with* that movement, giving rise to the movement by terminating *in* the movement's proper subject.

E. THE WILL AND CONDUCT

1. The Will as Passive and Active

Now, the tendency toward really possessing something wanted is not confined to tendencies initiating bodily movements. The movement by which a choice is arrived at, deliberation (a movement of reason), is itself a part of the process of attaining something wanted. For this very reason, Aquinas grants that one may speak of an act of use that *precedes* choice:

> since the will also moves reason in a certain way and uses it, 'the use of that which is for an end' can be understood according to the way in which it [that which is for an end] is in the consideration of reason referring it to the end.[123]

---

122. And in my will too. Since (by hypothesis) my arm is as much in my power at 3:00 as at 5:00, there must be some difference in my will to account for my not moving my arm at 3:00 and my moving it at 5:00. The difference is that at 3:00, I do not want to move my arm *now*, whereas at 5:00 (or when I think it is 5:00) I do want to move it *now*. So there is no difference in my will as regards the original object of choice, namely moving my arm at 5:00; but there is a difference in it as regards 'what to do with my arm now,' a difference corresponding to a change in what time it is 'now.' This difference requires no new deliberation on my part; my choice at 3:00 to ring the bell at 5:00 is itself a disposition to decide to ring the bell 'now' when the time 'now' is 5:00. Intentions for future actions include future willings in their objects.

123. I–II, q. 16, a. 4. This recognition that something like use can exist even prior to any 'external' movement helps confirm our inference from what Thomas says in I–II, q. 16, a. 4, that the two relations of the will to its object are not confined to the willing of things that are for the sake of an end. In particular, it shows that the will's second relation to the end can exist, in the form of intention, even when the end is too remote, or the means to it too vaguely determined, for the willing of it to result immediately in any action, i.e. any external movement toward the end. Intending is want-

This too is consistent with the general account of agency or efficacy. If use is an act of the will in its capacity as an active power, and so terminates in that which is being used, then *pari ratione* the acts that do terminate 'in the will,' and pertain to its first relation to its object, would seem to belong to it according as it constitutes a kind of *passive* power.[124] This means that they are acts by which a man gets determined or *formed* so as to tend toward the object; or, in accordance with the discussion in Chapter 3, acts by which he becomes one to whom the object stands as a genuine final cause, as an actual principle of inclination.

In the case of the act of choice, the agent-power initiating the will's formation is nothing other than the will itself. 'The will, through the fact that it wants an end, moves itself to wanting the things that are for the end.'[125] The will's power over itself is not confined to its power over its power to use the other powers in man. It also has power over its own formation. Since choice is deliberate willing, and since for Aquinas a human action in the chief sense is one that proceeds from deliberate willing,[126] it is thus in all strictness that he says that

---

ing to reach the end by some means, but this may be merely wanting to reach the end 'by some means or other.' Even while the agent is still deliberating, he is already intending the end; indeed, his deliberation is itself a kind of means. Intending is nothing other than tending to attain an end, *somehow*.

Finnis ('Object and Intention in Aquinas,' esp. pp. 8–10) goes to great lengths to downplay the distinction between intention and choice. He judges that at least in the typical case, an intention is always identical with a choice; the distinction between them is only 'formal' (a distinction of reason). In support of this he cites I–II, q. 12, a. 4, where Aquinas says that the intention of an end, and the choice of something for the sake of that end, form one act, and are distinct only in reason. But Aquinas is surely not trying to make the same point that Finnis is. Even if it is true that most intentions are formed by choice, the point of I–II, q. 12, a. 4 is to establish the unity of an intention and *any* choice for the end intended, even if the choice is formed through a deliberation which terminates long after the intention was formed. This comes out in the reply to the third objection, where Aquinas notes that intentions can exist even when the means to their objects have not yet been selected. He takes this as a sign that intention and choice are *distinct* (whereas see Finnis, n. 18). His thought is that an intention can exist without a choice for some means to what is intended; yet when the choice comes about, it forms one act with the intention, and the distinction between them is then only of reason; they form a kind of continuum. We have already seen how this is possible. Intention is a kind of active principle in the subject, an aiming of himself toward some end. Sometimes the pattern or the steps of the movement toward the end have yet to be determined; in this case, the intention is an aiming himself toward determining. This movement is deliberation, and its term is choice. So choice exists as a kind of passion, a being-determined toward something (the means); and this passion arises from the chooser himself, under the action of aiming himself toward the end. So, once the choice comes about, it is one (by continuity) with the intention, and the distinction between them is merely of reason; yet the intention existed before the choice. Evidently what Aquinas has in mind here corresponds closely to his more explicit account of the relation between command and *use*. Command precedes use, often in time (I–II, q. 17, a. 3); yet they form one act (a. 4), albeit one whose parts are separable and related as prior and posterior (ibid., ad 2 and 3). (See above, Chapter 2, Sections B.2 and D.2.)

124. See Brentano, *The Psychology of Aristotle*, p. 73 and corresponding note: 'the faculty of desire is something passive,' because 'the desires are in it.'

125. I–II, q. 9, a. 3. See also *De malo* q. 6, a. 1.

126. I–II, q. 1, a. 1. See also I–II, q. 85, a. 1 ad 3.

human acts can be considered as actions or as passions, 'since a man moves himself, and is moved by himself.'[127]

Undoubtedly, though, in its narrower and more ordinary acceptation, 'use' refers to acts which presuppose that the subject's appetite has already been fully formed or 'made proportionate' to an action; that is, it refers to action itself, in the sense of what begins only when *all* the steps of a given line of deliberation are finished.[128] That is, it refers mainly to something relative to which the will is a purely active power. It is with respect to other capacities that the agent, in acting, is 'being moved' by himself.

It is evidently along this line that Sellars insists that acts of will are not actions. What he is calling 'acts of will' are the acts that we have described as terminating 'in' the will, or acts concerning which the will is to some extent passive.[129] That this is the only sort of act of will that he recognizes, i.e. that everything else is merely 'physical,' shows only that he too shares in the general outlook discussed earlier. But given this restriction, his point is well taken: these are not actions. Recall Melden's claim that actions cannot be events caused by acts of will, since acts of will are themselves actions; they admit of moral evalua-

---

127. I–II, q. 1, a. 3.

128. A line of deliberation is finished when it is brought back to a determination as to what to do *now*. It is of course perfectly legitimate to speak of intermediate choices, i.e. choices of things which themselves require further deliberation before it is possible to begin attaining them; but until the process is brought back to something that one is able and willing to do now, and that one believes to be suitable to attaining the more remote goals and means, none of these more remote items can be said to have been chosen in the full and proper sense. Choice, taken without qualification, is about what to do now, because it is this that is without qualification in one's power. This means, among other things, that the proper difference between choice and use cannot be said to consist in the fact that choice is sometimes about future things, e.g. ringing the bell at 5:00, while use is only of what is present. If it is true that I can choose now to ring the bell at 5:00, this is because I can choose now to start something which I have some hope of finishing with my ringing of the bell at 5:00. This 'something' may be no more than waiting until 5:00; but that *is* something. It includes at least a determination to avoid doing anything (or better, anything 'unnecessary') that will prevent me from ringing the bell at 5:00. If there is no *separate* deliberation or choice of anything to be done between now and 5:00, that is simply because the whole process is obvious to me; I already know everything that has to be done if I am to ring the bell at 5:00. It would come closer to the essential difference between choice and use to say that choice takes place according to the condition of the chooser, whereas use takes place according to the condition of the thing used. Thus if the thing used is a body, its use takes time, and is a motion; but the choice to use it is not. (See Sellars, 'Volitions Re-affirmed,' p. 48, § 6.) This is why I can choose now to ring the bell at 5:00, but cannot now ring the bell at 5:00. Naturally, a particular object of choice may be something which I in no way do now. But it must be something which *enters into* what I start now, and it is what I start now that constitutes the principal object of my choice. The expression 'at 5:00' in the above example is an oblique way of referring the bell-ringing back to now, by setting it in definite relation to the present time.

129. 'Volitions Re-affirmed,' p. 48, § 2. He does not deny, of course, that even these are things which someone does or engages in; but they are not actions in the sense of giving an answer to the question 'what shall I do?' The answer to this question is always an *object* of such an 'act of will.' See above, pp. 176–77.

tion. Even if, on other grounds, that definition of action cannot be accepted, this objection calls for at least some qualification. 'The object of a human action is not always the object of an active power; for the appetitive power is in a way passive, insofar as it is moved by the appetible; and yet it is a principle of human acts.'[130]

What this means is that prior to performing an action, prior to using an active power to produce the effect by which that action is specified, the human agent has already produced an act that is specified by that object, and indeed a moral (voluntary) act: the act by which the agent *becomes* ordered toward performing such an action. It is true that this is voluntary, and moral, only because it also is caused by the will; it is a choice, or at least a willing of something in the agent's *power* to deliberate about. But this only shows that not every act or event caused by the will, and not everything moral, is an action. Sometimes it is only an event on the way toward the performance of an action.

2. Exterior Acts as Acts of Will

Sellars also insists that the acts of will, or volitions, whose existence he wants to defend are not parts of the actions of which they are causes, not the 'initial steps which bring the rest' of the action.[131] This is reasonable, again assuming that he is talking about acts like wanting or choosing. My choice to ring the bell is not part of my ringing the bell; my ringing the bell may begin long after the choice is adopted.

However, Sellars' refusal to acknowledge *any* acts of will that *are* parts of human actions and causes of the rest of the actions of which they are parts is in no way justified by his insistence that the action begins with the beginning of the exercise of the physical or executive power proper to it. 'Thus when I move my finger and my finger moves because I will to move it, the initial stage of the moving is exactly that; the initial stage of the moving begins when the finger begins to move.'[132] This is true, and it shows that my 'willing to move my finger' is not part of the action of moving it. But it does not show that the beginning of the finger's motion, the start of the exercise of the power to move it, is not also an act of will: a *use* of the finger.

Indeed, it rather supports that thesis; for the expression 'my willing to move my finger' means 'my willing that *I* move my finger.' The 'moving my finger,' or at least the application of the strength in my finger to *its* action of moving the finger, is not caused by an act of my will; it *is* an act of my will.[133] What the quotation from Sellars shows is that this act is altogether simultaneous with the event of the strength's being applied to the work of moving the finger. This is to be

---

130. I–II, q. 18, a. 2 ad 3.
131. Volitions Re-affirmed,' p. 49, § 9.
132. Ibid.
133. See Anscombe, 'Will and Emotion,' p. 105.

expected, since these are in fact the *same* act, at once the action of my will and something undergone by the strength in my finger.

Nor is it any objection that the object of *this* act of will is an action too, namely an 'exterior' action, one performed by a 'physical' power. Nothing prevents the parts of actions from being actions too, and it is only by being in continuity with the action of the will that the 'exterior' action itself forms part of a *human* action.[134] This point is well stressed by Donagan: neither interior nor exterior acts, by themselves, constitute a complete human act. A complete human act is a composite of the two. An interior act has an exterior act for its object; and an interior act that is *not* ordered to the exterior act that is its object in such a way as to be incomplete without the accomplishment of that act is not even a complete *interior* act.

This is not to deny that a merely interior act, one which fails to produce its exterior effect, suffices to constitute an unqualified piece of conduct. Nor is it to say that the morality of an exterior act can be fully determined by looking only to its object and circumstances.[135] An interior act can constitute a *fully definite* piece of conduct without thereby being a complete piece of conduct; not everything required for the completion of something is required for the completion of its specification. And if it is necessary to look outside (or behind) an exterior act in order to give full specification to the conduct that it instantiates, this shows only that by itself it is conduct in a merely secondary or participated way.[136] It does not show that an exterior act does not form *part* of something that is *essentially* conduct. Once again, it is illuminating to consider the analogy with the relation between the human soul and the human body, which together constitute one complete human being.

On the other hand, it is impossible for some action of mine to begin in something outside my body. If things that go on outside my body can be part of my conduct, this is only to the extent that they are subject to my body. I can set nothing else to work without setting my body to work; and my doing so is already my starting to perform an action, in any intelligible sense of 'action.' We may say that it is not possible for anything outside of me to be immediately subject to an interior act of my will. It is in just this sense that the term 'interior' is defensible. What is immediate to my will is always an act in me.[137] Actions of things outside

---

134. 'The will uses one's members for acting, as instruments; nor do exterior acts have the note of morality, except insofar as they are voluntary' (I–II, q. 18, a. 6).

135. See I–II, q. 18, a. 4, together with q. 19, a. 3.

136. This is also why, if someone's movements derive from his will in a defective way, for instance through ignorance, there may be no form of conduct which they instantiate in an unqualified way, and they may not be able to be placed straightforwardly in any determinate, moral species. See below, Chapter 5, Section D.3.

137. As Anscombe has shown (*Intention*, pp. 52ff.), this does not mean that the understanding through which I perform an action is always exclusively in terms of things intrinsic to me, i.e. according to descriptions that require no reference to things outside me. I would find it very difficult, for

me can be mine only by being subject to my own exterior acts, acts produced in me by my will. 'Whatever is done about the use of irrational things subject to a man is done through an act of the man himself moving such things.'[138]

Perhaps it is according to considerations such as these that Aquinas can lay down, as an altogether universal thesis covering both interior and exterior acts, that a human act can be considered both in the manner of an action and in the manner of a passion, 'because a man moves himself and is moved by himself.'[139] A human act is always a case of someone using *himself*.

This suggests that there is some truth in Davidson's thesis that all we ever do is move our bodies, the rest being up to nature. I argued in Chapter 2 that it is a mistake to say that a man's action *finishes* with what takes place in him or with something of which he is the subject; but it certainly *starts* there. It is only over acts inside the boundaries of our bodies that we have immediate control. But, even more interestingly, he is also right to put the limit at the boundary of a man's *body*, not at his will taken as a purely 'spiritual' faculty. One's will is the only thing over which one *necessarily* has immediate control, but it is not always the only thing over which one has immediate control. This is the sense of the series of questions raised by Aquinas in I–II, q. 17, arts. 5–9, concerning the powers whose acts can be 'commanded' by the will. These are the powers which, barring some impediment, a man can set to work voluntarily without having to set something else to work first.

It is not always true that one's will is the only thing in one's immediate control. But what is more, it is also altogether unnatural, against the nature of the *will*, for this to be the case. By this I do not mean only that it is natural for men to want to have control over other things besides their wills. I also mean that not to have such control is against the nature of that potential in human beings which serves as the main criterion for calling them good or bad human beings. It is against the nature of the will precisely because the will is this potential. Recall

---

instance, to form such a description of my present action of typing these words. But part of the understanding through which I perform an action is an understanding of the instruments employed in it; and even if I can *think* of using something outside myself without using any part of myself, I cannot act through such a thought. In her example (p. 54), even if it is true that I make my arm go down at the speed at which it would fall only by thinking in terms of keeping the ball level, I am at least thinking of keeping the ball level *with my arm*.

138. I–II, q. 93, a. 5. In this text Aquinas is contrasting the way in which men can make physical things (other than themselves) act, and the way God does so. Even though physical things are not part of him, their acts *are* immediately subject to his will; he can, as it were, make them act 'from inside.' If Aquinas restricts what he says about man to man's control over *irrational* things, this is because he is using the control exercised by one man over another, through command, as the least imperfect example available for illustrating God's control over nature. *In a sense*, or 'for all practical purposes,' to make someone else do something by simply telling him to is to make him do 'all' the work; one has not 'done' anything, or not made oneself do anything, 'but only said the word.'

139. I–II, q. 1, a. 3.

the point noted toward the end of Chapter 1: if we ask 'why is the will this potential?,' i.e. 'why are *we* (not just our wills) called good or bad mainly according to the dispositions of our wills, and not those of any other power?,' the answer is this: 'through the will we use all the things that are in our power.'[140]

Certainly the will must be able to use itself too; but if it could use nothing else, it would be useless. If it could use nothing else, and if it were still true that what makes a man to be a good man is a good will, then the upshot would be simply this: being a good man is no good. But being a good man *is* good, and is essentially having a good will, because it means being disposed to use oneself to accomplish what is good, being apt to *do* good. Naturally, room must be made for thwarted deeds; but not in such a way that one's being thwarted or not becomes a matter of indifference.

3. The Heart of Conduct

Now, so much stress on 'use' may start to give the impression that what is being proposed is some kind of 'utilitarianism,' treating human action as essentially a kind of means toward an end outside itself, something merely instrumental. In this final portion of the chapter, I shall try to show that this is not the case. Doing so will enable me to bring out what, it seems to me, may be regarded as the heart of human action or conduct: the use of one's choices.

The notion of 'use' being employed here is very broad. Not all use is merely technical or productive use. In that sort of use, the goal is indeed extrinsic to what is used, and as a consequence the use itself, the production, can never be a goal just in its own right. But moral use, or action, is not of this sort. Moral action is *immanent* action.

> Of acts, some pass into exterior matter, such as burning or cutting; and acts of this sort have for their matter and subject that into which the action passes.... But there are certain acts that do not pass into exterior matter, but remain in the agent, such as desiring and knowing; and all moral acts are of this sort, whether they be acts of virtues or of sins.[141]

---

140. See above, p. 44. See also I–II, q. 57, a. 1; a. 3 ad 2; a. 4.

141. *Actuum autem quidam transeunt in exteriorem materiam, ut urere et secare: et huiusmodi actus habent pro materia et subiecto id in quod transit actio. . . . Quidam vero actus sunt non transeuntes in exteriorem materiam, sed manentes in agente, sicut appetere et cognoscere; et tales actus sunt omnes actus morales, sive sint actus virtutum, sive peccatorum* (I–II, q. 74, a. 1). It is not to be supposed that the capacity, or the root of the capacity, for immanent acts cannot also be a source of transitive acts; quite the contrary. The capacity for immanent acts bespeaks a high degree of actuality or perfection, and hence of power generally. Consider these two texts. *Secundum Philosophum, in IX Meta., duplex est actio: una quae manet in agente et est perfectio ipsius, ut videre; alia quae transit in exteriora et est perfectio facti, sicut comburere in igne. Divina autem actio non potest esse de genere illarum actionum quae non sunt in agente: cum sua actio sit sua substantia. . . . Oportet igitur quod sit de genere illarum actionum quae sunt in agente et sunt quasi perfectio ipsius. Huiusmodi autem non sunt nisi actiones cognoscentis et appetentis* (*SCG* II, ch.

It is of the utmost importance not to conceive the will's being first passive, then active, as though the will were like a billiard ball, first being struck and receiving motion, and then striking something else and passing the motion on.[142] This would indeed make the will and its acts merely instrumental. But, first of all, the movement of the will by its object, which is the formation of its desire or its proportion to the object, is not at all the same kind of movement as that which it initiates through its use of the other powers. This movement does not 'pass through' the will to the power being used; rather, the will retains the desire formed in it, and this remains the same throughout the use of the power by which the desire is satisfied. The desire does not merely stimulate the use, but regulates it.

Moreover, the will itself has control over its own formation. It moves itself toward choice, through deliberation. Deliberation often presents several objects as choiceworthy or as potential objects of choice, from which the will selects freely; and the act of deliberation itself is subject to choice. Also, we have seen how the will's use of the other powers is at the same time its use of its own power over them. It initiates and controls its own causality. Its exercise of the chosen action is an exercise of itself and, through itself, of the other powers.

Indeed, the will's power over itself goes even beyond its power over its own formation, in choice, and beyond its power over its own act of moving the other powers in a man. It also has power over the *use* of its choice, the very application of its choice to the control of the movement of the other powers. That is, once the will's disposition has been formed, through choice, its subsequently acting according to the choice is not at all a mere 'natural result,' occurring automatically if there are no external obstacles (of whatever kind, including such things as the fact that it is not yet the chosen time to act). It belongs to the will itself to apply or exercise its choice. A person may very well select, from among his choices, the one to act upon *now*, just as he may select, from among the things he knows, which one to consider now. And he may also either adhere to his choice and carry through with it, or not do so, without ever considering repealing it—for instance in a case of incontinence.[143] Of course, incontinence is not so much an exercise of the will's dominion as a failure to exercise it.

23, § 993). *Quanto alicuius actionis principium est perfectius, tanto actionem suam potest in plura extendere et magis remota: ignis enim, si sit debilis, solum propinqua calefacit; si autem sit fortis, etiam remota. Actus autem purus, qui Deus est, perfectior est quam actus potentiae permixtus, sicut in nobis est. Actus autem actionis principium est. Cum igitur per actum qui in nobis est possumus non solum in actiones in nobis manentes, sicut sunt intelligere et velle, sed etiam in actiones quae in exteriora tendunt, per quas aliqua facta producimus; multo magis Deus potest, per hoc quod actu est, non solum intelligere et velle, sed etiam producere effectum* (SCG II, ch. 6, § 884).

142. I owe this consideration to Fr Lawrence Dewan.

143. The incontinent man never decides, for instance, that he was wrong to resolve (say) not to overeat; such a decision would not be incontinence, but a beginning of intemperance or gluttony. Between a *policy* of not overeating and one of self-indulgence, he still prefers the former. Only, when the pie is set before him, he decides not to live up to it this time. This is why Aristotle says (*Nico-

This last notion, that of the use of one's choices, is particularly significant. For here we have a genuine action which at the same time remains seated in the voluntary agent, *qua* voluntary and *qua* agent. Perhaps a choice, in itself, is more a disposition or state than an action, not answering the question 'what are you doing?' (though of course it may be the *result* of something that answers the question, namely deliberating). But surely the use or application of a choice is such an answer. For instance, one might answer the question by saying 'I am being merciful,' or 'I am just being fair.' Such an answer certainly asserts more than the subject's mere possession of the virtue of fairness. It asserts his exercise of the virtue. But the virtue of fairness is nothing other than a habitual form of choices, choices to exercise fairness or to act fairly (rather than unfairly). This form of choices is itself something which one may choose to adopt. The action of being fair is the exercise of a chosen form of choice, the application of this form to the control of one's movements.

Certainly, then, such an action also constitutes a principle or source of exterior acts, acts that terminate in something other than the will, and finds its complement there; it is an action which is only part of a complete action. For example, being fair, here and now, will involve listening to what someone has to say. But being fair, as such, does not consist *formally* in any exterior act. There is no one form of exterior action which, universally, constitutes an instance of being fair (though there may very well be forms of exterior action which *cannot* constitute instances of being fair or share in the nature of fairness). And if, through no fault of his own, the person is prevented from doing what being fair requires here and now (or what it would require if he could do it!), if he has actually tried to do it then he *has* been fair. The heart of being fair is an immanent action.[144] It is an action both initiated by and seated in the will.[145]

But of course a heart without the other members is an incomplete, indeed a mutilated entity. As I tried to argue earlier, the interior acts of the will are never

---

machean Ethics III, ch. 4, 1111b14) that the incontinent man does not choose his *praxis*, i.e. his incontinent conduct. He chooses the deed, but he does not directly choose being incontinent rather than continent. There is no such thing as a choice to be incontinent. There are only incontinent choices. By contrast, there are both wicked choices and a choice to be wicked.

144. This is corroborated by the fact that it is a 'perfect' action, not a motion; it is complete in its form while it exists. Being fair may involve writing out a check. But while one is writing a check, one is being fair in doing so, and has been fair the whole time.

145. It is also worth noting that for Thomas, the will is not the sole 'subject' of moral action. That is, although the other faculties only share in moral action or conduct, not being its proper source or possessing it *per se*, nevertheless not all of them share in it merely in the manner of instruments. The sense-appetites, too, are capable of immanent operations, namely passions or emotions, and these are moral to the extent that they are subject to the control of the will, i.e. to the extent that the sense-appetites are capable of being used. What are merely instrumental to moral action are the bodily members, since they are not subjects of immanent operation but only sources of transitive actions. See I–II, q. 74, arts. 2 and 3.

self-sufficient, but are always *ordered* to some exterior act; the *end* of essentially moral action is, or at least includes, something which is not an essentially moral action.[146] This is not contradicted, but rather corroborated, by the example of being fair. Someone may indeed end up being prevented from doing what fairness requires under the circumstances, and still have been fair. But he must at least have sought to do it; and hence his not doing it must be involuntary, against his will and inclination. His end includes something other than the purely being fair.

Speaking of fairness, Thomas makes striking use of the distinction between immanent use and merely transitive or productive use in the course of defending his classification of justice among the moral virtues.[147] The third objection he raises against this classification is that justice has to do with external (corporeal) things, and therefore ought to be numbered among the arts or skills. His reply is that justice has to do with external things not as regards making or producing them, but as regards 'using them, in relation to someone else.' Justice concerns external things, but it does so precisely to the extent that these mediate personal relations, i.e. to the extent that one's handling of external things puts *oneself* in a certain, specifically personal relation.

This relation is realized *in* the handling, not as a kind of extrinsic consequence of it, and can be good or bad in its very own right. Personal relations, which in the case of human beings are always embodied in or mediated by dealings with external things, are what form the heart of the matter of justice. This is why justice is not only one of the moral virtues, but also the chief among them.[148]

Obviously this does not mean that all personal relations are essentially matters of justice. Justice is a factor in human relations because external things form an inescapable circumstance of them, by forming necessities of human life. Through justice, in fact, a man provides for his own 'personal' needs precisely in the manner of one who has not lost sight of the elementary truth that the others too are persons, not mere tools. This is why personal relations outside the sphere of justice cannot be right if one of their subjects is unjust; and the most noble of them, the forms of what Aristotle calls true friendship, cannot exist at all.

Aristotle considers friendship to be a relation into which one enters by choice. He also regards true friendship as a kind of tendency to share one's life with one's friend, where 'life' means above all mental life, one's thoughts and affections. The fulfillment and exercise of the friendship lies precisely in that sharing. I mention this only in order to remove any remaining impression that Davidson's thesis was adopted solely or mainly to insist upon the will's control

---

146. For Thomas, the *true* end of moral action, i.e. the end of truly good moral action, as a whole, is something of a *higher* order than essentially moral action; it is not only not immediately from the will, but also not primarily dependent on the will, at least the human will. What depends on the human will is only a certain participation in it.

147. II–II, q. 58, a. 3.

148. I–II, q. 66, a. 4; II–II, q. 58, a. 12.

over the body. It would hardly be very Thomistic to treat the use of the bodily powers as the climax of human action, or as the domain in which human life finds its fulfillment.[149] The aim was merely to underscore once again the thesis that human life cannot find its fulfillment in the exercise of 'pure' acts of will, even when the will is looked upon as an *active* power; and that this fact must enter into the account of the will itself, as an active power, from the very start. The will is both a principle and an object of use.[150] But of course its most important applications are in the use a person makes—or fails to make—of his mind and heart.[151]

---

149. Besides, what Davidson means by 'moving our bodies' includes mental acts as well. His 'anomalous monism' allows him to use the term 'body' to refer globally to everything in somebody.

150. See Augustine, *De libero arbitrio* II, ch. 14, § 51; *De doctrina christiana* I, ch. 22, § 20 to I, ch. 40, § 44.

151. In this metaphorical usage, 'heart' denotes the same thing as the will, but seen in its character as a passive power, the power of engaging in 'spiritual passions' such as *dilectio* (see I–II, q. 26, a. 3). If the active power of the will cannot reach its term 'within' the soul itself, this is because the will is moved to act by love, and because the chief object of love cannot be the soul itself. Yet a good deal of one's love is also in one's power, and this precisely because not even one's own love is the soul's chief object or complete fulfillment. Rather, its fulfillment must reside in the act by which it is fully united to, fully possesses and is fully possessed by, the most fully lovable object (I–II, q. 3, a. 4; also q. 1, a. 1 ad 2; q. 4, a. 2).

Chapter 5
Praeter intentionem

INTRODUCTION: SOME TERMINOLOGY

The principal part of the goal of this study has now been reached. The goal was to contribute to an account of human or voluntary action by considering it in relation to features common to action generally, features cutting across the analogical spectrum embracing human and non-human action. The concern of this final chapter is to address, from the same perspective, a secondary but nevertheless inescapable dimension of human action. This is the dimension of actions which are not a direct effect of the will's agency, but only pertain to it in some sort of indirect fashion. This dimension is secondary, because indirect agency is a secondary sense of agency. The general background for these considerations was provided in Chapter 3, Section E.

In particular, I shall concentrate here on things which bear an indirect connection with an agent's *intention*. The root of human agency consists in a person's power to form his own intentions, in choices, and to exercise these intentions, in the use of his choices. It is by having a connection with this power that things have a connection with human agency as such. Something may have a connection with a person's intention without being its object. It may fall outside his intention, be *praeter intentionem*.

The topic of *praeter intentionem* is vast, and so is the literature on it. (Less vast, but still vast, is the literature on the topic in Thomas.) I have no intention of providing anything even close to an exhaustive treatment of either. I shall certainly not enter into the thicket of its application to moral issues; one or two issues will come up only to illustrate Aquinas's doctrine. My aim is limited to making some contribution to understanding the general notion of it and speaking about it coherently. It seems to me that a good deal of help is provided here by bringing in the more general notions of active efficacy and tendency.

Before entering into the analysis of indirect intention, it might be helpful to clarify certain pieces of terminology that Aquinas uses in discussing the specification of actions. This theme is of course intimately connected with that of objects of intention, since these are what specify acts. Aquinas's treatment of the specification of actions is complex, sometimes downright bewildering; and the source of the difficulty is not always merely his terminology. But often it is.

The first set of terms consists of two pairs, formal/material and *per se/per accidens*. It is important not to confuse these. Both what is 'formal' to an act's constitution and what is 'material' to it can belong to it *per se*. Only what is material to it can belong to it *per accidens*. Suppose I take some medicine, say some antibiotic, solely for the sake of restoring my health. In this case, my ingesting the antibiotic substance is chiefly or, in St Thomas's terms, 'formally' a health-procuring or medicinal act. But the immediate term of this act, which is simply the presence of the antibiotic inside my body, also pertains in some way to the very substance of what I am doing. St Thomas would say that, relative to the act's quality as health-procuring, its nature as the ingestion of this substance pertains to it 'materially.' But it certainly does not pertain to the act merely *per accidens*. It belongs to the act's very substance and is a cause of the act's health-procuring quality.

The distinction between formal and material elements in an act's species enables us to acknowledge, for instance, that two acts may both be healings, yet also include or at the same time embody acts which are specifically, not just accidentally different. The difference between taking an antibiotic and doing therapeutic exercises is hardly accidental, outside what their agents mean to be doing! The distinction also enables us to express the fact that the difference between taking an antibiotic for the sake of health and taking it for some other purpose, e.g. research, is in some way even greater than the difference between taking an antibiotic for the sake of health and doing exercises for the sake of health. The one difference is formal, the other only material.[1]

Another potential source of confusion is Aquinas's distinction between an act's 'natural' or 'physical' species and other sorts of species that might belong to it, e.g. a 'moral' species. This distinction has no direct relation whatsoever to the distinction between the descriptions of an act that are available to some external observer and those which only the agent himself necessarily knows. Rather, it is between species belonging to an act insofar as it proceeds from a physical agent, and species belonging to it insofar as it proceeds from some other kind of agent, e.g. a voluntary agent. The same act may possess both, since a physical agent may be set to work or used by a voluntary agent. A physical species is a description belonging *per se* to an act in virtue of the form or nature (from which follows the inclination or tendency) of a physical agent performing it. In the above example, the nature of the antibiotic yields such a description: (say) killing some bacteria. In this example, it would be perfectly legitimate to speak of an 'artificial' species belonging to the act:[2] the description that belongs to it *per se* in virtue of its pro-

---

1. See *Summa theologiae* I–II, q. 17, a. 4; q. 18, arts. 6 and 7; q. 72, a. 6.
2. The question of the moral species of an act of taking medicine, or of healing oneself, is a different one; it concerns the way in which the act is something desirable for the agent. My point in focusing upon an example of a distinction between a physical species and an artificial species belonging to an act, rather than on one between a physical and a moral species, is in part its relative simplicity, and in part its serving to indicate that the distinction between physical and moral is not a distinction between what goes on in the 'visible world' and what goes on in some 'inner' realm of the will.

ceeding from the art of medicine—its being an act of healing.³ Relative to the art of medicine, the stuff ingested is a kind of instrument. Its proper act, i.e. the *kind* of act proper to it (killing bacteria), is material relative to the kind of act proper to the medical art (healing). One indication of this is the fact that the act of healing does not necessarily *begin* with the taking of the medicine. It begins from the one who is the seat of the medical knowledge being exercised. It starts (say) with the prescription of the medicine. What the medicinal stuff itself carries out is only a part of an act of healing.

This in turn means that although the action of the medicinal stuff is an act of healing, and not by chance, it is not so *primarily* or *on its own*. Rather, it has the nature of an act of healing only as it were secondarily or by participation. The stuff's action is primarily one of (say) killing some bacteria. Its being an act of healing is only a supervenient condition or quality, a further modification of it.⁴ Indeed, the stuff's *being medicine* is only a supervenient condition of it, not *its* substance. The reason why these modifications do not belong to the stuff or its action merely by chance is that it has been prepared and applied under the control of the medical art.

On the other hand, although the act's being a healing is not something proportioned to the nature of the medicine, but only to the medical art, it is the medicine that does the actual execution of this part of the healing. This part of the healing derives immediately from the medicine, and only mediately or remotely from the doctor. This is to say, in Aquinas's terms, that the action of the medicine, whether described as killing this bacteria or as a healing, is an 'exterior' act of the medical art. It can be attributed to the medical art, but not as to its immediate or proximate source. As explained in the previous chapter, the acts that proceed immediately from some principle are called acts 'elicited' from it; those that proceed from it only by way of something else, acts that it 'elicits' from something else, are acts 'commanded' by it. These are also called 'exterior' acts of it, since their immediate source is something 'outside' of it. An example of a purely elicited act of the medical art would be a diagnosis or a prescription.

---

3. Of course, someone might ingest the same stuff, and so be healed, without any intention or expectation of that result; the healing might happen by chance. But then the act of ingesting the stuff does not have the nature of a healing; i.e. its being a healing is not part of its substance. It is not formally a taking of medicine.

4. See I–II, q. 18, a. 7 ad 1.

A. INDIRECT OBJECTS OF INTENTION AND ACT-SPECIFICATION*

1. Direct and Indirect Objects of Intention

To begin, let us recall the notion of indirect agent-causality laid out in Chapter 3, Section E. Several forms of such causality were distinguished. The general reason why all of them are cases of indirect causality is that a direct cause is conceived of as something whose causation of the effect is self-explanatory; that is, something which yields the effect by its own power and inclination, and to which the effect is apt to be conformed. A direct cause is one that intends, i.e. tends toward, the effect itself, and not just something that the effect accompanies.

Now, in the text from the commentary on the *Metaphysics* that we examined, we saw that Thomas calls the direct causes *per se* causes; the indirect ones, those of which the relevant effect is not the object of the cause's tendency, he calls causes *per accidens*. And he does so both when it is a matter of a chance cause, and when it is a matter of a cause having some sort of necessary (or *ut in pluribus*) order to the relevant effect.

Nevertheless, the very fact that the latter are not cases of chance causality sometimes leads Thomas to speak of the effect in such cases as resulting *per se* from the cause, or from the action of the cause. That is, he sometimes uses *per se* as the immediate opposite of 'by chance.' Nor is this merely an equivocation upon the expression *per se*. For what he evidently means is that such effects are not *wholly* outside the cause's tendency or intention.

> 'Cause *per accidens*' is said in two ways: in one way, on the part of the cause, and in another, on the part of the effect. . . . On the part of the effect, when something is taken that is accidentally conjoined to the effect. . . . And in this way, fortune is said to be a cause *per accidens*, from the fact that something is conjoined *per accidens* to the effect; for instance, if the discovery of a treasure be adjoined *per accidens* to the digging of a grave. For just as a *per se* effect of a natural cause is what follows according to the demand [*exigentiam*] of its form, so the effect of a cause acting deliberately [*a proposito*] is what occurs from the agent's intention; hence whatever comes about in the effect outside [the agent's] intention is *per accidens*.
>
> And I say this if what is outside the intention follows rarely [*ut in paucioribus*]; for what is always or frequently conjoined to the effect falls under the same intention. For it is foolish to say that someone intends something and does not want that which is adjoined to it frequently or always.[5]

---

* For a more thorough study of the textual and theoretical basis for some of the main points urged in this and the following two sections, together with further consideration of the issues raised in notes 17 and 57 below, see the Appendix, 'The Specification of Action in St. Thomas: Nonmotivating Conditions in the Object of Intention.'

5. *Causa per accidens dicitur dupliciter: uno modo ex parte causae; alio modo ex parte effectus. . . . Ex parte autem effectus, quando accipitur aliquid quod accidentaliter coniungitur effectui. . . . Et hoc modo*

The penultimate sentence of this quotation almost seems to say: what is outside the agent's intention is not always outside his intention. What it means is that what is not a direct or *per se* object of the agent's intention may still in a way fall under the intention. It does so if it is conjoined to the *per se* object not by chance. 'Sometimes something incidental accompanies the effect principally intended always or for the most part; and then what is incidental is not separated from the intention of the agent.'[6]

Something 'principally intended,' or what I would call a *per se* object of intention, is something intended *simpliciter*, taken by itself; something whose achievement *constitutes* the fulfillment of an intention; something around which the agent's action is designed or formed. This may or may not be something sought just for its own sake. The difference being noted here is not between intermediate and ultimate ends,[7] but between ends and their accompaniments. What marks the difference is whether or not it is possible to say of the thing, taken without any addition or qualification, that it is aimed at. I may intend to take medicine only because I want health, but it is still true that the taking of the medicine, just as such, is something I aim at, something according to which some movement of mine is formed.[8]

This does not necessarily mean some movement of mine other than the very taking of the medicine. It may mean simply that the form of my movement *is* that of a taking of medicine. That is, intending to do something does not always involve wanting to do something *else* in order to do it. Sometimes Thomas is taken to hold that it does. But what he says is that intention is an act of will regarding an end, 'insofar as it is the term of something that is ordered toward it.'[9] The 'something that is ordered to it' need not be an action; it may just be an agent or a power. Aquinas certainly speaks often enough of ordering some *thing* toward an action, and of ordering *oneself* toward an end.[10]

---

dicitur fortuna esse causa per accidens, ex eo quod effectui aliquid coniungitur per accidens; utpote si fossurae sepulcri adiungatur per accidens inventio thesauri. Sicut enim effectus per se causae naturalis est quod consequitur secundum exigentiam suae formae, ita effectus causae agentis a proposito est illud quod accidit ex intentione agentis: unde quidquid provenit in effectu praeter intentionem, est per accidens. Et hoc dico si id quod est praeter intentionem ut in paucioribus consequatur: quod enim vel semper vel ut frequenter coniungitur effectui, cadit sub eadem intentione. Stultum est enim dicere quod aliquis intendat aliquid, et non velit illud quod ut frequenter vel semper adiungitur (In II Phys. lect. viii, § 214). See also *In VII Meta.* lect. vi, § 1382, *In XI Meta.* lect. viii, §§ 2269, 2284.

6. *Aliquando accidens concomitatur effectum principaliter intentum semper vel ut in pluribus; et tunc accidens non separatur ab intentione agentis* (De malo q. 1, a. 3 ad 15).

7. See above, p. 97.

8. See *De malo* q. 2, a. 2 ad 8; Finnis, 'Object and Intention,' pp. 10–14.

9. I–II, q. 12, a. 1 ad. 4. Donagan comes close to saying that intending to do something always involves wanting to do something else in order to do it (*Choice*, p. 98).

10. See e.g. I–II, q. 17, arts. 1, 2; I–II, q. 89, a. 6. Along this line, there seems to be something to quarrel with in Wittgenstein's remark: 'When I raise my arm "voluntarily," I do not use any instrument to bring the movement about. . . . My wish is not such an instrument either.' (*Wenn ich meinen*

An example of something not (normally) a direct object of intention is the discomfort that accompanies taking some medicine. It would be incorrect simply to say that I am aiming at the discomfort. It does not determine the structure of the action by which I bring it about. Yet it *is* an accompanying object of my intention to take the medicine. I intend to take a medicine that happens to produce discomfort. My intention to take the medicine is some kind of tendency or order toward the discomfort, though only to the extent that it is a tendency to take the medicine. There is no distinct tendency toward the discomfort in its own right. A purely physical example is that of fire heating: the proper or principal object of its intention is the production of heat, but since this is inseparable from the removal of cold, that also falls under the fire's intention. We saw in Chapter 3 how this sort of efficacy involves a kind of indirect proportion between the agent and the effect.

Let us try to characterize more precisely the way such objects 'fall under' the agent's intention. Thomas says that 'it is foolish to say that someone intends something and does not want that which is adjoined to it frequently or always.' 'Foolish' (*stultum*) is a very strong word. Is it really *foolish* to say that I do not want the discomfort produced by the medicine? I certainly find it repugnant and have no desire for it; and if it turned out that the medicine restored my health but did not produce the discomfort after all, I would be delighted. It seems to me that if Thomas finds it foolish to say that the agent does not want such things, he can only be taking the expression 'not to want' (*non velle*) as equivalent to 'nill' (*nolle*).[11] It may not be foolish to say that the person does not positively want such things to be, but it is foolish to say that he positively wants them not to be. At most, he can only have a *velleitas*; he *would* want that they not be, if this were

---

Arm 'willkürlich' bewege, so bediene ich mich nicht eines Mittels, die Bewegung herbeizuführen. . . . Auch mein Wunsch ist nicht ein solches Mittel: Philosophical Investigations, § 614, p. 160.) The reference to 'my wish' suggests that what he means by 'an instrument' (*Mittel*) is some distinct act, and in this sense he is probably right. The raising of one's arm, as that is normally thought of, is an altogether homogeneous sort of act; one is not taking something other than the arm, making it perform some act that one thinks of as something other than a raising of the arm, and applying it to the arm to produce the further event of its rising. But surely I am using *something* to make my arm rise, however vague my understanding of it may be; I am using what I call my strength. Here one may object that according to Aquinas's doctrine of instrumental agency, the instrument has some act proper to itself, and the one using it accomplishes his own proper act by means of this. But the distinction between the act of the instrument and that of the principal agent, for Aquinas, is not always a distinction between individual events. It is primarily between forms or kinds of acts. An instrument of a certain kind performs acts of a certain kind; the principal agent, in using it, makes it perform an act of this kind *in a certain way*, a way relative to which the instrument, in itself, is merely indifferent or indefinite. Now, if I have the strength to raise my arm at all, I have the strength to raise it some distance; and since the distance is divisible, that same strength is the strength to raise it a part of that distance. Whether I raise it the whole distance that my strength allows or only part is not determined by my strength. Perhaps I determine it.

11. He does recognize such a usage for *non velle*: I–II, q. 6, a. 3 ad 2.

possible without losing the thing that he *does* positively want, e.g. to take the medicine. What is impossible, and foolish to say, is that while intending to take the medicine, and knowing that this involves the discomfort, I intend to avoid the discomfort. My intention to take the medicine *prevents* me from having the intention of avoiding the discomfort: I cannot be fully unwilling to suffer it.[12] (Naturally, this assumes that the discomfort is, or is believed to be, really inseparable from taking the medicine. If not, then of course I may have the intention of separating them.) The discomfort 'falls under' my intention to take the medicine in just this sense: the intention prevents me from intending to avoid it. So the intention's proper object and effect is the taking of the medicine; but the intention also spills over, or extends indirectly, to the discomfort.

It should be noted at once that it would be terribly misleading to lump the indirectly intentional together with the directly intentional under one generic term 'intentional.' The indirectly intentional is intentional only by analogy.[13] It is the directly intentional which is intentional *simpliciter* or without qualification. Only the directly intentional provides an *explanation* (as an end or a reason) for one's action. Thus, Anscombe says that foreseen concomitants of intentional acts are voluntary but not intentional; and it is reasonable that she does so. The notion of the intentional which governs her discussion is precisely that of something which is an explanation for the action embodying it. John Finnis even suggests throwing out expressions like 'oblique intention' altogether, and describing foreseen side-effects only as 'willful and not unintentional.'[14] Still, whatever they are called, it is important to see that for such things it is never a mere matter of fact, just happening to be the case, that they are not unintentional. They *cannot* be unintentional. And it is precisely the agent's intention that makes this so.

2. *The Indirectly Intended and Matter in the Species of Actions*

Now, in some of the places where Aquinas says that an effect falling outside the agent's intention results from the action *per se*, he also states explicitly that what belongs to something *per se* pertains in some way to its species. 'Whatever

---

12. Cf. Finnis, 'Intention and Side-Effects' (1991), p. 48: such effects are brought about 'not unintentionally.'
13. This point is brought out well by Duff, *Intention, Agency and Criminal Liability*, p. 27.
14. Anscombe, *Intention*, p. 89; Finnis, 'Intention and Side-Effects' (1991), pp. 44–61. See also Bennett, *The Act Itself*, pp. 201–03. Lumping together the directly and indirectly intentional is at least the drift of Bentham's theory of 'oblique intention,' and also of Sidgwick's doctrine that all consequences foreseen as certain or probable are to be regarded as intended. (On Bentham, see Flannery, 'Natural Law *mens rea* versus the Benthamite Tradition.') The only reservation that one might have about 'willful' is that it can also mean something like 'obstinate,' and so tends to connote a *bad* will; as should become clear below, the present notion of 'indirectly intentional' does not entail a bad will. It is a different kind of indirect intentionality that entails this.

things follow *per se* on a sin pertain in some way to the very species of the sin.'[15] We have already seen that it is his general doctrine that the species of an action is determined by the agent's intention. Evidently, then, he does not mean that such effects *constitute* the action's species; the species is taken from the intention's direct object. But they follow from the action in accordance with its species. This would seem to mean that, if not the effect itself, at least some principle of it *is* included in the intention's direct object. That is, a full description of the intention's direct object includes something which *connects* it with the effect, even if it does not include the effect itself. This 'something' is not identical with the object, but is nevertheless 'in' it. It is rather like matter for the object.

The direct object of an intention is the end that constitutes the completion of the action embodying that intention. What makes it an end is its having the form of some good of the agent's (whether the goodness of it be that of an end or that of a means). But this form is not the whole of the intention's direct object; rather, it is what the scholastics call the formal object of the intention, the reason why the object is an object. As in the case of physical things, what pertains to the intention's object, and so to the action's species, is more than its form or proportion to the agent. The object is that which *has* the form or proportion. As discussed in Chapter 3, in the case of actions that produce changes, the object also includes the patient, the thing acted upon, the subject in which the form is realized.[16] For it is in the patient that the end exists; and, to repeat the point insisted upon in Chapter 3, what is intended is the *existence* of the end. In other words, what is acted upon, the patient, contributes to the specification of action because and insofar as it is a direct object of intention, being the subject in which is realized the form according to which the agent acts. Since the patient is included in the action's species, what follows upon the accomplishment of such an action in such a patient also belongs to it according to its species.[17]

---

15. *Quaecumque per se consequuntur ad peccatum, pertinent quodammodo ad ipsam peccati speciem* (I–II, q. 73, a. 8). See I–II, q. 20, a. 5.

16. It should be obvious that 'matter' here does not necessarily mean physical 'stuff'; consider the action of changing someone's mind. For convenience, I focus the discussion here on transitive actions (and intentions for transitive actions), the ones that have real 'patients.' In the case of immanent actions, there is still an object, something that the action bears upon; but it is somehow in the agent (cf. I, q. 56, a. 1; *In IX Meta.* lect. viii, § 1864–65), and is not changed by the action. Nevertheless it has its own content, and makes its own contribution to the action's constitution. 'Matter' is used analogically in these instances, according to the common feature of that to which something is *applied*: some power, some form of activity, some order to an end.

17. For another and forceful way of putting this point, see Flannery, 'What is Included in a Means to an End?': in distinguishing an action from its side-effects, it is not plausible to go so far as to reduce the action to a merely abstract description, expressing only what its conduciveness to one's purpose formally consists in. Flannery's example is that of redescribing a craniotomy, performed on a fetus in order to remove it from the mother, as a 'cranium-narrowing.' (Thomas of course does not consider this case, but it serves well to illustrate his view.) With this description, the fact that the cranium is *crushed* may be presented as a mere side-effect. But in fact narrowing a cranium, in the way

For instance, the production of steam, by the action of fire on water, is an indirect effect of the fire. The intrinsic tendency of fire is not to produce steam; fire which is not producing steam is not thereby somehow frustrated or impeded in its action. Strictly speaking the fire's action does not consist in boiling the water. Calling it a boiling is naming it according to this indirect effect, the production of steam. But it does consist in heating, and what is being heated is water; and this entails the production of steam. This in turn means that when the fire is applied to water, the fire's tendency to heat yields a tendency to heat the water, and a tendency to produce steam. This is not the object of any distinct tendency in the fire, but it is an accompanying object of its tendency to heat, when what it is heating is water.

This same account is applicable to actions upon that particular kind of patient which is an instrument. Not every effect that an instrument is apt to have, once it is applied to a given matter by the principal agent, need contribute to what the agent properly intends in applying it, or enter into the species of his action. Yet those effects that result from the very facts that the instrument is such-and-such a thing, which the agent intends to use, and that the patient is such-and-such a thing, which the agent intends to act on, still follow from the species of the agent's action, and fall somehow within his intention. The earlier example of the medicine is a case of this sort. Although the taking of the medicine is not formally an act of 'making oneself uncomfortable,' it *is* formally an act of taking *that* medicine, and discomfort does follow on such an act. Another example would be that of a man's using force to defend himself from an aggressor. By its very nature, the use of force on someone can, and sometimes does, result in the person's death. Now if the one defending himself is not aiming at the aggressor's death, then even if the aggressor does die, this is not formally an act of killing; but it *is* formally an act of using force upon someone, and that is a sort of act to which some *likelihood* of death (if not death itself) belongs *per se*.[18] It has something lethal, or something in the direction of the lethal, about it.

---

that the surgeon intends in such a case, *is* crushing it. It is a narrowing *because* it is a crushing; he narrows the cranium by crushing it. Now, it seems to me that Thomas's view would allow us to suppose that the surgeon is not aiming at the fetus's death, not crushing the skull *in order* that the fetus die. But—also on Thomas's view—regardless of his *further* aim, his act is aimed at producing the crushed skull of an innocent person; and surely it is to that extent unjust. (On the fetus's innocence, see below, n. 60.) The skull *belongs* to the person, after all, and so does the skull's shape. How unjust is it? Well, what is the value of an intact skull? The person's *life* depends on it. (Cf. I–II, q. 73, a. 8: *si vero nocumentum per se sequatur ex actu peccati, licet non sit intentum nec praevisum, directe peccatum aggravat; quia quaecumque per se consequuntur ad peccatum, pertinent quodammodo ad ipsam peccati speciem.* Such aggravation can extend all the way to the gravity of murder: II–II, q. 64, a. 8.) Of course, if medicine can come up with a way of repairing the skull after crushing it in the required manner, the situation would be different. The crushing of it would then not be the surgeon's *whole* intended treatment of the skull (and of the person whose skull it is), and in any case the 'value' of the skull's remaining intact would be considerably reduced.

18. Thus the kind of *praeter intentionem* result that Aquinas has in mind in his discussion of killing in self-defense (II–II, q. 64, a. 7) is not the kind according to which death results by *chance*.

To repeat, it is of the utmost important to see that calling these things 'indirectly intended' means that it would be incorrect to say, without any qualification, that they are intended. Rather, they may only be *included* in an account of what the agent intends by way of having some principle in what he intends or having some order to it. They are not intended *secundum se* or *simpliciter* or *per se*, but *secundum ordinem ad aliud*: according to their order toward something else.[19] This 'something else' is the intention's direct object. It is by way of something in the object that the intention extends to them.

Thus the tendency of fire is not *simply* to consume air; it does tend to reduce the quantity of oxygen in the environment, but only to the extent that this accompanies what the fire chiefly intends, i.e. what it does tend to do 'simply,' which is to burn. So its tendency may be formulated as: a tendency to burn something, and, to that extent, to reduce the quantity of oxygen. Likewise, although the sailor who jettisons cargo in a storm, to lighten the ship, does simply intend to get the cargo off the ship (though only as a means to saving the ship), he certainly does not simply intend for the cargo to fall into the sea and become irrecoverable. Indeed, he would do anything he could to prevent this result—short of leaving the cargo on the ship. If he intended it simply, he would not wait for the storm (except perhaps to give him a pretext). Yet, assuming that he knows that this is what will happen, a full account of what he does simply intend should include it. He intends 'to throw the cargo off the ship and (since this is what "off the ship" here entails, in his own understanding of it) into the sea, to save the ship.' To place the cargo's falling into the sea *completely* outside the sailor's intention would be to say that he was a cause of it by chance; which would be nonsense.

In short, such things do not merely accompany the *execution* of the agent's aim. They also accompany the aim itself. They do so by way of the aim's object. And for that reason, they also belong to the action taken precisely as an action, i.e. as proceeding from the agent. This, again, is in accordance with the observations offered near the end of Chapter 2. The aim that an action embodies is an aim to act. Hence its full proper description requires more than the features that show it suitable or conformable to the agent, though these are the chief features and the ones that form the core of the explanation of the action's existence. These are what are 'formal' in the act's species. But the description also requires at least those features implied in the agent's aiming to *enact* what is suitable or conformable to him; even if, considered by themselves, these features are indifferent or even repugnant to him.

Once more, a guiding principle is that the action of the agent is in the patient. For the basic notion underlying the concept of indirect, non-casual

---

Killing someone by chance is discussed in the following article. He is talking about an action which *per se* (i.e. not just in virtue of some unknown circumstance) can produce the other's death. See below, Section C.2.

19. See I–II, q. 78, a. 1 ad 2.

agency is that of 'contraries.' Objects are called contraries relative to some subject in which they are apt to exist; its possession of one excludes its possession of the other. Now there is nothing impossible about wanting or desiring, or in general having a certain proportion to, contraries. The sailor may both desire to save the ship and desire not to lose the cargo. Indeed, he may both desire to jettison the cargo and desire not to lose it. They are not contraries in his desire. But there is no action available to him that can satisfy one of these desires without thwarting the other; for it is impossible for the *cargo* both to be jettisoned and not to be lost. So, it is impossible for him to aim at or intend both.[20] His intending to jettison the cargo does not *consist* in an intention to lose the cargo; but it does extend to the loss, indirectly. And this is because it *does* consist in an intention to jettison the cargo. For it is not the intention that determines what the per se effects of jettisoning the cargo are.

3. Indirectly Intended Effects and the Quality of the Will

Joseph Boyle finds it anomalous that Aquinas should say in one place (*SCG* III, ch. 6, § 1907) that a sailor 'who throws cargo into the sea for the sake of safety does not intend the throwing of the cargo but safety.' Boyle insists, rightly, that Aquinas's typical doctrine of intention would lead to the conclusion that 'the throwing overboard of the merchandise is the [direct] object of an intention; it is an end of sorts. One must aim to achieve it and might have to struggle to achieve it or to use means to achieve it.'[21] It is also true that the context of the *Summa contra gentiles* passage at least gives the impression that St Thomas is using the term 'intention,' atypically, to refer only to the aiming at something for its own sake.

But Boyle also criticizes (on what he takes to be Aquinas's own principles) the comparison drawn there between the jettisoning of the cargo and the *deordinatio* accompanying a sinful act, as objects of intention. Now, without doubt, the two cases differ in several respects. But there can be something misleading about neglecting the way in which they *are* comparable.

What is in question is the status of the act of jettisoning as an object of intention. This act has various features, and Boyle has focused on one that is slightly different from the one considered by Aquinas. The two features have different relations to the sailor's intention. What the sailor directly intends is (Boyle's feature) to throw the cargo *overboard*, i.e. off the ship; he needs to lighten the ship. But, because the ship is surrounded by the sea, his throwing the cargo overboard is simultaneously a throwing it *into the sea* (St Thomas's feature); and this is *not* something the sailor is intending or trying to bring about, except

---

20. See Donagan, *Choice*, p. 50: what intending something adds to wanting it is a determination to bring it about.
21. '*Praeter intentionem* in Aquinas,' p. 655.

indirectly. This is important, because it means that results not directly intended can be counted as falling somehow under one's intention even if one is not culpable for them. (Boyle seems to assume they cannot; this is why he rejects the comparison with the *deordinatio* of a sinful act.) The sailor is certainly not to be blamed for the loss of the cargo; quite the contrary. A man may be responsible for some generically bad result without having a bad will (see below, Section B.3). It may even be proof of the soundness of his will.

The difference between the loss of the cargo and the *deordinatio* of a sinful act is not that the latter is indirectly intended, according to the present understanding of 'indirectly intended,' while the former is not; it is that the loss of the cargo is not something which one should always *intend to avoid*, while the *deordinatio* is. The present sense of 'indirectly intended' is just that: what one's intention prevents one from intending to avoid. However, there is also another sense of 'indirectly intended.' The *deordinatio* of sin is something which the sinner *fails* to intend to avoid, when he could and should so intend. In *this* sense, the *deordinatio* is indirectly intended, while indeed the loss of the cargo is not. I shall explain this other sense more fully in Section C.

B. THE DIFFUSIVENESS AND NON-DIVISIVENESS OF INTENTION

1. Chisholm's Theses

The above account of indirect objects of intention seems to correspond to what Chisholm calls the principles of the 'diffusiveness' and 'non-divisiveness' of intention. The principle of the diffusiveness of intention is that if someone intends p, knowing that p entails q, then he intends the conjunction p and q. For instance, if a man intends to drive off in a car parked nearby, knowing that it belongs to someone else, then he intends this: to drive off in a car parked nearby that belongs to someone else. The principle of the non-divisiveness of intention is that if someone intends the conjunction p and q, he does not necessarily intend q by itself. The man may not intend just this: to drive off in a car that belongs to someone else.[22]

That is, he may not be doing what he is doing because it will deprive someone else of a car, but only because it will provide him with the quickest means of getting to his destination. Again, this is the difference between direct and indirect objects of intention: only the former are explanations of the action that fulfills the intention. But despite this difference, if the man knows that the car belongs to someone else, it would be ridiculous to say that he positively meant not to drive off in someone else's car.

22. 'The Structure of Intention.'

The point is subtle. Many authors disagree with the diffusiveness of intention principle.[23] Donagan, following Bratman, while not explicitly addressing Chisholm, uses this example: 'If you intend to run a marathon and believe that you will thereby wear down your sneakers, it does not in the least follow that you intend to wear down your sneakers.'[24] This example is similar to one used by St Thomas. 'If someone often or always gets his feet wet when he goes to a muddy place, then granted that he does not intend this, nevertheless it is not said to be by [bad] luck.'[25] But what Aquinas means is that although he does not intend simply to get his feet wet, this still falls under his intention. What Chisholm's critics seem to ignore is the other principle, the non-divisiveness of intention.[26] When taken together with it, the principle of the diffusiveness of intention appears to fit very well with the doctrine that actions are individuals, i.e. that one and the same action may admit many true descriptions whose combination is logically contingent.

The thesis that actions are individuals has been debated strenuously by analytical philosophers. It has been presented in various versions by its proponents, and some versions are more radical than others. Davidson's is one of the best known, and also one of the most radical. Arguing on formal semantic grounds (he points especially to adverbial modification), he appears to hold that actions must be regarded as irreducible subjects.[27] That is, for instance, sentences which posit individual substances—people or things—and go on to predicate action-verbs of them (strolled, kicked) cannot be successfully analyzed unless individual action-subjects (a stroll, a kick) are also posited. Donagan appears to hold a similarly radical version of the thesis. His reason is the need to account for the relation between things and time.[28] (This too would be an instance of adverbial modification, but Donagan's argument is not a semantic one.) On the other hand, Anscombe, who also upholds the thesis, appears only to want to say that there is nothing *wrong* with treating actions as individuals, and to indicate its usefulness as a way of expressing such things as the fact that some actions take on more and more descriptions as their results unfold, without 'any further effort' on the agent's part.[29] She has doubts about Davidson's line of argument,[30] and does not

---

23. See e.g. Boyle and Sullivan, 'The Diffusiveness of Intention Principle: a Counterexample'; Pitcher, ' "In Intending" and Side Effects.'
24. *Choice*, p. 106.
25. *In II Phys.* lect. viii, § 215.
26. Thus Boyle (*'Praeter intentionem* in Aquinas,' p. 649 and Boyle and Sullivan, 'The Diffusiveness of Intention Principle') identifies Chisholm's position with that of Sidgwick, who maintains that a man intends all the foreseen results of whatever he does intentionally. But the positions are not the same. Rather, Chisholm's seems to be very much like that of Boyle himself. What Boyle wants to say is that not all foreseen results are *directly* intended. But he does grant that they are at least intended *indirectly*; see '*Praeter intentionem* in Aquinas,' pp. 657–60. Cf. below, Section B.3.
27. See, *inter alia*, most of the essays in his *Essays on Actions and Events.*
28. See Chapter 2, n. 73.
29. See especially her 'Under a Description.' On 'no further effort,' see above, p. 52.
30. 'Under a Description,' pp. 216–19.

seem to insist on the 'irreducibility' of the individual action. Fortunately, however, it is not necessary here to enter into the thick of the debate. Jonathan Bennett has given a masterly treatment of it, and one which makes it a much less critical issue. The upshot appears to be that speaking of individual actions may be useful, but it is not indispensable.[31]

Thomas certainly finds it useful to speak of actions as individuals. This comes to the fore in his discussion of 'circumstances' (I–II, q. 7). Circumstances are, as it were, 'accidents' of actions. Through them, one and the same action can take on several names. For instance, an ablution might also be a warming or a cooling, and a healing or a harming.[32] Still, Thomas does not make individual actions into irreducible subjects; actions too are accidents. The only irreducible subjects are individual substances. Circumstances do not really 'inhere' in the actions, but in substances. They are accidents of actions in the sense that they accompany actions in the same subject.[33]

Particularly interesting is his account of why circumstances can enter into the scientific treatment of action. One objection to such treatment is that circumstances are accidents, and there is no science of accidental being. His reply is that not all the accidents that accompany action in a subject have the nature of circumstances, but only those which in some way 'touch' the action or have some 'order' to it; these are *per se* accidents of the actions, to be distinguished from the *per accidens* accidents that fall outside of science.[34] What falls outside of science is the 'accidental' in the sense of what is by chance. The expression *per se*, of course, was the very one Thomas used to distinguish between chance and non-chance effects of action; the latter have a certain order, necessary or *ut in pluribus*, to the action, and so pertain to it somehow *per se*. And of course, Thomas holds that circumstances can affect the moral goodness or badness of an action, and that they can do so even when they do not give the action its species, i.e. do not constitute conditions intrinsic to the action's very object. This could not be the case if circumstances did not somehow fall under the agent's will and intention. For then they would not be *per se* accidents of the action, but only *per accidens*. 'In the things that are for the sake of an end'—as are all voluntary actions—'that which is intended is what is called *per se*, whereas that which is outside of intention is *per accidens*.'[35]

2. Chisholm's Theses and Individual Actions

If a man intends an action which is a running a marathon, and if he knows that this same action will be one that results in worn sneakers, then it is hard to

---

31. See Bennett, *Events and their Names*, passim.
32. I–II, q. 7, a. 3 ad 3.
33. I–II, q. 7, a. 1 ad 2 and 3.
34. I–II, q. 7, a. 2, obj. 2 and reply; cf. I–II, q. 18, a. 3 ad 2.
35. *In his autem quae sunt propter finem, per se dicitur aliquid quod est intentum, per accidens autem quod est praeter intentionem* (II–II, q. 59, a. 2).

escape the conclusion that the wearing of the sneakers also falls under his intention. For what he intends is an action, not a description or feature of one, nor even 'an action under such-and-such description.'[36] The action is intended under all the descriptions he expects to be true of it, though he does not intend it *because* of all of the descriptions he expects of it. He may intend it *despite* some of them. The thought may be put this way: if you ask the man, 'Are you not aware that in running the marathon you will also be wearing down your sneakers?' and he says 'yes,' then if you ask, 'But you mean to do it anyway?' he can truthfully say 'no' only by giving up the intention to run the marathon.

In the terms of Aquinas's scheme of the typical moments in the genesis of a complete voluntary act, since the wearing down of the sneakers falls indirectly under the man's intention, it also falls indirectly under his consent and preference and choice. This may help to clarify the point, since we do readily speak of consenting to and choosing things that are repugnant to our wills, e.g. 'the lesser evil.' (Still, of course, the choice is only indirectly of the evil; it is chosen on account of being 'lesser.') The runner accepts the fact that the sneakers will get worn down, since this goes with his acceptance of the project of running the marathon; and he prefers that his sneakers get worn down rather than that he not run the marathon. Since he intends to run the marathon, while knowing that his sneakers will get worn down, he chooses the wearing down of them—not on its own account, but on account of its necessary connection with the running.[37] But once something required for the fulfillment of an intention is discovered and chosen, it too falls under the intention, in the same way that it falls under the choice.[38]

The principle of the diffusiveness of intention does not mean that all foreseen effects are directly intended. Nor does it mean that an intended action is directly intended under every one of its known descriptions *taken in isolation* or,

---

36. To say this, that the object of his intention is the act under such-and-such a description, is to misunderstand the grammar of the expression 'under a description.' The correct way to put it would be: it is under such-and-such a description that the act is the object of his intention. See Anscombe, 'Under a Description,' p. 208.

37. Not every object of choice, not everything desired *propter finem*, need be directly conducive to the end (the normal sense of 'means'). In order for something to fall under a choice, it suffices that (the agent believe that) the end cannot be attained unless this other thing is brought about. The nature of the connection between them does not matter. Far from being *per se* conducive to the end, what is chosen may in fact rather oppose it; as when a mountain climber deliberately does something that involves great risk to his life, in order to save his life. He chooses to take the risk.

38. See I-II, q. 12, a. 4. The principle is: *idem autem actus cadit super obiectum et super rationem obiecti*, the same act bears upon the object and the reason of the object. Hart puts the point well. In 'Problems of the Philosophy of Law,' pp. 97–98, he notes that in law, a man is held to have intended all the foreseen consequences of his conduct, whether or not he aimed at them. For, he says, the question is whether, at the time of acting, the agent had (i.e. could have made) 'a *choice* whether these consequences were or were not to occur' (p. 98). The concept of choice operative here is set forth by J. L. Austin in his description of what it is to act deliberately: 'I act *deliberately* when I have deliberated—which means when I have stopped to ask myself, "Shall I or shan't I?" and then decided to do X, which I did' ('Three Ways of Spilling Ink,' in *Philosophical Papers*, p. 286).

as the scholastics say, 'reduplicatively' (taking the description twice, with *qua* or its equivalent introducing the second instance). For example, suppose someone intends to run a marathon, knows that such an action will also be a wearing down of his sneakers, but is not aiming to wear down his sneakers. In this case the proposed action is not, *qua* a wearing down of his sneakers, directly intended by him. But the principle does mean that the proposed action taken *concretely*, as the *subject* of all its known descriptions, is directly intended. The *composite* of its known descriptions is directly intended. *Qua* a 'running a marathon and a wearing down of sneakers,' the action *is* directly intended, although it is intended only because it is a running of a marathon. 'Running a marathon' expresses only the formal object of the agent's intention. This also means that although he does not directly intend wearing down his sneakers, he does directly intend an action that is a wearing down of his sneakers.[39]

Or almost. A possible objection to this account is that foreseen but not directly intended results neither constitute nor form a part of the fulfillment of the agent's intention. That is, assuming that what he was directly aiming at comes about, the failure of other results that he expected in no way means that his aim was frustrated, wholly or even partially.[40] Their failure to come about may in fact be a relief to him. Presumably to say that something is directly intended means at least that it constitutes the whole or a part of an intention's fulfillment.

The answer to this would seem to be based on the distinction between descriptions that are true of an action according to what is intrinsic to it and those that are true according to something extrinsic to it. In the previous example, the man's action does not consist in wearing down his sneakers. It is not brought to completion in the sneakers' being worn down. That result is extrinsic to it. What is *not* extrinsic to it, however, is to be an action that the man *expects* to have that result. And the performance of an action that he expects to have that result *is* essential to, or rather is, the fulfillment of his intention.

The objection is instructive in two ways. First, it shows that it is not the case that the composite of an intended action and all of its foreseen results is something directly intended. Rather, we should say that something directly intended is directly intended under the composite of all the descriptions that the agent attributes to it. Secondly, it shows that not all of the descriptions of an action that

---

39. For an example of a study of the effects of the 'reduplication' of a description of a subject on predications, see III, q. 16, arts. 9–12. The notion of reduplicative predication is connected with the analytical philosophers' distinction between 'intensional' and 'extensional' functions, a distinction that is important for the analysis of intentional action offered by Davidson, Anscombe, Donagan and others. See below, Section D.

40. See *De malo* q. 2, a. 6 obj. 6: *voluntas non fertur super circumstantiam; sicut cum aliquis furatur vas aureum consecratum non curat de consecratione.* The reply grants the fact that the thief does not 'care' about the vessel's being consecrated, this not being what his will primarily (*principaliter*) bears on— he would take the vessel just as soon even if it were not consecrated. But Thomas insists that his will *fertur super rem sacram ex consequenti; magis enim vult rem sacram accipere quam auro carere.*

fall within the agent's intention do so as things which he intends to make true of his action. Some of them do so only as things which he expects to be true of what he intends. So, properly speaking, it is precisely as objects of his expectation that they fall within what he directly intends.[41] If the intention is fulfilled, he will have performed an action that is truly described as one which he expected to have those descriptions. This makes it possible to evaluate his action relative to those descriptions even if they turn out to be false, i.e. even if the expected results fail to occur, while not depriving him of his undeniable responsibility for those results, if they do occur.

3. Non-Fortuitous Side-Effects and Responsibility

As Boyle insists, foreseen side-effects cannot be outside the agent's intention in such a way as to remove his responsibility for them or their imputability to him.[42] A man cannot, strictly speaking, be *excused* for bringing about such results. To excuse is to withdraw accusation; it is to judge that the act or result in question cannot be imputed to the one excused.[43] If the act is imputable, then he is responsible for it; i.e. he is answerable for it, able to be called to account, fit to be asked *why* he did it. For this very reason, such results must in some way fall within his intention. The diffusiveness principle means simply that the question 'why?' is applicable to the bringing about of such results. But of course the agent's explanation, in terms of his end and of the (known) circumstances of his action, i.e. in terms of the *reasons* for his action, may very well give a *justification* of it too.[44] The point is simply that explanation and justification of results by way of an end would make no sense were those results not somehow intentional, brought about 'for the sake of' the end, though perhaps not as intrinsically conducive to it.[45]

However, everything else being equal, the fact that you have not aimed directly at some foreseen result does make you less responsible for it than you

---

41. That is, his expectation of what will be true if his intention is fulfilled. He may not have much expectation of fulfilling it.
42. See his 'Toward Understanding the Principle of Double Effect.'
43. See J. L. Austin, 'A Plea for Excuses,' in *Philosophical Papers*, p. 176.
44. Or it may not. As Davidson says, 'when we talk of reasons in this way, we do not require that the reasons be good ones' ('Intending,' in *Essays on Actions and Events*, p. 83).
45. See above, n. 37. On the distinction between excuse and justification, see D'Arcy, *Human Acts*, p. 172. The thought here is the same as what underlies Aristotle's distinction between two ways in which what one does may be 'compelled' (*Nicomachean Ethics* III, ch. 1): one is by physical force, the other by the fear of an evil which would result from not doing it. Only the former takes away voluntariness. What is done out of fear is still voluntary; it can be called 'compelled' only (1) in the sense that considered *by itself* it is against one's will, and (2) insofar as one's doing it under the circumstances is 'understandable.' (This, we may say, can be either because the danger is such as to justify the action, i.e. excuses the agent, or because the fear aroused is too strong to overcome, i.e. makes the agent pardonable.) This is why Aristotle can say that some acts are so heinous that nothing can 'compel' us to do them.

would be had you aimed at it. You are not so bent on bringing it about as is someone who aims at it directly.[46]

In accordance with the general distinction between direct and indirect causality, this means that you are a cause of it to a lesser degree. This is an important point. It means that the distinction between intended and merely foreseen results, or between results that specify one's action and those that merely follow upon it according to its species, is a distinction in the degree to which one can be said to have made those results certain to come about.

Consider the frequent objection to the moral significance of the question of the directness or indirectness of some result, e.g. someone's death. If what you do kills him anyway, what difference does it make whether or not you were aiming at his very death? It makes at least this much difference: if you did not aim at his very death, then, provided that you do succeed in bringing about what you *did* aim at, you will not mind if something happens to prevent him from dying after all.[47] That is, even if his death is a nearly certain result of your succeeding in what you are doing, it is not you who are making certain of it. Of the things that might happen to thwart the killing of someone, at least some are things that someone bent on killing him would take into consideration and try to stop, while someone not having that aim would not. At any rate, his death cannot be as certain, *on the supposition of your accomplishing your aim*, as it would be if it *were* your aim, again on the supposition of your accomplishing your aim. The certainty of your getting what you aim at, if you get what you aim at, is plainly greater than the certainty of the occurrence of something other than what you aim at, if you get what you aim at. Still, this difference, which is only one of degree of certainty, is perhaps not very significant morally. At any rate the fact that you are not directly aiming at anyone's death does not at all entail that no matter what you do, you cannot be guilty of murder.[48]

Chisholm's discussion is limited to voluntary agents, and concerns only the *believed* accompaniments of what the agent properly intends. But even assuming that the beliefs are true, these accompaniments may be only a portion of what follows on the nature of what the agent intends. Yet for Aquinas, everything of this sort, everything that naturally or generally accompanies what an agent intends, falls under his intention. It does not matter whether he considered it, or even whether he knew of it.[49]

In part, this is because falling indirectly under one's intention does not require one's having had any distinct apprehension or belief about them; for there

---

46. As Hart notes ('Problems of the Philosophy of Law,' p. 98), when examining the sheer fact of the imputability of a harm, the law does not consider what the accused was aiming at, but it does consider whether he aimed at the harm when assessing the gravity of the offense.
47. See above, n. 40.
48. See below, Section C.2.
49. See I–II, q. 20, a. 5; q. 73, a. 8.

is no *distinct* intention of them. For instance, raising my arm is generally accompanied by a host of changes inside my arm of which I have no clear understanding at all, nor could I have been expected to; but these are included in my intention to raise my arm.

Also, in part, the claim is based on the fact that what is at stake is what follows on the nature of what I *intend*. This is the same as what follows on the nature of what I actually do only if what I actually do is what I intend. So it is not a question of what generally follows according to the true circumstances of the case, e.g. the true condition of what I am acting upon, of which I may have been ignorant or mistaken. Only what I believe to constitute the circumstances of my action can enter into the proper object of my intention. Moreover, it is important to restrict the point to what *generally* follows on the nature of what I intend, and not extend it to things that what I intend merely makes possible or a little more likely. When a man does something with knowledge that it entails some sort of risk, what must fall under his intention is just the risk, not necessarily the thing risked.

As for a false belief that something generally follows upon what I intend, the point is that Aquinas's claim about what follows on the nature of what one intends is only about what must be *included* in my intention; it does not exclude things that do not truly follow upon what I intend from the possible scope of my intention.[50]

Finally, as for a false belief that something does *not* generally follow on the nature of what I intend, or ignorance that it does follow, there are two possibilities. One is that the mistake or the ignorance is itself included in my intention, as something I could overcome if I wanted.[51] The other is that I could not overcome it. In this case, it either would or would not make me refrain from acting if I knew of it. If it would not (e.g. one of the changes in my arm when I raise it), then it may be included in my intention as something that would fall under my intention if I knew of it. If it would, then the action is performed out of ignorance and is, simply speaking, contrary to my intention; so that what follows on *its* nature cannot necessarily be said to follow on the nature of what I intend. It does not have the nature of what I intend, except in a qualified way.

Two remarks to accompany this last point. First, to say that my action is contrary to my intention, by reason of some feature I did not know about it, does not mean that I must have thought of actions having such a feature and resolved to avoid them. It means only that the action must be repugnant to my 'overall'

---

50. On the other hand, things that do not follow on the nature of an action, and are known not to follow on it, do not necessarily fall under the agent's intention, even if they do come about and he *knows* they will come about. He has not in any way made them result. They will fall under his intention only if he could and should have intended to prevent them and did not. See I-II, q. 79, a. 1, corp. and ad 2; also below, pp. 218–20.

51. See I-II, q. 6, a. 8, together with II-II, q. 64, a. 8.

aim.⁵² Secondly, the fact that my action is, simply speaking, contrary to my intention does not mean that everything about it is contrary to my intention. Indeed, there must be something about it that fits my intention if I (not just some part of me) am to be called the agent of it at all. It means that the action as a whole is contrary to my intention. But I can still be held responsible for everything about it that is not contrary to my intention.⁵³

C. EVIL AS *PRAETER INTENTIONEM*

1. Indirectly Intending Evil

The notion of indirect objects of intention is of particular importance in Aquinas's account of the causes of evil (*malum*). Following pseudo-Dionysius, Aquinas holds that a bad effect is always *praeter intentionem*, 'outside the intention' of the agent that causes it. But whatever this meant for pseudo-Dionysius, for Aquinas it certainly does not mean that an agent cannot in any way aim at something bad. Indeed, insofar as *malum* is taken concretely, as 'something bad,' he does not even hold that an agent cannot aim *directly* at it. Rather, what cannot be directly aimed at is the very badness of something bad. The description according to which it is something bad cannot be the one under which it is directly intended. The badness of something bad is its lack of some perfection or good. The sheer lack of some good cannot be intended *per se*, for the simple reason that it cannot be good, apt to be desired, *per se*.⁵⁴ If it is desired and intended, this is only indirectly, by reason of some good that accompanies it. But it certainly can be intended in this way.⁵⁵ The very

---

52. Wittgenstein is very helpful here, with the analogy he draws between what one intends to do and what one means (*Philosophical Investigations*, §§ 633–93); see esp. § 692, where he notes that 'meaning' something does not mean 'thinking of it.' See D'Arcy, pp. 128–29.

53. See below, Section D.2, on things done out of ignorance.

54. Thus in *SCG* ch. 6, § 1907, and in I, q. 19, a. 9, Aquinas is taking 'intention' as aiming toward something directly. See the *quasi per accidens* and *per se intentam* in I, q. 49, a. 2. The thought in I, q. 19, a. 9 and q. 49, arts. 1 and 2 is that evil cannot be desired or intended except by accompanying something desired or intended.

55. By the same token, it can be consented to and chosen. The doctrine that evil is always *praeter intentionem* is sometimes thought not to give an adequate representation of some forms of evil, for instance malice. Aquinas certainly thinks there is such a thing as malice; he defines it as 'knowingly choosing (spiritual) evil,' taking 'evil' in the *abstract* sense—the privation itself of some (spiritual) good: I–II, q. 78, a. 1. (Thus it seems incorrect to say that *SCG* III, ch. 6 is the only text in which Aquinas suggests 'that he believes that what is formally evil (and thus *praeter intentionem*) is the object of an act of choice': Boyle, '*Praeter intentionem* in Aquinas,' p. 655, n. 28.) What Thomas denies is that even the malicious man chooses evil for the simple reason that it is evil or chooses the evil for its own sake. He may directly intend some concrete thing that he knows full well to be evil, and may even form an explicit preference to embrace the evil of it rather than to do without the perfection and goodness that it still has. But what he is primarily aiming at is the perfection in it, and if it is really true that he knows the evil of it (not just that others call it evil), then he still *wishes* that he could

enactment of some good may carry with it, sometimes unavoidably, the lack of some other good.[56]

In accordance with the discussion of indirect causality in Chapter 3, Thomas appears to conceive of two ways in which this is possible: according to causality *per removens prohibens* (or causality that can be assimilated to this), and according to the causality of an obstacle, causing something not to exist or not to happen. In the former way, the evil thing is a positive occurrence or result. This in turn can be something indirectly intended in one of two ways. In one way, what an agent properly intends to effect may have conjoined to it, in a necessary or general (i.e. foreseeable) way, some evil result; either as removing an obstacle to it, or as providing some necessary condition for it, or as disposing something for it. Again, however, the fact that something generically evil is conjoined to an action, according to its species, does not mean that the action itself is bad according to its species. It depends upon the relation between the action, according to its species, and the proper good of the agent. That is, it depends on whether performing such an action is a disorder for the agent; or, if you prefer, on whether the evil in question makes the action to be, relative to the agent, evil without qualification or evil only in a particular respect.

Since the bad cannot be the proper object of any intention or aim, it cannot constitute the principal term according to which any action is specified. Aquinas insists upon this point repeatedly. However, to the extent that the bad may still fall somehow under an agent's intention, it may pertain to his action according to its species. It pertains to the action's species by being conjoined, not by chance, to the good that properly specifies the action. Generally this is because it follows upon the exercise of the action in the matter in which the agent intends to realize the action's proper object. The matter is also a principle of the action's specification. Thus Aquinas distinguishes two things that belong to the notion of sin: a voluntary act, and a disorder in it, namely a deviation from God's law. Only the former, he says, is referred *per se* to the sinner, i.e. is something the sinner directly intends. But

---

enjoy the good of it without having to embrace the evil too. Or, he may *wish* that he could find the evil desirable in its own right, wish that the very being evil made it good. But in order to desire it, even Milton's Satan has to give it the name 'good.'

56. Even when an evil, in the abstract sense (privation), accompanies some good unavoidably, so that in some way it is needed for attaining that good, it is needed only indirectly. That is, the sheer lack of some perfection is not, by itself, something conducive to the possession of some other; what is directly conducive to that is the capacity for it in the perfection's subject. But sometimes the possession of one perfection is an obstacle to the exercise of the capacity for the possession of another. Hence the removal of one perfection is needed, not by the sheer fact of being such a removal, but because it is identical with the freeing up of the subject for some other perfection. The privation of one good is a cause of another good only indirectly, as a 'removed obstacle' to it. The freeing up of the subject may be identical with depriving it of something, but it can be aimed at only because it is a freeing up. This means that it cannot be a proper object of intention, even as a means (an intermediate end). Of course, not all removals are really deprivations; sometimes we speak of removing an evil.

Aquinas *is* careful to include, in what the sinner directly intends, the matter in which he intends to act: what the sinner directly intends is 'to perform such a voluntary act in such a matter' (*talem actum voluntarium exercere in tali materia*).[57]

2. Not Intending to Prevent an Evil

The second way in which an evil result can be indirectly intended is by its being something which the agent does not intend to prevent. In such a case, it is something indirectly intended if, on the basis of the consideration of the agent himself and not just something extrinsic to him, he could have been expected to do something to prevent it. This expectation requires two things. The first is that he have had it in his power to do something to prevent it; it must be he himself

---

57. I–II, q. 72, a. 1. See also I, q. 48, a. 1 ad 2; I–II, q. 18, a. 5 ad 2; q. 54, a. 3 ad 2; q. 79, a. 2 ad 3; *De malo* q. 2, a. 6 ad 3; *SCG* III, ch. 9, § 1930; *In II Sent.* d. 34, q. 1, a. 2 ad 3. According to Grisez, Finnis and Boyle, 'an action is intentional if it is part of the plan on which one freely acts. That is to say, what one tries to bring about in acting, whether it be the goal one seeks to realize or the means one chooses to realize that goal, is intended' (*Nuclear Deterrence*, p. 79). Grisez also says that one's action is defined by the intention that it embodies, the adopted proposal or plan upon which one acts (*Christian Moral Principles*, p. 233). All of this squares with Aquinas's view. But Grisez complains that 'Thomas often includes in its object anything which makes an act definitely wrong, for this settles its moral species (cf. *De malo* q. 2, a. 6 ad 2). On my account, the object only includes what one chooses even if the wrongness of the act arises elsewhere. For example, the object of an act of driving somewhere in an automobile is determined by the choice to travel to that place, and this remains so even if the auto belongs to another, is used without permission, and in using it one accepts the side effect of grave partiality toward oneself against the other' (ibid., p. 247, n. 3). Now, if 'definitely wrong' means 'intrinsically' wrong or wrong *per se*, then it is hard to see how one could say this and at the same time hold (as Grisez does) that there *are* any definitely wrong acts. Why would the act he describes be *inseparable* from the side-effect of grave partiality, such that one could not avoid 'accepting' that, if the connection between the act and the side-effect were not rooted in the act's object? In any case, Grisez's complaint about Thomas oversimplifies Thomas's position. Certainly, for Thomas, anything that makes an act definitely wrong (again, assuming that 'definitely' means *per se*) must be *included* in its object; but this feature is not what *principally* constitutes the act's moral species, precisely because it is not simply *identical* with the object, not *per se* the object. What principally constitutes an act's moral species and *formally* differentiates it can only be something directly intended. As regards specification, the role of a condition which renders an act definitely wrong is not to determine it absolutely as a species of moral action, but to determine it as a species of *evil* moral action. Prior to this is that by which the act is any sort of moral action at all. It is something directly intended, an end, that first enables an act to be placed in the genus of morals at all (cf. I–II, q. 18, a. 7). It does this by enabling the act to be an object of the will, i.e. by being a good. Moral specification is specification as an object of the will. The specificatory role of the 'bad condition' is merely material relative to the role of the end, and also relative to the role of what is *directly* intended as a means. The reason why the bad condition has *any* specificatory role is that calling an act 'moral' is also attributing it to the agency (the practical direction) of reason; something can be willed only if it is apprehended and ordered to the will by reason (I–II, q. 19, a. 2 ad 3, a. 3). To attribute an act to reason is to make it specifiable according to reason's judgment of its relation to (its compatibility with, its order to) the *primary* object of will, namely, the *perfect* good or the *last* end, as understood by reason (see I–II, q. 21, a. 1).

who prevented himself from preventing it. This in turn means that it must be by virtue of his own intentional activity, either concomitant or antecedent, that he does not act to prevent the result.[58]

The second requirement is that something he could have done to prevent the result, but did not, be something he should have done, something that it is bad for him not to have done. Otherwise, his preventing himself from preventing the result would not be contrary to his own (primary) inclination, which is toward what is good for him. This would mean that the prevention of the result is not expectable of him *per se*; he cannot be regarded as inimical to it. Assuming that he did not directly intend the result, its following upon what he intentionally does is only, as it were, by chance.

I say 'as it were,' because of course he may have foreseen the result. This is an important additional point as regards the 'diffusiveness of intention' principle. The principle is that all foreseeable results of what one intends to do are in some way included in one's intention. But this does not mean that everything which someone can foresee, and which he knows would not happen if he did something other that what he intends to do, falls under his intention. For not everything of this sort is a result *of* what he intends to do, something to which his intended action will in any way contribute, something having that 'necessary or *ut in pluribus* order' to his action. It may only be a result of his not doing something else instead; and if, notwithstanding that result, this is not something which he should do, then what he does do simply has no bearing on the result. It can only be said to have some sort of bearing on the result if it is a removal of some *per se* obstacle to the result (or, of course, if the result itself is directly intended); but, *ex hypothesis* he himself cannot be considered such an obstacle. No sort of proportion can be set up between his action and the result. The performance of his action coincides with the occurrence of the result, but the relation between them is just that: a coincidence. Unless he should have acted to prevent the result, the result does not pertain to or follow from what he did do, according to its species, either formally or materially.

The only appetitive act that might be said to bear upon such a result, assuming that it was foreseen, is that of consent. Unlike intention and choice, consent to something is not necessarily a disposition to bring it about. It only may be a disposition not to prevent it.

Indeed, results of this sort can be 'indirectly intended' only in a rather different sense from that which applies to foreseeable accompaniments to what some-

---

58. See I–II, q. 71, a. 5: *non enim est peccatum omissionis nisi cum aliquis praetermittit quod potest facere et non facere. Quod autem aliquis declinet ad non faciendum illud quod potest facere et non facere, non est nisi ex aliqua causa vel occasione coniuncta vel praecedente. Et si quidem causa illa non sit in potestate hominis, omissio non habet rationem peccati. . . . Si vero causa vel occasio omittendi subiaceat voluntati, omissio habet rationem peccati; et tunc semper oportet quod ista causa, inquantum est voluntaria, habeat aliquem actum, ad minus interiorem, voluntatis.*

one does intentionally. The latter are intended in the sense that they accompany something intended. In a way they fall within the scope of the agent's aim. The others, by contrast, are intended only in the sense that the agent is *not* aimed *away* from them as fully as he might be. They do not fall positively within the scope of his aim. It makes sense to speak of such things as intended only when, and to the extent that, the agent is not aimed away from them to the degree or in the way that he *should* be. He may be aimed *more* toward them than he should be, even though strictly speaking his aim is not really *toward* them at all, directly or indirectly.

For the same reason, to say that something was indirectly intended in *this* way *is* equivalent to blaming the agent for it.[59] Unless he is to blame for not doing something to prevent it, and assuming that it was not precisely because he wanted it to come about that he did not choose to prevent it, it cannot intelligibly be attributed to him as to an agent. He is not an origin of it at all. What he brings about intentionally does not carry this result with it; it merely coincides with this result. A sign of this is that no one ever gets *praised* for not preventing a *good*, unless he directly intended it; i.e. unless, for the sake of it, he withheld some action that might have prevented it.

Attributing results to someone in this way, of course, presupposes that a man can be a cause of his having or not having a certain intention. As we read in the passage from I–II, q. 6, a. 3, it must be that 'the will, by willing and acting, can impede that which is a not-willing and a not-acting, and sometimes should.' Indeed, it seems possible to say that things indirectly intended in the first sense (as known to be carried along by what is directly intended) are culpable only if they are also indirectly intended in this sense; for 'culpable' *means* 'could and should have been avoided.'

Aquinas's example in I–II, q. 6, a. 3 was that of a ship that sinks for lack of a steersman. A given steersman can be called the cause of the ship's sinking only if (1) he had it in his power to steer the ship, and (2) he should have done so. He would not be the cause if, for instance, he had been forcibly restrained, or had been assigned to some other ship. In the latter case, even if it was in his power to take the helm of the ship that sank, he could not have been expected to do so. Indeed, he could have been expected *not* to do so, since that would mean abandoning his own ship. This would hold even if he knew that the other ship lacked a steersman. His having this knowledge does not entail that in intending to steer his own ship, he also intends that the other sink. Perhaps he may be said to intend (indirectly) his own *letting* it sink; but it is a sheer coincidence that his not

---

59. See Kenny, *Aristotle's Theory of the Will*, p. 34: 'Very often the natural description of facts involves appeal to tacit evaluations. What a person is said to have done, for instance, may well depend on what he ought to have done.' Also D'Arcy, *Human Acts*, p. 49: 'if doing X would have prevented Y, Y will be called a consequence of not doing X, or of omitting to do X, only on the same condition,' namely, that 'doing X was expected or required of him.'

steering it is equivalent to letting it sink. His not steering it does not make him a cause of its having no one to steer it. It does not lack a steersman because *he* failed to give it one.

This sense of 'indirectly intended' plays a very important role, and one that is often overlooked, in the text of Aquinas most frequently adduced in discussions of the so-called doctrine of double effect: II–II, q. 64, a. 7, on 'whether it be licit for anyone to kill someone in defending himself.'

Thomas's answer to the question is very simple. It is never licit for a private person to aim to kill someone, i.e. to act precisely in order to bring about a person's death, even as a way of defending himself against an attack. But in defending oneself, it may be licit to use means which, in addition to having the effect of conserving one's life by putting a stop to the attack, also have the effect of the aggressor's death. This is licit when the use of such means is 'proportionate,' or not more violent than is necessary to stop the attack.[60] Having in mind the divine prohibition against killing, Aquinas is careful to point out that what he is thus calling licit is not an act whose very species is killing, is not *formally* killing. An act's species or kind is taken from what is directly intended in it.

Thus, his giving special importance to the question of what is directly intended, in cases like this, is the result of his holding that certain actions are universally prohibited or intrinsically bad, bad in virtue of their very kind. Nevertheless, as should be obvious, showing that an action is not formally of a certain prohibited kind does not suffice to show that it is not bad at all. In fact, it does not even suffice to show that the action falls entirely outside the scope (the 'spirit') of the prohibition. That is, even if one's action only indirectly tends to produce the object by which a certain bad kind of action is specified, it may still be bad, *with the very badness of that kind of action*.

This rests on two things. (1) A bad kind of action may be an action whose specifying object is bad in its own right, as the object of murder is a human death,

---

60. Of course, in Thomas's text, it is assumed that the aggressor really is one, i.e. that the threat to one's life truly comes from him. If not, then he is to that extent innocent (*innocens*, not harmful), even if using violence upon him might serve somehow to get at the real danger. Such would appear to be the case, for instance, in fetal craniotomy as a response to ectopic pregnancy. The fetus is not where it is because it has any inclination or tendency to be there; on the contrary, it is trapped. The danger is not the fetus, but rather the fetus's *being trapped in that place*. It is not in virtue of the fetus, but by accident, that the fetus is trapped in that place. But using lethal violence upon an innocent person is unjust, and unrectifiably so (you can do nothing to counterbalance it or compensate for it), since it kills him. (See above, n. 17.) For Thomas, it is never licit, even if it is not done *because* it is lethal, i.e. for the *sake* of killing the person. (Cf. *Nullo modo licet occidere innocentem* in II–II, q. 64, a. 6. The expression *nullo modo* would appear to cover indirect killing; i.e. 'indirectly,' too, would seem to count as a *modus*. Thus, the immediately subsequent article asks whether it is ever licit to kill someone in self-defense, and the answer is yes, it can be, if the killing is indirect. Indirect killing is a 'mode' of killing.) Moreover, even when the aggressor really is one, if one's being attacked by him is not something unjust, then for Thomas it is unjust (an 'unjust war') to counter-attack, though it would not be unjust to flee (II–II, q. 69, a. 4).

undeserved. (2) 'Bad' means 'ought to be avoided.' So, the universal prohibition of the action, or the judgment that it is an intrinsically bad *kind* of action, means that you should always *at least* avoid *aiming* at its object.[61] If you are not aiming at the object, then you are not performing that *kind* of action, and the action that you are performing may not be bad *in kind*. But the performance of it *may* still be bad, because it *may* entail your not avoiding the object as much as you should; for the object is, after all, something bad.

Thus, to establish the possible licitness of not-directly-intended killing in self-defense, Thomas is certainly not satisfied with saying only that it is not formally killing. He also sees a need to point out that 'neither is it necessary for salvation [hence for licitness] that a man set aside an act of moderate care, so as to avoid the killing of another; for a man is more bound to provide for his own life than for another's.' Here we have a question of whether something is indirectly intended in our second sense: what someone does not intend to prevent, when he could and should. What Thomas is saying is that a man is not bound to prevent himself from carrying through with such an act. Hence, he is not a cause of what follows upon it, *in the manner of* one who causes something by not doing what he could and should to prevent it. It is only with this point established that Aquinas can conclude that the man responsible for his aggressor's death, in the way described, is not culpable. It is also this sort of indirect causality that is at work in the case of someone who *is* culpable for a death brought about by *chance*, the case discussed in the subsequent article.[62]

There are, then, two very different senses of 'indirectly intended.' One refers to a foreseen and non-casual accompaniment of what someone intends. Such accompaniments may be good or bad, and the good ones do not necessarily make the action good, nor do the bad ones necessarily make it bad. The other refers to

---

61. It would be obvious madness to say that one must always do everything he physically can in order to avoid every conceivable bad state of affairs, or even every truly impending one. Judging which evils to avoid, and at what cost, is a matter of prudence. Laws—general commands and prohibitions—are rules of prudence. The question of intrinsically bad acts is the question whether there is anything that one should *at least* never *pursue*—and hence, whether there is any action, any *pursuit*, that one should always avoid. (This question is only interesting, of course, to the extent that it concerns things that one *could* possibly pursue.) I suspect that for Thomas, the affirmative answer to it depends on the existence of an end or an object of pursuit which constitutes the very principle of the whole practical order, i.e. which any voluntary agent *is* pursuing by the very fact of being a voluntary agent (cf. I–II, q. 1, a. 6, esp. ad 3; I–II, q. 73, a. 3 ad 3). This 'last end' or perfect good would constitute the principle of an order, and any pursuit deviating from it would be judged morally disordered (see above, n. 57).

62. If it is legitimate to measure one's own life against another's, and to prefer one's own, then why is it never licit to act with the aim of killing the aggressor? Evidently the answer is that acting with such an aim can *never* be 'proportionate' to the mere goal of defending oneself against attack. What is legitimate is to do what is necessary to quell the present threat to one's life. But to aim to kill the aggressor is to aim to put him out of the way *permanently*. This is more than what the proposed case makes necessary.

what someone fails to intend to prevent when he could and should. This is necessarily something bad, and saying that it is indirectly intentional of someone, in this way, is blaming him for it.[63]

Perhaps it would be useful to have different names for these two kinds of indirectly intended accompaniments. The first kind might retain the name 'indirectly intended,' though there may also be other grounds for avoiding this or similar names.[64] But for the second kind, it might be appropriate to reserve the expression 'indirectly *voluntary.*' This is how Thomas uses that expression in I–II, q. 6, a. 3. 'Voluntary' comes closer than 'intentional' to expressing the fact that *this* kind of indirectly intentional item is proper to the will, i.e. to human agents. For only a human agent has control of his intentions, such that it is possible to say that he could and should have adopted a certain intention, and was himself the cause of his not doing so.

3. Omissions

To complete the picture of the ways in which an evil result can fall indirectly within someone's intention, some attention should be given to omissions. An 'evil result' can itself be the sheer non-occurrence or non-existence of something, a 'negative' result. What was discussed in the previous subsection includes something of this sort: the non-prevention of an evil is itself an evil. Non-occurrences may also be evil in their own right, not merely on account of something that follows from them; e.g. not speaking when it is time to speak.[65]

Now, non-occurrences and non-actions, to the extent that they can be thought about and to that extent 'are,' can also be directly intended. For they can even be considered good, insofar as the corresponding occurrence or action is judged bad. As Aristotle says, the avoidance of evil is good. So, a man may intend not to do something; and there need not be anything definite that he intends to do instead.[66] Presumably only persons are capable of this.

Naturally, no one intends not to do something just by reason of what good there is in doing it, nor by reason of what evil there is in not doing it. However, if he intends not to do it, there is still some conduct involved (at least, if men are

---

63. Cf. Flannery, 'Natural Law *mens rea*,' p. 399: 'In determining what is and what is not within a person's intention, we do indeed presume that certain things are to be pursued, other things to be avoided.'

64. See above, p. 199.

65. There is ample literature on the subject of omissions. For an interesting study and some bibliography, see Patricia G. Smith, 'Contemplating Failure.'

66. See I–II, q. 71, a. 5: *actus [interior voluntatis] quandoque fertur in ipsam omissionem; puta cum aliquis vult non ire ad ecclesiam, vitans laborem.* This evidently corrects the (slightly?) earlier *De malo* q. 2, a. 1, where he had said that the will can never bear directly on an omission, *quia non ens et malum est praeter intentionem et voluntatem.* Evil is of course *praeter intentionem,* but a *non ens* can sometimes be judged good, e.g. if the *ens* in question is bad (see I–II, q. 8, a. 1 ad 3).

the agents of their own intentions) and to this extent the non-occurrence is pretty well assimilable to an action. It is an act of refraining from or withholding something, an action that consists in not doing something. That is, in this case the non-occurrence *formally specifies* some act, though of course the evil of it does not belong to the act's species, but only follows from it.

But it is also possible that instead of having a definite intention not to do it, he simply does not have any intention to do it. When there was some reason to expect him to do it, and when it is his own action that prevents him from intending to do it, he is a cause of his not doing it; and when he should have done it, and the action that prevents him from doing it does so not by chance, then he is not merely a chance cause of it. Nevertheless, in this case it is less plausible to say that the not-doing is itself an action. It is an effect of an action, and that action may be described relative to it; and if it is not a chance effect, then the action's order toward it somehow belongs to that action's species. But it does so only materially. A non-action does not formally specify any act. Its own species (simply the negation of the species of the occurrence) does not in any way include the act that occasions it.[67]

Anscombe quarrels with Davidson's thesis that something is a (human) action if and only if there is some description of it under which it is intentional, and she does so partly in consideration of omissions.[68] In her view, omissions may be actions, and yet not be (directly?) intentional at all. But this makes one wonder what she means by 'action.' If non-intended omissions are actions, what are they omissions of? Of actions, surely; but then if omissions too are actions, it seems possible to have an omission of an omission.

Perhaps her thought is simply that omissions, even unintended and uncontemplated ones, can be voluntary. But why limit the voluntary to actions, even human actions? Cannot other things besides actions be voluntary? Perhaps they can, but only by in some way depending upon voluntary action; we have just seen that this is what Aquinas holds. Their voluntariness derives from the voluntariness of some action, and they qualify that action.

It does, however, seem that at least directly intended omissions can be called actions, and not merely effects of action. But since this is evidently something that only rational beings are capable of, it also seems that actions which are directly intended omissions are always voluntary human actions. It was also sug-

---

67. See I–II, q. 71, a. 5.

68. 'Action, Intention and "Double Effect,"' p. 12. Her other objection is that tripping over the edge of the carpet, described as part of an intentional progress across the room, seems to be intentional, and yet Davidson denies that it is an action. Here the problem is just the term 'tripping.' She is using it as more or less synonymous with 'stumbling.' To be sure, stumbling part of the way across the room may be something intentional, but it also seems capable of being an action. But in another sense tripping means simply 'striking something with one's foot and losing one's balance'; and in this sense, it forms no part of one's progress across the room. Thus, instead of saying that someone 'tripped across the room' (where what is meant is a stumbling, and not a child's playful tripping) one would be much more likely to say that he 'tripped and stumbled across the room.'

gested, in passing, that it makes sense to speak of intentional omissions as actions, and to say that things that someone does not intend to prevent may be indirectly intended only if a man can be called the agent of his intentions. The whole 'actuality' of the actions that are omissions resides in the intention; and for that very reason, a result that someone does not intend to prevent can fall within what he does intend only if it was in his own power not to intend this and to intend instead to prevent the result. There can be omissions only where there is the power of forming one's own intention, which is the power of choice.

D. *PRAETER INTENTIONEM*, THE INVOLUNTARY THROUGH IGNORANCE, AND THE SPECIFIABILITY OF ACTION

This chapter is about things done *praeter intentionem*. Up to this point, the discussion has concentrated mainly on how something which an agent does not directly intend may still fall under his intention in an indirect fashion. Normally this is something which accompanies what he directly intends, on account of the circumstances, and which does so in a foreseen or at least a foreseeable way. But of course, not everything which is done *praeter intentionem* is foreseen or even foreseeable. It is humanly impossible to foresee absolutely everything which will accompany one's undertaking. This would require, among other things, being aware of absolutely all of the circumstances.

In traditional terms, when a rational agent does something which involves a circumstance of which he is unavoidably ignorant, he is said to do it in 'invincible' ignorance of the circumstance. If there is anything which is absolutely *praeter intentionem*, falling entirely outside the agent's intention, it would surely be what is done out of invincible ignorance and is simply unforeseeable. Such things are strictly accidental or casual. Since the exercise of human agency always involves a certain measure of ignorance, it is always mixed with accidental elements. It is never a *wholly* intentional affair, even taking 'intentional' to cover both the directly and the indirectly intentional.

But of course, if it is an exercise of human agency at all, then there must be *something* intentional, directly intentional, about it. This is a necessary condition for voluntary human action. Is it sufficient? If there is something intentional about what someone does, is it thereby a voluntary action, no matter what accompanies it *praeter intentionem*? I raise this question mainly with an eye to the fact that even when there is something intentional about what someone does, his ignorance of a circumstance may lead to a result which is not only accidental but also positively involuntary. As I shall try to show further on (Section D.2), the involuntariness in such a case does not belong exclusively to the unforeseen or accidental element in it; it also spills back onto the intentional element itself. In this case, I believe, the intentional element must be judged to be intentional only in a somewhat restricted or qualified way, according to some merely abstract consideration; absolutely speaking, it too is *praeter intentionem*.

As will be seen, this distinction between what is absolutely intentional and what is intentional only in a qualified way is not the same as the distinction between the directly and indirectly intentional. Drawing it will help to bring out one final point about the specification of human conduct, as a complement to the discussion in Chapter 4, Section E. This will bring to a close the present study of conduct in its relation to physical agency and agency in general. Before entering into the thick of the question, however, I will present (in Section D.1) a more technical account of the fact that human action is never a wholly intentional affair, drawing upon a position taken by Davidson, Anscombe and Donagan, among others, to the effect that a human action is an event or a doing which is intentional 'under some description.'

1. The Intensionality of the Intentional, and Causality

Human agency necessarily involves intention. At first glance, it even seems plausible to consider human actions, among actions generally, as belonging to a special class of actions, the class of *intentional* actions. But the fact that human actions have unintended accompaniments, especially unforeseeable accompaniments, raises a serious doubt about the existence of such a class. The doubt arises particularly in the context of the treatment of actions as concrete individual events.[69] It is very simple: depending upon how an action is described, or what feature of it is used to refer to it, it may be truly said to be intentional, and it may also be truly said not to be intentional. So if there were such a thing as the class of intentional actions, then one and the same action would both belong and not belong to the class. As Davidson concludes, there can be no such class.

There are things that are true of what Oedipus did which are not true of what he intended to do. He did not and could not foresee that in striking the old man, he would be striking his father. If both 'striking the old man' and 'striking his father' truly describe what he did, then what he did and what he intended to do are not entirely the same; only some descriptions of what he did match what he intended to do. What he did cannot be said to have been intentional of him in every respect. Otherwise, no matter what description is used to refer to it, 'intentional of Oedipus' would be true of it; just as no matter how you refer to a red apple, it is true to say of it that it is red.

Put in more technical language, the thought is that 'intentional,' as said of concrete individual actions, constitutes what is called an 'intensional' context. Intensional contexts are distinguished from extensional contexts. An expression constitutes an extensional context if the following obtains: the truth-value of the sentence in which it occurs remains the same when some other expression in the sentence is replaced by one having a different sense or meaning (intension) but

---

69. See Anscombe, *Intention*, pp. 37–43; Davidson, 'Agency,' in *Essays on Actions and Events*, pp. 43–61; Donagan, *The Theory of Morality*, pp. 118–19 and *Choice*, pp. 81–86.

the same reference or domain of application (extension). If this does not obtain, then it is an intensional context. 'Intentional' constitutes an intensional context for an action, because truth-value may vary according to the sense of the expression by which the action is designated. An action may be intentional according to some features, and not intentional according to others.

In cases like that of Oedipus, cases of things done involuntarily through ignorance, the action is in fact both intentional and *counter*-intentional. It was according to Oedipus's intention to strike the old man, and contrary to his intention to strike his father. This however is only an extreme example, in which the intensionality of 'intentional' is particularly clear. The judgment that 'intentional' is intensional, and the denial that it marks off a special class of actions, is not based solely on such extreme cases. As Donagan notes, even when there is nothing about one's action that is contrary to one's intention, there are always many things about it that are unknown or unforeseen, and so *outside* one's intention, *praeter intentionem*.[70]

Davidson and Donagan do hold, however, that 'action' marks off a class of events. An event either is or is not an action. (We may recall that 'action' here means human action.) They also want to hold that being intentional, under some description, is an essential component of being an action. They therefore characterize actions as events that are, under *some* description, intentional.

My aim here is not at all to quarrel with this line of reasoning. Instead, I will want to raise a further question, in Section D.2, precisely about those extreme cases in which the action is involuntary. The question will be whether, in such cases, it is still right to speak of something genuinely or *unqualifiedly* intentional, even *with* the addition of 'under some description.' But the discussion of the thesis that 'intentional' is intensional proves helpful in bringing the question forth, and it is worth carrying on a little further.

In presenting his own version of the claim, Donagan suggests that speaking of something as having a feature 'only under a certain description' is itself rather misleading, because it treats the feature as though it were a real *property* of the thing. He insists that intensional features, such as being intentional, are not real properties of what they are said of. Properties are extensional. 'No more than anything else can an action both have a property and not have it.'[71] As he sees it, when an action is called intentional, no real property is being attributed to it; instead, it is being considered in relation to some person who has a *propositional attitude* about it, namely the attitude of intending it.[72] To call it intentional is really only to say that the agent intended it. The relevant real property is the propositional attitude of the person, his intention, not the action's being intentional. Intensional features are generated by propositional attitudes.

---

70. See Donagan, *The Theory of Morality*, p. 118.
71. *Choice*, p. 85.
72. On the notion of propositional attitudes, see above, Chapter 4, Section C.1.

While genuine properties like being shot are possessed only by real individuals, properties like being believed to exist and being feared are merely apparent. Wherever there is good reason to say, of some property specified by means of a verb of propositional attitude, that something possesses it, but only under a certain description, what is thus misleadingly said is simply that somebody has a propositional attitude of the kind referred to by that verb, and that the proposition to which that attitude is taken can be expressed in terms of that description.[73]

Although I do not think that St Thomas's doctrine is in agreement with this position, it would appear to be possible to put it in his language by saying that what 'intentional' and other intensional predicates signify is (1) a certain relation, and (2) a mere relation of reason. The relation which 'intentional' signifies would be a relation to some agent; it signifies being the object of an agent's intention. But on the side of the thing which is called intentional, this would only be a relation of reason. Something's being the object of an agent's intention does not posit any special feature in the thing itself, any 'property.' Its being the object of an agent's intention does not consist in anything in it, but in something in the agent. The agent's intending the object posits something real in the agent, some propositional attitude. Whatever is real about the relation is on the side of the agent. But once we have grasped the agent's order of tendency toward the object, we can consider the object precisely as the other term of this order. It is from this consideration that the notion of the intentional arises.

Now, Donagan is surely right that expressions for objects of propositional attitudes, as such, do not posit any real property in what they are predicated of. By way of confirmation, it could be noted that the example which Aquinas gives of a relation that is only of reason on the side of one of its terms, although real on the side of the other, is a relation established precisely by what Donagan would regard as a propositional attitude, namely knowledge.[74] Yet it is not clear to me that Donagan is right to say that the term 'intentional' signifies nothing other than a relation to a propositional attitude. Or rather, it is not clear that what it signifies is nothing other than being the *object* of a certain propositional attitude. In addition to this, it would also seem to signify another relation to a propositional attitude, that of being its *effect*—which, I would say, is not a mere relation of reason.

Donagan's position treats 'intentional' as though it were synonymous with 'intended.' But this cannot be right. If I merely intend to go to the store, but have not done so, then we may say (perhaps rather awkwardly) that there is an 'intended' trip to the store, but not that there is an intentional one. When we speak of the mere object of someone's intention, i.e. what he intends, we do not

---

73. *Choice*, p. 84.
74. I, q. 13, a. 7.

necessarily have in mind any action actually performed or any term actually reached. The object of an intention is, as such, a merely potential action or event, one that may or may not also be actual. The condition for something's being an object of intention is not its having any actual existence of its own, but only the existence of some inclination toward it, based on some thought of it or some other sort of form corresponding to it, in the intending subject. But what are called intentional actions are actions actually performed. It is of things that someone actually does that one asks whether they were intentional or not.[75] There may be *nothing* intentional corresponding to a given intention. To use Donagan's example, Othello intended the 'justifiable vindication of his honour against his adulterous wife'; but no action of his even has that description, let alone is intentional of him under it.

Of course, if something is intentional, then presumably it is also the object of some intention, something intended. It must have some feature or form that is identical with an object of the agent's intention. But it is also more. Calling an action intentional means that it exists or happens *because* it is the object of an agent's intention. (Naturally there may be other 'becauses' too.) A sign of this is that otherwise things done by sheer good luck could be called intentional whenever they happen to correspond to some intention of the agent's. But 'intentional' is opposed to 'by sheer good luck.' This would not be the case if something's being intentional were not a way of being an effect, just as something's being by luck is. Things are intentional that are done *by* intention, and 'by' denotes a relation to a cause. Speaking in terms of concrete individual events, to say that an event was intentional of someone must mean that the event exists in virtue of being, under some description, the object of his intention.[76] Its conformity with his intention *explains* its existence.

---

75. Note that this account resolves the apparent circularity, remarked above (Chapter 2, Section E.3), involved in saying that an intention is specified by its object, which is often an action, and that an action is specified by the intention it fulfills. What specifies an intention is a *potential* action, (say) one that the agent has thought of. This is in some way prior to the intention. What an intention specifies, that of which it constitutes the chief unifying form, is an action actually performed (*if* the action is intentional: see below, Section D.3). The action is in some way posterior to the intention (not necessarily in time).

76. This formulation avoids the difficulty often posed by the consideration of 'deviant causal chains.' Donagan (*Choice*, p. 93) offers an example of this difficulty, slightly modifying one from Davidson. Suppose that a climber, wanting to rid himself of the weight and danger of holding another man on a rope, decides to loosen his hold on the rope. Then, imagine that before he even begins to execute this choice, the choice itself so unnerves or horrifies him that he loses control and lets go of the rope. In this case, what he does, the letting go of the rope, is exactly what he chose and intended to do, and is in fact explained by his intention; but it is neither intentional nor an action of his. Yet Donagan wants to call an action a doing that is explained by its doer's choice, which he regards as a certain type of intention (an intention that is sufficiently determinate to act upon: see *Choice*, pp. 50–51). Donagan's solution to the problem is to say that what is caused by a choice is an action when the choice's causality is itself the causality that was chosen (*Choice*, pp. 87–93). That is,

An effect's relation to its cause is a real relation. It does posit something real in the effect. More precisely, an *actual* effect's relation to its cause is a real relation. Although intending, as it has been treated throughout these pages, signifies some kind of causal disposition, the causal relation that it sets up between its subject and the object intended is, *per se*, only a relation between a potential cause and a potential effect. One can intend or tend toward something without yet having brought it about and without ever bringing it about. This is why being intended need not be regarded as a real property of something. But being intentional implies being caused, and to be caused *is* to be brought about. To say that this was caused by that is to say that this exists because of that; for something to be caused is for it to depend on the cause for its existence.[77] Surely if there is anything that belongs to a subject as it is 'in itself,' its existence does; and hence so does its dependence on its cause. The order between an effect and its cause belongs to the effect as it is in itself, not merely according to what accrues to it through reason's operation of considering it side by side with its cause. In short, 'intentional,' unlike 'intended,' does name something in the individual action to which it is attributed. It is not a mere relation of reason.

Now, none of this is to deny that 'intentional' is intensional. For it is not at all unreasonable to hold that causality itself is in some way intensional.[78] This is

---

you choose not only the doing, but also its being explained by your choice, and the manner in which it is to be explained by it; so that what you do is an action of yours only if it is explained by your choice in the manner in which you chose that it be explained. (This solution faces an objection taken from Donagan himself, who says that the 'capacity to intend and choose does not depend on having the concepts of intending and choosing': *Choice*, p. 158. It is hard to see how someone could choose the manner in which his doing be explained by his choice if he did not have some concept of choice. However, I suspect that the capacity to choose does in fact depend on having some notion of what a choice is. Choices are typically made in response to something like the question 'which of these shall I take?' Understanding the question is prior to making the choice, and already implies a grasp of what it is to prefer one thing to another. To prefer one thing to another *is* to choose.) I have already indicated my general agreement with the self-referentiality of the causality in human agency (see p. 178), but I wonder whether appeal to it is necessary in order to avoid the present problem. Deviant causal chains are not confined to the domain of human action; they are nothing but forms of indirect causality. So why not say simply that those doings which are human actions which are caused *directly* by the doer's choice, and not merely by something that accompanies the choice (e.g. the horror it inspires)? This is the sense of the formula 'exists in virtue of being an object of one's intention.' It means that the description according to which the doing is the object of the agent's intention is the description that gives the doing's 'substance,' the chief intrinsic cause of its existence. (Note, however, that here the indirectness is 'on the part of the cause'; see the quotation on indirect causality on p. 125. As we have seen, some doings which merely accompany an object of intention can still fall within the scope of human action, indirectly, by the fact that the agent does not prevent or withhold them when he can and should.)

77. See *In II Post an.* lect. vii, § 471: *propter hoc enim dicitur aliquid causatum, quod habet causam sui esse.*

78. See Anscombe, 'Causation and Extensionality.' In saying this, I am of course denying that intensional contexts pertain only to propositional attitudes.

a disputed issue, because causality itself is (to say the least) a controversial topic. So is the more special topic of agent-causality. But I am assuming the notion of agent-causality laid out in Chapters 2 and 3, according to which it breaks down, analogically, into *per se* and *per accidens*, or direct and indirect, causality. Once it is broken down in this fashion, its intensionality seems evident.

It may be true, as Chisholm argues in 'Query on Substitutivity,' that there is a sense in which causality is extensional. One concrete thing *can* truly be called a cause of another, and no matter how you designate them, the causal relation between them exists. But you have to designate them in a certain way in order to show *what* the causal relation is. For example, pointing to a statue, you say 'Michelangelo caused that.' This can be true in many different ways. Maybe Michelangelo carved it. Then Michelangelo, *qua* sculptor, directly caused it *qua* a statue. Maybe someone else carved it, but he excavated the marble (in pointing to the statue you are also pointing to the marble); then he *qua* excavator directly caused it *qua* a separate piece of marble, and only indirectly *qua* statue. Or maybe one of his rivals carved it, provoked by envy of his fame; etc. Even when cause and effect are concrete things, it is *in virtue of something* that the cause is the cause, and *with respect to something* that the effect is the effect.

Moreover, when something is said to have been done by someone intentionally, the very addition of 'intentionally' already specifies the agent's causality somewhat, signifying that it is direct or *per se*. What an agent does *per se* is precisely what he does according to his own tendency or intention. 'In things that are for an end,' as are all actions, 'it is something that is intended which is called *per se*; whereas what is outside intention is called *per accidens*.'[79] So there can be little doubt that attributions of intentionality are intensional.

How then are we to avoid the contradiction in saying that one and the same action is both intentional and non-intentional, if we wish to continue speaking of concrete individual actions, and at the same time hold that the action's relation to the cause, its being an intentional effect of the cause, posits a real property in it?[80] To be sure, a thing cannot both have and not have a property. But it is not necessary to deny that a real property is being expressed every time a contradiction crops up. It may be that the property is being expressed in a merely indefinite way. Socrates is both quick and not quick—a quick thinker, and not a quick hockey player. In the case of actions, could we not say that the term 'intentional,' taken by itself, does express a real property, but in a merely indefinite way? The

---

79. *In his autem quae sunt ad finem, per se dicitur aliquod quod est intentum; per accidens autem quod est praeter intentionem* (II–II, q. 59, a. 2).

80. It would hardly help Donagan's position to deny that relations are sometimes real properties or to insist that all relations are mere beings of reason. For this would also undercut the real property which he thinks *is* involved in saying that something is intentional, namely the propositional attitude in the agent. An attitude is an attitude toward something; it is relational, and the relation is intrinsic to it.

real property involved is not the action's simply being intentional, but its being an intentional such-and-such. That is, for instance, besides saying that Oedipus's action is intentional *qua* a striking of an old man and non-intentional *qua* a striking of his father, we could also say, and with greater precision, that it is an intentional striking of an old man and a non-intentional striking of his father.

The term 'intentional,' then, remains intensional; its applicability to an action may vary according to the senses of the terms with which it is combined, even if they have the same extension. And at the same time, the expression combining 'intentional' with the appropriate term, e.g. 'an intentional blow,' is extensional. It is true of the action no matter how the action is designated. This suggests, I think, that even if there is no such thing as the class of intentional actions, there could be such a thing as the class of intentional blows, utterances, offenses, etc. Intentional actions of a given *kind* might form a class. But this is not my present concern.

2. Praeter intentionem *in What is Involuntary through Ignorance*

My present concern is with the question whether every doing which has something intentional about it is an action, in the sense of a full-fledged voluntary human action. I am not now going back to the fact that there is a sense in which 'intention' is not the exclusive property of human agents; at present I am speaking of intention in the stricter sense, rational intention. In this sense, is a doing which is intentional under some description always voluntary? The answer at which I will eventually arrive is yes, if the doing is unqualifiedly intentional; but what I wish to bring out is the way in which a rational agent's doing may be involuntary and yet be intentional in a real, albeit merely qualified, manner.

Take a standard example of something done involuntarily out of ignorance. A hunter in the woods, having good reason to hunt, and after having exercised all due precaution, takes aim and shoots at a deer; but the projectile strays, striking a man concealed in the brush and killing him. When the hunter discovers what has happened, he is horrified. Had he been aware of the man's presence, he would certainly not have shot at the deer. And yet, is it not true that he wanted to shoot at the deer, intended to shoot at it, and shot at it directly on account of his intention to do so? If the voluntariness of a deed were simply a matter of its having something somehow intentional about it, then his shooting at the deer would have to be judged voluntary.

Still, it seems strange to say that in doing something because he wanted and intended to do such a thing, the hunter acts involuntarily. How are we to avoid it? Should we say that what is involuntary of him is something *else*, something other than the shooting at the deer? For instance, he also shoots when there is a man in the vicinity of the target, and indeed shooting when there is a man in the vicinity of the target is contrary to his will. Should we say then that he voluntarily shoots at the deer, but involuntarily shoots with a man in the vicinity of the target? Is his action a voluntary attempt to slay a deer, but an involuntary risk to another man's life? This would avoid attributing involuntariness to something which the hunter did because he wanted to.

But this account will not do. It breaks down the action into two abstract features or descriptions, saying that one is according to the agent's will, and the other contrary to his will. But it says nothing about how the *combination* of these features stands in relation to the agent's will, and this is decisive for the question of whether he acted involuntarily *at all*. Generally speaking, the hunter wants to shoot at the deer; and generally speaking, he also wants to avoid shooting when there is a man in the vicinity of the target. But what about shooting at the deer *even when* there is a man in the vicinity of the target? Is this something he is willing to do, or is it something he is determined to avoid? Until this question is answered, it cannot be determined whether or not *this* instance of shooting when there is a man in the vicinity of the target is genuinely involuntary.

The general point here is that the voluntariness or involuntariness of an individual action of a given kind does not always correspond to the voluntariness or involuntariness of the kind taken as a whole. It is not true that if an action is of a certain kind, and this kind of action is contrary to the agent's will, then if the agent does something of that kind it must be involuntary. An individual action of a given kind may be performed voluntarily, even if that kind, as a whole, is against the agent's will. As St Thomas says, a sailor's jettisoning cargo in a storm is voluntary, simply speaking, even though taken generally, jettisoning cargo is against the sailor's will and an involuntary kind of thing for him.[81] This jettisoning, jettisoning in a storm, is quite voluntary. At most it is involuntary only *secundum quid*, according to a certain abstract consideration: it has some feature which, considered in *isolation* from the concrete case, is against his will. Nor would it matter if the sailor jettisons the cargo in the storm out of ignorance, happening to let some cargo fall into the sea while he is about some other business; it would still not be involuntary of him, since he would be quite content with that result.

The expression *secundum quid* in the previous paragraph should not be confused with the expression 'under a description.' It is not that the sailor's action is involuntary under the description 'jettisoning cargo,' while voluntary under the description 'jettisoning cargo in a storm.' If anything, it is that the description 'jettisoning cargo' belongs both to something that is voluntary of him, namely jettisoning cargo in a storm, and to something that is involuntary of him, namely jettisoning cargo taken by itself or as a whole—that *kind* of action. Jettisoning cargo is quite voluntary of the sailor when it is jettisoning cargo in a storm. The action of doing so is not involuntary of him under any *definite* description of it.

---

81. See I-II, q. 6, a. 6. Cf. Aristotle, *Eudemian Ethics* II, ch. 8, 1125a11–13; *Nicomachean Ethics* III, ch. 1, 1110a8–9.

If the hunter's risking another man's life was involuntary of him, not just *secundum quid* but *simpliciter*, then what was against his will was not only jeopardizing another man's life, considered generally or abstractly, but also *this* instance of jeopardizing another man's life. This was involuntary of him despite the fact that it involved an opportunity to slay a deer. This in turn means precisely that had he known that in shooting at the deer he was jeopardizing another man's life, he would have refrained from shooting at the deer. Hence *this* shooting at a deer, the one which is identical with an act of jeopardizing another man's life, is involuntary of him, even though on the whole shooting at a deer is not so. There may be some general description of his action which is in accordance with his will; but it is not voluntary under any definite description.[82] At most, it is only something that *would have been* voluntary of him, had the circumstances been what he thought.

Yet there remains the troublesome fact that he seems to have wanted to perform *this* shooting at a deer and to have performed it intentionally. If he wanted to do it and it was intentional of him, how can it not have been voluntary of him? Instead of trying to distinguish the descriptions according to which his action is involuntary from those according to which it is voluntary, it seems to me that the correct answer is that not even the shooting at the deer was something he wanted, or something intentional of him *simpliciter*. It was intentional only *secundum quid*.

Even if it is true that the shooting at the deer is performed in virtue of an intention of the hunter's, and to some extent corresponds to that intention, this need not mean that it *fulfilled* or answered fully to any intention of his—*even the intention to shoot at the deer*. Let us grant that the hunter's intention to shoot at the deer is something distinct from his intention to avoid putting someone else's life in jeopardy. The latter intention is obviously something which he failed to fulfill, out of ignorance and involuntarily. But despite appearances, even the former is something which he only partially fulfilled. The reason for this lies in the nature of human intention.

Something becomes the object of someone's intention only through his judgment that pursuing it or applying himself to it suits him. Even if the hunter's intention to shoot at the deer is something distinct from his intention to avoid putting someone else's life in jeopardy, it cannot be something distinct from his intention to be doing what he judges to suit him *in* shooting at the deer. But he judges shooting at the deer, then and there, to suit him only because he judges it to be safe for him and everyone else. He would not want it or intend it if he did not judge it to be safe; his intention to shoot is inseparable from his intention to shoot safely. This is in fact another application of the principle of the non-divisiveness of intention.

---

82. This means that even if 'intentional' and 'voluntary' are predicated of actions intensionally, 'involuntary' is predicated extensionally. This involves no contradiction, since the contradictory of 'voluntary' is not 'involuntary' but 'non-voluntary.' An action may be both voluntary and non-voluntary under different descriptions, but it cannot be both voluntary and involuntary.

The hunter's intention to shoot at the deer is inseparable from his intention to shoot safely; and of course this is something which he failed to carry out. The shooting which he actually performs does not have the suitability for him which he judged it would have. It is not *formally* the same as the object of his intention, since it lacks the goodness and suitability in virtue of which the object of his intention, to shoot safely at a deer, became such an object. It only has some part or element, something material, in common with the object of his intention, namely its being a shooting at the deer.[83] It does have something intentional about it, but only *secundum quid*, according to this common element, abstractly considered. Properly speaking, it is outside his intention, *praeter intentionem*, and even contrary to his intention, involuntary. In general, we may conclude that when an unforeseen result of one's undertaking is genuinely involuntary, its involuntariness spills back onto whatever there is of one's undertaking that is foreseen and in some way according to one's intention.[84]

Indeed, does not the involuntariness spill back onto the intention itself? Would it not be correct to say that not only the hunter's shooting at the deer then and there, but also his very intention to do so, is involuntary? In explaining the nature of what is involuntary through ignorance, St Thomas says two things. One, which is obvious, is that what is done involuntarily through ignorance of circumstances is something which the agent would not have done, had he known the circumstances. But he also says that the ignorance of circumstances is a cause of the agent's *wanting* to do what he would not have *wanted* to do, had he known them.[85] So in some qualified sense he may very well do something he intends to do, and do it because he intends to; but it is out of ignorance, not only that he does it, but also that he intends to do it. We might say that his ignorance removes or diverts an obstacle to his acting as he does, and to his intending to

---

83. In saying that an action must possess the suitability in virtue of which it is intended, in order to be said properly to fulfill the intention, I do not mean that it must succeed in producing the *further* desired result for the sake of which it is chosen and intended. It is chosen because the chooser attributes to it some order toward the result; what it must have is that order. But it may have the order even if the result fails through some impediment. If a hunter shoots and misses, his shooting is not thereby rendered unintentional or only partially intentional of him; he shoots with perfect awareness that he might miss. A means to an end may be a fallible means, and it may be chosen with full awareness of its fallibility; so even if it does actually fail, it may still possess everything required for its being just what the agent chose. In other words, there is a difference between an unsuccessful action and a vain or futile action. A futile action, for instance, would be heating water with the intention of setting it on fire. The water may be getting hotter and hotter, and so the action might be said to conform imperfectly or partially to the agent's intention; but the action has no real order toward the water's catching fire, since there is no such thing, and it is something which could only be undertaken out of ignorance.

84. Of course, it is not really that the undertaking becomes involuntary retroactively. Rather, all the involuntariness in what an agent *does* out of ignorance has its root in the involuntariness of the ignorance itself, which is prior to his doing what he does and a cause of it.

85. I–II, q. 6, a. 8.

act as he does—the obstacle being *his own will*. His will would have impeded him not only from doing what he did but also from intending to do what he intended to do, if he had known the circumstances.

I am not saying that what is involuntary of the hunter is only his intention to shoot at the deer, as though I were now treating this intention as if it were something distinct from his intention to shoot safely. What is involuntary is precisely the intention to shoot safely. What shows that it is involuntary is that shooting safely, then and there, was *impossible* for him to bring about. The real 'matter' for the intended action was lacking, or was incomplete. The deer was possible to shoot at, but not possible to shoot at safely, except in the hunter's mistaken belief. The actual shooting which the hunter performed was not and could not be safe. And precisely because it was of something impossible to bring about, if for no other reason, it seems to me that we can speak of this intention—to shoot, safely, then and there—as involuntary.

Recall once again that in human beings, intention depends on a judgment of the suitability of the object. This means not only a judgment as to the suitability of *having* the object, but also a judgment as to the suitability of pursuing it or applying one's power to it; for intending something is nothing other than wanting to pursue it or to apply one's power to it.[86] But the judgment that something is suitable in this way depends on the judgment that it is possible to attain or to do. No one intends what he judges to be impossible to attain or to do; such an intention would be self-defeating and futile.[87] No one voluntarily aims at something impossible.[88] If what someone intends or aims to do is impossible to do, then his intention must be involuntary, through ignorance.

We could very well say, I believe, that there is a *natural* intention or tendency in the will not to intend what is impossible. Certainly people can and do have intentions about their intentions. This is implicit in the notion that people form their own intentions. The typical process by which they do so is that of deliberation and choice. In deliberating, a person intends to make a choice, and he intends that his choice be conducive to the end in view of which he is deliberating. The choice will be conducive to the end only if the action which is its object is conducive to the end. If the action chosen is impossible, then it cannot be conducive to the end,[89] and neither can the choice of it. Such a choice can only come about *praeter intentionem*.

---

86. See I–II, q. 12, a. 1 ad 4.
87. See above, n. 83.
88. More generally, *perfectio actus voluntatis attenditur secundum hoc, quod est aliquid bonum alicui ad agendum. Hoc autem est possibile. Et ideo voluntas completa non est nisi de possibili, quod est bonum volenti* (I–II, q. 13, a. 5 ad 1).
89. *Sic enim se habet id quod est ad finem, de quo electio est, ad finem, sicut conclusio ad principium. Manifestum est autem quod conclusio impossibilis non sequitur ex princio possibili. Unde non potest esse quod finis sit possibilis, nisi id quod est ad finem fuerit possibile. Ad id autem quod est impossibile, nullus movetur. Unde nullus tenderet in finem, nisi per hoc quod apparet id quod ad finem esse possibile* (I–II, q. 13, a. 5).

3. The Involuntary through Ignorance and the Specifiability of Action

At least two conceivable objections to this position should be addressed. They will lead into the final considerations, which concern the moral specifiability of action. The first objection is simply that it sounds absurd to speak of an intention as involuntary. After all, intention is an act of the *will*, and an *interior* act; how can such a thing be involuntary?

It is important to note that even though 'voluntary' means somehow from the will and somehow intentional, 'involuntary' does not necessarily mean in *no* way from the will and in *no* way intentional. 'Compelled' or 'forced' means that; the forced is 'that of which the principle is outside, with the one suffering it contributing nothing.'[90] But the involuntary is broader than the forced. It also includes things done out of ignorance. In contrast with what is done under force, acting out of ignorance *entails* that the agent intends to do something and applies himself to its accomplishment; it is through so applying himself that he brings about the accidental and unforeseen result. St Thomas says that the interior act of the will cannot be forced,[91] but as far as I know, he never says that it cannot be brought about through invincible ignorance and thereby involuntary.[92]

Granted, it is probably not very common to speak of interior acts of will as involuntary *or* voluntary; normally the question of voluntariness or involuntariness concerns actions or doings. But in general, a doing is involuntary for someone whenever it is done contrary to his will. As I have argued, there is no reason why a doing which, in some *qualified* way does proceed from an 'intrinsic principle' in the subject, originating somehow from his will and being somehow the object (or part of the object) of his intention, cannot also be unqualifiedly repugnant to his will. But if the realization of some portion of the object of one's intention turns out to be involuntary, and if it is realized *in virtue* of the intention itself, then it is difficult to see how the intention can fail to be involuntary as well.

The second objection is that to deny that a person's act is voluntary is to deny that it falls within the scope of morality. The domain of morality is the domain of the voluntary. Yet when someone acts involuntarily out of ignorance, may he not still be susceptible of moral judgment? One could still very well appraise Othello for engaging in what he *thought* was a justifiable vindication of his honor, or Oedipus for striking the old man, or the hunter for shooting at the deer. They

---

90. *Violentum est cuius principium est extra, nihil conferente vim passo* (I–II, q. 6, a. 6 ad 1). As discussed above (pp. 159–60), Thomas argues that a sufficient 'contribution' on the part of the patient, removing the involuntariness, would be his simply *wanting* to undergo the thing (I–II, q. 6, a. 5 ad 2).

91. I–II, q. 6, a. 4.

92. At least it should not be so difficult to grant that the agent's self-application to action, his *usus*, may be the result of ignorance and involuntary; but *usus*, too, is an interior act of the will. See above, Chapter 4, Sections D.1 and D.2.

have all made choices and can be evaluated accordingly. Must they not then be said to have acted voluntarily?

This objection may be handled by recalling the distinction between what is intentional *simpliciter* and what is intentional only in a certain respect. The same sort of distinction is applicable to the voluntary. Let us go back to the case of the hunter. I argued that his intention and choice to shoot were involuntary, since the ignorance which led to them was involuntary and he would not have adopted them had he known the truth. They were not voluntary *simpliciter*. But they were voluntary in a qualified fashion, namely, *supposing* his beliefs about the situation. He had control over his response to the *believed* situation, and this is sufficient for his response to possess moral quality, to display his character, and so forth. He does come to regret his choice, but what he regrets is not the choice considered merely as a response to certain beliefs, or considered merely according to the proposed course of action which moved it as its object. Rather, he regrets the choice considered as the origin or moving principle of the behavior which followed, i.e. considered according to its effect.[93]

But precisely because the *believed* situation was not the situation *simpliciter*, the effect of the choice was not and could not have been in conformity with its object; and this makes it involuntary, *simpliciter*, because to choose a proposed course of action *is* to want to bring about an effect in conformity with the proposal. The hunter's behavior, his exterior movements, were not fully informed by his choice, and it is of the very nature of a choice to tend toward informing the chooser's movements. There is no such thing as a choice which is satisfied by itself alone, even though an unsatisfied choice may be a morally good (or bad) choice. The fact that the moral domain is the domain of human acts, and that there is morality whenever there is choice, does not entail that there is a *complete* human act whenever there is choice or morality.[94]

This cuts two ways. It means that a choice is only a principle of action, not itself an action; the domain of complete human action extends beyond the agent's will and is a composite of interior and exterior acts. It also means that even when a person's movements are initiated by his choice, so that when he is moving there is morality involved, his movements may very well not constitute the completion or fulfillment of his choice, and the moral quality of the choice may not extend to them. They may not embody his choice and may not constitute an exterior *moral* act.

The latter point may be spelled out by means of a question, along the lines of Anscombe's use of the question 'why?' to get at the nature of intention. Sup-

---

93. This twofold way of considering the choice corresponds to its being an act of appetite. Appetite is essentially a 'moved mover,' moved by the good existing in apprehension and moving toward its real possession. See Aristotle, *De anima* III, ch. 10, 433b16, and above, Chapter 4, Section E.1. See also I. II, a. 13, a. 5, ad 1 (quoted above, Chapter 4, n. 2).

94. See above, Chapter 4, Section E.2.

pose we take the example of Othello, and ask: just *what* was he doing? Two incompatible answers can be offered: he was, as Donagan puts it, engaging in a 'justifiable vindication of his honour against his adulterous wife'; or he was killing his innocent wife.

The first answer expresses what he was 'up to' and the object by which his moral disposition is properly assessed. But of course it faces the rather difficult objection that it means that he was doing something which was impossible to do. His adulterous wife could no more be killed by him than the present king of France can be bald. He had no adulterous wife. The matter for such action was lacking.

The second answer, that he was killing his innocent wife, expresses something quite possible, and seems to tell us what 'really happened.' But it does not tell us what Othello was doing in his quality as a *human* agent, does not tell us about his *conduct*; and this is what the question 'what was he doing?' normally calls for.[95] That the second answer does not tell us about Othello's conduct is shown, at least in part, by Anscombe's test: the question 'why was he killing his innocent wife?,' in the sense of 'what for?,' is just not applicable. It seems to me that in fact, in cases such as that of Othello, the question of *what* he was doing is similarly inapplicable, or at least it is not applicable in an unqualified fashion. This is because such cases are simply not cases of complete human actions.

This is not an idle point. I have witnessed several disputes about whether it is correct to say that what a person did was or was not such-and-such a thing, this being the sort of thing he means to be doing but for which the matter is lacking. The question never seems to be resolved satisfactorily; and the reason, I believe, is that it assumes something which defeats its own application. There is *no* good answer to the question of what he did. Here is one of the disputed cases. Suppose a rich man disguises himself as a pauper and begs from a passer-by. Out of charity, the passer-by gives him something. We may assume the passer-by would be angry if he learned that he had been fooled. The question is then raised, is his action a case of giving alms to the poor, or not? The question asks for what sort of human act the passer-by has performed. But there can be no absolute answer, because he is acting out of ignorance and involuntarily. It is not a case of an unqualified, complete human act.[96]

---

95. See above, Chapter 1, at n. 6. Something both possible and indicative of Othello's conduct would be that he was *intending* to kill his adulterous wife; but this is still not an answer to the question 'what was he doing?,' because intending is not 'doing' something at all. (See Chapter 4, Section D.2.) To ask what he was doing is to ask what kind of action he was performing, and an intention is not an action, but only a principle of action.

96. Of course there can be qualified answers, but what is the value of them? One qualified answer which I have heard proposed would be that 'morally speaking' the passer-by has given alms to the poor. But what this means would be put more clearly, and with less risk of sophistical inferences, by saying simply that the passer-by has all the *merit* of one who has given alms to the poor. Someone can have all the merit of one who has given alms to the poor without actually having given

Earlier, in passing, I indicated my wish to defend the *general* legitimacy of asking for the 'what' or the 'essence' of an action.[97] But this is not always legitimate. Some things have no essence, and others have essence only up to a point. What has no essence is what is a being and a unity merely *per accidens*. An example in the domain of substances would be an object which is nothing more than a clump of things stuck together haphazardly. In the domain of actions, an example would be an event which is a mere coincidence. What is done out of ignorance is like this; e.g. to dig a grave and in so doing to find a treasure, or to kill a wife presumed guilty and in so doing to kill an innocent wife. Coincidences do not have essences, because they do not embody any intention. An event is an action, and is specified according to the intention it embodies, *if* it embodies one.

Of course, there is always some component in a coincidence which is not itself a coincidence. It was not a coincidence that Othello killed his wife. But even what is not a coincidence may not possess any essence fully and may be somewhat indefinite. Among substances, an example of this would be something which is still in the process of generation. Within the framework of Thomas's biology, such would be an embryo in its early stages. Thomas holds that before a man or a horse is generated, the embryo is just an 'animal,' indefinite or indeterminate in its species.[98] Among actions, what would be merely indefinite in species would be something which results from undertaking to execute an intention but which fails to embody any intention fully. Even if there is some measure of 'action' in it, it is impossible to say exactly *what* action it is; you can only say what it was meant to be, and perhaps what it seems to be. Aristotle says that when we act voluntarily, we are principles of our actions as parents are principles of their children.[99] We might say, then, that considered as a product of the will, what is done involuntarily out of ignorance is abortive, or a sort of freak.

At the risk of pushing the comparison with substances too far, and assuming that we now know that the early embryo is already a horse or a human being, as the case may be, can we find another example of a not fully determinate substance? We might consider a gamete, but this is already something *definite*, e.g. definitely human, even though it is not a *whole* human being but only a sort of part. The best example I can find of something which is merely on the way to having a determinate species, indefinite in itself, would be food in the process of digestion. It is 'organic' stuff, but it does not yet share fully in the nature of any definite species of organism. Of course food is on the way to being something

---

alms to the poor. Compare the case of a student who knows the subject well but does poorly in the examination because of a non-scientific factor: the examination contains gratuitously misleading questions. The fault is the exam-setter's, and the student deserves a good mark. But would there be any point in saying that 'scientifically speaking' the student has written a good examination?

97. See Chapter 2, n. 18.
98. I, q. 119, a. 2. See Anscombe, 'Embryos and Final Causes,' p. 300.
99. *Nicomachean Ethics* III, ch. 7, 1113b18.

definite only in the manner of part of an organism, not as a separate whole. But our concern is with actions; and many actions, too, while being quite definite in themselves, are only particular steps within larger projects. The present point is that things that are involuntary out of ignorance are not definite even in the manner of parts. And this is because their agents have not fully 'assimilated' the circumstances.

This leads to the last observation, aimed at restoring a balanced perspective in line with the previous chapter's insistence upon the naturalness of the interior act's order toward the exterior act. If what is done involuntarily through ignorance is a sort of freak product of the will, it is also exceptional. Normally people's particular steps, if not their larger projects, do in fact reach their goals. When the question 'what is so-and-so doing?' comes up, it usually does have application.

When someone *seems* to be acting intentionally and humanly, so that you want to know *what* it is that he is so doing, normally he *is* acting intentionally and humanly. There is something like a person's *looking as though* he is in control of his movements, which can be perceived even when the sense of the movements is not quite clear; and for the most part the look is genuine. Otherwise, how could there be such a look? The case is similar when the view is from 'inside': usually our movements truly have the unity and sense that we mean to be giving them. For instance, what we say is usually what we mean to say.

This is Anscombe's simple and (remembering Kant) very telling observation, which she expresses in various ways in *Intention*, that for the most part, what someone is doing is what he then intends to be doing. 'Surprising as it may seem, the failure to execute intentions is necessarily the rare exception.'[100] Certainly there can be intention, and choice, and morality even when the execution fails. But morality is something serious, as nature is something serious. What makes morality serious—what makes moral goodness really good, and moral badness really bad—is, among other things, the fact that for the most part, the execution does not fail.

---

100. *Intention*, § 48, p. 87; cf. § 4, p. 9.

Appendix
The Specification of Action in St. Thomas: Nonmotivating Conditions in the Object of Intention

In a lecture delivered in 1982, Elizabeth Anscombe voiced some reservations about the principle of double effect.[1] She said that she had come to realize that it was not really a single principle, but rather a "package deal," combining a number of principles or criteria that are not intrinsically connected.[2] She suggested splitting it up and keeping only a part, which she called the "principle of side-effects." This principle is rather modest. For one thing, it concerns only one kind of side-effect, namely death. Other harms or evils are not mentioned. What it says is that the exceptionless moral prohibition on murder "does not cover *all* bringing about of deaths which are not intended."[3] Of course it does not say that the prohibition covers no such cases. Nonintended killings can be murder too. But neither does the principle of side-effects determine which of them are murder and which are not. That requires other principles. Here Anscombe proposed only one, which she took to be obvious and to cover a good many cases: namely, that the "intrinsic certainty of the death of the victim, or its great likelihood from the nature of the case," would render the act murderous.[4]

Anscombe went on to protest against the ascription of the principle of double effect to St. Thomas Aquinas. Often, in fact, the principle is said to be present, at least implicitly, in Thomas's treatment of killing in self-defense.[5] In part, this is because of his requirement of "proportionate means" in defending oneself. But Anscombe insisted—quite rightly, I think—that this requirement has nothing to do with the double-effect "doctrine of a proportion of good over evil in the upshot."[6] She also declared that, if we want Thomas's view on responsibility for evil consequences generally (and not just death), the place to look is not his discussion of self-defense, but rather a passage earlier in the *Summa theologiae*—question 20, article 5 of the *Prima secundae*—in which he explains the

---

1. Anscombe, 'Action, Intention, and "Double Effect."'
2. Ibid., pp. 22–24.
3. Ibid., p. 21. She does think that the prohibition covers intentional killing, with only "the relevant 'public' exceptions" (ibid.).
4. Ibid., p. 24. By "the nature of the case" she seems to mean the nature of the action performed. Thus, immediately following this remark, she exemplifies it with a case of surgery aimed at getting an organ, in which the patient's death is "pretty certain from the nature of the operation."
5. II-II, q. 64, a. 7.
6. Anscombe, 'Action, Intention, and "Double Effect,"' pp. 24–25.

relation of a consequence (*eventus sequens*) to an action's goodness or badness.[7] She closed the lecture by quoting that passage, without comment.

A good way to begin my own discussion will be to summarize that very passage. Then, still in the first section, I shall summarize a related passage, also from the *Summa theologiae*, on whether sins are graver, the more harm they cause. In light of these two passages, I shall argue that Thomas's treatment of nonintended effects that follow *per se* on intentional action—I call them head-on effects—does not accord well with the usual understanding of the distinction between intended effects and side-effects. This is because he presents these effects as directly voluntary. In section 2, I try to correct two common readings, which I think mistaken, of Thomas's discussion of killing in self-defense. As it happens, they are readings to which at least one of the authors of the New Natural Law theory subscribes. Then, in section 3, I shall start to home in on the central thesis of this paper, which is that, for Thomas, features of an action that do not motivate the agent, or do not provide reasons for acting, can fall within the agent's intention, and can sometimes even specify the action. As a way of both arguing for this thesis and showing why it matters, I undertake to contrast Thomas and the New Natural Law theory on the question of the scope of the object of intention. Section 4 therefore presents some passages from writings by the theory's proponents that illustrate their view of the object of intention. Section 5 lays out my reading of Thomas on the matter. Here I argue, among other things, that for him something can be intended merely *per accidens* and nevertheless not be *praeter intentionem*, and that it can therefore be a factor in the specification of action. In section 6, I try to characterize the issue in general theoretical terms.[8]

1. Head-on Effects

The passage to which Anscombe refers is about whether a consequence can add to an act's goodness or badness. The answer that Thomas defends is no. Generally speaking, an act's consequences do not affect its own quality. But Thomas acknowledges important exceptions. If the agent of a bad act foresees bad consequences, yet goes ahead with it, that shows him to have an even more disordered will. Moreover, any consequence—even unforeseen—that "follows on such an act *per se* and for the most part," shows the act itself to be better or worse "in its kind" (*ex suo genere*).[9] This last point, that *per se* consequences reflect an act's kind, is what most interests me. The other passage that I wish to summarize—question 73, article 8 of the *Prima secundae*—will help bring out the interest of it.

---

7. Translations of Thomas in this paper are mine.
8. I wish to thank two anonymous reviewers of this article for their helpful comments and suggestions.
9. Perhaps his general answer is negative because he thinks most consequences are neither *per se* nor foreseen.

In the latter passage, Thomas is discussing whether a sin is graver, the more harm it causes.[10] This time his overall answer is yes. But he distinguishes four ways in which harm can aggravate sin. First, there is harm that is foreseen and intended, as by a murderer or a robber. Such harm is itself an object of sin, and so of course it aggravates the sin, quite directly. The second sort is harm that is foreseen but not intended. This also aggravates sin, but only indirectly, by showing a will so bent on the sin as to accept a harm that the agent would otherwise avoid. Here Thomas gives the example of someone who crosses a field in order to fornicate and thereby knowingly harms the crops. In the third place are harms that are neither foreseen nor intended and that follow on the sinful act merely *per accidens*. These do not directly aggravate the act itself. However, they are imputed to the sinner, as owing to his negligence: he fails to avoid them when he could and should do so (inasmuch as he could and should avoid the sin itself).[11] Finally, some harms are neither foreseen nor intended, but follow on the sinful act *per se*. An example is the scandal caused by fornicating publicly.[12] This sort of harm aggravates directly. "For whatever follows on a sin *per se*," Thomas explains, "pertains somehow to its kind."

It is important to understand what Thomas means by saying that something follows *per se*. He does not mean simply that it is foreseeable. Even results that can be foreseen with certainty—necessary results—may not be *per se*. Their certainty may be owing to extrinsic, merely accidental factors, rather than to anything intrinsic to the act itself, anything in the act's own kind. That is to say, to use Anscombe's phrase, the certainty may not be "from the nature of the case." For example, given a person's character, it may be quite certain that she will be scandalized by another's action, and yet the action itself not be intrinsically scandalous.[13] Most Catholic moralists hold that the nonintended death of a fetus resulting from a hysterectomy performed on a pregnant woman is like this. The hysterectomy itself does not constitute a lethal action upon the fetus. Indeed, it is not trained upon the fetus at all. It only, as it were, removes an obstacle to the fetus's death. The death of the fetus is certain and necessary, but nevertheless it is only a *per accidens* result, not *per se*.[14]

But let us consider more closely what Thomas is saying about unforeseen, nonintended harms. As we have just seen, those that follow *per se* on a sin aggravate the sin directly, while those that follow *per accidens* do not directly aggravate the sin, but they do so indirectly, being ascribed to culpable negligence. This difference is, I think, an application of a distinction drawn early in the *Prima secun-*

---

10. I-II, q. 73, a. 8. I am summing up the first two thirds or so of the corpus.
11. Cf. II-II, q. 64, a. 8.
12. Cf. II-II, q. 43, a. 1, ad 4.
13. See II-II, q. 43, a. 3. For other examples, see the *sed contra* of I-II, q. 20, a. 5.
14. On Thomas on necessary *per accidens* effects, see above, pp. 125–28.

dae, between two ways in which things may be voluntary.[15] Let me explain this distinction and why I think it applies here.

To be voluntary is to be caused by the will. But something may be caused by the will either directly or indirectly.[16] Directly voluntary effects proceed from the will inasmuch as it is active, as heating proceeds from heat.[17] Indirectly voluntary effects proceed from the will inasmuch as it does not act, as the sinking of a ship is attributed to the ship's pilot insofar as he leaves off steering the ship.[18] However, things are not attributed to the will in this indirect way, by its not acting, unless the circumstances are such that it could and should act in such a way as to prevent them. By contrast, things that result directly from the will's act are always attributed to the will as their cause. No special circumstances are needed.

Now as we saw, in question 73, article 8, harm that is ascribed to the sinner's negligence is said to aggravate his sin in an indirect way, by the fact that he fails to avoid it when he could and should. This is the language of the indirectly voluntary.[19] Contrasted with this is harm that follows *per se* on a sin. It directly aggravates the sin, even if it is unforeseen and not intended. The very contrast already suggests that this sort of harm is to be regarded as directly voluntary. Elsewhere, in fact, Thomas is quite clear that something can be said to result directly from the will's act even when the will does not directly bear upon or directly tend toward that result. This is the case when the will does directly bear upon or tend toward the result's cause—the so-called voluntary in cause.[20] (Presumably the cause itself must be direct or *per se*, tending of itself to produce such a result.)[21] Moreover, both in the article about consequences and in the one about harms, Thomas tells us that *per se* results somehow reflect or pertain to the act's own kind. He is obviously talking about the act's moral kind, which is to say, its kind

---

15. Thus in II-II, q. 64, a. 8, using language very similar to the relevant lines of I-II, q. 73, a. 8 ("*dare operam rei illicitae*," etc.), Thomas explicitly characterizes effects brought about through culpable negligence as indirectly voluntary.

16. I-II, q. 6, a. 3.

17. When he distinguishes between scandal that follows on an act *per se* and scandal that follows only *per accidens*, Thomas calls the former "active" scandal: II-II, q. 43, a. 1, ad 4. Of course, the example of an act of heating that proceeds from heat hardly serves to illustrate the idea of a *per se* effect that the agent does not intend. Thomas is not concerned with that idea in I-II, q. 6, a. 3.

18. I do not think the example in I-II, q. 73, a. 8 of crossing a field to fornicate and harming the crops is a case of indirectly voluntary harm. The harm to the crops seems to follow *per se* on the act of crossing the field. What is indirect is not the harm's voluntariness, but only its aggravation of the sin of fornication. It is not a function of this sin's own object or kind. By contrast, the scandal given by public fornication is a function of the act's being fornication.

19. See I-II, q. 6, a. 3.

20. See II-II, q. 77, a. 7. Here the voluntary in cause is explicitly distinguished from the indirectly voluntary. It is directly voluntary—a direct effect of the will, one attributed to the will's act—because the will's act does bear upon or tend toward it (*fertur in ipsum*), albeit not directly or in itself but in its cause.

21. In ibid., an example of the voluntary in cause is the behavior that results from intentionally getting drunk.

as a human, voluntary act. Since the act itself is directly voluntary, surely anything that pertains to its moral kind is as well. It seems clear, then, that in the passage on harms Thomas is saying that a harm that is not intended or even foreseen can be directly voluntary,[22] namely, if it follows *per se* on a voluntary act.

This is striking. As it is usually formulated, the principle of double effect supposes that all nonintended harms are either not voluntary at all or only indirectly voluntary (in the above sense), depending upon whether or not the agent could and should have acted in such a way as to avoid them. The principle gives criteria for deciding. But such criteria are irrelevant to directly voluntary harms, and what I am arguing is that, for Thomas, a nonintended and even nonforeseen harm may be directly voluntary.

A good example of this is offered in a passage from the disputed questions *De malo*:

> A necessity that is on the supposition of something subject to the will does not take away the quality of mortal sin. Thus, if a sword is thrust into someone's vital organs, the person necessarily dies; but the blade-thrust is voluntary. Hence the death of the person who is smitten by the blade is imputed to the one who smites as a mortal fault.[23]

Clearly Thomas means that the death's being intended or not is incidental. It is imputed to the agent in any case, and this means that it is voluntary of him in any case. This makes sense if indeed it is directly voluntary in any case.

I do not mean to suggest that Thomas's treatment of nonintended *per se* effects implies that there are kinds of actions which the principle of double effect would allow but which he would prohibit. His text, after all, is about harms following *per se* on sinful kinds of actions. There is no risk that the principle of double effect allow such actions, because it rules out all actions that are sinful in kind. But what especially interests me is the connection that Thomas posits, quite generally, between an act's *per se* results and its kind. Such results "somehow pertain" to the kind. Not everything that is outside an action's kind, then, is merely extraneous or incidental to it. The action is not, so to speak, hermetically sealed within its kind, such that nothing else can directly qualify it. Even though the public fornicator does not intend to scandalize, and his action's kind is not plain scandal, it is still an intrinsically scandalous act.[24] Anscombe provides another example: "Surgery would be thought *murderous*, even though it was not

---

22. I take it that Thomas is assuming that the agent does know (or at least could and should know?), in a general way, that such a result follows on that kind of act. What is not actually foreseen is this instance of the result, as following on this instance of the kind. The agent's not having bothered to consider the consequences of what he is doing does not exclude their being voluntary of him—even directly voluntary.
23. *De malo* q. 3, a. 10.
24. Cf. II-II, q. 43, a. 3, obj. 3 and ad 3.

done in order to kill, but, say, to get an organ for someone else, if the death of the subject were expected as a near consequence, pretty certain from the nature of the operation."[25]

Thomas even indicates that a nonintended result can aggravate "infinitely," that is, make an act be mortally sinful which without that result would not be so. He grants that remote and unforeseen results cannot do this, but a result that is conjoined (*coniunctus*) and foreseen can. "Thus, shooting an arrow is not a mortal sin, but shooting an arrow in conjunction with killing a man is a mortal sin; and likewise, not to repel a passion that inclines toward mortal sin is not without mortal sin."[26] I assume that "shooting an arrow in conjunction with killing a man" means shooting at what one knows to be a man—but not necessarily because it is a man or because he can thereby be killed. It does not matter whether one intends to kill the man with the arrow, or to commit the sin toward which the passion inclines. These results still aggravate the acts and make them mortal sins. Now, Thomas cannot be saying that the result is constitutive of the act's kind. He insists repeatedly that an action's kind is constituted by its object, and that this is something intended.[27] But a *per se* result is *per se* precisely because the act's order to it pertains somehow to the act's kind, and hence to the act's object. Acts with different *per se* results must differ correspondingly in their objects, and this difference may in turn make for different kinds, even kinds that differ infinitely in gravity.

It would be helpful to have terms that reflect the difference between *per se* and *per accidens* results of actions. I would suggest restricting the expression "side-effect" to *per accidens* results. Would anyone call a death resulting from a sword-thrust to the vitals a side effect, even if the agent did not intend it? For such *per se* results, I propose the term "head-on."[28]

---

25. Anscombe, 'Action, Intention, and "Double Effect,"' 24 (emphasis added).
26. *De malo* q. 3, a. 10, ad 5.
27. For example, in I-II, q. 1, a. 3; q. 72, aa. 1, 5, 8; II-II, q. 39, a. 1; q. 43, a. 3; q. 59, a. 2; q. 64, a. 7. Especially instructive, again, is the example of scandal in II-II, q. 43, a. 3. If one is not intending to lead another into sin, but this result follows *per se* on one's action, then one is guilty of active scandal (ibid., ad 4); yet one's action does not have the species of scandal. See also IV *Sent.*, d. 38, q. 2, a. 2, qcla. 2, ad 3. A description may be true of an action, even true of it *per se*, yet not express its essential species. (Here it is crucial to distinguish different senses of "*per se*"; see below, the first paragraph of section 2.) As Thomas explains in II-II, q. 43, a. 3, obj. 3 and ad 3, a sin's being performed in the presence of others is only a circumstance and does not give a species. Contrast this with cases in which there is a nonmotivating condition of the action's very object; see the examples of sacrilege cited below at nn. 70, 84, and 85, and in n. 92. That sort of condition does give a species.
28. I would gladly call them "direct." But this term is used in magisterial documents of disputed interpretation, and among Catholic moralists it is contentious. The New Natural Law proponents restrict it to intended effects.

2. Self-Defense Again

An objection to the very notion of nonintended results that follow *per se* can be drawn from Thomas's discussion of self-defense (*STh* II-II, q. 64, a. 7). Moral acts, he says, take their kinds from what is intended and not from what is outside intention, since this is *per accidens*.²⁹ If it is *per accidens*, how can it ever be *per se*? The answer, I believe, is simply that the terms *per se* and *per accidens* are equivocal. In one sense, only what is in a thing's essence or definition belongs to it *per se*, and everything else is *per accidens*. But in another sense, not only what is in a thing's essence, but also what follows on its essence either necessarily or for the most part belongs to it *per se*, and only what derives from an extrinsic source, as though by mere coincidence, is *per accidens*.³⁰ In this sense, what belongs to a thing *per se* is sometimes not a species of it, but rather some sort of property. To cite an old Scholastic example, this is how risibility—capacity for laughter—belongs to humans. Socrates' species is man, not risibility, but risibility follows upon the essence of man, and in this sense Socrates is risible *per se*. In the sphere of action, then, anything in an action's essence must be within the agent's intention. But something outside intention can follow on the essence necessarily or for the most part. It is not merely coincidental. It follows on the action in virtue of the action itself, and in that sense it belongs to the action *per se*. If it can fail in rare cases, this is because occasionally some extrinsic impediment can appear. Likewise, other results might follow on the action on account of the coincidental presence of some other cause.

Similarly equivocal, I think, is the notion of *praeter intentionem*, "outside intention." Thomas distinguishes between those things outside an agent's intention that are not intended at all, and those to which the intention does somehow extend. *Per se* consequences are among the latter.

---

29. See also the other texts cited in n. 27, as well as *In V Eth.* lect. xiii, §§ 1035–36, and *In VII Eth.* lect. ix, § 1438. I find it odd that, on this point, editions and discussions of II-II, q. 64, a. 7 usually point only to II-II, q. 43, a. 3 (the text on scandal), or I-II, q. 72, a. 1 as well. Surely, if we want to stay within the *Secunda secundae*, more pertinent than q. 43, a. 3 is q. 59, a. 2, which is nearer to q. 64, a. 7 and regards the same virtue, justice. And if we look back to the *Prima secundae*, we find what is surely the most important text on this point, standing almost at the beginning of the entire *Secunda pars* and therefore indicating just how fundamental the idea is in Thomas's moral thought: I-II, q. 1, a. 3. It is true that the term "intention" and its cognates are not given great prominence there (although there are two instances). But the article's very thesis is that "human acts properly take their species from an end," and to function as an act's end is nothing other than to be intended.

30. See I-II, q. 7, a. 2, ad 2: some accidents are "altogether *per accidens*," while others are "*per se*." Here Thomas is discussing the so-called circumstances of actions, which are treated by the arts and sciences that deal with actions, as accidents of actions (cf. the previous article). He says that they are of the *per se* type, this being the type that can be considered by an art or a science. On circumstances, see also I-II, q. 18, a. 3, ad 2. Earlier references, in the *Summa theologiae*, to the general distinction between *per se* accidents and those that are *per accidens* include I, q. 3, a. 6; and I, q. 77, a. 6. On the fact that no science treats of what is entirely *per accidens* and in no way *per se*, see *In VI Meta.* lect. ii, §§ 1172–79; *also In I Post. an.* lect. xiv, §§ 120–24. On the fact that the same science treats a subject and its *per se* accidents, see *In II Phys.* lect. iii, § 158; and *In IV Meta.* lect. i, § 529.

> Just as a *per se* effect of a natural cause is what follows according to the demand of its form, so the effect of a cause acting deliberately is what occurs by the agent's intention; hence whatever comes about in the effect outside the intention is *per accidens*. And I say this if what is outside the intention follows rarely; for what is always or frequently adjoined to the effect falls under the same intention. For it is foolish to say that someone intends something, and does not will that which is often or always adjoined to it.[31]

That last sentence further corroborates the view that such effects are directly voluntary. Again,

> sometimes an accident of some effect is joined to it in few cases and rarely; and then the agent need not in any way intend the *per accidens* effect while he intends the effect *per se*. But sometimes an accident of this type is attached either always or for the most part to the effect principally intended; and then the accident cannot be separated from the intention of the agent. If, therefore, something evil is joined only infrequently to the good that the will intends, it is possible to be excused from sin; for example, if someone cutting down a tree in a forest where people rarely pass kills a person by cutting down the tree. But if the evil is joined either always or for the most part to the good that is intended *per se*, one is not excused from sin although he does not intend this evil *per se*.[32]

Following Joseph Boyle, I think we can say that such effects are intended *per accidens*.[33]

Surprisingly, however, in the face of the very passage just quoted, Boyle asserts categorically that question 64, article 7 allows a private person to defend himself in such a way that the aggressor's death follows "naturally"—that is, *per se*. Boyle grants that the "use [in ad 4] of '*quandoque*' [sometimes] to describe the frequency of the deadly consequence's following from an act of self-defense suggests that the aggressor's death is not a natural and totally predictable consequence of the defensive act as such."[34] But as Boyle sees it, since Thomas seems to be permitting, in private self-defense, any killing that is outside intention and that involves no greater use of force than is needed to stop the attack, and since sometimes a use of force that is naturally (or *per se*) lethal is needed, Thomas must also be allowing that.

On this question, I find Steven Jensen's arguments to the contrary persuasive.[35] His strongest argument, I think, is that a use of force upon which the aggressor's death follows naturally must be one in which at least some serious

---

31. *In II Phys.* lect. viii, § 214.
32. *De malo* q. 1, a. 3, ad 15.
33. Boyle, '*Praeter intentionem* in Aquinas,' p. 660.
34. Ibid., 658. *Quandoque* connects well with the way accidental nonintended harms, as opposed to *per se* ones, are described in q. 73, a. 8: "*quae consequi possent*"—"which might follow."
35. Jensen, *Good and Evil Action*, pp. 62–64.

harm to the aggressor is intended,[36] and that, for Thomas, it is illicit for private agents ever to harm (let alone kill) anyone intentionally.[37] This means that the defender's action itself is a sin, and that therefore, as we gathered from question 73, article 8, the *per se* result of the aggressor's death directly aggravates it and is directly voluntary of the defender.

In question 64, article 7, in fact, Thomas says flatly that "to kill a man is not licit except by public authority for the common good." This is to say that no voluntary killing at all is licit for private persons, no matter whether the voluntariness be direct or indirect.[38] Thomas does indeed allow that a "moderate" defensive action, in which the force used is no more than is needed, can be licit. The defender is not bound to set such action aside so as to avoid killing the aggressor. In other words, in such a case, the aggressor's being killed is not indirectly voluntary of the defender. It is not something that he causes by failing to avoid it when he could and should.[39] But this is only to say that it may be licit for the private agent to do something upon which the aggressor's death follows *per accidens*.[40] If it follows *per se*, it cannot be licit. In fact we find a clear indication that this is what Thomas means at the beginning of the article's corpus, where he says that an effect of action that is outside intention is *per accidens* (and so does not specify the action). This is what he goes on to allow, in some cases, to private agents: *per accidens* killings. As we have just seen, the effects of action that are

---

36. It is crucial, though, not to confuse being lethal *per se* with being in circumstances such that death results certainly or inevitably (see above, at n. 14). For instance, if the aggressor is on a cliff-edge, pushing him away may inevitably result in his death, but it is not lethal *per se*, and it need not involve any intention even to injure. Boyle, in 'Praeter intentionem in Aquinas,' does not seem to see much difference between the notions of a *per se* result and a certain result. Moreover, although he does refer to q. 73, a. 8 (ibid., 653, 662), he is silent about its treatment of nonintended *per se* results.

37. Thomas says this just four articles prior to q. 64, a. 7 (II-II, q. 64, a. 3, ad 3). He had also said it earlier, in his discussion of *rixa*, strife (II-II, q. 41, a. 1). Finnis agrees that it is never licit to intend to injure someone (Finnis, *Aquinas*, pp. 276, 278; also Finnis, *Moral Absolutes*, pp. 54–55.

38. If it is not voluntary in any way, then properly speaking it is neither licit nor illicit. See II-II, q. 64, a. 8. To say that it is not voluntary in any way is to say that the defender's will is in no way its cause. Evidently it would be important to distinguish between the range of the causality of the defender's will and the range of its mere power and consent. That is, the fact that the defender could avoid the aggressor's death by willing not to defend himself as he does, and that he therefore in some way consents to the aggressor's death or to letting the aggressor die, does not make him a cause of the death. For a comparable case, see together the following texts: I, q. 19, a. 9, ad 3; q. 49, a. 2, ad 3; I-II, q. 79, a. 1.

39. I explain this point at greater length above, pp. 218–19.

40. Here I am correcting something I say above, pp. 201–02 n. 18. There, having in view the fact that Thomas treats killing by chance in II-II, q. 64, a. 8, and taking "by chance" to mean the same as *per accidens*, I concluded that any result that is not by chance must be *per se*, and that q. 64, a. 7 was allowing killings that result *per se*. But clearly what Thomas means by a chance killing is one that is not only *per accidens* but also unforeseen. *Per accidens* killings may be foreseen, and q. 64, a. 7 allows some of those. This error led me, in those pages of the book, to adopt an unnecessarily complicated explanation of the impermissibility of craniotomy; on this see the first paragraph of section 3 below.

per accidens are those that are *wholly* outside the agent's intention, being intended neither *per se* nor even *per accidens*. By contrast, *per se* effects are intended at least *per accidens*, and they are directly voluntary. Directly voluntary killing in self-defense can be licit only for a public agent.[41] And even this is only if the aggressor is a malefactor—a criminal or an unjust belligerent.

It is sometimes suggested that, for Thomas, the objective justice or injustice of the aggression is incidental to the morality of killing in self-defense.[42] This, however, is not altogether true. Not long after question 64, article 7, Thomas asks whether someone condemned to death may licitly fight the executioner. He says that, if the condemnation is unjust, the answer is yes; but if the condemnation is just, then since clearly in that case the executioner may licitly fight the condemned man, the condemned man's fighting the executioner amounts to "unjust war."[43] Thomas is not saying that one is bound to accept a death to which he has been justly sentenced. Even a justly condemned man may licitly flee execution, if he can, because he is not bound "to do that whence death would follow."[44] But Thomas is saying that it is not licit forcibly to resist an agent acting justly. An objection argues that it is always licit to follow natural inclination, and that there is a natural inclination in all things to resist what can destroy them. He replies: "Man is given reason so as to follow natural inclination, not indiscriminately, but according to the order of reason. And so not just any self-defense is licit, but that which is done with due moderation."[45] So the "moderation" that Thomas requires in self-defense is not, after all, only a matter of using force sufficient to stop the attack and no more. Any use of force at all is immoderate, if it is upon an undue object—in this case, upon an executioner or other public authority acting justly.

If this holds where there is a just assault, it surely holds where there is no assault at all—and all the more so if the force is used in a way that is naturally or *per se* lethal.[46] I say this because the topic that I shall take up next is craniotomy.[47]

---

41. Not even a public agent may licitly kill someone in an indirectly voluntary way, since indirect voluntariness by its nature implies culpability, being failure to avoid or prevent the thing in question when one could and should.

42. "Aquinas's analysis of the intention in self-defence does not depend upon there being an unjust aggression" (Finnis, Grisez, and Boyle, ' "Direct" and "Indirect" ' (2001), p. 28 n. 46). See also n. 47 below.

43. II-II, q. 69, a. 4.

44. Ibid., ad 2. By the same token, someone sentenced to starvation may eat food brought to him secretly, since "not to eat would be to kill himself" (ibid.).

45. II-II, q. 69, a. 4, ad 1.

46. Thomas condemns killing the innocent in absolutely any way: "*nullo modo licet occidere innocentem*" (II-II, q. 64, a. 6). On this, see above, p. 217 n. 60.

47. Immediately prior to the sentence quoted in n. 42, the authors assure us that "we in no way suggest that the baby in the craniotomy is an unjust aggressor or any other kind of aggressor. (Indeed, we deny that the unborn baby is ever an aggressor.)" In an earlier piece, Boyle had said this: "St. Thomas, unlike many other scholastic moralists, does not introduce the question of the injustice of the

The issue is both vexed and tired, and so I beg the reader's indulgence. I also beg indulgence for dredging up something I wrote about it more than two decades ago. It offers a good case study for the topic that is my central interest here.

3. Craniotomy Again

In that old discussion, although I did not mention the New Natural Law theory, I said things having an obvious bearing on its proponents' position on craniotomy.[48] I agreed with them in part, saying that the surgeon performing craniotomy need not be intending the fetus's death. I also disagreed with them in part, seconding Kevin Flannery's view that a craniotomy cannot be seen as essentially nothing but a cranium-narrowing, with the cranium's being crushed regarded as a mere side-effect and not part of the act's essence or kind. I further held (citing q. 73, a. 8) that acting with the aim of producing the crushed skull of an innocent person is unjust, and that the injustice of it has the gravity of murder, because the person's death follows on it *per se*.[49]

In an article published not long afterwards, John Finnis, Germain Grisez, and Joseph Boyle took notice of my remarks.[50] Addressing what they said will help me to define the issue better than I originally did.

Their first remark was that I failed to show that craniotomy is better described as "producing the crushed skull of an innocent person" than as "cranium-narrowing for the purposes of removal from the birth-canal." I shall return to this point after addressing their other remarks.

---

attack into his analysis [of killing in self-defense]. What's more those who do make use of this feature of the self-defense case, use it to justify direct killing—that is, the killing is a means to saving one's life. What is at stake here, of course, is whether the craniotomy is indirect killing and so the argument about whether the fetus is a 'materially unjust aggressor' is not to the point; that argument assumed that if the fetus were shown to be a materially unjust aggressor it could be directly killed" (Boyle, 'Double-Effect and a Certain Type,' p. 312). I agree that Thomas is not saying that directly killing an unjust aggressor can be licit for a private agent. But I am talking about what Thomas does allow to a private agent in q. 64, a. 7, namely, the direct use of violence upon the aggressor. This cannot be licit if the aggression is just (though the point is made explicit only in q. 69, a. 4). Even less can it be licit if the person undergoing the violence is no kind of aggressor at all—especially if the violence is such as can sometimes result in death, and very especially if it does so naturally or *per se*.

48. See above, pp. 200–01 n. 17. For their view, see Boyle, 'Double-Effect and a Certain Type'; also Grisez, *Living a Christian Life*, pp. 502–03.

49. The reading of Thomas on "head-on" effects that I am proposing in this paper makes that account of the impermissibility of craniotomy unnecessarily complicated (see above, n. 40). It is sufficient to see that the fetus's death is directly voluntary. Moreover, since the fetus is the very object of the action of craniotomy, it seems that the death can be said to specify the action (making it to be murder) and not merely to add a nonspecifying qualification, as in the case of nonintended active scandal. It is more like the case of theft from a sacred place, which is specified as sacrilege, evidently because the very thing stolen somehow shares in the place's sacredness (see below, n. 92).

50. Finnis, Grisez, and Boyle, ' "Direct" and "Indirect"' (2001), p. 26 n. 38.

Then they said that I seem "to be perhaps conceding, *sub silentio*, that the craniotomy need not be excluded by the exceptionless moral norm against killing the innocent, and therefore letting the assessment of its moral character rest on an assessment of its fairness, its justice." Initially I could not make sense of this. For (as was surely obvious) my remarks reflected what I took to be Thomas's view, and (as is surely no less obvious), for him the exceptionless norm against killing the innocent *is* an assessment of such action's justice. His best-known treatment of it falls squarely within the *Summa*'s treatise on justice.[51] Eventually I realized that they were speaking in the terms of their own theory, in which the morality of (intentional) killing is framed, not primarily as a matter of justice or injustice toward the person killed, but as a matter of how one's will is related to the basic good of human life.[52] In any case, I certainly was not making that concession. What I was driving at was simply that there can be "murder where death foreseeably results from one's action, without the actual intention of killing,"[53] and that this would be such a case. And I took it that there is indeed an exceptionless moral norm against murder, which of course they too hold.

The authors went on to repudiate my use of question 73, article 8. They said that this text was not to the point, "since it deals only with the way in which consequences, even though unintended, can aggravate the gravity of what is already judged to be wrongful." But that is exactly the point I was urging. Having (as I thought) established that what is intended in craniotomy is unjust, because the fetus has a right to its intact skull, I observed that the fetus's life depends on its intact skull—which is to say, its death follows *per se* on the craniotomy—and I appealed to question 73, article 8 to argue that this aggravated the injustice, making it tantamount to murder.

Their last comment was this: "Note that whether and to what extent the life of the unborn child 'depends on' not being subjected to the craniotomy is far from clear in the obstetric emergency we are considering—a situation in which the child is expected to die no matter what is done." This I find astonishing. Taken at face value, it means the child's being certain to die soon anyway casts doubt on whether the craniotomy kills it.

In sum, I think that all but the first of their responses missed the target. The first, however, was a hit, and it was also the most important: that I failed to show my description of craniotomy to be better than theirs. This is so. I merely asserted it. More precisely, I merely asserted the more general thesis from which I derived it. The thesis is that while a human action's object—the object constituting its kind—always has (or seems to have) the form of some good (either as end or as means) for the agent, the object is not that form all by itself. It is rather that

---

51. II-II, q. 64, a. 6. He also says that all of the precepts of the Decalogue—including the fifth, of course—regard justice: II-II, q. 100, a. 3, obj. 3 and ad 3.
52. See Finnis, *Moral Absolutes*, p. 81.
53. Anscombe, 'Action, Intention, and "Double Effect,"' 20.

which has (or seems to have) the form. In other words, although the object must have some feature that moves the agent to apply himself to it as he does, the object is not this feature alone. It is that to which the agent thinks the feature belongs, the feature's subject. It is relatively concrete. Nor is it only the feature's subject taken "as such," that is, as described or named according to that feature. It also includes whatever other features the agent ascribes to it. It can be truly described or named according to any of them.

In the case of craniotomy, this would mean that the act's object is indeed, as they would say, a cranium able to be removed from the birth-canal.[54] They would also call it a narrowed cranium. These descriptions rest on features that move the surgeon's will, reasons why he acts as he does. But I am saying that the object can also be called a damaged, even a lethally damaged cranium. For the surgeon knows that this description is true, intrinsically, of the narrowed cranium. He knows that the cranium's being narrowed (in the way he intends) is one with its being lethally damaged. That he is not interested in its being lethally damaged is incidental. His action's object is a lethally damaged cranium, and he intends to bring this about—even though he does not intend it because of its being that, but only because of its being something that he can go on to remove from the birth-canal.

In assuming, however, that the specifying object of a human act, and what an agent intends, includes more than what motivates him to act or constitutes a reason for his acting, I assumed just what the New Natural Law proponents deny.[55] The cranium-narrowing's being a damaging is, on their view, *per accidens*. It belongs to the procedure considered as a mere piece of external behavior and as subject to natural conditions, but not considered as an intentional, human action. Indeed, on their view, the very fact that the cranium is a *true* cranium—a living, properly functioning part of a living human fetus[56]—is *per accidens*. What is *per se* is only that it is a hard, cranium-sized and cranium-shaped object that must be crushed and narrowed if it is to be removed from the birth-canal. This alone constitutes a reason why the surgeon acts on it as he does. And since, on their view, not only the fetus's death, but also the harm to it, is outside the surgeon's intention, the death cannot be deemed a *per se* effect of his action or

54. But on the term *cranium*, see below, at n. 56.

55. They could even grant that the craniotomy's object is a *crushed* cranium. For they can still deny that it is a damaged cranium. In fact, Boyle seems to have no objection to calling it a crushed cranium: Boyle, 'Who Is Entitled to Double Effect?,' p. 480. However, he must be taking the term *cranium* itself somewhat loosely. He can hardly mean that the object is or includes precisely a true, living cranium (on which see the next note and the text associated with it). This is because its being a true, living cranium does not (or need not) enter into what motivates the procedure.

56. I am alluding to Aristotle's view that it is false to predicate *man* of a dead man (*De interpretatione*, ch. 11, 21a22–23), except in an equivocal sense (*Meteorology* IV, ch. 12, 389b31–32; *Parts of Animals* I, ch. 1, 640b34–36), and that, likewise, if a part of a man, for instance an eye or a finger, dies or loses the capacity for its proper function, what results is no longer the same kind of thing and bears the name of that part only in an equivocal sense (*Meteorology* IV, ch. 12, 390a10–13; *Parts of Animals* I, ch. 1, 641a4–6; *De anima* II, ch. 1, 412b19–22; *Metaphysics* VII, ch. 10, 1035b23–25).

regarded as pertaining to its kind. In general, the crushing and narrowing of hard objects does not usually or naturally result in death. So the fetus's death only follows *per accidens* on what the surgeon intends, and it cannot be imputed to the surgeon as something directly voluntary of him. At most, there may be a question of its being imputed to him as something indirectly voluntary (in Thomas's sense), something that he fails to prevent when he could and should do so—for example, when the procedure is not really necessary to save the mother's life. Circumstances will decide this question. This, I take it, is the New Natural Law view of the case.

What is required, then, is a comparison of that general view of the scope of intention with Thomas's view.

4. The New Natural Law Theory on the Object of Intention

Sometimes the proponents of the New Natural Law theory characterize the object of intention simply as a determinate state of affairs that the agent's practical reason has proposed as an end or a means.[57] In their more rigorous discussions of the matter, however, they qualify this characterization or offer a more restricted one. The following is a representative passage, by Joseph Boyle.

> Whatever does not function as an end of action or a means to the end can be *praeter intentionem*, even if it is a natural consequence or a property of what is within the intention, if it can be separated from the goodness of the end intended or the resolve to achieve that good. . . . It is possible to distinguish what is within the intention from what is foreseen but is not within the intention and this distinction can be drawn at the point where ends and means are separated from concomitants and non-essential properties of ends and means.[58]

By "non-essential," I take it, Boyle means not essential to the goodness of the end or to the resolve to achieve that good. He is ascribing this view to Thomas. Other representative passages are as follows.

> Foreseen effects of what one does are intended only if they actually are among one's reasons for acting. If they are not, they are part of neither the proposal one adopts in choosing the purpose(s) for the sake of which one chooses: they are part of neither the means nor the end(s). . . . Intentions are constituted by acting persons' reasons for making their choices and by precisely what they choose to do.[59]
>
> The means are included in the proposal under the description that makes them intelligibly attractive as a means.[60]

---

57. See, for example, Boyle, 'Toward Understanding the Principle of Double Effect,' pp. 534–36.
58. Boyle, '*Praeter intentionem* in Aquinas,' p. 665.
59. Finnis, Grisez, and Boyle, ' "Direct' and "Indirect" ' (2001), p. 8. Similarly, "If short-term financial gain was not part of the director's reasons for their decision, they do not intend it" (ibid., p. 6).
60. Finnis, *Moral Absolutes*, p. 68.

> The description under which what is done is intended is . . . settled by one's practical reasoning as an agent, by the intelligible benefit one seeks and the means one chooses under the description which promises to yield that benefit.[61] What is *being done* is not settled simply by looking at behaviour, to see what movements are being made, with what awareness and what results. Rather, that is settled by what one chose, under the description which made it attractive to choice (not: the description which makes it acceptable to onlookers, or to 'conscience').[62]
>
> Now, in choosing, one adopts a proposal to bring about certain states of affairs. And the states of affairs which one commits oneself to bringing about—one's instrumental and basic purposes—are precisely those identified under the intelligible description which made them seem rationally appealing and choosable.[63]

The following are two case types other than craniotomy in which this account clearly plays a role.

> By my reformulation of the principle of double effect, some additional operations involving the removal of a nonviable fetus could be justified. An example would be when the pregnancy itself was dangerously overloading an ill mother's heart and kidneys. In such a case, I think the fetus may be removed, because although it will certainly die, the very same act (through a humanly indivisible process) lessens the strain on the mother and contributes to the mother's safety, which alone need be intended by an upright agent.[64]
>
> If a baby, by falling asleep, will fall onto a button which will bring about the incineration of a school full of children, and the only way to stop the baby from falling is to shoot it so that it topples the other way, that can be done without intent to kill or injure even though the effect on the baby is mutilating or lethal and 'deliberate,' that is, caused with full knowledge and control.[65]

Sometimes I do wonder whether the New Natural Law authors are applying their own account consistently. For instance, Finnis takes up the example of an eccentric surgeon who, while operating on an appendix, removes the patient's heart for the purpose of a later experiment. Finnis says that, although the surgeon does not intend to kill the patient, this is still murder. He explains:

---

61. Finnis, 'Intention and Side Effects' (2011), p. 190.
62. Ibid., p. 191.
63. Ibid., p. 194. I find it hard to tell from this passage whether states of affairs that are identified under different descriptions can be the same states of affairs. But I take it that, if they can, they are intended only as identified under the description(s) making them seem choosable, and not according to all the descriptions that are true of them, nor even all those that the agent ascribes to them. See Boyle, 'Toward Understanding the Principle of Double Effect,' pp. 534–35.
64. Grisez, 'Toward a Consistent Natural-Law Ethics,' p. 94. For a similar, more recent discussion, see Grisez, *Living a Christian Life*, 502–03.
65. This passage is from a long endnote added in Finnis, Grisez, and Boyle, '"Direct" and "Indirect" in Action' (2011), 266–67n†. The passage is on p. 267. It is not entirely clear whether the passage should be ascribed to Finnis alone or to all three authors.

The surgeon intends to and does deal with the body, that is, the very person of the patient, as his own to dispose of. Though his choice is not, precisely, to kill or even, perhaps, to impair the functioning of the patient/victim—that is, though death and impairment of functioning are side-effects—the surgeon's choice *is* precisely to treat the bodily substance and reality of that other human person as if that person were a mere subhuman object. The moral wrong, on a precise analysis of the surgeon's intent, is a form of *knowingly death-dealing enslavement*; one who inflicts death, even as a side-effect, in order to effect such an instrumentalisation of another has, in the fullest sense, 'no excuse' for thus knowingly causing death.[66]

I do not see why the surgeon's intention or choice is any more to enslave or instrumentalize the patient than it is to harm or kill the patient. What makes the surgeon's action favor the end of experimentation is not the action's enslaving the patient. It is simply the action's obtaining something fit to experiment upon. Moreover, would it constitute enslavement if it did not harm the patient? If not, then if the harm is not intentional, how can the enslavement be so?

In a note added to the reprint of this essay, Finnis says that, in the original article, he failed to consider sufficiently whether the surgeon's intent, which does not include death, does nevertheless include mutilation—violation of bodily integrity—as a means. Evidently he judges that it does. He also mentions other cases of intentional mutilation: as a means (to facilitate begging), or as an end (when done out of a grudge), and he refers to the issue of the separation of conjoined twins. He then offers a general reflection:

> What is decisive for the intention- and act-analysis in such cases is whether the bodily position or activity of person V is itself a threat to another's well-being and the cutting into or dismemberment of V is a means of mitigating that threat. That is why war-like acts in legitimate defence of self, others, or common good can be brought under Thomas's analysis of defensive intent, in respect not only of the good of life . . . but also of the good of bodily integrity.[67]

I do not see why the mere fact that the end is to mitigate the sort of threat described entails that intending V's dismemberment does not constitute intending the violation of V's bodily integrity. As is well known, Thomas certainly recognizes the possibility of intending to kill or to harm as a means (a legitimate one) to defense of the common good, and also as a means to self-defense (this being illegitimate for private agents).[68] Nor do I see why the end's *not* being to mitigate that sort of threat entails that, *ceteris paribus*, the violation of V's bodily

---

66. Finnis, 'Intention and Side Effects' (2011), 194.
67. Finnis, 'Intention and Side Effects' (2011), 197. See also Finnis, Grisez, and Boyle, ' "Direct" and "Indirect" in Action' (2011), 267.
68. See II-II, q. 64, a. 7 itself; also II-II, q. 64, a. 2; q. 65, a. 1.

integrity necessarily *is* being intended as a means. Perhaps, with any other end, the action cannot fail to be "unfair" to V. But if we are given only what the end is not, and not what it is, how can we possibly judge, from a mere description of behavior, what is or is not being intended as a means to it?

In any case, the main point I wish to make here is simply that, from Thomas's viewpoint, the proponents of the New Natural Law theory unduly narrow the scope of intention.

5. Thomas on the Object of Intention

These authors do seem to recognize that their view differs from Thomas's somehow. Grisez says:

> Thomas often includes in its object anything which makes an act definitely wrong, for this settles its moral species (cf. *De malo*, q. 2, a. 6, ad 2). On my account, the object only includes what one chooses even if the wrongness of the act arises elsewhere. For example, the object of an act of driving somewhere in an automobile is determined by the choice to travel to that place, and this remains so even if the auto belongs to another, is used without permission, and in using it one accepts the side effect of grave partiality toward oneself against the other.[69]

If I understand rightly, Grisez is claiming that such an act, although wrong, is not properly of the kind called theft. It would only be "thievish" or something like that. Its proper kind would be theft only if the automobile's belonging to another and the agent's lacking permission to use it somehow furnished him with a reason for taking it. Grisez is quite correct, I believe, to suggest that Thomas would include those factors in the act's object and would specify the act as theft. But I do not think Thomas would grant that he is thereby including in the act's object or kind anything not included in what the agent chooses. Rather, Thomas differs from Grisez on what is included in what an agent chooses (and intends).[70]

Boyle says that the state of affairs that he calls the object of intention is what the Scholastics call the "formal object" of the act, which gives the act its essential

---

69. Grisez, *Christian Moral Principles*, 247 n. 3. On this passage see also above, p. 214 n. 55.

70. With regard to the passage that Grisez cites, however, I suspect that he was looking at a version of it that contains a highly pertinent textual error. In *De malo*, q. 2, a. 6, ad 2, the Marietti edition (p. 481) has this: *Fit species furti quae est sacrilegium, ex circumstantia loci, et non ex conditione obiecti.* "The species of theft that is sacrilege comes about from the circumstance of place and not from a condition of the object." This would actually be saying that the species of the act is taken from something outside the object. But in the more recent critical edition (Leonine ed., vol. 23, p. 48, l. 273), the *non* has been replaced with *tamen*, "yet," so that the passage runs: "The species of theft that is sacrilege comes about from the circumstance of place and yet from a condition of the object." This version also fits far better with the rest of the passage.

character.[71] The alternative to this view, he says, presents intentional actions as the initiation of concrete causal sequences with indefinitely many descriptions and effects.[72] But it seems to me that Thomas's position lies between these alternatives, and that for him the object of intention is indeed something definite, but nevertheless not as abstract as the New Natural Law authors make it.

Thomas's use of the expression "formal object"—or, more usually, "formal proportioning (*ratio*) of the object"[73]—is somewhat variable. Sometimes, for instance, he says the formal *ratio* of sight is color.[74] At other times he says it is light. In either case the idea is clear. Light makes color visible, and illuminated color makes what has it visible.[75] But Thomas does not mean that only light, or only luminous color, is properly seen or an object of sight. In fact he says that, properly speaking, what is seen is not (luminous) color, but rather, the concrete "a colored."[76] The difference is not just grammatical. He holds that there can be other features of a thing, besides its luminosity and its color, that fall within the scope of the act of seeing it: size, shape, distance, and so on. These features can enter into a thing's look. Not all of its features can; for instance, its flavor cannot (though we may associate a flavor with a look). Of course, a thing's size and shape get their visibility from its color, and not vice-versa. And the size or the shape are not seen by themselves, in abstraction from the colored thing. Yet not even the color, taken separately or abstractly, is properly seen either. What is properly seen is the colored, sized, shaped (etc.) thing.

The case with intention and its scope is similar. One can intend only what one has judged somehow good (or "attractive" or "beneficial" or "appealing" or "choosable"), either on its own account or on account of its order to something else judged good; and one judges a thing good according to some (real or apparent) feature of it. Being judged good according to some feature, together with being judged attainable through one's action, is what makes a thing apt to be intended, by furnishing a sufficient reason or motive for intending it. But other

71. Boyle, 'Double-Effect and a Certain Type,' 317 n. 22.

72. Boyle, 'Double-Effect and a Certain Type,' 307; 'Toward Understanding,' 535; 'Praeter intentionem in Aquinas,' 664.

73. *Ratio formalis obiecti*. The thought is that what an action or a power bears upon always has some feature that proportions it to the action or the power and that functions as the reason why the action or power bears on it.

74. For example, I, q. 1, a. 3; q. 59, a. 4.

75. For example, II-II, q. 1, a. 3.

76. I, q. 45, a. 4, ad 1. A helpful text on this matter is I *Sent.*, d. 17, q. 1, a. 5. There Thomas distinguishes quite sharply between the notion of the object of an act and the notion of the *ratio* in virtue of which the act bears on the object. At the same time, he is clear that one and the same thing can function now as object, now as *ratio*; and sometimes an object is its own *ratio*, sometimes not. But it is quite clear that the object sometimes includes a good deal more than the *ratio*. Here, for example, he says that the object of an act of love may be a *person*, while the *ratio* may be God's dwelling in the person, or the person's charity, or some other feature. In other words, the motivating feature does not exhaust the object.

features of the thing can also fall within the scope of the act of intending it. In fact all the features that the agent ascribes to it do so.[77] The only features that do not do so are those of which the agent is ignorant. To be sure, those features that the agent ascribes to the thing, but that furnish no reason for intending it, fall under his intention only by virtue of their connection with the feature(s) that motivate the intention. They are not intended by themselves. But that which is intended includes them. They do not fall outside intention, any more than size and shape fall outside sight.

To use an example from Thomas, suppose a sawmaker intends to make a saw out of iron.[78] His reason for making it out of iron is that iron is hard. The hardness is the feature that motivates his intention. But the sawmaker also ascribes other features to iron, for instance, aptitude to rust and to wear out. These are not reasons why he intends to make the saw out of iron—quite the contrary. Yet they fall within the scope of his intention. His intention is not merely to make the saw out of something hard. The object of his intention is more concrete. What Thomas says is that his intention is to make the saw out of *iron*. So at least the hard thing's *being iron* falls within the intention. But, as the sawmaker understands it, to be made out of iron *is* to be made out of something apt to rust and wear out. Of course these features do not fall within his intention apart from their connection with the iron's hardness, just as size and shape are not seen apart from their connection with color. But size and shape are included in what the sighted person sees, and the iron's aptitude to rust and wear out are included in what the sawmaker intends.

This is a delicate point.[79] All the features that an agent ascribes to the effect that he intends fall within the scope of his intention, but this does not mean that all the further results to which he thinks his intended effect leads must fall within the scope of his intention as well. The sawmaker intends to make an iron saw, and hence he intends to make a saw that is apt to rust, but he need not intend the further result, the saw's actually rusting. Still, as we saw earlier, *per se* effects do somehow "pertain" to an action's species, which again is a function of the agent's intention. If they are foreseen, then at least the action's order toward them cannot be wholly outside the scope of the agent's intention. The saw's aptitude to rust must somehow fall within the sawmaker's intention.

Similarly, not all of the circumstances that an agent associates with what he intends need fall within the scope of his intention. But the thing's being so circumstanced must do so. For instance, Thomas says that in the case of washing someone

---

77. If, however, the thing is an action, it is important not to slip from a feature of that action to a mere effect of it, or even to a distinct action that is merely circumstantial to it. The two actions cannot simply be identified, even if one somehow qualifies the other.

78. See I, q. 76, a. 5, ad 1; *Quaestiones disputatae de anima*, q. 8 (= a. 8 in the Marietti edition).

79. For a more complete treatment, see my discussion of Roderick Chisholm's principles of the "diffusiveness and non-divisiveness of intention" above, pp. 204–12.

by pouring water on him, the cooling that results is a circumstance of the washing.[80] That act of washing is not simply identical with the act of cooling, any more than being clean is identical with being cool. But the washing can be qualified, as it were adjectivally, by the cooling: it is a refreshing washing, or something like that. Or, to use the now familiar example, giving scandal by fornicating publicly does not mean that the act of fornicating is itself an act of giving scandal. But it is a scandalous act of fornicating. And even if the agent does not fornicate publicly in order to give scandal, he intends to fornicate publicly, and so scandalously.[81]

In other words—and this may be my most controversial claim—although, taken by themselves, nonmotivating features are intended only *per accidens*, they are not always *praeter intentionem*. Boyle says, "Aquinas identifies what is related *per accidens* to the agent's intention and what is *praeter intentionem*."[82] I do not think this is quite accurate. Granted, what is *praeter intentionem*, if intended at all, must be so only *per accidens*. But the converse, I believe, does not always hold. That is, not everything intended *per accidens* is *praeter intentionem*. "*Praeter intentionem*" means *outside* what the agent directly intends. But it is possible for something to be *inside* what an agent intends, and yet not be something that he intends directly, but only *per accidens*.

We can compare what is intended to what is moved. Anything outside of what a mover directly moves will be moved by it, at most, only *per accidens*. But there may also be things moved by it only *per accidens* that are inside what it directly moves. When the wind moves a ship, it also moves a nail inside the ship, though only *per accidens*.[83] Likewise, things that are intended only *per accidens* may still, for Thomas, be within the intention.

In line with this point, places abound in which Thomas ascribes something to the object of a voluntary action, and to the action's resulting species or kind, that does not furnish the agent with a motive or reason for the action. The following text is quite explicit about it. It is on whether a circumstance can give a sin its kind.

> [Objection] Every sin is voluntary. . . . But the will does not bear on a circumstance; as when someone steals a golden consecrated vessel, he does not care about its being consecrated. So this circumstance does not give the sin its kind; and likewise with others.
> [Reply] Although the thief's will does not bear chiefly on the sacred object but on the gold, it bears on the sacred object as a result; for he wills rather to take the sacred object than to do without the gold.[84]

---

80. I-II, q. 7, a. 3, ad 3.

81. By contrast, if the scandal is only a *per accidens* result, as in pharisaical scandal, then even if it is foreseeable, an action from which it results is neither an act of giving scandal nor even a scandalous act. It is simply an act that foreseeably results in scandal. An act is qualified by its effect according to the nature of its order to the effect.

82. Boyle, '*Praeter intentionem* in Aquinas,' 660.

83. The example of the nail in the ship is taken from Aristotle, *Physics* IV, ch. 4, 211a17–23.

84. *De malo*, q. 2, a. 6, obj. 6 and ad 6. See also IV *Sent.*, d. 16, q. 3, a. 2, qcla. 3.

In this article from *De malo*, and also in the parallel *Summa* passage, where the example is an object stolen from a sacred place, Thomas explains that a circumstance can constitute a kind of action insofar as it can be considered as something more than a circumstance, namely, as a "principal condition of the object."[85] A condition's being "principal," however, does not consist in its giving the agent a motive.[86] It consists in the fact that the condition "regards a special order of reason, whether for or against."[87]

I do not think that Thomas is hereby rejecting the idea that moral actions always get their kinds from ends and things intended. He is not saying that the condition in question *is* the object or that it is intended *per se*. It is only a condition of the object. The object is indeed an end.[88] But this end, this object, must be taken concretely, as having all the features that the agent ascribes to it, and not just as having those that make it attractive to him or constitute a reason for acting. And any feature, whether or not it constitutes a reason, can determine a moral kind, simply by making the end especially due, or especially undue, according to reason.

Another good example is drunkenness.

> The sin of drunkenness . . . consists in the immoderate use and desire of wine. Now this may happen to a man in three ways. First, such that he does not know the drink to be immoderate and intoxicating: and then drunkenness may be without sin. . . . Secondly, such that he perceives the drink to be immoderate, but without knowing it to be intoxicating, and then drunkenness may involve venial sin. Thirdly, it may happen that a man is well aware that the drink is immoderate and intoxicating, and yet he would rather fall into drunkenness than abstain from the drink. Such a man is a drunkard properly speaking, because morals take their species not from things that occur accidentally and beside the intention, but from that which is directly intended. In this way drunkenness is a mortal sin, because then a man willingly and knowingly deprives himself of the use of reason, whereby he performs virtuous deeds and avoids sin, and thus he sins mortally by running the risk of falling into sin.[89]

Thomas says that there is drunkenness, not just when the drinker's direct aim is to be drunk, but whenever the drinker's aim is to drink what he knows to be an immoderate and intoxicating amount of drink. The formulation is like that of the

---

85. *De malo*, q. 2, a. 6, ad 2 and ad 9; I-II, q. 18, a. 10.

86. In I-II, q. 72, a. 9, ad 2, he says that a circumstance never transfers an act to some other species unless it is connected with some other motive. There he is evidently talking about circumstances that are nothing but circumstances and that do not constitute principal conditions of the object. We might say that a circumstance qua circumstance does not specify except by connection with a motive. But a condition of the object can specify on its own.

87. I-II, q. 18, a. 10.

88. Even the exterior act's object specifies the act only insofar as it is an end, that is, intended: I-II, q. 72, a. 3, ad 2.

89. II-II, q. 150, a. 2.

passage from *De malo* on sacrilegious theft: it is enough that the drinker's will bear on being drunk in such a way that he would rather "fall into" (*incurrere*) drunkenness than abstain from the drink.[90] He gets drunk willingly, but neither being drunk nor even the amount's being intoxicating need be something that he intends *per se*.[91]

A great many of the kinds of acts that Thomas discusses fit the same analysis. One example is that of the man condemned to starvation who is secretly provided with food. As we saw, Thomas says flatly that not to eat it would be suicide. He does not make it depend on the man's having an interest in dying. He never says that in order properly to be guilty of theft, one must be taking what is another's because it is another's; or that there is true adultery only if conjugal condition is a motive of the act; or that it is not really murder if the victim's innocence (or whatever factor makes his being killed undue) is not a reason for killing him; and so on.

It can also happen that a nonmotivating condition of the object affects the morality of an act without putting it into a distinct kind. This is what happens in the example in question 73, article 8 of fornicating publicly. The condition of being public does not specify the act. The act's kind remains simply fornication, and this condition only aggravates it, by making it tend *per se* toward scandal.[92] Still, such a condition aggravates, and is voluntary, directly, proceeding from the agent inasmuch as he acts.

But it should not be too surprising that things indirectly intended sometimes specify actions, if indeed it is true that even nonintended *per se* effects—head-on

---

90. Also pertinent is I-II, q. 76, a. 4, corp. and ad 2: a man who wants only to drink an immoderate amount, but who thereby gets drunk, loses discretion, and consequently kills a man, is guilty of *two* sins, killing *and* drunkenness.

91. Preferring one thing to another and so choosing to bring it about when the only alternative is the other thing does not entail that the thing chosen is intended *per se*; see I-II, q. 78, a. 1, ad 2. The thing chosen is "willed" or done "willingly" in the sense used in the passage from the *Physics* commentary above at n. 31.

92. See II-II, q. 43, a. 3, ad 3. The act's being scandalous depends on this circumstance and yet belongs to the act *per se*. As we saw earlier, Thomas says that *per se*, nonintended effects pertain somehow to the act's kind. The scandal example suggests that he does not mean that such effects follow on the kind universally; rather, they may follow on the kind only under certain conditions. Obviously the act's being fornication is quite pertinent to its being scandalous, even though its being scandalous also requires the further condition of being public. But why does this further condition not specify the act as scandal, in the way that the condition of being in a sacred place does specify an act of theft as sacrilege (I-II, q. 18, a. 10)? Is it because only the latter condition relates the act's own object to a "special order of reason" (I-II, q. 18, a. 10)? That is, a thing's being in a sacred place makes the thing itself somehow sacred, and so makes the act of stealing the thing be in itself a violation of a sacred thing (that is, a sacrilege); the sacrilege is not a mere further result of the act. But being in public does not make an act of fornication be a scandalizing of the very person with whom one fornicates (that person being the object of one's act of fornicating; the scandal is a result that affects only some other person or persons. In order to specify the act, this result would have to be intended, or at least associated with a distinct motive (see above, n. 86).

effects—somehow "pertain" to an action's species. If the indirectly intended item is included within the very object that is directly intended, then it can be a specifying factor, even if it is not a motivating one (in which case, at least usually, it would be directly intended); that is, even if it does not fall *per se* under the inclination of the agent's will. For it may still "regard a special order of reason, whether for or against," and it may do so *per se*.

6. Theoretical Issues

Have I now proved that I have a better description of craniotomy, and a better theoretical basis for it, than do the New Natural Law authors? No. I have only tried to show that they do not have Aquinas on their side. Nor, I believe, do they have the man on the street. I think most people would say that taking what is another's property can be genuine theft even if the thing's being another's furnishes the taker with no reason for taking it; and likewise for the other cases. Of course the authors have no duty to agree either with the man on the street or with Thomas.

I wish, however, to formulate a little more precisely how I understand the general theoretical issue. Regarding my own position, I would insist that I am not adopting (or foisting on Thomas) what the New Natural Law authors sometimes call physicalism. I am not simply identifying the object of intention with an externally observable piece of behavior or result. This is because I hold that the object of intention is essentially something conceived or understood by the intention's subject. Thus, for instance, an externally observable result of which the agent is invincibly ignorant is not within his intention. Nor is every result that he can or does foresee. Moreover, I am certainly not saying that a human action's kind is constituted only partly ("formally") by what is within the agent's intention, and partly ("materially") by other, purely physical or natural determinations ("teleologies").[93] It is constituted entirely by what is within the agent's intention. My claim is that I am looking at intention and its object, and at human action and its specification, from the properly moral perspective, that of the acting person.

Regarding the New Natural Law authors, I would stress that I am not charging them, as some have, with exaggerating the role of intention in the specification of action. I think Thomas gives it no less of a role. Only, I think he has a different view of its scope. How might we characterize the disagreement?

---

93. For one thing, not every natural tendency is really teleology at all, that is, order toward a *telos*, an end. An end is a perfection, a good, and it *explains* the tendency, as its final *cause*. There is such a thing as tendency (in the sense of noncasual order) toward results that are accidental to the agent's end; see above, n. 14. And even when the result in question is a true end, Thomas is very clear that natural ends, merely as natural, do not specify moral acts. Only moral ends, which are ends of the will, do so. "For a movement does not take its kind from that which is a terminus *per accidens*, but only from that which is a terminus *per se*. But moral ends are accidental to a natural thing; and conversely, being a natural end is accidental to a moral end" (I-II, q. 1, a. 3, ad 3).

If we want a label, I would propose that, from Thomas's point of view, the New Natural Law theory is rather too intellectualist. By this I mean that it makes the proper object of an act of will as abstract as even an object of intellect can be. Thomas says, "the object of intellect is simpler and more absolute than the object of will; for the very concept [*ratio*] of appetible good is an object of intellect; but the object of will is the appetible good whose concept is in intellect."[94] Thomas is explaining why the intellect's object is nobler and higher than the will's. It is simpler and more abstract. This is why, and how, intellect moves will. It works to form the will's very object. It does so by applying the *ratio* of will's object—the *ratio* of good—to the judgment of something. This is what properly moves the will: not the *ratio* of good by itself, but something judged to possess this *ratio*. The *ratio* of good is indeed the formal *ratio* of the object of the will. But it is not the whole object. The object is more concrete, including not only the *ratio* itself but also that to which it is understood to apply.

Intellect can bear on the very reason for desiring something, all by itself, in abstraction from the thing's other conditions, according to the sort of existence that things can have in an intellectual soul. But the will bears only on the real thing that is understood to be desirable for that reason, and it bears on this thing according to and together with all the conditions that are understood to pertain to the thing in its real being. Not all of these conditions are reasons for willing, but they are all included in what is willed, and they even condition the one who wills it. "For the action of intellect consists in this, that the *ratio* of the thing understood is in the one who understands; but the act of will is completed in this, that will is inclined to the very thing, as it is in itself."[95] Here Thomas speaks generally of the will's inclination, not specifically of the act of will called intention. But among the acts of the will that regard something taken as an end, intention seems to be the most practical, since it bears on an end as something to be attained by some means.[96] And so it also seems to have the most concrete object, since human actions regard concrete particulars.[97]

In this respect, the will's intention is rather like a nature's. "A [human] nature does not intend to produce a [human] nature except in a concrete subject, and hence it does not intend to generate humanity, but a man.[98] Of course the two sorts of intention are not simply identical. The object of the will's intention is, if anything, even more concrete—more determined by particular conditions—than that of nature's. In fact, the will's object is always potentially open to determination by further conditions. This is precisely because the will's object is pre-

---

94. I, q. 82, a. 3.
95. I, q. 82, a. 3; see I-II, q. 13, a. 5, ad 1.
96. I-II, q. 12, a. 1, ad 4.
97. I, q. 29, a. 1; I-II, q. 9, a. 2, ad 2.
98. III *Sent.*, d. 8, q. 1, a. 2, ad 2. On the notion of intention in (irrational) nature, see I, q. 2, a. 3 (*Quinta via*); I-II, q. 12, a. 5.

sented by reason—practical reason, which is not confined to universal considerations, as speculative reason tends to be, but which can and must extend to singulars.[99] Reason's capacity for very abstract objects goes together with its being open to absolutely all forms, and this in turn means that there is no limit to its power to combine forms into more and more concrete composites.[100] Even though the will's act is always motivated by a universal reason, the fact that it is inclined toward things as they are in themselves means that it is inclined toward them as concrete singulars.[101] So instead of saying merely that it is too intellectualist, perhaps it would be more accurate to say that, from Thomas's point of view, the New Natural Law theory's account of intention and its object is too speculative, not sufficiently practical.

As for the principle of double effect, it is concerned, not with what motivates the will, but with the will's effects. The principle's main job is to distinguish between those bad results of action that are in no way effects of the agent's will and those that are its indirect effects by his failing to avoid them when he could and should. What I have argued is that, for Thomas, a result, the thought of which does not motivate the will, can still be the will's direct effect and can even specify its action. In order to judge such cases, a principle of *side*-effects is not needed.

---

99. I-II, q. 9, a. 1, ad 2; II-II, q. 47, a. 3. Universal considerations can be principles of action, but only as applied to particular considerations; see *In III De an.* lect. xvi, §§ 845–46.

100. I-II, q. 18, a. 10.

101. I, q. 80, a. 2, ad 2.

Bibliography

Ackrill, J. L. 'Aristotle's Distinction between *energeia* and *kinēsis*,' in *New Essays on Plato and Aristotle*, pp. 121–41. Edited by R. Bambrough. London: Routledge & Kegan Paul, 1965.

———. 'Aristotle on Action,' *Mind* 87 (1978), pp. 595–601.

Anscombe, G. E. M. 'Action, Intention, and "Double Effect,"' *Proceedings of the American Catholic Philosophical Association* (1983), pp. 12–25.

———. 'Aristotle,' in G. E. M. Anscombe and Peter T. Geach, *Three Philosophers*, pp. 1–63. Ithaca: Cornell University Press, 1961.

———. 'Causality and Determination,' Inaugural Lecture, Cambridge University, 1971; reprinted in Anscombe, *The Collected Philosophical Papers of G. E. M. Anscombe*, vol. II, pp. 133–47. Oxford: Basil Blackwell, 1981.

———. 'Causality and Extensionality,' *Journal of Philosophy* 66 (1969); reprinted in *Collected Papers*, vol. II, pp. 173–79.

———. 'The Causation of Action,' in *Knowledge and Mind. Philosophical Essays*, pp. 174–90. Edited by Carl Ginet and Sydney Shoemaker. Oxford: Oxford University Press, 1983.

———. 'Embryos and Final Causes,' in *Finalité et intentionnalité: doctrine thomiste et perspectives modernes*, pp. 293–303. Edited by J. Follon and J. McEvoy. Louvain-la-Neuve: Editions de l'Institut Supérieur de Philosophie, 1992.

———. *Intention*. Southampton: Basil Blackwell, 1976.

———. 'Modern Moral Philosophy,' *Philosophy* 33 (1958); reprinted in *Collected Papers*, vol. III, pp. 26–42. Oxford: Basil Blackwell, 1981.

———. 'On Brute Facts,' *Analysis* 18 (1958); reprinted in *Collected Papers*, vol. III, pp. 22–25.

———. 'On Promising and Its Justice, and Whether It Need Be Respected *in foro interno*,' in *Collected Papers*, vol. III, pp. 10–21.

———. 'Thought and Action in Aristotle,' in *New Essays on Plato and Aristotle*. Edited by R. Bambrough. London: Routledge & Kegan Paul, 1965; reprinted in *Collected Papers*, vol. I, pp. 66–77. Oxford: Basil Blackwell, 1981.

———. 'The Two Kinds of Error in Action,' *Journal of Philosophy* 60 (1963); reprinted in *Collected Papers*, vol. III, pp. 3–9.

———. 'Under a Description,' *Nous* 13 (1979); reprinted in *Collected Papers*, vol. II, pp. 208–19.

———. 'War and Murder,' in *Nuclear Weapons: a Catholic Response*. Edited by W. Stein. London and New York: Sheed & Ward, 1961; reprinted in *Collected Papers*, vol. III, pp. 51–61.

———. 'Will and Emotion,' *Grazer Philosophische Studien* 5 (1978); reprinted in *Collected Papers*, vol. I, pp. 100–07.

———. 'You Can Have Sex without Children,' *Proceedings of the Canadian Centenary Theological Congress*, Toronto, 1968; reprinted in *Collected Papers*, vol. III, pp. 82–96.

Aquinas, St Thomas. *S. In XII libros Metaphysicorum expositio.* Edited by R.-M. Spiazzi, O.P. Taurini: Marietti, 1964.

———. *Quaestiones disputatae de potentia*, in *S. Thomae Aquinatis quaestiones disputatae*, vol. II, pp. 1–276. Edited by P. M. Pession *et al*. Taurini: Marietti, 1965.

———. *Scriptum super libros Sententiarium.* 4 vols. Edited by P. Mandonnet and M. Moos. Paris: P. Lethielleax, 1929–47.

———. *S. Thomae Aquinatis opera omnia.* Iussu impensaque Leonis XIII P.M. edita. Roma: ex typographia polyglotta et al., 1882–.

Arregui, Jorge V. 'Wittgenstein on Voluntary Actions,' *International Philosophical Quarterly* 32 (1992), pp. 299–311.

Austin, John L. 'A Plea for Excuses,' *Proceedings of the Aristotelian Society* 57 (1956–57); reprinted in J. L. Austin, *Philosophical Papers*, pp. 175–204. Oxford: Clarendon Press, 1961.

———. 'Three Ways of Spilling Ink,' *The Philosophical Review* 75 (1966); reprinted in *Philosophical Papers*, pp. 272–87.

Bennett, Jonathan. *The Act Itself.* Oxford: Clarendon Press, 1995.

———. *Events and their Names.* Indianapolis/Cambridge: Hackett Publishing Company, 1988.

Berti, Enrico. 'Soggetto, anima e identità personale in Aristotele,' in *Peri Psyche, De homine, Antropologia. Nuovi Approcci*, pp. 1–14. Edited by Marcello Sánchez Sorondo. Roma: Herder-Università Lateranense, 1994.

Bourke, Vernon J. *Ethics. A Textbook in Moral Philosophy.* New York/London: The Macmillan Company, 1966.

Boyle, Joseph. 'Double-Effect and a Certain Type of Embryotomy,' *Irish Theological Quarterly* 44 (1977), pp. 303–18.

———. '*Praeter intentionem* in Aquinas,' *The Thomist* 42 (1978), pp. 649–65.

———. 'Toward Understanding the Principle of Double Effect,' *Ethics* 90 (1980), pp. 527–38.

———. 'Who is Entitled to Double Effect?' and 'Further Thoughts on Double Effect: Some Preliminary Responses,' *The Journal of Medicine and Philosophy* 16 (1991), pp. 475–94 and pp. 565–70.

——— and Sullivan, T. 'The Diffusiveness of Intention Principle: a Counterexample,' *Philosophical Studies* 31 (1977), pp. 357–60.

Boyle, Joseph, John Finnis, and Germain Grisez. *Nuclear Deterrence, Morality and Realism.* Oxford: Clarendon Press, 1987.

Bratman, Michael. 'Davidson's Theory of Intention,' in *Essays on Davidson: Actions and Events*, pp. 13–26. Edited by B. Vermazen and M. B. Hintikka. Oxford: Clarendon Press, 1985.

Brentano, Franz. *The Psychology of Aristotle.* Edited and translated by Rolf George. Berkeley: University of California Press, 1977. Original: *Die Psychologie des Aristoteles.* Darmstadt: Wissenschaftliche Buchgesellschaft, 1967.

Brock, Stephen L. 'The Specification of Action in St. Thomas: Nonmotivating Conditions in the Object of Intention,' *The Thomist* 83 (2019), pp. 321–55.

———. 'What is the Use of *Usus* in Aquinas' Psychology of Action?,' in *Les philosophies morales et politiques au Moyen Age*, vol. II, pp. 654–64. Edited by B. C. Bazán, E. Andújar and L. G. Sbrocchi. Publications du Laboratoire de la pensée ancienne et médiévale. New York/Ottawa/Toronto: LEGAS, 1995.

Candlish, Stewart. 'Inner and Outer Basic Action,' *Proceedings of the Aristotelian Society* 84 (1983–84), pp. 83–102.
Carr, David. 'Practical Inference and the Identity of Actions,' *The Review of Metaphysics* 34 (1981), pp. 645–61.
Chisholm, Roderick M. *Person and Object*. London: George Allen & Unwin Ltd., 1976.
———. 'Query on Substitutivity' (comments on Føllesdal, 'Quantification into Causal Contexts'), in *Boston Studies in the Philosophy of Science*, vol. II, pp. 275–77. Edited by R. S. Cohen and M. W. Wartofsky. New York: Humanities Press, 1965.
———. 'The Structure of Intention,' *The Journal of Philosophy* 67 (1970), pp. 633–47.
Danto, Arthur C. *Analytical Philosophy of Action*. Cambridge: Cambridge University Press, 1963.
———. 'Basic Actions,' *American Philosophical Quarterly* 2 (1965), pp. 141–43.
———. 'Basic Actions and Basic Concepts,' *The Review of Metaphysics* 32 (1979), pp. 471–86.
D'Arcy, Eric. *Human Acts. An Essay in their Moral Evaluation*. Oxford: Clarendon Press, 1963.
Davidson, Donald. *Essays on Actions and Events*. Oxford: Clarendon Press, 1980.
de Finance, Joseph. *Essai sur l'agir humain*. Rome: Presses de l'Université Grégorienne, 1962.
Dewan, Lawrence, O.P. 'The Real Distinction between Intellect and Will,' *Angelicum* 57 (1980), pp. 557–93.
———. 'Saint Thomas and the Principle of Causality,' in *Jacques Maritain: Philosophe dans la Cité/A Philosopher in the World* (Philosophica 28), pp. 53–71. Edited by Jean-Louis Allard. Ottawa: University of Ottawa Press, 1985.
———. 'St Thomas, Our Natural Lights, and the Moral Order,' *Maritain Studies* 2 (1986), pp. 59–92.
Donagan, Alan. *Choice: The Essential Element in Human Action*. New York: Methuen Press, 1988.
———. *The Theory of Morality*. Chicago: University of Chicago Press, 1979.
———. 'Thomas Aquinas on Human Action,' in *The Cambridge History of Later Medieval Philosophy*, pp. 642–54. Edited by Norman Kretzmann, Anthony Kenny and Jan Pinborg. Cambridge: Cambridge University Press, 1982.
Duff, R. A. *Intention, Agency and Criminal Liability*. Oxford: Blackwell, 1990.
Finnis, John. *Aquinas: Moral, Political, and Legal Theory*. Oxford: Oxford University Press, 1998.
———. 'Intention and Side-Effects,' in *Liability and Responsibility. Essays in Law and Morals*, pp. 32–64. Edited by R. G. Frey and Christopher W. Morris. Cambridge: Cambridge University Press, 1991. Reprinted, with some additions, in John Finnis, *Intention and Identity*, pp. 173–97. Vol. II of *Collected Essays*. Oxford: Oxford University Press, 2011.
———. *Moral Absolutes: Tradition, Revision, and Truth*. Washington, D.C.: The Catholic University of America Press, 1991.
———. 'Object and Intention in Moral Judgments According to Aquinas,' *The Thomist* 55 (1991), pp. 1–27.
Finnis, John, Germain Grisez, and Joseph Boyle. ' "Direct" and "Indirect": A Reply to Critics of our Action Theory,' *The Thomist* 65 (2001) pp. 1–44. Reprinted, with some additions, as ' "Direct" and "Indirect" in Action,' in John Finnis, *Intention and Identity*, pp. 235–68. Vol. II of *Collected Essays*. Oxford: Oxford University Press, 2011.

Flannery, Kevin, S.J. 'Natural Law *mens rea* versus the Benthamite Tradition,' *The American Journal of Jurisprudence* 40 (1995), pp. 377–400.

———. 'Practical Reason and Concrete Acts,' *Natural Law and Moral Inquiry. Ethics, Metaphysics, and Politics in the Work of Germain Grisez*, pp. 107–34. Edited by Robert P. George. Washington, D.C.: Georgetown University Press, 1998.

———. 'What is Included in a Means to an End?,' *Gregorianum* 74 (1993), pp. 499–513.

Føllesdal, Dagfinn. 'Quantification into Causal Contexts,' in *Boston Studies in the Philosophy of Science*, vol. II, pp. 263–74. Edited by R. S. Cohen and M. W. Wartofsky. New York: Humanities Press, 1965.

Geach, Peter. 'Aquinas,' in G. E. M. Anscombe and P. T. Geach, *Three Philosophers*, pp. 65–125. Ithaca: Cornell University Press, 1961.

———. *Logic Matters*. Oxford: Basil Blackwell, 1972.

Goldman, Alvin. *A Theory of Human Action*. Englewood Cliffs, New Jersey: Prentice-Hall, 1970.

Grisez, Germain. *Christian Moral Principles*. Vol. I of *The Way of the Lord Jesus*. Chicago: Franciscan Herald Press, 1983.

———. *Living a Christian Life*. Vol. II of *The Way of the Lord Jesus*. Quincy, Ill.: Franciscan Press, 1993.

———. 'Toward a Consistent Natural-Law Ethics of Killing,' *The American Journal of Jurisprudence* 15 (1970), pp. 64–96.

Hart, H. L. A. 'Problems of the Philosophy of Law,' in Hart, *Encyclopedia of Philosophy*, vol. VI, pp. 264–76. Edited by Paul Edwards. London: Macmillan, 1967. Reprinted in *Essays in Jurisprudence and Philosophy*, pp. 88–119. Oxford: Clarendon Press, 1983.

Hume, David. *A Treatise of Human Nature*. Edited by T. Greene and T. H. Grose. London: Longmans, Green & Co., 1886. (Reprint Aalan: Scientia Verlag, 1964.)

Jensen, Steven J. *Good and Evil Action: A Journey through Saint Thomas Aquinas*. Washington, D.C.: The Catholic University of America Press, 2010.

Jonas, Hans. *The Phenomenon of Life. Toward a Philosophical Biology*. New York: Harper & Row, 1966.

Kenny, Anthony. *Action, Emotion and Will*. London: Routledge & Kegan Paul, 1979.

———. *Aquinas on Mind*. London: Routledge, 1993.

———. *Aristotle's Theory of the Will*. London: Duckworth, 1979.

———. *The Metaphysics of Mind*. Oxford: Clarendon Press, 1989.

MacIntyre, Alasdair. 'The Antecedents of Action,' in *British Analytical Philosophy*. Edited by B. Williams and A. Montefiore. London: Routledge & Kegan Paul, 1966. Reprinted in MacIntyre, *Against the Self-Images of the Age*, pp. 191–210. London: Duckworth, 1971.

Makin, Stephen. 'Aquinas, Natural Tendencies and Natural Kinds,' *The New Scholasticism* 63 (1989), pp. 253–74.

McInerny, Ralph. *The Logic of Analogy*. The Hague: Martinus Nijhoff, 1971.

Melden, A. I. *Free Action*. London: Routledge & Kegan Paul, 1961.

Meyer, Susan Sauvé. *Aristotle on Moral Responsibility. Character and Cause*. Oxford UK/Cambridge USA: Blackwell Publishers, 1993.

Nussbaum, Martha. 'The "Common Explanation" of Animal Motion,' in *Zweifelhaftes in Corpus Aristotelicum: Studien zu einer Dubia. Akten des 9.ten Symposium Aristotelicum*, pp. 116–56. Edited by P. Moraux and J. Wiesner. Berlin/New York: De Gruyter, 1983.

———. *The Fragility of Goodness. Luck and Ethics in Greek Tragedy and Philosophy.* Cambridge: Cambridge University Press, 1986.
Penner, Terry. 'Verbs and the Identity of Actions—a Philosophical Exercise in the Interpretation of Aristotle,' in *Ryle*, pp. 393–460. Edited by Oscar P. Wood and George Pitcher. London: Macmillan & Co., 1970.
Pitcher, G. '"In Intending" and Side-Effects,' *The Journal of Philosophy* 67 (1970), pp. 663–68.
Polo, Leonardo. 'Tener y dar. Reflexiones en torno a la segunda parte de la Encíclica *Laborem Exercens*,' in *Estudios sobre la encíclica 'Laborem exercens*,' pp. 201–30. Edited by F. Fernández Rodríguez. Madrid: BAC, 1987.
Ramírez, Santiago. *De hominis beatitudine* and *De actibus humanis*, in *Edición de las Obras Completas de Santiago Ramírez, O.P.*, vols. I and IV. Edited by V. Rodriguez. Madrid: Consejo Superior de Investigaciones Científicas, 1972.
Rodriguez Luño, Angel. *La scelta etica.* Milano: Edizioni Ares, 1988.
Sellars, Wilfrid. 'Volitions Re-affirmed,' in *Action Theory. Proceedings of the Winnipeg Conference on Human Action, May 1975*, pp. 47–66. Edited by M. Brand and D. Walton. Dordrecht: D. Reidel, 1976.
Smith, A. D. 'Agency and the Essence of Actions,' *The Philosophical Quarterly* 38 (1988), pp. 401–21.
Smith, Patricia G. 'Contemplating Failure,' *Philosophical Studies* 59 (1990), pp. 159–76.
Spaemann, Robert. *Glück und Wohlwollen.* Stuttgart: Ernst Klett Verlag, 1990.
Sweeney, Eileen C. 'From Determined Motion to Undetermined Will and Nature to Supernature in Aquinas,' *Philosophical Topics* 20 (1992), pp. 189–214.
Taylor, Charles. *The Explanation of Behaviour.* London: Routledge & Kegan Paul, 1964.
Veatch, Henry B. 'Is Kant the Gray Eminence of Contemporary Ethical Theory?,' *Ethics* 90 (1980), pp. 218–38.
Waterlow, Sarah. *Nature, Change and Agency in Aristotle's Physics.* Oxford: Clarendon Press, 1982.
Weisheipl, James A., O.P. *Nature and Motion in the Middle Ages.* Edited by William E. Carroll. Washington D.C.: Catholic University of America Press, 1985.
Westberg, Daniel. *Right Practical Reason: Aristotle, Action, and Prudence in Aquinas.* Oxford: Clarendon Press, 1994.
Wittgenstein, Ludwig. *Philosophical Investigations.* Translated by G. E. M. Anscombe. Oxford: Basil Blackwell, 1967.
Wojtyła, Karol. *I fondamenti dell'ordine etico.* Città del Vaticano: Libreria Editrice Vaticana, 1980 (esp. the articles 'Il problema della volontà nell'analisi dell'atto etico,' pp. 49–68, and 'Il ruolo dirigente o ausiliario della ragione nell'etica nel contesto del pensiero di Tommaso d'Aquino, Hume e Kant,' pp. 91–106).

Index of References to Works of St Thomas Aquinas

(For passages quoted or discussed in the text, footnote references are given in parentheses.)

Summa theologiae

I, q. 1, a. 1	5 n. 2	I, q. 29, a. 3 ad 2	93 n. 5
I, q. 1, a. 3	6 n. 8, 256 n. 74	I, q. 29, a. 4	20
I, q. 2, a. 3	262 n. 98	I, q. 30, a. 4	18 n. 30
I, q. 3, a. 6	245 n. 30	I, q. 33, a. 1	107 n. 40
I, q. 4, a. 1	12 n. 19	I, q. 37, a. 1	167 (n. 77)
I, q. 5, a. 1	97 n. 18	I, q. 41, a. 1 ad 2	22 (n. 44), 39 (n. 82), 76 (n. 58)
I, q. 5, a. 1 ad 1	12 n. 19	I, q. 41, a. 2	154 n. 35
I, q. 5, a. 3	97 n. 18	I, q. 44, a. 2	119 n. 73
I, q. 5, a. 3 ad 4	47 n. 1	I, q. 44, a. 4	114 n. 63
I, q. 5, a. 4	7 n. 14, 12 n. 19, 105 n. 35, 115–122	I, q. 45, a. 4 ad 1	256 n. 76
		I, q. 48, a. 1 ad 2	37 n. 80, 214 n. 57
I, q. 5, a. 4 ad 3	44 (n. 91), 144 n. 22	I, q. 48, a. 6	45 n. 91
I, q. 6, a. 1	97 n. 18	I, q. 49, a. 1	128 (n. 90), 129 n. 94, 155 n. 44, 212 n. 54
I, q. 6, a. 1 ad 2	98 n. 19		
I, q. 13, a. 5 ad 1	9 n. 15	I, q. 49, a. 2	212 n. 54
I, q. 13, a. 7	72 n. 50, 224 n. 74	I, q. 49, a. 2 ad 3	247 n. 38
I, q. 16, arts. 1–2	159 n. 56	I, q. 56, a. 1	200 n. 16
I, q. 16, a. 4 ad 2	113 n. 58	I, q. 58, a. 2	58 n. 21
I, q. 16, a. 7 ad 2	18 n. 29	I, q. 59, a. 1	164 n. 70
I, q. 16, a. 8 ad 4	160 n. 57	I, q. 59, a. 2	114 n. 62, 164 n. 70
I, q. 18, a. 1	33 n. 71	I, q. 60, a. 1	98 n. 19, 178 n. 114
I, q. 18, a. 3	33–34 (n. 72), 166 n. 76	I, q. 60, a. 1 ad 2	23 n. 46, 45 n. 97
		I, q. 62, a. 8 ad 3	166 n. 76
I, q. 19, a. 1	139 n. 7	I, q. 63, a. 1	165 n. 72
I, q. 19, a. 9	212 n. 54	I, q. 66, a. 2	10 n. 17
I, q. 19, a. 9 ad 3	247 n. 38	I, q. 67, a. 3 ad 3	28 n. 59
I, q. 19, a. 10	166 n. 76	I, q. 75, a. 2 ad 1	19 nn. 33 & 34
I, q. 21, a. 1 ad 3	31 (n. 64)	I, q. 75, a. 2 ad 2	19 nn. 33 & 34, 20 n. 36, 24 (n. 48)
I, q. 22, a. 2 ad 4	6 n. 10, 35 n. 75		
I, q. 25, a. 5	166 n. 76	I, q. 76, a. 2 ad 1	21 n. 39
I, q. 25, a. 5 ad 1	143 (n. 20)	I, q. 76, a. 5 ad 1	257 n. 78
I, q. 26, a. 1 obj. 2	144 n. 23	I, q. 77, a. 1	110 n. 51
I, q. 27, a. 1	48 n. 4	I, q. 77, a. 6	245 n. 30
I, q. 27, a. 4	165 (n. 71), 179 n. 118	I, q. 77, a. 6 ad 3	50 n. 7
		I, q. 77, a. 7 ad 1	50 n. 7
I, q. 28, a. 1	76 n. 57	I, q. 78, a. 1	164 (n. 67)
I, q. 29, a. 1	6 n. 10, 14–35, 262 n. 97	I, q. 78, a. 1 ad 3	173 n. 99
		I, q. 79, a. 1 ad 2	164 n. 68
I, q. 29, a. 2 ad 5	21 n. 38	I, q. 80, a. 2 ad 2	263 n. 101

272 *Action and Conduct*

I, q. 82, a. 3	173 n. 101, 262 nn. 93 & 94	I–II, q. 6, a. 2 obj. 2	23 n. 46
I, q. 82, a. 4	166 n. 73	I–II, q. 6, a. 3	130–31 (nn. 96 & 97), 155 n. 44, 216–17, 219, 242 nn. 16, 17, & 19
I, q. 83, a. 1 ad 3	31 n. 67		
I, q. 83, arts. 1 & 3	166 n. 75		
I, q. 85, a. 3 ad 1	117 n. 67	I–II, q. 6, a. 3 ad 2	198 n. 11
I, q. 85, a. 6	117 n. 67	I–II, q. 6, a. 4	172 n. 95, 233 n. 91
I, q. 103, a. 1 ad 1	35 n. 75, 98 n. 19	I–II, q. 6, a. 5 ad 2	153 n. 33, 233 n. 90
I, q. 103, a. 1 ad 3	98 n. 19	I–II, q. 6, a. 6	229 n. 81
I, q. 103, a. 4	117 n. 69, 182 n. 114	I–II, q. 6, a. 6 ad 1	153 n. 33, 233 (n. 90)
I, q. 105, a. 3	178 n. 114		
I, q. 105, a. 4	178 n. 114	I–II, q. 6, a. 8	211 n. 51, 231 n. 85
I, q. 105, a. 5	6 nn. 10 & 11, 178 n. 114	I–II, q. 7, a. 1	17 n. 28
		I–II, q. 7, a. 1 ad 2 & 3	206 n. 33
I, q. 115, a. 1	105 n. 36		
I, q. 115, a. 1 ad 5	28 n. 59	I–II, q. 7, a. 2 ad 2	206 n. 34, 245 n. 30
I, q. 119, a. 2	236 n. 98	I–II, q. 7, a. 3 ad 3	89 n. 90, 206 (n. 32), 258 n. 80
I–II, q. 1, a. 1	5 n. 2, 182 n. 126		
I–II, q. 1, a. 1 ad 2	140 n. 10, 141 n. 15, 177 n. 113, 191 n. 151	I–II, q. 7, a. 4 ad 2	89 n. 90
		I–II, q. 8, a. 1	158 (n. 53)
		I–II, q. 8, a. 1 ad 3	158 (n. 54), 159 (n. 55), 219 n. 66
I–II, q. 1, a. 2	8 nn. 10 & 11, 96 (n. 1)	I–II, q. 9, a. 1	44 (n. 92), 163 n. 73, 179 n. 119, 263 n. 99
I–II, q. 1, a. 2 ad 1	35 n. 74		
I–II, q. 1, a. 3	45 (nn. 93 & 96), 88 n. 88, 183 (n. 127), 186 (n. 139), 244 n. 27, 245 n. 29	I–II, q. 9, a. 2 ad 2	262 n. 97
		I–II, q. 9, a. 3	45 n. 95, 175 (n. 109), 182 (n. 125)
		I–II, q. 9, a. 4	45 n. 97, 110 n. 53
I–II, q. 1, a. 3 ad 1	79 n. 69	I–II, q. 9, a. 6	110 n. 53
I–II, q. 1, a. 3 ad 3	106 n. 38, 261 n. 93	I–II, q. 10, a. 1	45 n. 97, 123 n. 82, 141 n. 16, 178 n. 114
I–II, q. 1, a. 6	218 n. 61		
I–II, q. 1, a. 7	144 n. 23	I–II, q. 11, a. 2	177 n. 113
I–II, q. 2, a. 1	36 (n. 78)	I–II, q. 11, a. 3	177 n. 113
I–II, q. 2, a. 1 ad 1	36 n. 78	I–II, q. 12, a. 1	95 (n. 10), 175 n. 107
I–II, q. 2, a. 2 obj. 1	144 n. 23	I–II, q. 12, a. 1 ad 4	175 nn. 106 & 107, 197 (n. 9), 232 n. 86, 262 n. 96
I–II, q. 2, a. 7	144 n. 23		
I–II, q. 3, a. 1	144 n. 23		
I–II, q. 3, a. 2 ad 1	144 n. 24	I–II, q. 12, a. 2	97 n. 17
I–II, q. 3, a. 2 ad 4	140 n. 13	I–II, q. 12, a. 2 ad 3	175 n. 107
I–II, q. 3, a. 4	140 n. 12, 191 n. 151	I–II, q. 12, a. 3	97 n. 17
I–II, q. 3, a. 5	142 n. 16	I–II, q. 12, a. 4	175 n. 110, 181 n. 123, 207 n. 38
I–II, q. 4, a. 1 obj. 3	144 n. 23		
I–II, q. 4, a. 2	141 n. 14, 191 n. 151	I–II, q. 12, a. 5	95 (n. 10), 262 n. 98
I–II, q. 4, a. 4	145 (n. 25)	I–II, q. 13, a. 4	174 n. 103
I–II, q. 4, a. 5 obj. 4	144 n. 23	I–II, q. 13, a. 5	232 n. 89
I–II, q. 4, a. 7	144 n. 23	I–II, q. 13, a. 5 ad 1	135 (n. 2), 147 n. 28, 173 n. 98, 175 nn. 106 & 108, 232 n. 88, 262 n. 95
I–II, q. 5, a. 5 ad 1	145 (n. 27)		
I–II, q. 5, a. 8	145 n. 23		
I–II, q. 6, proem.	170 n. 86		
I–II, q. 6, a. 2	34 n. 72, 155 n. 40	I–II, q. 13, a. 6 ad 3	162 n. 66

Index of References to Works of St Thomas Aquinas

I–II, q. 14, a. 6 ad 2	129 n. 93	I–II, q. 56, a. 3	44 n. 92
I–II, q. 15, a. 1 ad 3	173 n. 100	I–II, q. 57, arts.	
I–II, q. 15, a. 3	153 n. 34	1, 3, 4	187 n. 140
I–II, q. 15, a. 4 ad 2	156 n. 49	I–II, q. 66, a. 4	190 n. 148
I–II, q. 15, a. 4 ad 3	165 n. 72	I–II, q. 66, a. 5 ad 4	117 n. 68
I–II, q. 16, a. 1	171 nn. 93, 172 n. 95, 177 n. 114	I–II, q. 71, a. 5	130 n. 96, 155 n. 44, 215 n. 58, 219 n. 66, 220 n. 67
I–II, q. 16, a. 2 ad 2	178 n. 116		
I–II, q. 16, a. 3	177 n. 113	I–II, q. 72, a. 1	214 (n. 57), 244 n. 27, 245 n. 29
I–II, q. 16, a. 4	45 n. 94, 172–74, 181 (n. 123)	I–II, q. 72, a. 3 ad 2	87 (n. 86), 259 n. 88
I–II, q. 16, a. 4 ad 3	178 n. 117	I–II, q. 72, a. 5	244 n. 27
I–II, q. 16, a. 5	172 n. 95	I–II, q. 72, a. 6	130 n. 95, 194 n. 1
I–II, q. 17, a. 1	178 n. 114, 197 n. 10	I–II, q. 72, a. 7 ad 3	63 n. 28, 79 n. 70
I–II, q. 17, a. 2	197 n. 10	I–II, q. 72, a. 8	244 n. 27
I–II, q. 17, a. 3	171 nn. 93 & 94, 178 n. 114, 182 n. 123	I–II, q. 72, a. 9 ad 2	259 n. 86
		I–II, q. 73, a. 3 ad 1	88 (n. 87)
I–II, q. 17, a. 4	28 (n. 58), 82 n. 77, 182 n. 123, 194 n. 1	I–II, q. 73, a. 8	200 (n. 15), 201 n. 17, 210 n. 49, 241–43 (nn. 10, 15 & 18), 246 n. 34, 247 n. 36, 249
I–II, q. 17, a. 5	174 n. 88, 170 n. 91		
I–II, q. 17, a. 5 ad 3	45 n. 97, 110 n. 53		
I–II, q. 17, a. 6	170 n. 88		
I–II, q. 18, a. 2 ad 3	82 n. 79, 184 (n. 130)	I–II, q. 73, a. 8 obj. 1	53 n. 11
I–II, q. 18, a. 3 ad 2	206 n. 34, 245 n. 31	I–II, q. 74, a. 1	187 (n. 141)
I–II, q. 18, a. 4	89 n. 90, 185 n. 135	I–II, q. 74, arts. 2 & 3	189 n. 145
I–II, q. 18, a. 5 ad 2	214 n. 57	I–II, q. 74, a. 7 ad 2, 3, 4	155 n. 44
I–II, q. 18, a. 6	82 n. 77, 185 n. 134, 194 n. 1	I–II, q. 75, a. 1	129 n. 94
I–II, q. 18, a. 6 ad 2	106 n. 38	I–II, q. 75, a. 1 ad 2	107 (n. 42), 112
I–II, q. 18, a. 7	106 n. 38, 194 n. 1, 195 n. 4, 214 n. 57	I–II, q. 75, a. 2	128 n. 90, 130 n. 95
		I–II, q. 76, a. 4	260 n. 90
I–II, q. 18, a. 10	259 nn. 84 & 86, 260 n. 92, 263 n. 100	I–II, q. 76, a. 4 ad 2	260 n. 90
		I–II, q. 78, a. 1	212 n. 55
I–II, q. 19, a. 2 ad 3	214 n. 57	I–II, q. 78, a. 1 ad 2	202 n. 19, 260 n. 91
I–II, q. 19, a. 3	185 n. 135, 214 n. 57	I–II, q. 79, a. 1	211 n. 50, 247 n. 38
I–II, q. 19, a. 9	143 (n. 21), 144 (n. 22), 247 n. 39	I–II, q. 79, a. 2 ad 3	214 n. 57
		I–II, q. 85, a. 1 ad 3	182 n. 126
I–II, q. 20, a. 3 ad 3	169 n. 82	I–II, q. 89, a. 6	197 n. 10
I–II, q. 20, a. 4	43 n. 89, 173 n. 98, 173 n. 103	I–II, q. 91, a. 2	141 n. 16
		I–II, q. 93, a. 5	6 n. 10, 186 (n. 138)
I–II, q. 20, a. 5	200 n. 15, 210 n. 49, 241 n. 13	I–II, q. 94, a. 3	178 n. 114
		I–II, q. 109, a. 8	155 n. 44
I–II, q. 21, a. 1	214 n. 57	II–II, q. 1, a. 3	256 n. 75
I–II, q. 21, a. 1 ad 2	111 n. 56, 123 n. 83	II–II, q. 23, a. 1	145 (n. 26)
I–II, q. 25, a. 1	98 n. 19, 214 n. 57	II–II, q. 39, a. 1	244 n. 27
I–II, q. 26, a. 3	191 n. 151	II–II, q. 41, a. 1	247 n. 37
I–II, q. 27, a. 2	113 n. 58	II–II, q. 43, a. 1 ad 4	241 n. 12, 242 n. 17
I–II, q. 51, a. 1	178 n. 114	II–II, q. 43, a. 3	241 n. 13, 244 n. 27, 245 n. 28
I–II, q. 54, a. 3 ad 2	214 n. 57		

274 *Action and Conduct*

II–II, q. 43, a. 3 ad 3	243 n. 24, 244 n. 27, 260 n. 92	*In libros Metaphysicorum expositio*	
II–II, q. 43, a. 3 ad 4	244 n. 27	IV, lect. I, § 529	245 n. 30
II–II, q. 47, a. 3	263 n. 99	IV, lect. iv, § 574	70 n. 48
II–II, q. 58, a. 2	6 n. 8, 18 (n. 31), 24 (n. 47)	V, lect. ii, § 775	114 n. 61
		V, lect. iii, § 789	126–28
II–II, q. 58, a. 3	190 (n. 147)	V, lect. ix, § 889	69 n. 43, 70 n. 45
II–II, q. 58, a. 12	190 n. 148	V, lect. ix, § 897	69 n. 44
II–II, q. 59, a. 2	87 (n. 85), 123 n. 81, 206 (n. 35), 227 (n. 79), 244 n. 27, 245 n. 29	V, lect. xi, § 910	17 n. 28
		V, lect. xvii, § 1124–27	10 n. 17
		VI, lect, ii, §§ 1172–79	245 n. 30
II–II, q. 59, a. 3	154 n. 36	VI, lect. iii, § 1192–93	108 n. 45
II–II, q. 64, a. 2	254 n. 68	VII, lect. vi, § 1382	87 n. 85, 197 n. 5
II–II, q. 64, a. 3 ad 3	247 n. 37	VII, lect. vii, § 1443	105 (n. 35)
II–II, q. 64, a. 6	217 n. 60, 248 n. 46, 250 n. 51	VII, lect. xvi, § 1633	21 (n. 40)
		VII, lect. xvii, § 1658	9 n. 16
II–II, q. 64, a. 7	201 n. 18, 217–19, 239 n. 5, 245–49, 254 n. 68	IX, lect. viii, § 1864–65	200 n. 16
		XI, lect. iii, § 2204	9 n. 16
II–II, q. 64, a. 8	201 n. 17, 211 n. 51, 241 n. 11, 242 n. 15, 247 nn. 37 & 39	XI, lect. viii, § 2269	87 n. 85, 197 n. 5
		XI, lect. viii, § 2284	87 n. 85, 197 n. 5
		XII, lect. vii, § 2522	139–40
II–II, q. 65, a. 1	254 n. 68		
II–II, q. 69, a. 4	217 n. 60, 248 n. 43, 249 n. 47	*Commentaria in libros Physicorum*	
		II, lect. iii, § 158	245 n. 30
II–II, q. 69, a. 4 ad 1	248 n. 45	II, lect. viii, § 214	87 n. 85, 196–97 (n. 5), 246 n. 31
II–II, q. 69, a. 4 ad 2	248 n. 44	II, lect. viii, § 215	205 (n. 25)
II–II, q. 77, a. 7	242 n. 20 & 21	II, lect. X, § 229	6 n. 9
II–II, q. 100, a. 3 ad 3	250 n. 51	II, lect. xiv, § 268	94 n. 9
		III, lect. i, § 280	65 (n. 34)
II–II, q. 123, a. 6	156 (n. 48)	III, lect. i, § 281	70 n. 46
II–II, q. 124, a. 3	156 (n. 48)	III, lect. ii, § 285	72–73
II–II, q. 141, a. 6 ad 1	89 n. 91	III, lects. iv–v	6 n. 11
		III, lect. v, § 316	77–78 (n. 64)
II–II, q. 145, a. 1 ad 2	142 n. 17	III, lect. v, § 322	76–78 (nn. 60, 61, 65), 81 n. 74
II–II, q. 145, a. 2	113 n. 58	III, lect. v, § 324	68–74
II–II, q. 150, a. 2	259 n. 89	VIII, lect. viii, § 1035	126 n. 87
II–II, qq. 155–56	165 n. 72		
III, q. 16, arts. 9–12	208 n. 39		
III, q. 19, a. 1	27 nn. 54 & 56	*Summa contra gentiles*	
III, q. 19, a. 1 ad 5	27 n. 57	II, ch. 6, § 884	188–89 n. 141
III, q. 19, a. 2	6 n. 5, 27 n. 54	II, ch. 23, § 993	13 n. 22, 188–89 n. 141
III, q. 62, a. 1	27 n. 54		
III, q. 62, a. 1 ad 2	27 n. 57	II, ch. 47, § 1238	23 n. 46
III, q. 62, a. 4	27 n. 55, 106 n. 37	II, ch. 48, § 1243	34 n. 73
III, q. 62, a. 5	28 n. 60	II, ch. 48, § 1244–46	166 n. 75

III, chs. 2–3	96 n. 15	*Sententia libri Ethicorum*
III, ch. 6, § 1902	126 n. 85	III, lect. i, § 387 156 n. 47
III, ch. 6, § 1907	203–04, 212 nn. 54	III, lect. v, § 443–44 147 n. 29
	& 55	V, lect. xiii, § 1035 245 n. 29
III, ch. 9, § 1930	214 n. 57	V, lect. xiii, § 1036 123 (n. 81), 245 n.
III, ch. 69, § 2458	105 (n. 33)	29
III, ch. 112, § 2856	92 n. 4	V, lect. xiii, § 1037 152–53 n. 32
III, chs. 112–13	31 n. 66	VII, lect. ix, § 1438 245 n. 29
		IX, lect. xi,
Quaestiones disputatae de malo		§ 1903–04 111 n. 57
q. 1, a. 3 ad 15	197 (n. 6), 246 n. 32	
q. 2, a. 1	219 n. 66	*In libros Peri hermeneias expositio*
q. 2, a. 2 ad 8	197 n. 8	I, lect. ii, § 13, 15, 19 9 n. 16
q. 2, a. 4 ad 9	89 nn. 90 & 91	I, lect. x, § 121 15 n. 26
q. 2, a. 6 ad 2	214 n. 57, 255 n. 70,	
	259 n. 85	*Expositio libri Posteriorum analyticorum*
q. 2, a. 6 ad 3	214 n. 57	I, lect. iv, § 38 102 n. 25
q. 2, a. 6 ad 6	208 n. 40, 258 n. 84	I, lect. xiv,
q. 2, a. 6 ad 9	259 n. 85	§§ 120–24 245 n. 30
q. 3, a. 10	243 n. 23	II, lect. vii, § 471 226 n. 77
q. 3, a. 10 ad 5	244 n. 26	
q. 6, a. 1	182 n. 125	*De ente et essentia*
q. 6, a. 1 ad 15	108 n. 45	ch. 1 70 n. 47, 121 n. 75
q. 16, a. 3 ad 9	147 n. 28	
		De principiis naturae
Scriptum super libros Sententiarum		(Leonine edn., vol. 47)
I, d. 17, q. 1, a. 5	256 n. 76	p. 41, § 3, II. 1–5 119123 n. 72
I, d. 19, q. 5, a. 2		
ad 1	13 (n. 17)	*Quaestiones disputatae de veritate*
I, d. 23, q. 1, a. 1	30 n. 63	q. 22, a. 1 97 n. 16
II, d. 1, q. 2, a. 1	89 n. 91	
II, d. 1, q. 2, a. 4	89 n. 91	*Quaestiones disputate de anima*
II, d. 34, q. 1,		q. 8 (= a. 8) 257 n. 78
a. 2 ad 3	214 n. 57	
III, d. 8, q. 1, a. 2		*Sententia libri De anima*
ad 2	262 n. 98	III, lect. xv, § 821 43 (n. 90)
IV, d. 16, q. 3, a. 1,		III, lect. xvi,
qqa. 2, 3	89 n. 91	§§ 845–46 263 n. 99
IV, d. 16, q. 3, a. 2,		
qcla. 3	258 n. 84	*Sententia libri Politicorum*
IV, d. 38, q. 2, a. 2,		Proemium 116 n. 67
qcla. 2 ad 3	244 n. 27	

Quaestiones disputatae de potentia
q. 1, a. 1   7 (n. 13), 104 n. 31
q. 2, a. 1   104 (n. 32)
q. 7, a. 9   73–74
q. 7, a. 10   77 n. 62
q. 9, a. 5   159 n. 56

Index of Names

Ackrill, J. L., 15
Anscombe, G. E. M., xii, 2, 5, 6, 9, 36, 53–55, 57, 59, 67, 68, 75, 79, 81–83, 86, 89, 92, 95, 101, 108, 129, 136, 149, 154–55, 157, 160–61, 174, 178, 184–85, 199, 205–08, 220, 222, 226, 234–37, 239–241, 243–44, 250
Aristotle, ix, xii, 2, 6, 7, 9, 11–12, 15, 17, 19–23, 25–26, 29, 31–32, 34, 36, 39–40, 42, 43, 48, 50–51, 58–59, 62, 67–68, 75, 81, 88, 94, 98, 100, 105–07, 109, 111, 113, 116, 128–29, 137, 147, 150, 153–56, 174, 188, 190, 209, 219, 229, 234, 236, 251
Arregui, Jorge V., 157
Augustine, St, 113, 133, 140, 143, 177, 191
Austin, John L., 207, 209
Bennett, Jonathan, 52, 82, 199, 206
Bentham, Jeremy, 199
Berti, Enrico, 23
Boethius, 14, 19
Bourke, V. J., 175
Boyle, Joseph, 2, 126, 203–05, 209, 212, 214, 246–49, 251–56, 258
Bratman, Michael, 162, 205
Brentano, Franz, 78, 113, 182
Brock, Stephen L., 172
Candlish, Stewart, 63
Carr, David, 82–83
Chisholm, Roderick M., ix, 2, 204–06, 210, 227, 257
Damscene, St John, 23
D'Arcy, Eric, 5, 7, 209, 212, 216
Davidson, Donald, 20, 53, 61, 82, 86, 109, 123, 162, 186, 190–91, 205, 208–09, 220, 222–23, 225
de Finance, Joseph, 113
Descartes, René, 98
Dewan, Lawrence, 116, 121, 164, 188
Donagan, Alan, 2, 4, 17, 29, 48, 53, 58, 64–67, 80, 83, 109–11, 123, 125, 136, 142, 146, 157–58, 160–62, 167, 169–70, 172, 174, 177–78, 185, 197, 203, 205, 208, 222–27, 235
Duff, R. A., 199
Finnis, John, 89, 182, 197, 199, 214, 247–50
Flannery, Kevin, 41, 199–200, 219, 249
Geach, Peter, 2, 80, 104
Goldman, Alvin, 57–58
Grisez, Germain, 214, 248–49, 252–55
Hart, H. L. A., 207, 210
Heidegger, Martin, 71, 94
Hume, David, 4, 65–69, 75, 79, 98–100, 103–04, 106–08, 116–17, 122, 142, 157
Jonas, Hans, 34
Kant, Immanuel, 4, 43, 103, 135–44, 145–48, 237
Kenny, Anthony, 2, 5, 12, 29, 36, 152–54, 156, 169, 176–77, 216
MacIntyre, Alasdair, 157, 168
Makin, Stephen, 95, 123
McInerny, Ralph, 14, 69–70, 118
Melden, A. I., 167, 183
Meyer, Susan Sauvé, 25, 150, 153
Nussbaum, Martha, 106
Penner, Terry, 12
Pitcher, G., 205
Polo, Leonardo, 114
pseudo-Dionysius, 212
Ramírez, Santiago, 6, 22, 32, 92
Rodriguez Luño, Angel, 166
Russell, Bertrand, 157
Ryle, Gilbert, 157
Scheler, Max, 136
Sellars, Wilfrid, 183–84
Sidgwick, Henry, 199, 205
Smith, A. D., 61, 63
Smith, Patricia G., 219
Spaemann, Robert, 90
Sullivan, T., 205
Sweeney, Eileen C., 13
Taylor, Charles, 91, 93–98, 100, 103, 107, 113, 147

Veatch, Henry, 4, 141
Waterlow, Sarah, 74, 79, 104–05, 109
Weisheipl, James A., 49
Westberg, Daniel, 169

Wittgenstein, Ludwig, 59, 67, 83, 157, 161, 168, 180, 197, 212
Wojtyla, Karol, 136, 142, 15

Index of Subjects

absence, and indirect causality, 128–31, 214–18
accidental change, and substantial change, 119–22
accidents, and substances, 15–25, 76–77, 79–80, 206
act
  as form, 8–9
  meaning of, 5–9, 38
  and potency, in motion, 68–74
action (*see also* actions; agents; motion), 3, 4, 6, 9, 154
  analogy of, 14, 35–39
  as causation (*see also* causality), 64–65, 74–81
  and change, 47–49
  concept of, connected with change and motion, 39, 47–49, 68, 74–77, 100–02
  distinction from activity in the agent, 51–52, 81–83
  as effecting a likeness of the agent, 106–08, 113, 115–16, 127–28
  and efficacy (*see also* efficacy), 39–45, 47–49
  and finality (*see also* final causality), 39–41, 91–98, 103, 122–23
  as forming, 104–06
  as giving, 114–17
  human *see* human action; conduct
  and individuals, 16–23
  and intention (*see also* intention), 85–90
  meaning of, 5–9, 22, 35–39, 100
  moral *see* human action; conduct
  in non-living beings, 29, 35, 49–51, 119–20, 123
  in non-rational beings, 6, 23–24, 27–39, 91–93
  as opposition or avoidance, 40–41, 126, 202–03, 219–20
  and passion, 39, 44–45, 47, 51–60, 65, 68–69, 77–90, 141–42, 153–54, 171–72, 179–84, 186
  and thought, 41–43
  voluntary *see* voluntary
action-description, 53–59, 81–90, 206–08
  essential, 55–56, 234–37
  and the object of intention, 84–90, 206–09, 222–32
action-theory, 1–6, 37–39, 45, 99, 156–58
actions (*see also* action; agents)
  as accidents of substances, 16–23, 76–77, 206
  as the domain of the voluntary, 43–45, 133–56
  complete and incomplete, 52–57, 60–63, 77–83, 185–86, 189–90, 234–35
  description of *see* action-description
  determined by intention, 87–90, 196–99, 225
  as ends and means, 96–97, 175–76
  as events, 49, 64–65, 78–79, 123–24, 168, 222–23
  immanent and transitive, 13, 37, 52, 187–91
  as individuals, 205–09
  involuntary *see* involuntary
  irreducibility of, 77–81
  and motions, 59–81
  role of body in, 185–86, 189
  specification of, 79–90, 193–95, 199–203, 214, 220, 233–37, 239–63
  and verbs, 11–13, 64–65, 176–77
acts of will *see* will, acts of
actus, 7–8, 38
agent-causality (*see also* causality; direct causality; indirect causality)
  in Aquinas and Hume, 99–108
  and finality, 91–99, 111–22
  and other kinds of causality, 114–22
agent-patient relation *see* action, and passion
agents
  and events, as causes, 108–10
  free *see* freedom
  hierarchy of, 27–30, 33–36

279

meaning of, 25–26, 35, 50
perfect and imperfect, 114–15
power of, distinguished from nature, 108–10
principal and instrumental, 27–33, 81–85, 97–98, 105–06, 172, 198, 201–03
agere, 6, 23
aim *see* intention
analogy, 7–13
of action, 35–39
angels, free will in, 45; distinction of intellect and will in, 164
appetite *see* inclination; will
appetitive attitudes, and cognitive attitudes (*see also* propositional attitudes), 156–63

beasts, as agents, 30–31, 33, 34
beatitude, 144–45
body (*see also* soul, and body)
in action, 185–86, 189
as analogous term, 10–11, 13
boulesis, 147–48
Buridan's Ass, 162–63

categories
individuals and universals in, 15–16
pertaining to motion, 68–70, 76–78
causa sui, 31, 37
causality (*see also* agent-causality; direct causality; final causality; indirect causality)
deviant chains of, 225–26
divisions of, 98, 114–22
and explanation by regularities, 102–04
and Hume's view, 65–68, 75–77, 99–103, 106–08
and intensionality, 222–28
and laws of nature, 109–10, 157
logical relationship between cause and effect, 106–08, 127
meaning of, 99–100
and motion, 75–77
per se see direct causality
primacy of formal, in understanding, 117–22
sufficient, 108, 129
and the will *see* will, acts of
chance causality (*see also* indirect causality), 102, 126–27, 130–31, 195, 196, 201–02, 206, 218, 247

change (*see also* motion)
and action, 47–48
accidental and substantial, 118–22
existence of, 100–01
choice
and action, 176–77, 183
causality of, 188, 225–26
and conduct, 36, 155, 187–91
and deliberation, 181–84, 188, 232
difference from wanting, 147–48
as exercise of the will, 186–91
freedom of, 166
and intention, 181–82, 232
and morality, 233–37
object of, direct and indirect, 207
in the relationship between the will and its object, 174–75
and use, 174–84, 188–91
chresis (*see also* use), 32, 174
circumstances
as accidents of actions, 17, 206, 245
ignorance of, and voluntariness, 221, 230–32, 237, 242
and specification of action, 211, 244, 255, 257–60
command, 177–78
and use, 171, 182
commanded acts *see* exterior acts
compulsion *see* force
conduct (*see also* action; human action; *praxis*; voluntary; will, acts of), 35–37, 43–45, 52
and choice, 36, 155, 187–91
and consent, 154–56
and exterior acts, 43–45, 168–69, 184–87, 233–37
as immanent action, 37, 52, 187–91
consent, 153–56, 173, 215
consequences, 199, 207, 216, 239–46, 250, 252
continence, 165
contingency
and involuntariness, 149–50
in relation of cause and effect, 106–08
continuity, in action and motion, 60–63, 74–79
culpability, and side-effects, 204, 209–12, 216–19

death, and the voluntary and involuntary, 150

INDEX OF SUBJECTS   281

deliberation (*see also* choice)
   and choice, 181–84, 188, 232
   and conduct, 36, 155
   as a movement, 83
desire *see* inclination; will
diffusiveness of intention, principle of, 204–09, 215
direct agency *see* direct causality
direct causality (*see also* causality; chance causality; indirect causality), 98–108
   and indirect causality, 101–04, 122–31, 196–99, 210–11
dominus sui actus see freedom, as mastery of one's act
double effect, principle (or doctrine) of, 217, 239, 243, 253, 263
drunkenness, 259–60

effects (*see also* side effects)
   head-on, 240–44, 249, 260–61
   per se
      and *per accidens*, 125, 196
      as directly voluntary, 242–43
      as intended at least indirectly or *per accidens*, 247
      as pertaining to an action's species, 241–44, 251, 257, 260–61
efficacy (*see also* agent-causality; causality)
   as a common feature of action, 39–49
   and finality, 40, 91–99, 102, 115–17
efficient causality *see* agent-causality
electio see choice
elicited acts *see* interior acts
ends (*see also* final causality; *finis operis*; inclination; intention)
   and goods, 96–98
   present in all actions, 91–94
   special place in human action, 35–37, 94–95
   and specification of action, 86–90, 243, 259
energeia, 11–12
enjoyment, 175–77
ens rationis, 69–71
equivocation, 6–9, 11–13
essences, of actions, 55–56, 87–90, 193–94, 200–03, 234–37
ethics, 1, 13
events
   actions as, 49, 64–65, 78–79, 123–24, 168, 222–23

   and acts of will, 167–69
   as causes, 64–65, 98, 108–10
   descriptions of, 79–81
   motions as, 74–77
   and relations, 65–68, 79–81
evil
   and moral specification, 213–14
   as *praeter intentionem*, 203–04, 212–21
exterior acts (*see also* interior acts; will, acts of), 87, 194–95
   and acts of will, 62–63, 168–72, 184–87, 189–91
   and morality, 43–45, 169, 186–89, 233–37

faculty, meaning, 110
   distinguishing one from another, 163–67
final causality (*see also* causality; ends; teleology), 40–41, 91–99, 110–22
   and efficacy, 40, 91–98, 101–02
   and goodness, 96–98
   and need, 114–15
finality *see* final causality
finis operis, and *finis operantis*, 89–90, 97–98
force, 155–56, 210, 233
foreseen results, responsibility for, 206–12
form
   as act, 8–9
   and matter, in actions, 84–90, 193–94, 200–03, 235–37
   as principle of action, 104–08, 112–15
formal causality (*see also* causality), 40, 117–22
freedom
   of choice, 166
   Kant's view, 142–43
   as mastery of one's act, 4, 6, 14–16, 23, 30–35, 37–38, 45, 91–92, 178
   and nature, in the will, 45, 178
   and non-rational agents, 34–35
friendship, 145, 190

God
   control of physical things by, 35, 92, 95, 186
   efficacy of, and will in, 142–43
   goodness of, and will in, 139, 142–43
   and human understanding, 117
   intellect and will in, 48, 142, 164–66
   life of, 135
   production by, vs. human production, 98

Triune, 111, 164–65
  will of, and human will, 142–45
good
  as cause, 115–22, 173–74
  as definite, 111
  as end, 96–98, 115–17, 123
  judgment of, 113
  in moral specification, 214
  as object of the will, 137–45, 158–60

happiness, 138, 140–41, 144–45
harm, 53, 254
  as aggravating, 210, 240–43, 246–47, 251
head-on effects (*see also* side-effects), 240–44, 249, 260–61
heart, metaphorical sense, 191
human action (*see also* action; conduct; *praxis*; voluntary; will, acts of)
  as intentional under some description, 222–32

identity thesis, 61, 82–83
ignorance
  and the accidental, 221
  and intention, 211–12, 229–32
  and involuntariness, 228–37
  and specification of action, 4, 233–37
immanent action, 13, 37, 52, 187–90, 200
imperfect operation *see* motion
inclination (*see also* ends; final causality; intention; will)
  as principle of action, 41, 94, 97, 110–15, 117, 128
incontinence, 162–63, 165, 188–89
indirect agency *see* indirect causality
indirect causality (*see also* chance causality; direct causality; *praeter intentionem*; side-effects), 98–104, 122–31, 196, 225–26
indirect effects *see* side-effects
individuality
  and matter, 16
  and substantial form, 21–22
individuals
  action as property of, 16–23
  definition of, 20
  and universals, 16–20
inertia, law of, 49
instrumental agency, 27–33, 82–86, 97, 105–06, 145, 171–72, 198, 201–03

intellect
  ability to grasp order proper to, 69
  acts of, and acts of will, 134
  distinguished from will, 160–67, 172–74, 179
  and finality, 94
  object of, and that of will, 262
intensionality, 208, 222–28
intention (*see also* ends; final causality; inclination; *praeter intentionem*)
  active and passive senses, 94–95, 180–81
  and choice, 181–82
  direct and indirect, 196–209, 214–19
  and evil, 212–21
  and explaining action, 101–02
  and ignorance, 228–37
  as intensional, 222–28
  in nature and will, 94–95, 262–63
  object of, 230–34, 239
    as principle of specification of action, 84–90, 123
    conditions of, and specification, 206, 214, 244, 255, 259–60, 262
    direct and indirect (or *per se* and *per accidens*), 196–212, 246
    in the New Natural Law theory, 252–55
    nonmotivating conditions in the object of, 244, 258–60
    outside, *see praeter intentionem*
  and omissions, 219–21
  and practical knowledge, 160–61
  principle of diffusiveness of, 204–09, 215
  principle of non-divisiveness of, 204–09, 230
  and the quality of the will, 203–04
  and specification of action, 56, 84–90, 196–200, 225
  as tendency, 85, 88, 91, 94–97, 122–25, 175–77, 180, 203
  and 'under a description', 207–09, 222–32
interference, 104, 125–31
interior acts, 169–70, 195
  and exterior acts, 62–63, 167–72, 184–86, 189–90
  and morality, 43–45, 186–90, 233–37
involuntary
  and contingency, 149–50
  and force, 155–56, 209, 233
  and ignorance, 233–37

INDEX OF SUBJECTS   283

and intention, 221, 228–32
and the voluntary, 151–56, 228–34
and wanting, 148–50

justice, 190

killing, 52–54, 56–58, 60, 64, 82–83, 85, 244, 253–54
in self-defense, 200–02, 217–18, 239–40, 245–52, 253

living beings
as agents, 29–30, 33
finality in, 93–96
freedom in, 34
love (*see also* wanting), 256
as appetite, 141
difference from understanding, 166–67, 179–80
and will, 140, 191

machines, and finality, 93–94
malice, 212–13
materia circa quam, 87
mathematics, and action, 47
material causality, 82, 118, 121, 145
matter
and form, in actions, 84–90, 193–94, 200–03, 235–37
as part of quiddity, 121
as principle of individuation, 16
means
and ends, 96–98, 197–200
relationship to the will, 175–77
mechanical causality, 93, 122–25
moral action *see* conduct
moral law, and the will, 141
morality, will as proper subject of, 43–45, 135–45, 186–91, 233–37
and nature, 237
motion (*see also* action; change)
and categories, 68–71, 76–78
comparison with action, 61–63, 68, 77
and concept of action, 39, 68, 74–77, 99–101
existence of, 68, 75, 100
as imperfect operation, 11–12, 37, 68–74, 95
as involving relation, 68–74
as irreducible event, 74–77

specification of, 44, 74–75, 87
subject of, 75–76, 78, 119
murder, 201, 210, 217–18, 239, 243, 249–50, 253, 260

natural agents *see* physical agency
nature
as effect of divine art, 94
meaning of, 49–50
and will, 45, 141–42, 178, 262–63
necessity, and causality, 107–08
New Natural Law theory, 240, 249–256, 258, 261–63
nilling, 146, 198
non-contradiction, and action, 41
non-divisiveness of intention, principle of, 204–09, 230
non-living things, as agents, 29, 35, 49–51, 119–20, 123
non-rational agents, 6, 23–24, 27–39, 91–93
non-voluntary agents *see* non-rational agents

object
meanings of the term, 13, 42, 86–87
of action (*see also* patient)
direct and indirect, 126, 128–31
of intention, *see* intention, object of
of will, *see* will, object of
oblique intentions, 199
obstacles, 126–31
occurrent causes, 108–09
omissions, 219–21
omne agens agit sibi simile, principle, 97, 105–08, 114–17, 128

parts
of substances, 18–28, 236–37
of actions, 28, 52–59, 62–63, 73, 169, 172–91, 236–37
passion
and action *see* action, and passion
in the will *see* will, action and passion in
patient (*see also* action, and passion; object)
in the specification of action, 56–59, 84–90, 199–203
per se causes *see* direct causality
perfect operation (*see also* motion), 11–12, 37, 98, 189
person, 14–26, 30, 190
perspective of the acting, 252, 261

284 *Action and Conduct*

physical agency, 27–35, 44, 47–51, 115, 169
   and finality, 88, 91–96, 110–16, 122–31
plants, and action, 13, 29, 33–35, 105
poesis, 40
potency and act, in motion, 69–79
potentially divisible, 62–63
power, 28, 42–43, 52, 94, 99–114, 116–20, 137
practical knowledge, and intention, 160–63
praeter intentionem or outside intention (*see also* indirect causality; intention; side-effects), 4, 40, 87, 126, 193–237, 245–47, 252, 257
   and ignorance, 221–23, 228–37
   not everything intended *per accidens* is, 240, 257–58
   nonmotivating conditions of the object as not, 258–60
   two senses of, 245
praxis (*see also* conduct), 32, 36, 154, 174, 189
prevention, 48, 104
   and evil, 214–19
principal agency, and instrumental *see* instrumental agency
privation, as principle of change, 119
propositional attitudes, 156–63
   and intentions, 223–24
purpose *see* ends; final causality; inclination; intention

rational agency (*see also* conduct; will)
   and autonomy, 135–45
   and non-rational, 27–39, 91–96
rational appetite *see* will
reason, practical, 3, 135–39, 142
   agency of, 214
   and intention, 252, 263
   and speculative, 42, 263
reduplication, 208
relations, in motion and action, 65–81
removens prohibens (*see also* indirect causality), 125–31
reproduction, 33, 105, 236
responsibility, and side-effects, 204, 209–12, 215–18, 239

sacrilege, 244, 249, 255, 260
scandal, and act-specification, 241–44, 249, 258, 260
self-defense, 200–02, 217–18, 239–40, 245–52, 253

sense-appetites, as subjects of moral action, 189
side-effects (*see also* effects, head-on effects; indirect causality; indirect intention; *praeter intentionem*), 86, 97, 101–02, 123–31, 196–237, 239–40, 244, 249, 254, 263
soul, 1, 3, 19–28, 31, 34
   and body, comparison with action, 28, 63, 90, 185, 241
   powers of, distinction among, 163–64
specification, of actions, 79–90, 193–95, 199–203, 214, 220, 233–37
   by ends, 86–90, 243, 259
   by intention, 87–90, 196–99, 225
spiritual acts, 61–62, 94
substances
   and accidents, 16–28, 76–77, 80–81, 206
   and actions, 27–30, 117–22, 205–06, 236
   parts and wholes, 18–28, 236
substantial change, and accidental, 119–21
substantial form, 10, 16, 29, 116
   as cause, 119–22
   and individuation, 21–23
sufficient cause, 108, 129

teleology (*see also* ends; final causality; inclination; intention)
   as irreducible form of explanation, 91–96, 107, 123–25
   natural, incidental to specification of human acts, 261
tendency (*see also* intention; will)
   as mere regularity, 102–04, 122–23, 196–07, 201–02
theft, 249, 255, 260–61
time
   and events, 80–81, 205
   and motion, 71–73
transitive actions, 13, 52–59, 187–90, 200
truth, practical, 160
trying, 61–62, 149, 151

understanding *see* intellect
unforeseen results
   and *praeter intentionem*, 221–23, 231, 233
   and voluntariness, 240–44, 247
universals, and individuals, 15–21
unmoved mover, 22

use (*usus*)
    as action, 3, 32, 44, 177–78
    active and passive, 172
    and choice, 174–84, 187–91
    in immanent actions, 187–91
    as interior act of will, 171–84, 233
    as a tendency, 172–77

velleitas (velleity), 43, 139, 147, 149, 173, 175, 198
verbs, 11–13, 176, 205
violence *see* force
volitions *see* will, acts of
voluntary, 133–91
    action, as primary analogate of action, 35–39
    action and passion, 151–54
    as attribute of effects, 145–56
    and autonomy, 133–45
    and choice and consent, 155–56
    directly, 240, 242–43, 246–47, 249, 251, 260
    in cause, 242
    indirectly (*see also* indirect causality; indirect intention; *praeter intentionem*), 219, 242–43, 247–48, 252
    and the involuntary, 151–56, 228–32
    and wanting, 145–48

wanting (*see also* will)
    as act of will, 175–77
    as a causal disposition, 145–56
    and the involuntary, 148–50, 230–34
    and the possible, 146–48, 175, 232
    and *velleitas*, 147–49
will
    action and passion in, 44, 141–42, 179–91
    acts of, 3, 43–45, 62–63, 94, 156–91
        as actions, 176, 183–86
        and causality, 43–45, 138–39, 156–61, 167–78
        interior and exterior, 62–63, 87, 167–72, 184–87, 189–91, 195, 233–34
        and propositional attitudes, 156–60
        as volitional relations, 169–70
    as appetite, 43–45, 139–41
    and autonomy, 135–45, 156–60
    and continence and incontinence, 162–63, 165, 188
    as faculty of agency, 43–45, 133–45
    as faculty of tendency, 43–45, 139–41, 164–65
    and intellect, 159–67, 173–74, 179
    and the involuntary, 152–56, 230–34
    and morality, 43–45, 135–45, 186–87, 213–15, 233–37
    natural operations of, 45, 95, 178, 232
    and nature, 262–63
    object of, 43–45, 137–45, 196–204
        twofold relation to, 172–84
    and that of intellect, 262
wish, 147–50

www.ingramcontent.com/pod-product-compliance
Lightning Source LLC
Chambersburg PA
CBHW050306010526
44107CB00055B/2121